THE PSYCHOLOGY OF
THE PEACEKEEPER

Recent Titles in Psychological Dimensions to War and Peace

THE PSYCHOLOGY OF THE PEACEKEEPER

Lessons from the Field

Edited by

Thomas W. Britt and Amy B. Adler

Psychological Dimensions to War and Peace

Harvey J. Langholtz, Series Editor

Westport, Connecticut
London

Library of Congress Cataloging-in-Publication Data

The psychology of the peacekeeper : lessons from the field / edited by Thomas W.
 Britt and Amy B. Adler
    p.   cm.—(Psychological dimensions to war and peace, ISSN 1540–5265)
    Includes bibliographical references and index.
    ISBN 0–275–97596–7 (alk. paper)
    1. Peacekeeping forces. 2. Peace—Psychological aspects. I. Britt, Thomas W., 1966– .
 II. Adler, Amy B., 1963– .   III. Series
 JZ6374.P79   2003
    341.5'84—dc21   2002044961

British Library Cataloguing in Publication Data is available.

Library of Congress Catalog Card Number: 2002044961
ISBN: 0–275–97596–7
ISSN: 1540–5265

First published in 2003

Praeger Publishers, 88 Post Road West, Westport, CT 06881
An imprint of Greenwood Publishing Group, Inc.
www.praeger.com

Printed in the United States of America

The paper used in this book complies with the
Permanent Paper Standard issued by the National
Information Standards Organization (Z39.48–1984).

10 9 8 7 6 5 4 3 2 1

To Robin and our incredible twin sons, Noah and Jordan.—T. B.

To Matthias, Jason, and Dylan.—A. A.

Contents

Series Foreword

Most of the books written on peacekeeping examine the topic from the perspectives of diplomacy, geopolitics, conflict resolution, or the military. And most books on psychology examine behavior as it can be predicted to exist in a range of settings and environments. But here in *The Psychology of the Peacekeeper: Lessons from the Field,* Britt and Adler examine some of the specific psychological and sociological aspects of what soldiers face when they serve on peacekeeping missions.

This is certainly a timely topic and a timely book. With 45,000 military peacekeepers and civilian police representing 87 nations serving on 15 UN peacekeeping missions as of the summer of 2002, it is an opportune time for those who plan and lead peacekeeping missions to benefit from what psychologists and other social scientists have to offer. What are the challenges peacekeepers face? How can peacekeepers best be prepared to deal with the psychological ambiguities of their unique and complex tasks? Do soldiers easily make the transition from war-fighter to peacekeeper and back? Does peacekeeping duty actually interfere with or enhance war-fighting skills? In the 18 chapters that follow, Britt, Adler, and 23 other contributing authors representing 7 nations examine these questions and for the first time take a systematic view of military peacekeeping from a psychological perspective. They first discuss some of the fundamental problems in conducting psychological research on peacekeeping. They then examine social-psychological issues in peacekeeping and address peacekeeping from the perspectives of industrial-organizational, health, and clinical psychology. They then examine some of the cross-cultural issues that can arise when a peacekeeping force is composed of soldiers from different nations, and they offer recommendations for planners of peacekeeping operations and areas for future research directions.

The 10 years between 1992 and 2002 saw a fundamental change in what the international community was willing to attempt in an effort to bring peace and relief to troubled regions. Most peacekeeping missions prior to 1992 were mounted only with the consent of the parties to the dispute, and it was the role of peacekeepers to monitor an agreed-upon cease-fire. In many cases, the biggest psychological challenge peacekeepers faced was boredom. But following 1992, peacekeepers were deployed in the absence of a cease-fire, without the consent of the parties to the conflict, where civilian populations were caught in the crossfire, and there was in fact no peace to keep. The assumptions and definitions of traditional peacekeeping were no longer valid because peace-keeping was being pulled simultaneously in two opposite directions—peace enforcement imposed through force, and humanitarian relief provided to ci-vilian victims. Peacekeepers deployed on these complex and multifaceted emer-gencies faced a new set of issues that were as much psychological as they were military or diplomatic.

Soldiers in war and soldiers on peacekeeping missions face completely dif-ferent key challenges. In war, soldiers face a clearly defined foe and use all force available to prevail on the battlefield through the application of violence. This is the war-fighter's psychology. But soldiers on peacekeeping missions are not supposed to participate in the conflict. Instead they are supposed to use per-suasion and their diplomatic skills to contain or limit violence and seek a peace-ful resolution to the conflict. This is not an easy task, and it poses a different set of demands—especially psychological demands—on the individual peace-keeping soldier. In many cases research psychologists examine questions that can be studied in a laboratory through structured and controlled experiments. Participants are assigned to treatment groups, the independent variables are administered, the dependent variable is measured, and the research psycholo-gist draws inferences based on the data. But psychologists studying peacekeep-ing do not have the luxury of conducting controlled laboratory experiments. They must deal with reality as it exists, seeking information through ques-tionnaires, surveys, and interviews. In war-fighting or peacekeeping, scientific research is never the highest priority on a soldier's mind, making this a difficult topic to study. But in this book, the contributing authors have faced this chal-lenge and have been as rigorous and scientific as possible. The reader will find a thorough and detailed discussion of a topic that is by its nature confusing, complex, and evolving with each new international emergency.

Harvey J. Langholtz
Series Editor, Psychological Dimensions to War and Peace

Preface

Across the globe, military personnel come together to serve as peacekeepers in regions where war and conflict have raged. The importance of these attempts at sustaining peaceful resolutions to conflict is reflected in the amount of resources, personnel, and international attention that such efforts require. Understanding the determinants of these complex operations and identifying the framework behind the implementation of peace initiatives involves analytical tools from a wide range of disciplines applied to a wide range of elements involved in peacekeeping. In this book, our focus is on the individuals who are sent to these potentially volatile regions to help create the conditions for peace. These peacekeepers are deployed to situations foreign to them, and they must attempt to preserve a fragile peace under what can be unclear and difficult conditions.

Many questions can be asked regarding the experiences of these peacekeepers: How do peacekeepers respond and adapt to the various stressors they encounter? How do peacekeepers view their participation in peacekeeping operations? What determines whether peacekeepers will be effective in carrying out their various tasks? How do peacekeepers from different countries work together to accomplish their mission? What distinguishes peacekeepers who grow and thrive as a result of participation in peacekeeping operations from those who develop psychological difficulties following their deployment?

This book brings together a multinational team of researchers from different specialties within psychology for a comprehensive examination of peacekeepers. By combining psychological theory and research conducted with peacekeepers, this text provides both an academic and applied perspective. The book is structured by subspecialties within psychology to ensure a level of depth and breadth in covering the topic of the psychology of peacekeepers. Specialists in social, industrial-organizational, health, clinical, and cross-cultural psychology use principles in their field to understand the determinants of health and performance among individuals involved in peacekeeping operations. It is our hope that by understanding the psychological issues affecting peacekeepers, recommendations can be made for optimizing the health and performance of individuals deployed in support of peacekeeping operations, thereby increasing the likelihood that the operations will achieve their goal of creating a stable peace in which rebuilding can occur.

Putting together an international volume that seeks to apply the lessons from diverse fields in psychology would not be possible without the dedicated contributions of the authors in this volume. We thank each of them. We would also like to thank Carl A. Castro for his support and insights throughout the development of this project. We are also grateful to Coleen Crouch, research assistant extraordinaire, for her positive attitude and careful attention to detail. Finally, Debbie Carvalko has been incredibly supportive throughout the project.

Work on this project was funded in part by the U.S. Army Medical Research and Materiel Command, Fort Detrick, Maryland, and we are grateful for this support. However, the views expressed in this volume are those of the authors and do not reflect the official policy or position of the Department of the Army, Department of Defense, or the U.S. government.

Finally, thousands of peacekeepers responded to the surveys and interviews that form the basis for this volume. We appreciate their time and effort in participating in this research. The underlying purpose of this volume is to support peacekeepers and the effectiveness of their operations. Peacekeepers deploy far from home, place themselves in harm's way, and confront challenges from boredom to danger in the service of peace. It is with the deepest respect that we acknowledge their contributions and sacrifices.

I
Fundamental Issues in Studying the Peacekeeper

1

The Psychology of the Peacekeeper: An Introductory Framework

Thomas W. Britt and Amy B. Adler

Individuals from over 110 nations have been called on to deploy to areas around the globe to maintain the peace among former warring factions and nations (United Nations Department of Public Information [UNDPI], 2001a). The United Nations (UN) has participated in over 50 peacekeeping operations in all parts of the world since 1948, and the prevalence and importance of peace-keeping missions show no signs of abating. In 2001 alone, the UN deployed 47,000 personnel in support of 15 peacekeeping missions (UNDPI, 2001a), and the North Atlantic Treaty Organization (NATO) has continued to devote significant resources to peacekeeping operations, including 21,000 troops to Bosnia-Herzegovina (NATO On-line Library, 2000) and 38,000 troops to Kosovo (Piatt, 2002).

These international peacekeepers must often do their job in a chaotic and uncertain environment. Among UN peacekeeping operations alone, 1,219 peacekeepers have been killed in the service of keeping the peace (UNDPI, 2001b). Not only do they confront traditional stressors associated with being deployed to foreign locations (such as family separation and the chance of being wounded or killed), but peacekeepers must also deal with stressors specific to the mission of peacekeeping, such as remaining impartial when dealing with members of the former warring factions, and refraining from aggression when being taunted or ridiculed. Despite the various stressors and challenges associated with peacekeeping, there is also the potential for peacekeepers to take personal pride in helping maintain peace and prevent bloodshed, and to use their skills in a real-world mission.

The job of the peacekeeper, by its very nature, is complex and yet vitally important to the success of multinational peace support operations. The emerging field of peacekeeping studies, introduced in the edited volume by Langholtz (1998), encompasses many crucial elements that are rooted in a range of social science disciplines from political science and economics to anthropology. These disciplines provide a basis for understanding the many-layered dynamics of supporting peace on a global scale. In developing the field of peacekeeping studies, specific areas of research deserve detailed examination. This volume addresses one of these areas. The goal of this book is to apply principles from the discipline of psychology to an understanding of the individuals actually engaged in the task of peacekeeping: the peacekeepers themselves.

In the spirit of the classic study of the American soldier during World War II (Stouffer et al., 1949), this volume illustrates how research-based principles from different areas of psychology can be applied to understanding the thoughts, feelings, and behaviors of individuals attempting to establish peace. In this volume we take an "outcome variable" approach toward understanding the well-being and performance of peacekeepers. That is, our ultimate goal is to draw from as many areas of psychology as possible to provide a complete account of the psychological issues relevant to peacekeepers. The focus of each chapter is how psychological theories and research can inform our understanding of the fundamental outcome variables of importance to peacekeepers: well-being and performance.

CLARIFICATION OF TERMS

Before reviewing the specific layout of the volume, we address the various terms that have been applied to the arena of military operations in which peacekeepers do their work. One of the reasons for detailing the different strategies of conducting peacekeeping operations is that how these operations are carried out has implications for the health and performance of peacekeepers. There is currently some controversy and inconsistency regarding how to refer to operations involving the monitoring or enforcement of peace in a troubled region (Diehl, 1993; Jakobsen, 2000). A useful starting point for clarifying the terminology is provided in a report of the Panel on United Nations (UN) Peace Operations (Brahimi, 2000). According to this report, peace operations are classified into three principal activities: (1) conflict prevention and peacemaking, (2) peacekeeping, and (3) peace-building. Of these three activities, peacekeeping describes the activities and operations of interest included in this volume. Peacekeeping reflects a broad range of operations, from observing cease-fires and separations, to attempts to establish peace following civil wars. As outlined in the Brahimi report, the bedrock principles of a peacekeeping operation include consent of the local parties, impartiality, and the use of force only in self-defense. Brahimi points out that military forces involved in such operations have traditionally been lightly armed. Military operations characterized by these principles are usually referred to as "peacekeeping operations" or "traditional peacekeeping."

In contrast to traditional UN peacekeeping, a relatively recent emphasis has been placed on conducting peacekeeping operations with large forces that are heavily armed and authorized to use force in addition to self-defense (e.g., to enforce aspects of the peace accord or to prevent the killing of civilians). These missions have been termed "complex peacekeeping" (Brahimi, 2000), peace enforcement, or peace restoration (Jakobsen, 2000). The NATO-led missions in Bosnia and Kosovo typify this new strategy of conducting peacekeeping operations. These missions represent a change in thinking about peacekeeping, both by the UN and other countries (Brahimi, 2000; Jakobsen, 2000). Many analysts now argue that peacekeeping operations may fail if the deployed military force is not sufficiently strong, and the rules of engagement are not sufficiently robust, to deter former warring factions from violating aspects of the accord or to respond with sufficient force when aspects of the accord are in fact violated (Brahimi, 2000; Jakobsen, 2000). Participants on such operations are still to remain impartial, and if force is used in response to the violation of a peace accord, the goal of the response is not to demolish the enemy completely, but rather to let the warring factions know that such violations will not be tolerated.

Given that the line between peacekeeping and peace enforcement may become blurred even within a single operation, "peacekeeping operations," "peace support operations," or "peace operations" are useful general terms for military operations whose objective is to aid in establishing peace in a region. Some chapter authors use the term "peace enforcement" when referring to a specific military operation characterized by the use of force to facilitate adherence to the peace agreement (e.g., Olonisakin, this volume), or they make reference to a particular operation as "traditional peacekeeping" when it is characteristic of traditional UN operations (e.g., Weisæth, this volume). In contrast to the diversity of terms used to characterize peacekeeping operations, all of the authors in the present volume refer to the individuals involved in the various missions as "peacekeepers."

Regardless of the categorization of peacekeeping operations themselves, we must recognize there is an even greater spectrum of military operations. We believe it is useful to think about military operations as consisting of three basic mission types: humanitarian, peace support (traditional peacekeeping and peace enforcement), and combat. Furthermore, the complexity of recent military operations reveals that the same mission can contain elements of two or three types of operations.

For example, humanitarian missions occurred during the Gulf War, and at the conclusion of the combat mission, a strong (i.e., complex) peacekeeping presence remained to enforce the peace treaty. In a similar example of moving from combat to peacekeeping, U.S. military personnel deployed in support of the U.S.-led operation in Haiti initially believed they would be engaging in a combat operation to remove the military leader of Haiti, but upon arriving in Haiti found out they would be serving as peacekeepers while a change of power occurred in the country. The operation can also move from a humanitarian to a combat mission. As described in several of the chapters in this volume, the U.S. operation in Somalia was initially humanitarian but turned into a combat operation designed to facilitate peace in the region. Clearly, these missions defy classification as a single type of operation. The important point to recognize is that military operations develop over time and can shift from one type of operation to another, running the gamut from humanitarian aid to combat. In general, these evolving missions with their changing guidelines, rules of engagement, and objectives challenge military personnel to adjust their expectations, attitudes, and behaviors quickly to meet the shifting mission requirements. The challenge of these missions lies not only in the fluid nature of the operational environment but also in the contrast between the goals of peacekeeping and the expectations and training of combat-ready military forces. It is in this ambiguous and demanding context that peacekeepers operate (see Britt, 1998).

OVERVIEW OF THIS BOOK

This volume is organized around five areas of psychology that have been applied to peacekeeping operations: social psychology, industrial-organizational psychology, health psychology, clinical psychology, and cross-cultural psychology. Within each area, a multinational group of scientists analyzes how principles in their specialty within psychology can be used to understand the peacekeeper experience. As a reflection of the multidisciplinary nature of peacekeeping research, many of the chapters overlap several areas in psychology. Ultimately, the chapters address three central questions regarding peacekeeping missions: What are the challenges and demands that peacekeepers face?, How can these challenges and demands affect the peacekeeper and the accomplishment of the mission?, and What can be done to facilitate peacekeeping adaptation in the face of these challenges?

Table 1.1 provides a descriptive framework for the psychological issues addressed by the various chapters. Although this list does not exhaustively describe all of the issues addressed by the chapter authors, it does serve as a framework for organizing many of the central ideas presented in the volume. As seen in Table 1.1, psychological factors relevant to peacekeeper adjustment and performance can be categorized at the level of the specific peacekeeping operation, the unit to which the peacekeeper belongs, and attributes of the individual peacekeeper. Factors associated at the level of the peacekeeping operation deal with issues that are likely to affect all of the peacekeepers participating in a given operation. For example, the strength of the rules of engagement and public support for the operation are issues at the operational level that may ultimately influence the peacekeeper's morale and performance. Past military research has emphasized qualities of the individual's unit, such as good leadership and group cohesion, as critical determinants of adjustment and coping during military operations (see Bliese & Castro and Thomas & Castro, this volume). Finally, attributes of the individual peacekeeper should influence the extent to which they adapt and perform well during the operation.

Table 1.1
Organizational Framework for Factors Hypothesized to Influence Peacekeeper Well-Being and Performance

---

Factors at the Level of the Specific Peacekeeping Operation
Presence or absence of a signed peace treaty
Details of the peace treaty (e.g., disarming time frame, unit withdrawal, presence of civilian military police)
Size of the proposed peacekeeping force
Rules of engagement for peacekeepers (robust vs. restrictive)
Operation-specific stressors (e.g., extreme hot or cold climate; highly antagonistic vs. supportive local population)
Number of and cultural differences among nations participating in the peacekeeping force
Public support for the operation
Maturity of the theater for peacekeepers (e.g., living conditions, opportunities for recreation and exercise)

Factors Relevant to Peacekeeper's Unit
Unit cohesion and morale
Quality of unit leadership (e.g., communication, support)
Collective efficacy (unit's belief in their ability to accomplish the mission)
Quality of predeployment training for the mission

Factors Relevant to the Individual Peacekeeper
Clinical history (e.g., prior psychological difficulties)
Predeployment stress level (e.g., recent major life events, family problems)
Source of motivation for participation (e.g., intrinsic vs. extrinsic)
Subjective perceptions of stressors on the deployment
Attitudes toward the operation (e.g., "Is the mission worthwhile?")
Style of coping with stress (e.g., avoidance vs. problem focused)
Individual self-efficacy (individual belief in ability to accomplish tasks)
Experience with and knowledge of the local population
Family support for the peacekeeper
Peacekeeper's past history of deployment

For example, peacekeepers with a history of clinical disorders are more likely to develop psychological problems following the operation (see Litz, Gray, & Bolton, this volume).

The second chapter in this first part addresses methodological issues in how peacekeeping researchers conduct research that will have relevance to peacekeepers on the ground. In Part II on social psychology, the chapters illustrate how a peacekeeper's social identity shapes his or her view of peacekeeping operations, the importance of stereotyping and prejudice in peacekeeping, and how peacekeepers' attitudes are related to deriving benefits from participation in the operation. In Part III on industrial-organizational psychology, the chapters consider aspects of job performance that are carried out by peacekeepers, the various sources of work motivation that drive the peacekeeper, and organizational variables predictive of job satisfaction and performance among peacekeepers. In Part IV on health psychology, the chapters consider the nature of stress during peacekeeping operations, how peacekeepers are able to cope with different types of stressors, and factors that may help protect peacekeepers from the negative effects of stress. In Part V on clinical psychology, the chapters focus on psychological problems that may develop for some individuals involved in peacekeeping operations, as well as the prevention and treatment of these problems. In Part VI on cross-cultural psychology, the chapters address the important issues of how peacekeepers from different nations work together, how value differences between cultures can contribute to cooperation or conflict, and the rather unique situation faced by African peacekeepers who attempt to maintain peace on their own continent. The final chapter summarizes the themes present across the various sections of the volume, provides recommendations for planners and leaders of peacekeeping operations, and highlights areas for further research.

The goals of this book are to identify psychological principles that help explain the adaptation of the peacekeeper in past, present, and future peacekeeping operations. Although the missions themselves may change, it is hoped the research and principles discussed in this volume will have relevance to peacekeepers as peacekeeping operations change and evolve. For example, some of the chapters in the present volume note the differences in stressors faced by soldiers who deploy on traditional UN peacekeeping operations characterized by a smaller force with more restrictive rules of engagement compared to those soldiers who deploy on NATO-led peacekeeping operations characterized by a large force with robust rules of engagement. Although the severity of certain stressors associated with the type of operation may be different, the same underlying stress dimensions may be present in both types of operations (see Adler, Litz, & Bartone, this volume). In another chapter, Olonisakin describes the case of African peacekeepers promoting peace on the African continent. Although such peacekeeping missions are unique, she cites some of the same stressors and sources of motivation that appear in other peacekeeping operations.

The reality of peacekeeping operations is that they can be complex and can change rapidly. This reality highlights the significance of another characteristic of the chapters in this volume, namely the importance of conducting research with actual peacekeepers on actual operations. Although important lessons may be learned from reflecting on how current psychological principles might be applied to peacekeeping in theory, each chapter either reports or cites data collected from peacekeepers on peacekeeping operations. By using such data, the information presented in the chapters is rooted in an ecologically valid approach to applying psychology to peacekeepers.

In keeping with this contextual approach, it is critical for research to be grounded in both quantitative and qualitative methods. Some authors in this volume focus on rich qualitative data gathered from participants on peacekeeping operations. Other authors take a more quantitative approach, developing standardized instruments to assess a variety of psychological variables relevant to the peacekeeper, and testing theoretical models that predict outcomes associated with peacekeeper attitudes, health, and performance. Taken together, these two research methods provide a more complete account of psychological factors relevant to the peacekeeper.

We hope these chapters serve the dual purpose of illustrating the utility of psychological principles to real-world problems and providing planners of peacekeeping operations with information and recommendations that will help promote the healthy adaptation and performance of peacekeepers. If psychological research is useful in developing healthy and high-performing peacekeepers, then not only may peacekeepers benefit, but their effective performance may also benefit the local populations by establishing a stable framework for peace.

NOTE

This chapter was funded in part by the U.S. Army Medical Research and Materiel Command, Fort Detrick, Maryland, and we are grateful for this support. However, the views expressed in this volume are those of the authors and do not reflect the official policy or position of the Department of the Army, Department of Defense, or the U.S. government.

REFERENCES

Brahimi, L. (2000). *Report of the panel on United Nations peace operations.* Retrieved May 1, 2002, from http://www.un.org/peace/reports/peace_operations/docs/summary.htm

Britt, T. W. (1998). Psychological ambiguities in peacekeeping. In H. J. Langholtz (Ed.), *The psychology of peacekeeping* (pp. 111–128). Westport, CT: Praeger.

Diehl, P. F. (1993). *International peacekeeping.* Baltimore and London: Johns Hopkins University Press.

Jakobsen, P. V. (2000). The emerging consensus on gray area peace operations doctrine: Will it last and enhance operational effectiveness? *International Peacekeeping,* 7, 36–56.

Langholtz, H. J. (Ed.). (1998). *The psychology of peacekeeping.* Westport, CT: Praeger.

North Atlantic Treaty Organization On-line Library. (2000). Kosovo—facts and figures. Retrieved May 10, 2002, from http.//www.nato.int/docu/facts/2000/kosovo-ff.htm

Piatt, G. (2002, April 28). NATO plans to cut Balkans force by 10,000. *Stars and Stripes,* p. 3.

Stouffer, S. A., Lumsdaine, A. A., Williams, R. B., Smith, M. B., Janis, I. L., Star, S. A.,
    & Cottrell, L. S. (1949). *The American soldier: Combat and its aftermath*
    (Vol. 2). Princeton, NJ: Princeton University Press.
United Nations Department of Public Information. (2001a). *United Nations peace*
    operations in 2001. Retrieved April 2, 2002, from http://www.un.org/Depts/
    dpko/dpko/pub/year_review01/index.html
United Nations Department of Public Information. (2001b). *United Nations peace-*
    keeping: In the service of peace. Retrieved January 28, 2002, from http://
    www.un.org/Depts/dpko/dpko/home_bottom.htm

2

Considerations When Conducting Psychological Research during Peacekeeping Missions: The Scientist and the Commander

Carl Andrew Castro

The best peacekeeping research arguably addresses practical problems confronted by the peacekeepers and advances the development of scientific theory. Whereas the military scientist is generally more concerned about the testing and development of theory and hypotheses, the operational commander is typically more concerned with identifying practical solutions to current problems. These two goals of peacekeeping research, however, are not mutually exclusive, and both can be achieved. This chapter presents some suggestions for how future peacekeeping research can improve the likelihood of simultaneously accomplishing both of these goals: (1) solving practical problems that arise on peacekeeping missions and (2) developing scientifically based peacekeeping theory.

This chapter is organized into six sections. In the first section, the importance of defining the research problem in terms of peacekeeping application is emphasized. It is further suggested that the involvement of the operational commander in this early stage of the research process can ensure that relevant peacekeeping issues are considered. In the second section, a framework for viewing the various classes of general theories are presented, with exemplars of these theories applied to peacekeeping missions. Given the importance of developing predictive models of peacekeeper performance and well-being that generalizes to other peacekeeping operations and military cultures, the next two sections address these issues. In the fifth section, the key research procedures, the survey and interview that psychologists employ in conducting peacekeeping research, are discussed. Here it is recommended that both the survey and the interview be used in peacekeeping research. In the final section, the role of theory and the commander is briefly discussed. In this section it is argued that the military scientist plays a critical role in providing scientifically valid findings to inform the commander when making decisions on how to improve soldier and unit readiness.

DEFINING THE SCIENTIFIC PROBLEM TO BE RELEVANT TO PEACEKEEPING MISSIONS

All scientific endeavors begin with a problem. As Northrop (1947) rightly notes, "no inquiry can ever get under way until and unless *some difficulty is felt* in a practical or theoretical situation" [italics in original] (p. 11). Although most of us agree that science should be problem oriented, all too often we become method oriented. The best way to ensure problem-oriented research is by clearly stating the problem, or the research question if you like, that the study will directly address. When conducting peacekeeping research, the operational commander (and the staff) should also be included in this phase of the process. This is extremely important to do, especially if the researcher has never been on a peacekeeping deployment or has not been to the deployed environment where the study is to take place. Often the commander and/or the staff will provide a unique perspective on issues concerning the peacekeeping mission that can only be obtained by those currently on the mission. Most importantly, though, and as discussed later, including the commander and the staff in deciding what peacekeeping issues to investigate ensures that the study addresses practical problems the commander cares about.

Stating the Problem

Stating the problem is by no means easy. Indeed, the most difficult portion of any inquiry, whether it be scientific or nonscientific, is its initiation. It is the analysis of the problem that provides the criterion for selecting out of the infinite number of facts in the world that are relevant to the problem at hand. One may have the most rigorous of methods during the later stages of investigations, but if a false or superficial beginning has been made, rigor later on will never correct the situation. The danger is in plunging into a subject matter, sending out questionnaires, gathering a tremendous amount of data, even performing experiments, only to come out at the end wondering what it all proves or means (see Platt, 1964).

Briefly, a complete analysis of the problem involves (1) stating clearly what the problem is, (2) identifying all of the relevant facts relating to the problem, and (3) designating all relevant hypotheses suggested by the relevant facts. An analysis of the problem must precede all scientific inquiry. Science does not begin with facts, with hypotheses, or even with a method, but instead with a clearly defined and articulated statement of the problem. This simple truth should always be kept in mind, especially when proposing research projects to field commanders who are not particularly interested in supporting an investigator's "curiosity" or "scientific hunch." At the very least there should be some uncertainty regarding the current situation or state of affairs that the commander will immediately agree with. Otherwise, the researcher is not likely to gain access to the peacekeepers to conduct the proposed study, or even if the researcher is able to gain access to the peacekeepers and conduct the study, when it comes time to brief the commander on the importance of the findings the researcher will be hard pressed to explain why the study was conducted to begin with or why other factors were not considered. Stating the problem clearly and up front, before the study begins, will help the peacekeeping researcher avoid these awkward moments.

Study the Peacekeeper

The proper study of peacekeeping is the peacekeeper. This means that peacekeeping researchers should focus on the behavior, attitudes, and well-being of the peacekeeper. To the extent that the peacekeepers' needs, wants, and desires are determinants of effective performance, they should also be assessed. After all, the goal of peacekeeping research is to create or establish an enabling environment for peacekeepers that maximally benefits their well-being and their ability to perform the mission, and this can only be accomplished if the focus is on the peacekeeper. This means two things. First, clear indicators of peacekeeper well-being and performance need to be identified. And second, those dimensions in the environment that influence the well-being and performance of the peacekeeper need to be identified.

All those factors in the environment that either individually or collectively affect the well-being and performance of the peacekeeper are the human dimension factors of peacekeeping. These human dimension factors may either enhance or decrement the well-being or performance of the peacekeeper. It is just as important to identify those aspects of human dimensions that affect performance and well-being in a positive manner (see Britt, Alder, & Bartone, 2001; Mehlum, 1995). Thus a complete analysis of the peacekeeper will include both the positive and the negative aspects of the deployment. Indeed, in my research of peacekeepers deployed to Bosnia, Kosovo, or Kuwait, the operational commanders always insisted on hearing both the good news and the bad news. This has led me to believe it is essential that we let commanders know what is working so they continue to do it, as well as letting commanders know what is not working so it might be improved.

THE IMPORTANCE OF THEORY AND CURRENT PEACEKEEPING THEORETICAL RESEARCH

The most important aspect of science is the development of theoretical explanations of natural phenomena that can be tested against the real world. That peacekeeping research is usually nonexperimental does not mean it is atheoretical. Theoretical studies can and must be conducted during peacekeeping missions. Thus peacekeeping research can be explanatory in nature. That is, peacekeeping studies can assess the causes or bases of behavior. Priority of studies should be given to those that address important ideas, which are linked to hypotheses, derived from theory. Lest we forget, "The function of a hypothesis is to direct our search for the order among facts. The suggestions formulated in the hypothesis may be solutions to the problem. Whether they are, is the task of the inquiry" (Cohen & Nagel, 1934). A crucial study is one that not only confirms an existing scientific theory, but also confirms one theory as it repudiates others (Platt, 1964). Such studies are impossible to define without recourse to at least two theoretical possibilities. Whenever possible all peacekeeping studies should attempt to test two or more theories simultaneously. By providing support for one theory, while showing deficiencies in another, we begin to exclude one theoretical approach while simultaneously advancing the development of another. We should never forget that ultimately science *is* about exclusion. Scientific progress is achieved the quickest, the faster we determine what is not useful and relevant.

This emphasis on theory should not discourage the conduct of peacekeeping studies that also address atheoretical issues, such as studies designed to answer practical problems. But it should always be made very clear that this is the case. The hallmark of atheoretical research is that the research is not based on statements drawn from a theory (hypothesis), and the research ideas, when tested, will not necessarily support, clarify, or refute a theory. Although such research may be found to have some relevance to theory after it is completed, this is usually not intended. In fact, the data from such an atheoretical study may end up being just a bit of scientific data that has no meaning or relevance to any given theoretical formulation at all. That said, never forget that the purpose of theory is to integrate existing knowledge and to obtain new knowledge. New knowledge results from the test of hypotheses derived from such theories. Thus theory-related research always has the promise of providing information that expands our understanding of peacekeeping missions that atheoretical-based research does not.

In the remainder of this section, a framework for conceptualizing the various theories tested during peacekeeping missions is presented, followed by examples from peacekeeping missions involving U.S. soldiers.

Factual and Normative Theory

Basically two general classes of theory apply to all peacekeeping research: factual theory and normative theory. Factual theory "designates a form of social organization which corresponds exactly to what is in fact the case in a specific society or culture to which the theory purports to refer," whereas normative theory "defines the ideal society at which we are aiming" (Northrop, 1947, p. 21; see also Weimer, 1979). Normative theory then concerns questions of what ought to be the case as opposed to what is indeed the case. Thus normative theory seeks to introduce change in the situation, at least in part, rather than conforming to it. One should also appreciate that typically the so-called hard scientists, that is, the physicists and chemists, deal in the domain of factual theories, whereas the so-called soft scientists, for instance, psychologists and sociologists, deal in both domains. This important distinction is due to the nature of the problems that each discipline addresses. The physical scientists are concerned primarily with the discovery of reality or facts if you prefer; the social scientists are concerned with both the discovery of reality and with the discovery of ways to improve it. That social scientists deal with both problems lends credibility to the belief of many social scientists that their scientific task is much more difficult than that of the physical scientists. After all, it is much more difficult to explain *and* improve a phenomenon, as opposed to just explaining it.

The distinctions between factual and normative theories are critically important for psychological peacekeeping research. If the purpose of the research was simply to "describe" the environment the peacekeepers are experiencing and how the peacekeepers are responding (or adapting), a factual theory would be adequate. However, if instead, the goal of the research is to improve the situation for the peacekeepers, and thereby induce change, a normative theory needs to be used. If one is not available, one must be developed. It is important to appreciate that normative theory depends on the use and/or development of an adequate factual theory because it is impossible to recommend changes for improvement unless one knows the facts of the current situation. This distinction is also important if the commanders of peacekeeping operations are expecting recommendations for improvement. If commanders are expecting the findings from the peacekeeping research to lead to specific recommendations, the guiding theoretical framework for the investigations should be normative in form; otherwise, the researchers will be at a loss for what to recommend.

Natural History and Deductively Formulated Theory

Within both the factual and normative classes of theories are two major stages of scientific inquiry: the natural history stage (inductively formulated) and the deductively formulated theory stage (Kuhn, 1996; Northrop, 1947). The goal of theory developed in the natural history stage is to describe the facts under investigation. Specifically, the methods of the natural history stage are inductive, involving observation, description, and classification; thus the concepts are necessarily largely descriptive and excessively qualitative in character. Such concepts are referred to as concepts by intuition, which means not a speculative hunch, but concepts that emerge or are developed as a result of direct observation.

In the deductively formulated theory stage, basic assumptions or postulates are proposed to exist from which theory and hypotheses are derived and developed. To this proposal or hypothesis, formal logic is then applied to deduce theorems or consequences (see Hawking, 1996). Thus it is much more mathematical in its approach. It is only by means of such concepts that unobservable entities and relations are introduced into scientific theory (see Hume, 1963). The task of the deductive scientist is to begin with the postulated entities, describe how the postulated entities are related, and then to find empirical data with which certain of the postulated entities can be correlated so the existence of the latter entities can be put to an experimental test. The deductively formulated theory stage is viewed as the more mature stage of scientific inquiry that every science tries to attain; and physics is viewed to be at this stage of scientific development (see Hawking, 1996, for excellent examples of how this approach was applied in physics to confirm the general theory of relativity).

We must appreciate that science in the natural history stage does not require the use of formal logic, although it may be used. Thus predictive power and quantitative science are not to be found in this stage of inquiry. Instead, qualitative science is the method used. But this fact should in no way result in a deprecation of the inductive method because it is not as effective in its predictive power as the deductively formulated type of science in the next stage. Instead, the development of a natural history stage of science is a necessary prerequisite for the deductively formulated theory stage. Indeed, if one proceeds immediately to the deductively formulated type of scientific theory without first passing through the inductive method of scientific inquiry, the result is likely to result in theory that fails to account adequately for all of the facts under investigation.

Viewed within this epistemological perspective, there are then four types or categories of theories: (1) factual–natural history theory, (2) factual–deductively formulated theory, (3) normative–natural history theory, and (4) normative–deductively formulated theory. These categories of theory are important for peacekeeping researchers because the stage of inquiry determines both the generalizability and the predictive power of the theory. Table 2.1 compares each of these four categories of theories, as well as providing exemplars from U.S. peacekeeping research. Each of these is discussed in more detail later.

Factual Peacekeeping Theories

Clearly, most of the peacekeeping research conducted to date with U.S. peacekeepers involves the testing and development of factual peacekeeping theories (e.g., Applewhite & Segal, 1990; Harris & Segal, 1985; Ritzer, Campbell, & Valentine, 1999). One of the best examples of peacekeeping research conducted within the factual–natural history stage is that of Harris and Segal (1985) in their analysis of boredom in U.S. peacekeepers deployed to the Sinai. In their careful and thorough report, these investigators describe four important factors that contribute to this important deployment stressor: underutilization, cultural deprivation, lack of privation, and social isolation. Their method of inquiry was inductive, involving observations, interviews, and descriptions. Thus

Table 2.1
Key Characteristics (with Examples from the Peacekeeping Literature) of Factual and Normative Theories as a Function of the Stage of Theory Development

	Stage of Theory Development	
Types of Theory	Natural History	Deductively Formulated Theory
Factual	Describe Reality	Describe Reality
	Intuition	Deduction
	Description, Categories, Classification e.g., Harris & Segal (1985)	Theory and Hypotheses Testing e.g., Rothberg et al. (1985)
Normative	Change or Improve Reality	Change or Improve Reality
	Intuition	Deduction
	Description, Categories, Classification e.g., Bartone et al. (1998)	Theory and Hypotheses Testing e.g., Dolan et al. (2001)

it was qualitative in nature. Indeed, these investigators provided a very detailed qualitative description of the life of these peacekeepers during the deployment. Harris talked to the soldiers and commanders before and during the deployment in order to better understand the issue of boredom and how it was affecting the deployed force. Notice that this approach was only possible because Harris was deployed to the Sinai on the peacekeeping mission. That this research approach can be productive is evidenced by the fact that these findings have since been replicated by other investigators in U.S. peacekeepers deployed to Croatia (Bartone, Vaitkus, & Adler, 1998) and Swedish peacekeepers serving in Lebanon (Carlstrom, Lundin, & Otto, 1990), indicating that boredom is not specific to a particular peacekeeping deployment or confined to a single nationality.

Factual theories in the deductively formulated theory stage have also been tested in peacekeeping operations. Perhaps the best exemplar of peacekeeping research testing a factual–deductively formulated theory is the stressor transition theory described by Rothberg and colleagues (Rothberg, Harris, Jellen, & Pickle, 1985). According to the stressor transition theory, when people move or transition to a new physical environment, their health and well-being is adversely affected. Note that the stressor transition theory does not distinguish between whether the transition involves going on a training exercise for several days or deploying for six months to another country; that is, neither location nor duration is important because it is only the transition process that is postulated to be stressful. Rothberg et al. tested this theory in U.S. peacekeepers deploying to the Sinai for six months and compared the deployment findings with those of soldiers participating in a field training exercise in the United States. Their measure of health and well-being was the number of sick call visits to the health clinic. Their approach was to correlate the number of sick call visits to the changed physical environment, that is, the peacekeeping deployment. As predicted, these investigators found increased sick call visits at both the time of deployment and at the time of transition to the field. However, for those soldiers returning from the peacekeeping deployment, the number of sick call visits again increased after they returned to their home station; this was not true for soldiers returning from the field. Thus, although empirical support was obtained for the stressor transition theory, there does appear to be important differences between a peacekeeping deployment and a field training exercise, at least in terms of the recovery period. Importantly, because the stressor transition theory is a factual theory, as opposed to a normative theory, appropriately, no prescriptions for change in order to improve the health of the deployed peacekeepers were offered.

Normative Peacekeeping Theories

This now brings us to the normative theories of peacekeeping research. Recall that normative theories seek to introduce change into the situation, either totally or partially, in order to improve the well-being of the peacekeeper. An excellent example of peacekeeping research conducted within the normative–natural history stage is the report by Bartone and colleagues (1998) in which they identify and describe the key dimensions of the psychological stressors encountered by a medical unit deployed on a six-month peacekeeping mission to Croatia. The basic premises of these investigators were that peacekeeping missions contain stressors and these stressors adversely affect peacekeeper well-being. Bartone et al. reported that the important peacekeeping stressors for the Croatia peacekeeping mission included isolation, ambiguity, powerlessness, boredom, and threat/danger. Note that the peacekeeping stressor model developed by Bartone and colleagues also involved direct observations, interviews, and description—that is, intuition, the methodology that defines the natural history stage of scientific theory. This study also used the survey in order to classify the various peacekeeping stressors into their appropriate dimensions. The peacekeeping stressor model is a normative model because clearly the intent is to identify the stressors present during the various phases of conducting a peacekeeping mission and then to either attenuate or eliminate the stressors, if possible. In fact, these investigators do offer a number of recommendations for improving the environment of the peacekeepers, either by removing or lessening the identified stressors. However, there are no other identified variables in the model other than the stressors and the effects of the stressors. Instead, such variables are to be found in the list of recommendations that the authors provide.

This brings us to the second type of normative theory: deductively formulated theory. Clearly, the predominant conceptual framework guiding much of the peacekeeping research in the United States, which falls into this theoretical category, is the research being conducted under the umbrella of what I refer to here as the stressor adjustment model (see Thomas & Castro, this volume; Bliese & Castro, this volume; see also Cooper, Dewe, & O'Driscoll, 2001; Jex, 1998). The basic premises of this model include the following: (1) there are stressors in every environment (see Castro & Adler, 1999) that affect the well-being and performance of the peacekeeper based on the peacekeeper's appraisal of the environment; (2) the response of the peacekeeper to the environment can take many forms to include changes in physical health, psychological well-being, behavioral performance, or cognitive capacity (note that the peace-keeper's response could also include biochemical and physiological changes as well that might result in changes to their behavior, and even their personality); and (3) the relationships among the peacekeeping environment, the peace-keeper's appraisal of the environment, and the peacekeeper's response can be affected by numerous variables including individual-level moderators such as coping (Dolan et al., 2001) and self-engagement (Britt & Bliese, 2003), as well as unit-level leadership and organizational-level behavior (Thomas & Castro, this volume).

The peacekeeping research that falls into the normative–deductively formulated theory stage is very much tied to hypothesis testing, which is directly derived from theory. Although not excessively mathematical, formal logic is applied to deduce predictions or outcomes from the peacekeeping adjustment model. Further, the stressor adjustment model, and its subsumed theories, is also clearly normative in form. Explicit in the conceptualization of this model is change, which theoretically can occur at every component of the model, and in both directions. That is, a change in one of the components can result in either an increase or decrease in the well-being or performance of the peace-keeper. This makes the stressor adjustment model quite dynamic in scope. (See Bliese & Castro, this volume, for a further discussion of the implication of this model.) Suffice it to say, this model has the potential to serve as a unifying framework for not only peacekeeping research, but for human dimension research in general.

PEACEKEEPING THEORY AND PREDICTIONS

It is often said that the most important criterion of a scientific theory is its predictive power. Predictive power depends on established connections between the present and the future. The more connections that can be shown to exist between the present and the future, the greater and the more unequivocal is the predictive power. As previously noted, peacekeeping psychological research is presently in the early stages of the development of deductively formulated theories in that we are unable to predict with any degree of accuracy the configuration of data to any particular point in time. This is not to assert that peacekeeping researchers do not assess and study important empirical knowledge concerning changes in time. We certainly do. However, our approach tends to be rather speculative as we attempt to generalize future social states based on the empirical curves of past social states (Northrop, 1947). Even the commonly held belief that longitudinal methods and data are a panacea for establishing causality within the social sciences are unfounded, because inferences regarding causality are quite complex. As Menard (1991) rightly notes, the two reasons for conducting longitudinal research are to describe the pattern of change and to determine the direction and magnitude of the causal relationship. Thus, although longitudinal designs do contribute to the development of predictive models, causality is not established based solely on longitudinal designs, but also require the use of deductively derived theory.

An additional requirement for predictive power is that the factors defining the state of the system at any time must obey the laws of conservation. This means the subject matter of the science in question must remain constant over time. Only if this is true will the knowledge of the current specific properties of the state of a given system enable us to deduce all future states; and this is what we really mean when we say we have a dynamic theory as opposed to a static one. Northrop (1947) concluded that the social sciences could never achieve a dynamic theoretical framework because our subject matter violated the laws of conservation. Initially, this assertion seemed true because we appear to live in an open system, with numerous feedback loops. After all, human thoughts, wants, desires, opinions, attitudes, and feelings do not remain constant over time but are always in a state of flux. However, if instead of focusing on the "absolute values" of these concepts we instead focus on their "meaning," which is certainly less susceptible to changes over time, we can then begin moving away from the "open system" of our subject matter. Indeed, there are statistical procedures that enable us to determine if the meaning of our concepts under investigation are relatively stable (see, for example, Chan, 1998). Clearly, such a conceptualization will be essential to develop highly predictive models of the peacekeeper.

PEACEKEEPING THEORY AND THE MILITARY CULTURE

The stage of theory development is critically important when attempting to generalize peacekeeping theory or hypotheses to other settings or cultures. For the natural history stage of theory development, we must always keep in mind the empirical and contextual environment of any concept developed by intuition. In contrast, concepts developed in the deductively formulated theory stage possess only those meanings that the postulates of the specific deductive theory in which they occur confer on them. The meaning of a concept by postulation, then, has nothing whatsoever to do with the previous historical, social, or cultural circumstances that led the scientist to postulate it. This means that theories (or hypotheses) developed in the natural history stage will not be as useful as those developed in the deductively formulated theory stage when generalizing to other cultures or social organizations.

Consider this example from the natural history stage of theory development. Early in a peacekeeping deployment, U.S. soldiers routinely complain about their living conditions, which usually consist of 10 to 20 persons sharing a single tent where lack of privacy is common (Halverson, Bliese, Moore, & Castro, 1995). It is not hard, if you are from the United States, to imagine how such living arrangements might adversely affect the morale of U.S. peace-keepers. However, if the peacekeepers are from a culture where communal living is the norm, such living arrangements probably would not be as stressful, if stressful at all. Furthermore, even for U.S. peacekeepers deployed to the same theater of operations, lack of privacy might not be an issue, depending on how developed the theater is at the time of deployment. Thus, when considering models or theories developed within the natural history stage of development, not only does culture need to be considered, but the deployment context as well.

In contrast, a deductively derived theory of peacekeeping has the advantage that it will be applicable to both civilian and military populations regardless of the culture or the type of organization, or even the type of deployment (i.e., combat, peacekeeping, or humanitarian). For example, although the origins of the stressor adjustment model are found in the social and industrial-organizational psychology literature using nonmilitary populations (see Katz & Kahn, 1978), its applicability to military populations has been firmly established by Bliese and colleagues (Bliese & Britt, 2001; Bliese & Castro, 2000; Bliese & Jex, in press). Similarly, the transition stressor model of Rothberg et al. (1985) was also first tested in a nonmilitary population involving first-year college students moving from home to the university campus (Gortmaker, Eckenrode, & Gore, 1982). It is only because these theories were deductively derived that they have the possibility of transcending culture, social organization, and prior history. And it is this aspect of a deductively derived theory that makes it such a powerful theory. Moreover, it is this constancy of meaning provided by these theories, formulated in terms of concepts by postulations, which permits them to be normative, that is, to prescribe an ideal good and acceptable type of human behavior and organization with respect to which actual society may be judged. For peacekeeping research, deductively formulated theory is essential if the goal is to develop or test a peacekeeping theory or hypothesis that will have meaning and relevance across cultures. The greater the differences between the cultures under study, the more important it becomes that the theory be deductively derived.

THE USE OF THE SURVEY AND THE INTERVIEW IN PEACEKEEPING RESEARCH

Today we preach that science is not science unless it is quantitative. In the learned world there exists a hierarchy of sciences, with physics and mathematics at the top and psychology and sociology at the bottom. Arguably, the test that sustains these gradations is the test of exactness. It is commonly supposed that a discipline grows more exact as it grows more mathematical and a precise correspondence exists between exactness and truth. Some believe this is true even for combat (see Dupuy, 1975). Beguiled by the criterion of exactness, many physical scientists, including social scientists, have helped propagate this view. By exactness, of course, we mean numbers; and in peace-keeping research, numbers mean surveys. However, there are many misconceptions about the use of the survey in science. In this section, a brief review of the advantages and disadvantages of the survey is presented. It is argued that the disadvantages of surveys can be mostly offset by conducting interviews.

Over the past 50 years, thousands of survey scales and items have been developed covering an extremely wide range of topics, and hundreds more continue to be developed every year. Although the U.S. military began using surveys during World War I to assess soldier mental functioning and job aptitude, the widespread use of surveys did not become part of the U.S. military culture until World War II. From late 1941 to the summer of 1945, Stouffer and his colleagues (1949) obtained, during a period of about 3.5 years, over 573,900 completed surveys from soldiers stationed in the United States and throughout the world, including the Pacific, the Middle East, and Europe. In Europe alone, approximately 299,500 completed surveys were obtained. The topics of these surveys included attitudes toward the British, fear of enemy weapons, psychiatric screening tests, attitudes of combat infantry officers and infantrymen, attitudes toward the war, and soldiers' attitudes about length of time in combat, to name but a few of the hundreds of subjects surveyed.

Surveys are typically self-administered, and they are most often used when one is interested in people's reports or recollections, values, attitudes, or other unobservable information. For these reasons, survey data is often subjective in nature, although rarely acknowledged as so by those peacekeeper researchers who routinely use them. Always keep in mind that responses to survey questions are not expected to correspond directly to actual behavior (e.g., Finlay, Trafimow, & Moroi, 1999) because people forget, distort, or do not really know the answers to various items on the survey. Similarly, neither behavior nor performance is "a transparent guide to sensations, thoughts, or feelings" (Blackburn, 1999, p. 67).

Because such a large number of valid scales and items are already in existence, no peacekeeping scientists should ever seek to develop their own scale until a complete literature review has been conducted and it has been determined that no existing scale will meet their research needs, by which I mean address the research problem under consideration. This, of course, does not mean survey scales should be utilized just because others have used them. Issues frequently arise during peacekeeping missions for which there are no existing scales. In these cases, certainly, new scales will be required (see Converse & Pressor, 1986). Indeed, numerous investigators have attempted to capture the attitudes and experiences of peacekeepers via the survey. In our research of peacekeepers deployed to Kosovo, we used scales specific to peacekeeping missions and, in some instances, developed scales unique to the U.S. experience in Kosovo (Adler, Dolan, & Castro, 2000; Castro, Bienvenu, Huffman, & Adler, 2000).

The consistent use of the same survey scale or items permits peacekeeping researchers to compare their findings across different military deployments. Certainly one of the best examples of this is the research conducted at the Walter Reed Army Institute of Research, which was reported by Stuart and Halverson (1997). In this report, the psychological status of U.S. soldiers was compared across six different military environments to include nondeployed garrison, Somalia, the Gulf War, Haiti, Kuwait, and Bosnia. We must appreciate that these comparisons were only possible because *identical* measures of psychological symptoms and demographic variables were used for all the assessments. Had this not been the case, direct comparisons would not have been possible.

Despite these obvious advantages of the survey in field research, it also possesses some important disadvantages as well. First, surveys are fairly impersonal. Unlike interview research, which allows the peacekeeping researcher and the respondent to get better acquainted, survey research generally does not enable the investigator to get to know the participants. Second, surveys are fairly static in that they are not easily changeable once data collection begins. Interviews, however, permit the researcher to probe issues or change directions in the midst of data collection. Finally, survey research tends to oversimplify the complexities of human thoughts, emotions, opinions, and attitudes. Once again, interviews provide an effective countermeasure here. In our research of U.S. peacekeepers deployed to Kosovo, we used both interviews and surveys (Castro et al., 2000). During the interviews, important peacekeeping issues emerged that we had not anticipated. However, because we had planned for multisurvey administrations, we were able to modify subsequent surveys to capture these unexpected issues. Had we not conducted interviews, we would have missed aspects of the Kosovo deployment that were important to the U.S. peacekeepers serving there that we were not astute enough to think of ahead of time.

This leads one to the obvious conclusion that survey research is most effective when used in conjunction with interviews, because interviews and surveys balance quite nicely the strengths and weaknesses of the other (see Hemingway, 2000). From a more practical perspective, my experience has been that commanders like numbers, and whenever possible they insist on them. Somewhat paradoxically, however, commanders also place a great deal of emphasis on the qualitative data that we obtain through the soldier interviews and through our own observations (see also Dupuy, 1975). Thus both survey and interview data appear to provide the operational commanders the right combination of information they need to assess the well-being of the peacekeeper.

THE ROLE OF THEORY AND THE COMMANDER

The commander's primary responsibility is the commitment of present resources to an unknown and unknowable future (see Clausewitz, 1976). Drucker (1964) tells us that only two things about the future are certain: One, "it can not be known," and two, "it will be different from what exists now and from what we now expect" (p. 173). He further informs us that "Any attempt to base today's actions and commitments on 'predictions of future events' is futile. The best we can hope to do is to anticipate 'future effects of events' which have already irrevocably happened." Because the future is going to be different than today and it cannot be predicted, the commander's job is to work systematically to anticipate the unexpected and unpredicted inasmuch as possible and to prioritize the level of risk.

Long-range planning does not and cannot aim at eliminating risks and uncertainties. Neither is it the goal of the scientist or of peacekeeping research to eliminate risk. To remove all risk would be impossible (Slovik, 1987; Wilson, 1979; Zeckhouser & Viscusi, 1990). Furthermore, when we remove one risk, we may inadvertently cause others to appear. The one thing the commander can do is to try to find, and occasionally to create, the right risk and to exploit uncertainty. (This is indeed what is generally referred to as the "art of warfare.") The peacekeeping scientist can assist the commander by identifying and prioritizing the risks and potential risks encountered on a peacekeeping mission. Said differently, risks are potential problems. It is the job of the peacekeeping scientist to determine how important current and potential problems are in relation to other problems. Without asking the essential question "how important?" we cannot prioritize and use our resources where they will have the greatest impact. The peacekeeping researcher can assist the commander in determining the priority of the problems and where existing resources are best utilized.

The commander, when he or she acts scientifically and wisely, must think and operate in literally two worlds. Here is where the importance of both factual and normative theories becomes so critical. The commander must know things as they are (i.e., possess a factual theory) and know things as they ought to be (i.e., possess a normative theory). In addition, the commander must also possess the intellect to know what is achievable with the current resources. The scientifically grounded commander possesses scientifically verified factual theory concerning what is the case and scientifically verified normative theory of what ought to be the case and then achieves as much of the ideal as possible.

To demand more than is possible may mean the defeat of one's ideals completely; whereas to ask less than perfection may be to achieve more. It is the responsibility of the peacekeeping scientist to provide the commander with the necessary theory to act. Theory that links human action to a clearly defined problem is certainly ideal.

FINAL THOUGHTS

More than three decades ago, Will and Ariel Durant (1968) noted that in the 3,421 years of recorded history, the world has only known peace during 268 of them. It would take little effort to update these numbers because the total number of years of peace remains unchanged; and given the current world events, it does not appear likely to change anytime soon. I believe this fact alone speaks to the continued importance of conducting scientifically valid social science research that aims to improve the well-being of the peacekeeper. On the surface, the research issues are quite straightforward: what is the problem, what are the theories and hypotheses being tested, what data will be collected, and what will the findings tell us? But I hope I have shown that these questions are deceptively simple, and the critical issues are much more complex—science is, indeed, hard.

There is perhaps very little difference between one scientist and another, but what little there is, is very important. In describing the thinking process, Blackburn (1999) also provides an excellent description of the effective peacekeeping scientist: one that is able "to avoid confusion, detect ambiguities, keep things in mind one at a time, make reliable arguments, become aware of alternatives, and so on" (p. 5). As I have already noted, this is no easy task, but our peacekeepers deserve nothing less.

NOTE

The views expressed in this paper are those of the author and do not necessarily represent the official policy or position of the Department of Defense or the U.S. Army Medical Command. During the writing of this manuscript, the author was funded by the Research Area Directorate for Military Operational Medicine (Karl E. Friedl, director), U.S. Army Medical Research and Materiel Command, Fort Detrick, Maryland.

REFERENCES

Adler, A. B., Dolan, C. A., & Castro, C. A. (2001). U.S. soldier peacekeeping experiences and well-being after returning from deployment to Kosovo. *Proceedings of the 36th International Applied Military Psychology Symposium* (pp. 30–34). Split, Croatia: Ministry of Defense of the Republic of Croatia.

Applewhite, L. W., & Segal, D. R. (1990). Telephone use by peacekeeping troops in the Sinai. *Armed Forces & Society, 17,* 117–126.

Bartone, P. T., Vaitkus, M. A., & Adler, A. B. (1998). Dimensions of psychological stress in peacekeeping operations. *Military Medicine, 163,* 587–593.

Blackburn, S. (1999). *Think: A compelling introduction to philosophy.* Oxford: Oxford University Press.

Bliese, P. D., & Britt, T. W. (2001). Social support, group consensus and stressor-strain relationships: Social context matters. *Journal of Organizational Behavior, 22,* 425–436.

Bliese, P. D., & Castro, C. A. (2000). Role clarity, work overload and organizational support: Multilevel evidence of the importance of support. *Work and Stress, 14,* 65–73.

Bliese, P. D., & Jex, S. M. (in press). Incorporating a multi-level perspective into occupational stress research: Theoretical, methodological, and practical implications. *Journal of Occupational Health Psychology.*

Britt, T. W., Adler, A. B., & Bartone, P. T. (2001). Deriving benefits from stressful events: The role of engagement in meaningful work and hardiness. *Journal of Occupational Health Psychology, 6,* 53–63.

Britt, T. W., & Bliese, P. B. (2003). Testing the stress buffering effects of self engagement among soldiers on a military operation. *Journal of Personality, 72,* 245–265.

Carlstrom, A., Lundin, T., & Otto, U. (1990). Mental adjustment of Swedish UN soldiers in South Lebanon in 1988. *Stress Medicine, 6,* 305–310.

Castro, C. A., & Adler, A. B. (1999, Autumn). OPTEMPO: Effects on soldier and unit readiness. *Parameters,* pp. 86–95.

Castro, C. A., Bienvenu, R. V., Huffman, A. H., & Adler, A. B. (2000). Soldier dimensions and operational readiness in U.S. Army forces deployed to Kosovo. *International Review of the Armed Forces Medical Services, 73,* 191–200.

Chan, D. (1998). The conceptualization and analysis of change over time: An integrative approach incorporating longitudinal means and covariance structures analysis (LMACS) and multiple indicator latent growth modeling (MLGM). *Organizational Research Methods, 1,* 421–483.

Clausewitz, C. von (1976). *On war.* M. Howard & P. Paret (Eds. and Trans.). Princeton, NJ: Princeton University Press.

Cohen, M. R., & Nagel, E. (1934). *An introduction to logic and scientific method.* New York: Harcourt, Brace.

Converse, J. M., & Pressor, S. (1986). *Survey questions: Handcrafting the standardized questionnaire.* Newbury Park: Sage.

Cooper, C. L., Dewe, P. J., & O'Driscoll, M. P. (2001). *Organizational stress: A review and critique of theory, research, and applications.* Thousand Oaks, CA: Sage.

Dolan, C. A., Huffman, A. H., Adler, A. B., Wright, K. M., Thomas, J. L., & Castro, C. A. (2001). Coping with the stress of a military deployment: Psychological and physical health. Paper presented at the annual meeting of Stress and Anxiety Research, St. Andrews, Scotland.

Drucker, P. F. (1964). *Managing for results.* New York: Harper & Row,

Dupuy, T. N. (1975). *Numbers, predictions and war: Using history to evaluate combat factors and predict the outcome of battles.* Indianapolis: Bobbs-Merrill.

Durant, W., & Durant, A. (1968). *The lessons of history.* New York: Simon & Schuster.

Finlay, K. A., Trafimow, D., & Moroi, E. (1999). The importance of subjective norms on intentions to perform health behaviors. *Journal of Applied Social Psychology, 29,* 2381–2393.

Gortmaker, S. L., Eckenrode, J., & Gore, S. (1982). Stress and utilization of health services: A time series and cross-sectional analysis. *Journal of Health and Social Behavior, 23,* 25–38.

Halverson, R. R., Bliese, P. D., Moore, R. E., & Castro, C. A. (1995). Psychological well-being and physical health symptoms of soldiers deployed for Operation Uphold Democracy: A summary of human dimension research in Haiti. Defense Technical Information Center (ADA 29812–5).

Harris, J. J., & Segal, D. R. (1985). Observations from the Sinai: The boredom factor. *Armed Forces & Society, 11,* 235–248.

Hawking, S. (1996). *A brief history of time* (10th anniversary ed.). New York: Bantam.

Hemingway, M. A. (2000). Qualitative research in I-O psychology. *The Industrial-Organizational Psychologist, 44,* 45–51.

Hume, D. (1963). *The philosophy of David Hume.* V. C. Chappell (Ed. and introduction). New York: The Modern Library.

Jex, S. M. (1998). *Stress and job performance.* Thousand Oaks, CA: Sage.

Katz, D., & Kahn, R. L. (1978). *The social psychology of organizations* (2nd ed.). New York: Wiley.

Kuhn, T. S. (1996). *The structure of scientific revolutions* (3rd ed.). Chicago: University of Chicago Press.

Mehlum, L. (1995). Positive and negative consequences of serving in a UN peacekeeping mission. A follow-up study. *International Review of Armed Forces Medical Services, 68,* 289–295.

Menard, S. (1991). *Longitudinal research.* Sage University Paper Series on Quantitative Applications in the Social Sciences, series no. 07–076. Newbury Park, CA: Sage.

Northrop, F. S. C. (1947). *The logic of the sciences and the humanities.* New York: Macmillan.

Platt, J. R. (1964). Strong inference. *Science, 146,* 347–353.

Ritzer, D. R., Campbell, S. J., & Valentine, J. N. (1999). Human dimensions research during Operation "Joint Guard," Bosnia. *Army Medical Department Journal, 8,* 5–16.

Rothberg, J. M., Harris, J. J., Jellen, L. K., & Pickle, R. (1985). Illness and health of the U.S. battalion in the Sinai MFO deployment. *Armed Forces & Society, 11,* 413–426.

Slovik, P. (1987). Perceptions of risk. *Science, 236,* 280–285.

Stouffer, S. A., Lumsdaine, A. A., Lumsdaine, M. H., Williams, R. M., Smith, M. B., Janis, I. L., Star, S. A., & Cotrell, L. S. (1949). *The American soldier: Combat and its aftermath.* Princeton, NJ: Princeton University Press.

Stuart, J. A., & Halverson, R. R. (1997). The psychological status of the U.S. Army soldiers during recent military operations. *Military Medicine, 162,* 737–743.

Weimer, W. B. (1979). *Notes on the methodology of scientific research.* Hillsdale, NJ: Erlbaum.

Wilson, R. (1979). Analyzing the daily risks of life. *Technology Review, 81,* 41–46.

Zeckhouser, R. J., & Viscusi, W. K. (1990). Risk within reason. *Science, 248,* 559–564.

II

Social Psychological Issues in Peacekeeping

3

The Social Identity of Peacekeeping

Volker C. Franke

INTRODUCTION

In November 1994, Lieutenant General Michael Ryan, NATO air commander in Southern Europe, organized what was at the time the largest bombing raid in Europe since the end of World War II. The target, an airfield in Croatia, served as a launching base for Serb aircraft conducting bombing raids into Bosnia. Ryan's task, however, was not to make war on Croats or Serbs, but to support UN peacekeeping forces in Bosnia (Keaney & Douglass, 1999). Almost from the inception of the mission, U.S. forces operated in relatively uncharted territory. Having trained to confront communist forces in the Fulda Gap for nearly half a century, American soldiers were rapidly forced to wrestle with the political, diplomatic, social, cultural, and military demands of a peace operation. Although operations other than war (OOTW) are not new (see Breed, 1998; Moskos, 1976; Segal, 1995), the experience of U.S. soldiers with such operations had not been extensive, given the Cold War exclusion of major powers from participating in peacekeeping.

After prospects of open warfare had faded, it became increasingly obvious that the skills that had guided American forces so effectively in the Gulf War provided insufficient preparation for the challenges soldiers were confronting in the Balkans. "We were taught how to sneak around these tanks quietly, surprise the enemy and destroy him in combat," a second lieutenant explained. "But here we are supposed to stay out of combat by being obvious. To me, it's like teaching a dog to walk backwards" (quoted in O'Connor, 1996, p. A-3).

Over the past decade, peacekeepers have been deployed to more than 30 trouble spots around the globe to conduct missions ranging from disaster relief to deadly combat. Since dramatic television footage of a dead American soldier being dragged through the streets of Mogadishu by a rioting Somali mob in October 1993 resulted in termination of the operation and the speedy withdrawal of U.S. forces, conducting peace operations has become increasingly routine for the American military. Recent reports from Kosovo showed that peacekeepers never opened fire despite being pelted by baseball-size rocks and attacked with Molotov cocktails (Kitfield, 2000a; Ricks, 2001). But these soldiers were military police, trained to patrol and interact with a sometimes hostile population. Although on many occasions, soldiers have refrained from responding to provocations with violence, it might be more difficult to adjust to the demands of peacekeeping missions for troops trained to use deadly force in combat (see Franke, 1999, 2000). As an operations officer explained, "they [combat units] get trash thrown at them and they want to hit somebody" (quoted in Ricks, 2001, p. A-21).

The disconnect between aggressive warrior identity and the mission objectives of a peace operation can be observed, for instance, in confirmed allegations of misconduct, including illegal detentions and excessive use of force, by American soldiers toward local nationals during the Kosovo peacekeeping mission (Burlas, 2000; Collins, 2000). At the extreme, this cognitive dissonance may lead to such calamitous behaviors as the torture and murder of a Somali youth by members of the elite Canadian Airborne Regiment (CAR) or the strangling of an 11-year old Albanian girl by an American paratrooper during his deployment in Kosovo (Erlanger, 2000; Kitfield, 2000b; Ricks, 2001). Fortunately, such drastic misbehaviors have been only isolated incidents within the rapidly expanding arena of peace operations. Nevertheless, these instances illustrate most vividly the challenges that peace operations may pose for soldiers' identity images and their self-conceptions as military professionals. Understanding the general processes by which aspects of social identity have relevance to combat-trained soldiers who are charged with fulfilling peacekeeping tasks and resolving identity tensions and cognitive dilemmas that may arise from the operational context becomes increasingly critical to ensuring accomplishment of mission objectives.

After a brief description of the nature of post–Cold War peace operations, I examine identity tensions in the context of peace operations in Somalia and in the former Yugoslavia. Next, I review the theoretical presuppositions of the social identity approach and assess its utility for understanding the identity demands of contemporary peacekeeping operations and for improving the cognitive preparation of soldiers participating in those operations. Finally, I analyze the effectiveness of different strategies for resolving cognitive inconsistencies in the context of peace operations.

THE CONTEXT OF PEACE OPERATIONS

Like war, peace operations are military enterprises serving political ends. But unlike war, they lack a focal enemy and, oftentimes absent clearly defined mission objectives, are typically conducted in an environment that is not well defined. There is much debate in military circles on how to differentiate among the growing array of "peace operations," that is, the spectrum of military operations other than war (MOOTW) encompassing humanitarian assistance, preventive diplomacy, peacemaking, peacekeeping, peace-building, and peace enforcement (Chopra & Watson, 1997; Diehl, 1993; Hardesty & Ellis, 1997; Kegley, 1998; Minear, 1997).

Although it is quite possible to delineate peace operations on paper, in reality these distinctions are often much less clear. The international community's intervention in Somalia, for instance, included three distinct operational phases with different mandates and sets of resources (Thomas & Spataro, 1998; Winslow, 1997, 1999). UNOSOM I began in mid-1992 as a humanitarian relief and peacekeeping operation in accordance with Chapter VI of the UN Charter to alleviate the suffering that, by then, had already taken the lives of nearly half a million people. With the effects of the civil war worsening, the UN Security Council authorized a U.S.-led Chapter VII peace enforcement operation in December 1992 (UNITAF) with a mandate to enforce peace by "using all necessary means to establish as soon as possible a secure environment for humanitarian relief operations in Somalia" (UN Security Council Resolution 794). By March 1993 it appeared the situation in Somalia had stabilized. As a result, the Security Council authorized UNOSOM II, which took the character of a peace-building mission covering the whole country and relying on the help of a reestablished Somali police force.

For the forces on the ground, transitioning between operational assignments meant continuous change in the mission and its objectives. To make matters worse, as mission objectives changed so did the rules of engagement (ROE), that is, the norms and regulations that define the legitimate use of force and guide behavior during an operation. As a result, soldiers were oftentimes confused and frustrated and felt unprepared to conduct the mission. In her study of the Canadian Airborne Regiment, anthropologist Donna Winslow (1997) observed tensions that arose from deploying combat soldiers to a peace operation. She concluded that "because civilized military training incorporates into its standards the notion that it is permissible to kill certain people but not others, feelings of ambivalence are likely to result among combat troops when faced with their ROE. This ambivalence may create an environment within which concepts of morality and legality become abstract, subject to varying situational definitions" (p. 210).

It is not surprising that in the constantly changing Somalia mission environment, some soldiers, confused by the mission's objectives, searched for new cognitive frames of reference to come to terms with their peacekeeping assignment and to preserve stable self-conceptions. A number of U.S. soldiers, for instance, employed a "warrior strategy," generalizing the behavior of local rioters to all Somalis (e.g., stereotyping them as lazy and uncivilized) and treating the entire population as potential enemies (Miller & Moskos, 1995). Others relied on a "humanitarian strategy," making conscious efforts to refrain from using negative stereotypes and to understand the behavior of the Somali people. The "warrior" strategy was adopted most readily by white male soldiers (more than 70%) who served in combat units, who "were trained intensively to operate against a foreign enemy and who did not wish to appear vulnerable to the Somalis" (p. 633). Miller and Moskos also found that soldiers became frustrated when, according to the rules of engagement, they were not allowed to respond to attacks by locals and were instructed to "return fire only if they saw exactly who among the rioters had shot at them, and if no other Somalis stood between them and the aggressor" (p. 622).

Although mission objectives in the former Yugoslavia were quite different from those in Somalia—from the outset UNPROFOR was designed as a peace enforcement operation and not as a humanitarian mission—personal accounts of U.S. peacekeepers still confirm the suggestion that participating in peace operations may challenge the stability of established self-conceptions. A sergeant deployed in Bosnia explained, "I'm a tanker, that's what I do, been one for 14 years. But let me tell you, those skills are perishable. You got to use them, and all I'm doing here is checking people's driver's licenses" (quoted in O'Connor, 1996, p. A-3). Interviewed about his peacekeeping duties in Kosovo, an American paratrooper confessed, "no, this is not what I envisioned as a staff sergeant. I thought I would be jumping out of planes and leading my section into combat" (Ricks, 2001, p. A-21).

A recently released report by the U.S. Army on the conduct of the 82nd Airborne Division during the Kosovo mission detailed difficulties some soldiers experienced adapting from a combat mentality to a peacekeeping operation. For example, the report stated that "the unit had an aggressive slogan, along the lines of 'shoot 'em in the face.' And the soldiers had a standard procedure of pointing their weapons or flashlights in the face of local nationals" (see Collins, 2000). The army investigation into alleged misconduct by members of the 82nd Airborne further determined that unit members violated the rules of their military assignments by intimidating, interrogating, abusing, and beating ethnic Albanians and by inappropriately touching Kosovar women (see Burlas, 2000; Collins, 2000). However, the report concluded that the actions of these few soldiers were isolated incidents and "should not detract from the exceptional job another 6,000 soldiers are doing in difficult circumstances as part of Task Force Falcon in Kosovo" (Burlas, 2000).

More than four decades ago, Janowitz (1960) already warned that professional soldiers would resist peacekeeping, because they were likely to view these policelike activities as less prestigious and less honorable than traditional combat tasks. These sentiments, expressed at the height of the Cold War, are still common among many combat-trained soldiers. An American peacekeeper, passing the time playing gin rummy while protecting a border area in Kosovo where ethnic Albanian guerrillas had been operating, admitted, "Being in the infantry, we're flexible. But this is an MP mission" (Ricks, 2001, p. A-21). One report synthesized the comments of 12,500 U.S. service members surveyed around the world in similar fashion: "We are doing some good work for these people, but I joined the Army to be in a combat-ready unit, not to be a policeman" (quoted in Kitfield, 2000b, p. 3952).

Note that the extent to which military professionals support peace operations and view peacekeeping as a central part of their military identity may vary by operational specialty. For instance, in my research on military socialization at the U.S. Military Academy, I found that cadets who desired careers as officers in traditional combat arms branches tended to be significantly more warrioristic and patriotic and at the same time less supportive of global institutions such as the UN and of peacekeeping missions than their peers who opted for combat support or combat service support branches. Moreover, military socialization in preparation for service in a combat arms branch increased cadets' propensity to identify with military reference groups (Franke, 1999).

Ironically, the most important skill needed in many post–Cold War peace operations remains war fighting. According to former NATO commander General George Joulwan, "I'd look for the best warfighter in the world. I'd look for the best guy that can fight. You ought not to think that you can develop somebody that's got this political-military experience that can't go quickly to the next step. I want a warrior. I'll train him to the mission. We have no hostile deaths in Bosnia, because we have warriors who are able to understand the next step." (quoted in Olson & Davis, 1999, p. 5).

However, the Somalia and Kosovo missions have shown that simply throwing combat-ready soldiers into peacekeeping missions may backfire. Many U.S. military leaders acknowledge that peace operations present a major challenge. General Montgomery Meigs, a former commander of the U.S. Army in Europe, admitted that "the army has a wonderful ability to adapt to a crisis, but we have to be better than that and adapt to the environment before the crisis hits, because in the twenty-first century, the crisis may be so different that you will not be able to adapt quickly enough. Just having good soldiers isn't going to cut it" (quoted in Olson & Davis, 1999, p. 9). The unique nature of many post–Cold War missions calls into question what it has traditionally meant to be a soldier and may require adjustments not only in military doctrine, but also in the military's combat-oriented warrior identity. Soldiers are trained to possess a combat identity and a strong commitment to their country. However, as the interview excerpts just cited indicate, the identity demands of peace operations may conflict with the social identity of the soldiers participating in these operations. Before exploring the particular case of identity tensions in peacekeeping further, it seems useful to discuss briefly the premises of social identity theory in more detail.

CONCEPTUALIZING SOCIAL IDENTITY

Identifying with others who share common attributes is an important part of deriving one's sense of self. Social identity, Henri Tajfel (1981) suggested, is "that part of individuals' self concept which derives from knowledge of their membership in a social group (or groups) together with the value and emotional significance attached to that membership" (p. 255). Theories of social identity are based on three premises: (1) people are motivated to create and maintain a positive self-concept; (2) the self-concept derives largely from group identifications; and (3) people establish positive social identities through normative comparisons between favorable ingroups and unfavorable outgroups. The evolution of social identity research can be illustrated by discussing three distinguishable, yet highly interrelated theoretical approaches.

Social Identity Theory

In a series of "minimal group" experiments, Tajfel and his colleagues (Tajfel, 1978, 1981; Turner, Hogg, Oakes, Reicher, & Wetherell, 1987) discovered that even artificially created, trivial group labels significantly affected individuals' perceptions of one another. Most test subjects consistently favored anonymous members of "their own group" at the expense of outgroup members. Because the experiments were set up so group designation caused attraction, subjects liked or disliked others not as individuals but merely as members of ascribed groups.

Outside the controlled experimental setting, individuals draw on multiple, sometimes even competing identity images to derive their self-conceptions. More important identities form a core that influences most decisions, whereas peripheral identities may affect decision making only in certain circumstances (Abrams, 1999; Brewer, 1991; Deaux, 1993; Dubin, 1992; Hofman, 1988; Hogg & Abrams, 1988; Sherman, Hamilton, & Lewis, 1999). More than half a century ago, Lecky (1945) suggested that an individual's self-conception is "his only guarantee of security, its preservation becomes a goal in itself. He seeks the type of experience that confirms and supports the unified attitude and rejects experiences which seem to promise a disturbance of his attitude" (p. 123). Individuals have a fundamental need to feel certain about their world and their place within it. Consequently, certainties and those factors responsible for consensus on which certainty rests (i.e., ingroup members, reference group norms) are imbued with positive valence, whereas factors that create uncertainties are valenced negatively (Abrams, 1999; Hogg & Mullin, 1999; Kahneman, Slovic, & Tversky, 1982).

Consistent with the need for uncertainty reduction, Swann and Ely (1984) discovered that individuals are significantly influenced by tendencies to verify their self-views and to confirm their expectations of others. Entering interactions with independent and sometimes conflicting agendas, people tend to resolve cognitive inconsistencies through a process of identity negotiation, enabling them to assume an identity for the duration of the interaction consistent with their self-conceptions (Swann, 1987). Whether or not a particular identity image (male, Jewish, black, warrior, peacekeeper, etc.) is invoked in a given situation depends on how salient or accessible that group identity is in the context. A number of experimental studies demonstrated that the self-perceptions, norms, beliefs, attitudes, feelings, and behaviors associated with salient identities motivate individuals to behave consistently with a group prototype—that is, the central tendency of members of a category—to satisfy the individual's need for both positive self-evaluation and the reduction of uncertainty (see Hogg, 1996; Rosch, 1978; Sherman et al., 1999). For instance, Terry, Hogg, and Duck (1999) found that subjects were more likely to engage in attitudinally congruent behavior when they received normative support for the attitude from a relevant ingroup and that the effect of ingroup normative support was stronger under high than low group salience conditions.

Sheldon Stryker (1968) conjectured that an individual's various identities exist in a hierarchy of salience that becomes consequential when a context invokes evaluations based on conflicting identity images (see also Abrams, 1999). In these situations, Stryker argued, invoking one identity over others is a function not only of its salience, but also of the level of commitment to that identity. He hypothesized that the stronger the identity commitment, the more individuals perceived the identity as instrumental to their "wants." At the same time, the more committed individuals are to a particular identity, "the higher the probability of role performance consistent with the role expectations attached to that identity" (p. 563) and the greater the probability they will seek out opportunities to perform consistent with the identity image. Extending Stryker's conception of identity, Hofman (1988) specified salience as the probability by which a subidentity is remembered and activated in a given context. Prolonged salience enhances its "centrality," that is, its importance among subidentities and the degree to which it interconnects with other subidentities. The stronger the identity's centrality, the more committed individuals will be to preserving and enhancing that identity. Centrality and commitment influence the "potency" of a subidentity, that is, how meaningful it is normatively and, consequently, how great its potential is for shaping attitudes, values, and behaviors.

Categories are particularly salient if recently or frequently activated or if people are motivated to use them. Hogg and Mullin (1999) demonstrated that salience is an interactive function of chronic or situational accessibility and structural/comparative and normative fit. Chronically accessible categories (e.g., sex or race) are more readily made salient by situational primes and primed categories are more salient if they are relevant to the context of the social categorization. Similarly, Sherman et al. (1999) argued that people have "chronic" group identifications that are always potentially accessible. These chronic identifications are "particularly likely to influence momentary self-conceptions in any given situation, and because of their ongoing importance to the individual, the social identity values associated with these group memberships seem likely to be continually important for the individual's self-conception" (p. 92).

Self-Categorization Theory

Researchers working in the social identity tradition would agree that human behavior is most immediately shaped by the cognitive frames—that is, the categories, meanings, and beliefs—that individuals rely on to understand a given context. The stronger individuals' commitment to a particular group, the more potent the group identity becomes and the more they will perceive group norms and values as part of their self-conceptions. Turner and colleagues (1987) advanced the basic social identity model that had developed out of minimal group experiments to account for specific ideological and contextual influences on behavior and found that social contexts can create meaningful group boundaries and that identities, as socially constructed categories, may shift depending on the situational context. Turner et al. conceptualized the process of self-categorization in three stages: (1) individuals define themselves as members of social groups; (2) they learn the stereotypical norms of those groups; and (3) under conditions where a particular ingroup category becomes salient, they tend to employ the ingroup attributes to decide on the appropriate conduct in the given context. According to self-categorization theory, "categorization works to align the person with the realities of the social context, to produce dynamic, context-specific definitions of self and others which both reflect and make possible the almost infinitely variable pattern of human social relations" (Oakes, Haslam, & Reynolds, 1999, p. 58).

The three stages are interdependent, that is, the individual, as a group member, also shapes group norms and, subsequently, contributes to a dynamic conception of the group identity. At the same time, behavior (e.g., participation in combat training exercises) that is consistent with a particular social identity (e.g., combat soldier) may affirm that identity, whereas behavior inconsistent with the identity (e.g., fulfilling peacekeeping duties) may impair the commitment to that identity (Franke, 1999, 2000). Analyzing the effects of intergroup images on stereotype changes, Oakes and colleagues (1999) found that stable contexts, in particular stable intergroup realities, produced stable, that is, certain, categories. By contrast, subjective uncertainty is produced by "contextual factors that challenge people's certainty about their cognitions, perceptions, feelings, and behaviors, and ultimately, certainty about and confidence in their sense of self" (Hogg & Mullin, 1999, pp. 256–257). Uncertainties prevalent in the peacekeeping context render adaptation of a specific, stable and certain identity image difficult.

Optimal Distinctiveness Theory

Based on social identity theory, Brewer (1991) developed a theory of optimal distinctiveness and argued that "social identity derives from a fundamental tension between human need for validation and similarity to others (on the one hand) and a countervailing need for uniqueness and individuation (on the other)" (p. 477). She viewed social identity as a compromise between assimilation with and differentiation from others, "where the need for deindividuation is satisfied within in-groups, while the need for distinctiveness is met through *inter*-group comparisons." This way, she conjectured, group identities enable individuals to be "the same and different at the same time." Of course, the degrees of assimilation and differentiation vary depending on the salience of particular identity images in a given context.

In previous research, I extended the applicability of the social identity approach from the experimental laboratory environment to genuine social field settings and tested its assumptions for normatively meaningful identifications (Franke, 1999, 2000). In this research, I conceptualized identity as a dynamic process of self-categorization and social comparison considering both the salience and centrality of values and attitudes and the potency of multiple subidentities. The empirical results confirmed that members of a social group (e.g., cadets at West Point) can perceive particular identity images as more or less potent. In turn, the data indicate that potency of specific identity images significantly affected respondents' attitudes.

These findings are corroborated by Britt's (1998) research on psychological ambiguities in peacekeeping. Based on the triangle model of responsibility, Britt conceptualized responsibility as a transaction between a specific event (context) that has occurred or is anticipated (e.g., exam, mission, battle, training exercise), the prescriptions or rules (norms) that govern the event (e.g., ethical codes, group norms, rules of engagement), and the identity images the individual invokes to make sense of the event and/or prescriptions (e.g., warrior, humanitarian, peacekeeper, Christian, parent). Events that allow soldiers to recall previous training experiences, rely on clear mission objectives and unambiguous rules of engagement, and invoke uncontested identity images will render operational decisions fairly straightforward. Consequently, as trained warriors, soldiers may perform exceptionally well during combat or peace enforcement operations (because their central identity image remains unchallenged in this context). As missions shift to peacekeeping or peace-building, however, the new identity image of peacekeeper may conflict with their core warrior identity. The next section examines identity tensions in peacekeeping more closely.

IDENTITY TENSIONS IN PEACEKEEPING

What decisions soldiers make and how they perform during a mission will depend to a large extent on how they understand the mission. If the mission makes sense and confirms their self-conceptions, if members of their most important reference groups (family, friends, company, platoon, etc.) share this meaning, and if society at large supports the operation, motivation and performance will be high. If, however, soldiers invoke cognitive frames (e.g., warrior) that are ill suited for a particular assignment (e.g., peacekeeping), morale, motivation, and performance might suffer (Britt, 1998; Miller & Moskos, 1995;

Segal & Segal, 1993). Individuals tend to internalize categories such as nationality, ethnicity, gender, social class, occupation, religion, political ideology—or military occupation specialty, unit, or regiment—and focus on similarities with other members of the group. As a result, attitudinal and behavioral choices will be influenced by the correlation between group identification and group norms and values (Levin & Sidanius, 1999; Oakes, Haslam, & Turner, 1994; Sidanius, Feshbach, Levin, & Pratto, 1997; Tajfel, 1978; Turner et al., 1987; Winslow, 1999; Woodhouse, 1998).

Military socialization illustrates the importance of reference group identifications and the process of self-categorization. Basic training, for instance, disconnects recruits from past social networks and established identities and develops new identities. For instance, cadet candidates at the U.S. Military Academy begin basic training as complete strangers. The extreme isolation from civilian society, an almost complete lack of privacy, and shared socialization experiences create a strong normative group bond. Depriving recruits of any alternative sources of meaning, basic training almost invariably forces them to adopt the "soldier" frame of reference (Franke, 1999; Priest & Beach, 1988). In her study of group bonding in the Canadian Airborne, Winslow (1999) showed that during initiation into One Commando, new recruits were first systematically stripped of their former identities, then subjected to rites of passage including parodies, testing, and humiliation, and finally they were reincorporated into the group as members of the regiment.

Exploring the process of social identity formation during military socialization at the United States Military Academy (USMA), I found that cadets who displayed potent military identity images tended to be more warrioristic and patriotic and were more committed to a professional career in the military than cadets whose military identity was less potent (Franke, 1999, 2000). This research also confirmed the assumption that self-categorization in terms of a social group enhances potency of the group identity, which, in turn, can affect value orientations and stimulate or constrain behavior. Overall, USMA appeared to prepare the majority of its graduates effectively "to fight and win the nation's wars" and successfully instilled in them (particularly the approximately 70% of graduates who will be assigned to combat arms branches) the traditional "warrior" identity image. However, based on their responses, cadets' West Point experience neither strengthened their support of the UN nor their commitment to peacekeeping missions.

These findings can easily be extended to the operational context of peacekeeping missions. Whereas peacekeeping is a relatively recent task for the U.S. military (Somalia was among its first post–Cold War peace operations), Canada has had a long and much cherished record of peacekeeping going back to the end of World War II. Nevertheless, like its southern neighbor, "the Canadian army socializes members to its ideal (institutional) ethos of combat." Winslow (1997) found that "in this type of army [warriors assigned to peacekeeping] it is natural for some men to feel frustrated and unchallenged" (p. 66). One

Airborne soldier observed, "The Airborne are trained to kill. Getting used to that is hard. They were a hard combat unit and they trained hard. An infanteer has to know everything about throwing a grenade or building road blocks or digging a trench" (p. 64). Winslow concluded that "in a highly stressed environment and with leaders giving mixed messages about aggressive behavior, perspective can be lost and extreme attitudes adopted" (p. 248).

In contrast, in Somalia, soldiers experienced what Britt (1998) described as a "conflict between the desire to follow orders to not help members of the local population and their own convictions that it is important to help others who are less fortunate" (p. 119). One peacekeeper affirmed,

It's a deep, personal dilemma. We all wanted to go to Somalia, not just to go to war. We would have hoped to go into battle, but it's very simple, we wanted to go bring food to the good guys and kill the bad guys. That's about it. If it had only been that simple, once we got there. They're all Black, who's who? They all look alike. Who's our friends, who's the enemy? (quoted in Winslow, 1997, p. 249)

Preparing military professionals for multinational missions and for the unique cognitive and behavioral requirements of peace operations might increase their identification with noncombat roles and their commitment to OOTW (see also Franke, 1997, 1998). Shaping military identity during socialization and training to reflect mutual adherence to combat and noncombat values might be one way to strengthen force morale and improve mission performance. Preparing soldiers to resolve cognitive inconsistencies that may arise in the context of peace operations may be another way.

RESOLVING IDENTITY TENSIONS IN PEACEKEEPING

More than two decades ago, Moskos (1976) already detected identity tensions among UN blue helmets assigned to peacekeeping duties in Cyprus:

A British Officer: One thing makes a soldier different and better than anybody else. The thing which gives that dignity which nobody else can have is his respect for the man he is fighting. No civilian can ever have that. No soldier who hasn't fought can have it either. In peacekeeping the trouble is that you don't have any enemy, and this means you don't have any dignity as a soldier.

A Canadian Officer: Even in peacekeeping you need some trouble to keep the men happy. The more trouble there is, the more everybody enjoys peacekeeping. Without trouble peacekeeping runs against the grain of the soldier. (pp. 126–129)

How can possible tensions between the peacekeeper and the warrior identities be resolved? In a classic study of belief dilemmas, Abelson (1959) suggested four modes for resolving cognitive inconsistencies. I will assess in turn each strategy within the peacekeeping context.

Denial

The commitment to one of the conflicting identities is either denied (i.e., the valence of that identity is reversed) or identification with an outgroup is asserted (see Figure 3.1). In a number of experiments on uncertainty reduction, Hogg and Mullin (1999) found that certainty-oriented people were primarily concerned with self-verification and the maintenance of existing beliefs. As a result, they tried to avoid situations of uncertainty and, if confronted with uncertainty, they tended to fall back on simple heuristics rather than attempts to resolve the uncertainty. Employing a "warrior strategy" during the Somalia operation certainly served to deny soldiers' identity image as peacekeeper (Miller & Moskos, 1995). The idea that anyone could be an "enemy" was reinforced right at the beginning of the mission. The handbook handed to CAR members prior to deployment stated, "always remember, yesterday's allies can turn on non-vigilant groups if it is in their interest and they can get away with it. This is an unfortunate aspect of trust building in Somalia" (quoted in Winslow, 1997, p. 246).

Bolstering/Hyperinvestment

Using this strategy, one of the conflicting identities is related to other central identity images so as to reduce dissonance. To bolster self-esteem and reduce uncertainty, individuals may attempt to enhance the stature of the ingroup and of ingroup norms, attitudes, and behaviors either through derogation of the outgroup or by redefining the prototypicality of the situational context (see Oakes et al., 1999; Pelham & Swann, 1994; Rosch, 1978; Sherman et al., 1999; Tajfel, 1978, 1981). Soldiers may justify decisions to use force by claiming to act in pursuit of some greater good (e.g., restore peace and democracy, terminate an unjust regime, end civilian suffering) or by establishing congruities with previously experienced situations (see Figure 3.2). For instance, many of the U.S. peacekeepers deployed to the Balkans had initially been trained for combat missions. To resolve cognitive inconsistencies with their peacekeeper role and to maintain their self-conceptions as warriors, these soldiers sought identifications with more "appropriate, honorable roles." As a result, many

Figure 3.1 Denial: The commitment to one of the conflicting identities is denied by reversing the valence of that identity (peacekeeper).

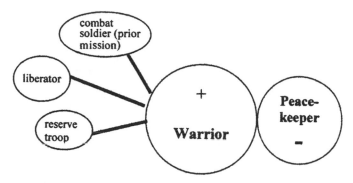

Figure 3.2 Bolstering: One of the conflicting identities (warrior) is related to other central identity images that enhance the valence of associated norms, attitudes, values, and behaviors of that identity.

imagined they were stationed in Macedonia as reserve troops that could be quickly mobilized to fight in Bosnia if necessary (Miller, 1997).

Similarly, Winslow (1997) concluded that the training conditions in the Canadian Airborne Regiment deployed to Somalia led to a "hyper-investment" in the warrior identity. One of her interviewees noted, "a peace-making mission in Somalia finally offered an opportunity for some gung-ho members of the CAR to prove themselves in battle" (p. 24). Another soldier reported, "I felt that members of 2 Commando were very gung-ho. Basically saying: 'I can't wait to kill my first black!' Some of them were trigger-happy and too aggressive" (p. 123). Although hyperinvestment or bolstering may be adaptive during a war when the self needs to be sufficiently alienated from the enemy in order to justify his destruction and to live with the emotional and cognitive consequences, this strategy is not readily adaptive to peace operations. As individuals become progressively invested in the group identity, their "capacity to relate to others outside of the group becomes significantly diminished and the potential for xenophobia increases" (p. 86).

In one study, Levin and Sidanius (1999) discovered that exhibiting negative affect toward the low-status outgroup (i.e., local Somalis) and increasing identification with the high-status ingroup (the CAR or the individual commando unit) may enable high-status group members to meet social dominance and social identity needs simultaneously, thereby stabilizing their self-conceptions (see also Sidanius et al., 1997; Sidanius, Devereaux, & Pratto, 1992). For instance, Haslam and colleagues (1996; see also Abrams, 1999) found that in the presence of consistent normative information from other ingroup members (i.e., the unit or regiment), the stereotypes and ingroup identity images and the norms, values, and behaviors associated with the group were bolstered. Among U.S. peacekeepers deployed to Somalia, white male combat soldiers showed the greatest propensity for stereotyping Somalis and adopting the warrior strategy, clearly bolstering their identity images as masculine warriors

(Miller & Moskos, 1995). Sadly, the brutal torture and death of the Somali teenager illustrates perhaps the most excessive effects of bolstering and out-group denigration—the CAR was predominantly white and exclusively male (see Winslow, 1997, 1999).

Differentiation

In the differentiation strategy, one identity is split into discordant subiden-tities. Individuals acknowledge incongruities and establish continuities with other situations and/or prior experiences. This way, they can focus on a posi-tively valenced subidentity and related values and, in so doing, preserve their self-conceptions (see Figure 3.3). In his research on stereotyping, Hewstone (1996), for instance, found that, when confronted with disconfirming evidence, individuals can internally differentiate their cognitive images by developing subtypes within the higher level category (e.g., black lawyer, aggressive woman, heroic or patriotic peacekeeper). This way, individuals can assimilate disconfirming information without revision of the overall stereotype or iden-tity image (see also Oakes et al., 1999).

Although combat soldiers may feel unfavorably toward peacekeeping as-signments or toward serving under UN command (see Franke, 1997, 1999), they have sworn an oath to support and defend their nation. U.S. soldiers, for instance, pledge commitment to "political authority, loyalty, duty, selfless ser-vice, courage, integrity, respect for human dignity, and a sense of justice" (De-partment of the Army, 1993, pp. 1–2). Differentiation enables them to interpret their peacekeeping role as concordant with their identity image as military professionals. Segal and Segal (1993) have termed this process "normalization."

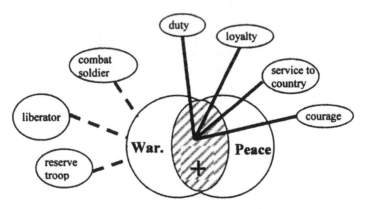

Figure 3.3 Differentiation: One identity is split into discordant subidentities and indi-viduals focus on positively valenced values, attitudes, and prior experiences to preserve their self-conception (e.g., the heroic peacekeeper). Soldiers may view peacekeeping as concordant with their identity image as military professionals.

They found that most soldiers interpreted peacekeeping not as part of a soldier's job, but as requiring qualities that only soldiers possessed, "most particularly, obedience and discipline" (pp. 52–55).

Britt (1998) found that soldiers often attempted to minimize threats to their self-conceptions resulting from psychological ambiguities they experienced in peacekeeping. Many either engaged in distracting activities (i.e., denial) or reinterpreted the situation in terms that provided them with a nondirect form of control (i.e., bolstering). However, he argued that, when soldiers "are faced with taunts and have to restrain their natural tendency toward aggression they should be encouraged to reinterpret the situation in a way that provides some form of secondary control over their situation" (pp. 122–123). For example, invoking previous experiences, they could justify not using aggression to prevent a potential escalation of the conflict. Clear ROE and prior peacekeeping training will help provide certainty and develop cognitive frames for officers and soldiers, enabling them to interpret mission objectives without undermining their identity images (see Sniderman, Brody, & Tetlock, 1991).

Transcendence/Integration

In transcendence/integration, both conflicting identities are combined and subsumed under a superordinate identity, and the dilemma is resolved by embedding the discordant identities into a comprehensive "superidentity" that, when potent, either resolves the tension or provides a cognitive justification for identity congruent behavior (see Figure 3.4). Similar to social identity theory, self-affirmation theory (Steele, 1988), for instance, proposes that individuals strive for an integrated and consistent self-image, "and that therefore evaluative challenges to one aspect of self motivates affirmation of another

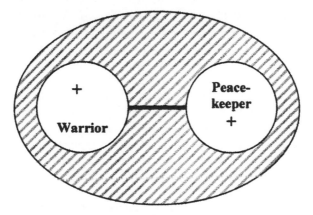

Figure 3.4 Integration: Both conflicting identities are combined and subsumed under a superordinate identity (post–Cold War military professional).

positive aspect in order to maintain the overall integrity of self" (Hogg & Mullin, 1999, p. 258). Military socialization and training that encourages positive evaluations of nonconventional assignments might prepare soldiers to view the peacekeeper subidentity as an integral part of their professional self-conceptions rather than merely as "a job that it takes a soldier to do." Although integration strategies may not always resolve severe moral dilemmas, military socialization and training that exposes soldiers continually to employ different strategies for resolving cognitive inconsistencies may make them more effective peacekeepers (see Franke, 1999, 2000).

Integrating the identity images of warrior and peacekeeper may help avoid identity tensions. Winslow (1997) argued that a strong group identity (e.g., with the regiment or unit) could be offset by discipline and leadership. She concluded, "a truly elite unit with a strong sense of professionalism and discipline would, in fact, be less likely to commit aggressive acts against members of the out-group. This is because the individuals are invested in an [integrated] identity which has components of self-discipline and ethics embedded in it" (p. 266). Individual soldiers and officers who view war fighting and peacekeeping as equally important to their central identity images will more easily be able to switch among mission requirements without jeopardizing their self-conceptions or mission accomplishment.

CONCLUSION

Empirical research on cognitive inconsistencies has demonstrated that when conflicting values are unequal in strength or when one subidentity is significantly more central to the individual's self-conception than another, individuals tend to employ denial or bolstering strategies. The more individuals rely on monistic belief systems or ideologies, that is, the more they view choices in black and white terms, the more they will tend to employ these simplistic strategies (Abrams, 1999; Hogg & Mullin, 1999; Tetlock, 1986). However, simplistic strategies may be ineffective in situations where individuals perceive two discordant identity images as central and rank them as close to equal in importance. In situations of high value pluralism, people tend to turn to the more effort-demanding strategies of differentiation (distinguishing the context-specific impact of alternative choices on one's values and self-conception) and integration (developing rules or schemata for coping with value trade-offs or identity dilemmas independent of a specific context). Although socialization may not resolve identity tensions completely, differentiation and especially integration strategies, once learned, may be invoked more readily and may help prevent indecision, resolve moral dilemmas, and avoid suboptimal behavioral outcomes.

Both Tetlock (1986) and Britt (1998) illustrated the context-dependent nature of human information processing. Their research findings point to the importance of the interaction between contextual, social, and personological factors that may influence some soldiers to rely on warrior strategies while others may invoke their identity as peacekeeper to make sense of mission requirements. The relative uncertainty of the Somalia mission combined with a lack of cognitive preparation encouraged many soldiers to employ denial or bolstering strategies to overcome conflicting identity images. But these strategies do not provide lasting solutions. By contrast, repeated exposure to scenarios that require soldiers to employ more complex cognitive strategies will encourage them to negotiate among central identity images and to avoid or resolve identity tensions more effectively in new contexts, as the more recent mission experience in Kosovo indicates (see Kitfield, 2000a, 2000b; Ricks, 2001).

Facing identity dilemmas for the first time on mission duty may stimulate denial or bolstering strategies. Early military socialization should stress the importance of combat and noncombat roles for the professional identity of post–Cold War soldiers. Training in differentiation and integration strategies may equip soldiers with more effective cognitive tools, helping them resolve cognitive inconsistencies and make mission congruent decisions across operational assignments. Military socialization that teaches soldiers to invoke positively valenced identity images that are congruent with different mission objectives would add certainty to behavioral choices, especially in the fluid context of peace operations. Such cognitive preparation could diminish the need to bolster the warrior identity or to deny or normalize the peacekeeper identity and could motivate soldiers to negotiate a new military identity reflecting both combat and noncombat roles. The implication is that soldiers could then rely on previously practiced integration strategies to help them resolve identity dilemmas more quickly and more effectively. The present analysis is based primarily on qualitative data taken from secondary field reports. Future research should attempt to test these resolution strategies empirically and examine more specifically the extent to which the social identity of military professionals might influence their motivation, well-being, and performance in differing operational contexts.

Although individuals may identify with different social groups in one context, they may share the same identity in another (e.g., the peacekeeper allied in a joint operation with soldiers from former enemy states). Recognizing shared bases of identification will allow them to accentuate similarities rather than differences. Focusing on a common identity, a shared purpose, or similar role commitments may permit members of conflicting groups to emphasize common experiences and comparable life interests rather than the differences that motivated the conflict in the first place. Learning to employ differentiation and integration strategies may not only help individuals to resolve cognitive inconsistencies without destabilizing their self-conceptions, it may also be an effective way of conflict resolution or at least mitigation by increasing intergroup tolerance and compassion for others.

REFERENCES

Abelson, R. P. (1959). Modes of resolution of belief dilemmas. *The Journal of Conflict Resolution, 3*(4), 343–352.

Abrams, D. (1999). Social identity, social cognition, and the self: The flexibility and stability of self-categorization. In D. Abrams & M. A. Hogg (Eds.), *Social identity and social cognition* (pp. 197–229). Oxford: Blackwell.

Breed, H. (1998). Treating the new world disorder. In H. J. Langholtz (Ed.), *The psychology of peacekeeping* (pp. 111–128). Westport, CT: Praeger.

Brewer, M. B. (1991). The social self: On being the same and different at the same time. *Personality and Social Psychology Bulletin, 17*(5), 473–482.

Britt, T. W. (1998). Psychological ambiguities in peacekeeping. In H. J. Langholtz (Ed.), *The psychology of peacekeeping* (pp. 111–128). Westport, CT: Praeger.

Burlas, J. (2000, September 22). Report finds incidents of misconduct toward Kosovars. *Army News Service.* [http://www.fas.org/man/dod-101/ops/2000/kosovo-000922.htm]

Chopra, J., & Watson T. (1997). Background paper: Political peace-maintenance in Somalia. In N. Azimi (Ed.), *Humanitarian action and peace-keeping operations: Debriefing and lessons* (pp. 99–123). London: Kluwer Law International.

Collins, R. T. (2000, September 21). Army report details Kosovo misdeeds. *Stars and Stripes.*

Deaux, K. (1993). Reconstructing social identity. *Personality and Social Psychology Bulletin, 19*, 4–12.

Department of the Army, Headquarters. (1993). *Field manual (FM) 100–5: Operations.* Washington, DC.

Diehl, P. F. (1993). *International peacekeeping.* Baltimore and London: The Johns Hopkins University Press.

Dubin, R. (1992). *Central life interests: Creative individualism in a complex world.* New Brunswick, NJ: Transaction.

Erlanger, S. (2000, April 2). The ugliest American. *New York Times Magazine,* pp. 52–56.

Franke, V. C. (1997). Warriors for peace: The next generation of military leaders. *Armed Forces & Society, 24*(1), 33–59.

Franke, V. C. (1998, Winter). Old ammo in new weapons?: Comparing value-orientations of experienced and future military leaders. *Journal of Political and Military Sociology, 26*, 1–22.

Franke, V. C. (1999). *Preparing for peace: Military identity, value orientations, and professional military education.* Westport, CT: Praeger.

Franke, V. C. (2000). Duty, honor, country: The social identity of West Point cadets. *Armed Forces & Society, 26*(2), 175–202.

Hardesty M., & Ellis, J. (1997). Training for peace operations: The U.S. army adapts to the post-cold war world. *Peaceworks 12.* Washington, DC: United States Institute of Peace.

Haslam, S. A., Oakes, P. J., McGarty, C., Turner, J. C., Reynolds, K. J., & Eggins, R. A. (1996). Stereotyping and social influence: The mediation of stereotype applicability and sharedness by the views of in-group and out-group members. *British Journal of Social Psychology, 35*, 369–397.

Hewstone, M. (1996). Contact and categorization: Social psychological interventions to change intergroup relations. In C. N. Macrae, C. Stangor, & M. Hewstone (Eds.), *Stereotypes and stereotyping* (pp. 323–368). New York: Guilford.

Hofman, J. E. (1988). Social identity and intergroup conflict: An Israeli view. In W. Stroebe, A. W. Kruglanski, D. Bar-Tal, & M. Hewstone (Eds.), *The social psychology of intergroup conflict: Theory, research and applications* (pp. 89–102). Berlin: Springer Verlag.

Hogg, M. A. (1996). Intragroup processes, group structure and social identity. In W. P. Robinson (Ed.), *Social groups and identities: Developing the legacy of Henri Tajfel* (pp. 65–93). Oxford: Butterworth-Heinemann.

Hogg, M. A., & Abrams, D. (1988). *Social identifications: A social psychology of intergroup relations and group processes.* London and New York: Routledge.

Hogg, M. A., & Mullin, B. A. (1999). Joining groups to reduce uncertainty: Subjective uncertainty reduction and group identification. In D. Abrams & M. Hogg (Eds.), *Social identity and social cognition* (pp. 249–279). Oxford: Blackwell.

Janowitz, M. (1960). *The professional soldier: A social and political portrait.* Glencoe, IL: The Free Press.

Kahneman, D., Slovic P. & Tversky, A. (Eds.). (1982). *Judgment under uncertainty: Heuristics and biases.* Cambridge: Cambridge University Press.

Keaney, T. A., & Douglass, S. (1999). *The UN-NATO coalition: Diplomatic and military interaction in Bosnia.* Maxwell/SAIS National Security Studies Case Study (CS 1299–16), Syracuse, NY: Syracuse University.

Kegley, C. (1998). Thinking ethically about peacemaking and peacekeeping. In T. Woodhouse, R. Bruce, & M. Dando (Eds.), *Peacekeeping and peacemaking: Towards effective intervention in post–cold war conflicts* (pp. 17–38). London: Macmillan.

Kitfield, J. (2000a). Lessons from Bosnia. *National Journal, 52–53,* 3936–3943.

Kitfield, J. (2000b). Peacekeepers' progress. *National Journal, 52–53,* 3947–3953.

Lecky, P. (1945). *Self-consistency: A theory of personality.* New York: Island Press.

Levin S., & Sidanius J. (1999, March). Social dominance and social identity in the United States and Israel: Ingroup favoritism or outgroup denigration. *Political Psychology 20,* 99–126.

Miller, L. L. (1997). Do soldiers hate peacekeeping?: The case of preventive diplomacy operations in Macedonia. *Armed Forces & Society, 23*(3), 415–450.

Miller, L. L., & Moskos, C. (1995). Humanitarians or warriors?: Race, gender, and combat status in operation restore hope. *Armed Forces & Society, 21*(4), 615–637.

Minear, L. (1997). Introduction to case studies. In N. Azimi (Ed.), *Humanitarian action and peace-keeping operations: Debriefing and lessons* (pp. 43–66). London: Kluwer Law International.

Moskos C. (1976). *Peace soldiers: The sociology of a United Nations military force.* Chicago: University of Chicago Press.

Oakes, P. J., Haslam, A., & Reynolds, K. J. (1999). Social categorization and social context: Is stereotype change a matter of information or of meaning? In D. Abrams & M. Hogg (Eds.), *Social identity and social cognition* (pp. 55–79). Oxford: Blackwell.

Oakes, P. J., Haslam A. S., & Turner J. C. (1994). *Stereotyping and social reality.* Oxford: Blackwell.

O'Connor, M. (1996, December 13). Does keeping the peace spoil G.I.'s for war? *New York Times*, p. A-3.

Olson, H., & Davis, J. (1999). *Training U.S. army officers for peace operations: Lessons from Bosnia.* Washington, DC: United States Institute of Peace.

Pelham, B. W., & Swann, W. B. (1994). From self-conception to self-worth: On the sources and structure of global self-esteem. *Journal of Personality and Social Psychology 57,* 672–680.

Priest, R. F., & Beach, J. (1988, August). *Cadets' values, changes after basic training: A ten-year comparison.* Paper presented at the 96th Annual Convention of the American Psychological Association, Atlanta, GA.

Ricks, T. (2001, March 25). U.S. military police embrace Kosovo role. *The Washington Post,* p. A-21.

Rosch, E. (1978). Principles of categorization. In E. Rosch and B. B. Lloyd (Eds.), *Cognition and categorization* (pp. 27–48). Hillsdale, NJ: Erlbaum.

Segal, D. R. (1995). Five phases of United Nations peacekeeping: An evolutionary typology. *Journal of Political and Military Sociology, 23,* 65–79.

Segal, D. R., & Segal, M. W. (1993). *Peacekeepers and their wives: American participation in the multinational force and observers.* Westport, CT: Greenwood.

Sherman, S. J., Hamilton, D. L., & Lewis, A. C. (1999). Perceived entiativity and the social identity value of group memberships. In D. Abrams & M. Hogg (Eds.), *Social identity and social cognition* (pp. 80–110). Oxford: Blackwell.

Sidanius, J., Devereux, E., & Pratto, F. (1992). A comparison of symbolic racism and social dominance theory as explanations for racial policy attitudes. *The Journal of Social Psychology, 132*(3), 377–395.

Sidanius J., Feshbach, S., Levin, S., & Pratto, F. (1997). The interface between ethnic and national attachment: Ethnic pluralism or ethnic dominance? *Public Opinion Quarterly, 61,* 102–133.

Sniderman, P. M., Brody, R. A., & Tetlock, P. E. (1991). *Reasoning and choice: Explorations in political psychology.* Cambridge: Cambridge University Press.

Steele, C. M. (1988). The psychology of self-affirmation: Sustaining the integrity of the self. *Advances in Experimental Social Psychology, 21,* 261–302.

Stryker, S. (1968). Identity salience and role performance: The relevance of symbolic interaction theory for family research. *Journal of Marriage and the Family, 30,* 558–564.

Swann, W. B. (1987). Identity negotiations: Where two roads meet. *Journal of Personality and Social Psychology, 53*(6), 1038–1051.

Swann, W. B., & Ely, R. J. (1984). A battle of wills: Self-verification versus behavioral confirmation. *Journal of Personality and Social Psychology, 46*(6), 1287–1302.

Tajfel, H. (Ed.). (1978). *Differentiation between social groups: Studies in the social psychology of intergroup relations.* London: Academic Press.

Tajfel, H. (1981). *Human groups and social categories: Studies in social psychology.* Cambridge: Cambridge University Press.

Terry, D. J., Hogg, M. A., & Duck. J. M. (1999). Group membership, social identity, and attitudes. In D. Abrams & M. Hogg (Eds.), *Social identity and social cognition* (pp. 280–314). Oxford: Blackwell.

Tetlock, P. J. (1986). A value pluralism model of ideological reasoning. *Journal of Personality and Social Psychology, 50*(4), 819–827.

Thomas, L., & Spataro, S. (1998). Peacekeeping and policing in Somalia. In R. B. Oakley, M. J. Dziedzic, & E. M. Goldberg (Eds.), *Policing the new world disorder: Peace operations and public security* (pp. 175–214). Washington, DC: National Defense University Press.

Turner, J. C., Hogg, M. A., Oakes, P. J., Reicher, S. D., & Wetherell, M. S. (1987). *Rediscovering the social group: A self-categorization theory.* London: Basil Blackwell.

Winslow, D. (1997). *The Canadian airborne regiment in Somalia: A socio-cultural inquiry.* Ottawa: Canadian Government Publishing.

Winslow, D. (1999). Rites of passage and group bonding in the Canadian airborne. *Armed Forces & Society, 25*(3), 429–457.

Woodhouse, T. (1998). Peacekeeping and the psychology of conflict resolution. In H. J. Langholtz (Ed.), *The psychology of peacekeeping* (pp. 153–166). Westport, CT: Praeger.

4

Prejudice and the Peacekeeper

Kurt A. Boniecki and Thomas W. Britt

Peacekeepers are increasingly deployed to areas of the world torn by civil war between various tribal, ethnic, and/or religious groups (Kimmel, 1998; United Nations Department of Public Information [UNDPI], 2001). From fighting between Christians and Muslims in Lebanon to mass genocide in Rwanda to ethnic cleansing in Kosovo, peacekeepers have witnessed some of the most virulent results of prejudice. The arduous job of the peacekeeper is to bring stability to these regions so humanitarian aid and peace negotiations can proceed unabated. To accomplish their mandate, peacekeepers must maintain impartiality toward the warring parties and empathy toward the local citizens (Greenberg, 1992; Latorre, 1984; UNDPI, 2001). However, peacekeepers are soldiers and, foremost, human beings that come to these conflicts with their own prejudices and the capacity to learn new ones. If their prejudices go unchecked and are allowed to affect their judgments and actions, their presence may only add fuel to the existing conflagration. In this chapter, we discuss how the specific environment and stress of peacekeeping operations can create and exacerbate the prejudices of peacekeeping soldiers, thereby endangering the success of their mission.

The roots of prejudice are multifaceted and can be examined from various historical, sociological, and psychological perspectives. Each perspective offers a different understanding of the problem, and neither is more or less valid than the other. However, given the focus of this volume, we limit our analysis to the psychological determinants of prejudice. Specifically, we draw on research and theory from social psychology and show how they relate to the motivation, performance, and well being of peacekeepers. We also present research from peacekeeping missions and apply social psychological theories of prejudice to understanding the actual experiences of peacekeepers and their attitudes toward the local population. For example, we often use data reported by Miller and Moskos (1995) concerning the self-reported experiences of U.S. peacekeepers during Operation Restore Hope in Somalia. This peacekeeping operation involved African American and European American U.S. soldiers being sent to a region in Africa to help provide humanitarian assistance and defuse a tense situation. As we will see, the utility of theories and research on prejudice to understand the issues faced by peacekeepers becomes especially salient in this operation. Furthermore, in cases where specific peacekeeping research has not yet been conducted, we attempt to show how the principles of prejudice could potentially be used to illuminate the issues that might have been faced by peacekeepers in those operations. In addition, we discuss how the principles of prejudice and stereotyping are relevant to future peacekeeping operations. Even when peacekeepers have no prior experience with the population they have been assigned to aid, the tendency to form stereotypes and exhibit potential prejudices is still prevalent.

In the social psychology literature, prejudice is typically defined as a negative evaluation of an entire social group (see Stephan, 1985). Stephan and Stephan (2000) have proposed the integrated threat theory of prejudice that incorporates different determinants of prejudice into a single model. This theory suggests that prejudice results from the perception that the members of the outgroup pose a threat to the ingroup. There are four types of threat: realistic threats, symbolic threats, intergroup anxiety, and negative stereotypes. We use the integrated threat theory as the framework for discussing the specific causes of prejudice as they apply to the peacekeeper.

REALISTIC THREATS

Realistic threats refer to the perception that the outgroup threatens the power or well-being of the ingroup (Stephan & Stephan, 2000). Perhaps more than any other source of prejudice, realistic threats are the most apparent in peacekeeping operations. Peacekeepers are sent to some of the most volatile regions of the world, and their presence is not always met with open arms by the warring factions or the local population. Peacekeepers have been robbed, stoned, shot, and killed, often by the very people they are mandated to protect. To date, more than 1,700 military and civilian peacekeepers have lost their lives during peacekeeping operations (UNDPI, 2001). In addition to the threat of physical assault, the local population may challenge or ignore the authority of the peacekeepers, thereby threatening their power. The loss of power may engender feelings of frustration in peacekeepers over an inability to control the conflict and accomplish their mission. The possible consequences of peacekeepers not being able to address the sources of such frustration have been noted by Litz and colleagues (Litz, King, King, Orsillo, & Friedman, 1997) and Weisæth (1990, this volume), and include the possibility of postmission psychological difficulties.

The idea that realistic threats lead to prejudice dates back to Sherif's (1966) realistic group conflict theory. According to Sherif, prejudice results from a competition between groups for scarce resources. Although Sherif's original theory and research focused primarily on competition between groups, later revisions broadened the theory to include real or imagined physical threats, conflicting economic and political interests, and challenges to group status and power (Bobo, 1983; Jackson, 1993; Levine & Campbell, 1972). Realistic threats promote feelings of frustration because the outgroup is perceived as blocking the goals of the ingroup, and frustration often leads to anger and hostility (Berkowitz, 1989; LeVine & Campbell, 1972). Indeed, Stephan and his colleagues (Stephan et al., 2002; Stephan, Diaz-Loving, & Duran, 2000; Stephan & Stephan, 1996; Stephan, Ybarra, & Bachman, 1999; Stephan, Ybarra, Martinez, Schwarzwald, & Tur-Kaspa, 1998) have found that perceptions of realistic threat predict people's negative attitudes toward other groups.

Howcvcr, the outgroup need not always be the source of the frustration. Hovland and Sears (1940) reported that, between the years of 1882 and 1930, lynchings of African Americans in the southern United States increased as economic frustrations grew over falling cotton prices. Thus frustration can arise from other sources, such as economic hardship, and the resulting anger may be displaced against a lower status outgroup that is unlikely to retaliate (i.e., a scapegoat). Peacekeepers, in particular, may be unable to direct their anger at the various sources of their frustrations (Litz et al., 1997). For example, peacekeepers under orders to "hold fire" when attacked by members of the warring parties are unable to direct their anger at the source of the assault (Britt, 1998). Furthermore, peacekeepers may experience frustration due to feelings of relative deprivation when comparing themselves to other peacekeeping contingents. During Operation Restore Hope in Somalia, many U.S. soldiers expressed anger over hearing that civilian personnel and UN troops from other countries were receiving higher pay (Miller & Moskos, 1995). Because military personnel are compensated by their own country, rather than the UN, real discrepancies in pay and privileges exist among the various contingents, adding to the frustration of many peacekeepers (Kimmel, 1998; Segal & Gravino, 1985). However, directing anger toward other peacekeeping contingents who make more money may seem irrational and counterproductive to the mission. As a result, peacekeepers may displace their anger toward specific targets who are unable to retaliate, such as unarmed local citizens. Indeed, Miller and Moskos (1995) reported observations of some UN troops during Operation Restore Hope beating Somalis and making jokes about wanting to injure or kill them indiscriminately (see also Franke, this volume).

SYMBOLIC THREATS

Symbolic threats stem from the perception that the outgroup violates or does not support the values, beliefs, or norms of the ingroup (Stephan & Stephan, 2000). In contrast to realistic threats, which jeopardize the ingroup's well-being, symbolic threats challenge the ingroup's worldview and sense of

morality. The very nature of the conflicts that peacekeepers are asked to monitor and control are likely to promote symbolic threats. These conflicts are often
the result of ethnic or religious differences, which may violate peacekeepers'
values of freedom, equality, and tolerance. The ironic consequence is that peacekeepers themselves may feel hostility toward those parties who appear to violate these fundamental values. For example, during Operation Restore Hope,
a number of U.S. soldiers expressed moral indignation over the Somalis fighting each other "for no apparently good reason" (Miller & Moskos, 1995).
Furthermore, the possibility of such moral indignation may be present whenever soldiers are involved in a peacekeeping operation where the country shares
values different from their own.

The notion that symbolic threats lead to prejudice originated from the symbolic and modern racism theories used to explain racism toward African Americans in the United States (Kinder & Sears, 1981; McConahay, 1986). According
to this perspective, European Americans' prejudice toward African Americans
results from the perception that African Americans violate the values of hard
work and fairness (also see Biernat, Vescio, Theno, & Crandall, 1996; Katz,
Wakenhut, & Hass, 1986). A number of studies have demonstrated the link
between these particular values and European Americans' racial attitudes and
behaviors (Biernat, Vescio, & Theno, 1996; Katz & Hass, 1988; Sears, 1988).
Similarly, considerable research has shown that threats to the values and beliefs
of the ingroup predict negative attitudes toward a variety of outgroups (Esses,
Haddock, & Zanna, 1993; Stephan et al., 2002; Stephan et al., 2000; Stephan
& Stephan, 1996; Stephan et al., 1999; Stephan et al., 1998).

Symbolic threats can result from real cultural differences in values and
norms. For example, many Islamic countries have banned the consumption of
alcohol and require women to cover their face and body to prevent temptation
in men. Soldiers from Western countries may reject such norms as extreme
and a violation of personal freedom, whereas local Muslims may view the
soldiers as dissolute for not following the norms. For instance, many soldiers
stationed in Saudi Arabia during Operation Desert Storm remarked that the
strict rules they were required to observe prevented them from really feeling
and living like Americans (Wright, Marlowe, Martin, Gifford, Belenky, &
Manning, 1995).[1]

Symbolic threats may also derive from the ingroup's tendency to attribute
the disadvantaged status of the outgroup to some disposition of the outgroup
as a whole—what Pettigrew (1979) termed the ultimate attribution error. Indeed, European Americans' belief that African Americans do not value hard
work means that European Americans attribute the higher rate of joblessness
and poverty in the African American community to laziness, rather than to
the situational constraints of institutional racism. Similarly, some peacekeepers
in Operation Restore Hope viewed the Somali people as lazy and uncivilized,
believing the Somalis preferred a life of drug use, killing each other, and poverty (Miller & Moskos, 1995). As a result, the outgroup is perceived to be

responsible for their fate and are therefore undeserving of aid (c.f., Bobocel, Hing, Davey, Stanley, & Zanna, 1998). Furthermore, the disadvantage of the outgroup may threaten an important symbolic belief—the belief in a just world. Most people need to feel the world is just, that people get what they deserve and deserve what they get (Lerner, 1980). Thus peacekeepers may blame the suffering of the local people on the people themselves as a means of protecting this fundamental worldview.

INTERGROUP ANXIETY

Intergroup anxiety refers to the threat that current or anticipated interactions with members of an outgroup may result in rejection, ridicule, exploitation, or embarrassment (Stephan & Stephan, 1985, 2000). Research has shown that intergroup anxiety predicts people's negative attitudes toward other groups (Islam & Hewstone, 1993; Stephan et al., 2002). Britt, Boniecki, Vescio, Biernat, and Brown (1996) suggest that intergroup anxiety stems from people's outcome expectancies for future intergroup interactions. Outcome expectancies are beliefs concerning one's ability to attain certain desired outcomes from specific social situations (Schlenker & Leary, 1982). When people are uncertain they can attain the desired outcome or believe they will be unable to do so, they experience anxiety. In peacekeeping operations, peacekeepers try to be fair, firm, and friendly with the indigenous people (Greenberg, 1992). If peacekeepers question their ability to present this image, intergroup anxiety results.

One determinant of intergroup anxiety is a lack of knowledge about the outgroup, particularly their culture and norms (Britt et al., 1996; Stephan & Stephan, 1985). Although most peacekeepers are briefed before their missions on the history and culture of the target region, the information they receive is most likely minimal and insufficient to prepare peacekeepers for all contingencies (see Britt, 1998, this volume). Indeed, one high-ranking U.S. officer blamed the failures of Operation Restore Hope partly on the "lack of experts on Somalian culture [and] values to help us understand the Somalian people" (Miller & Moskos, 1995, p. 630). Language differences also present a barrier to communication. As a result of these barriers, peacekeepers may be concerned about doing or saying something inappropriate. Given the diversity of locations to which peacekeepers from various cultures deploy, they must have accurate information about the local population and combatants, so views of these groups are less affected by negative experiences with a few select members of the population.

Another determinant of intergroup anxiety is prior negative experiences with members of the outgroup (Islam & Hewstone, 1993; Stephan et al., in press; Stephan & Stephan, 1985). Because of real cultural differences and animosity from certain locals, peacekeepers are likely to experience several, even periodic, unpleasant encounters with the indigenous population. For example, in their study of U.S. service members deployed on a humanitarian mission to

Kazakhstan, Britt and Adler (1999) reported that many service members were surprised at the level of dishonesty when dealing with members of the local population. Also, Miller and Moskos (1995) reported that, during Operation Restore Hope, some Somalis called African American soldiers "niggers" and "slaves," and some of the Islamic women referred to female peacekeepers as "whores" for not covering their faces in public. Such encounters promote anxiety over future intergroup interactions, and create uncertainty over who is a friend and who is not.

NEGATIVE STEREOTYPES

Negative stereotypes are perhaps the most complex aspect of the integrated threat theory. In the original theory, negative stereotypes were viewed as a threat because they provided negative expectations about future intergroup encounters (Stephan & Stephan, 2000). As a threat, negative stereotypes are seen as directly promoting prejudice toward the outgroup; if members of the outgroup are expected to be aggressive, lazy, and rude, the ingroup is certainly not going to like them. However, negative stereotypes may also serve as an antecedent to the other threats. For example, an outgroup believed to be aggressive would be viewed as a realistic threat to the well-being of ingroup members. Therefore, in the revised version of the integrated threat theory, negative stereotypes not only directly promote prejudice toward the outgroup, but also indirectly do so through the other threat variables (Stephan et al., 2002). Furthermore, negative stereotypes may also result from prejudice by serving to justify people's negative feelings toward the outgroup (Allport, 1954; Boniecki, 1997; Campbell, 1967). Thus a cycle may exist in which negative stereotypes cause feelings of threat that cause prejudice, which causes negative stereotypes, and so on.

Peacekeepers may come to the target region with preexisting stereotypes of the local population. In many cases, these stereotypes are based on information from the media rather than firsthand experience. At times, peacekeepers may apply a well-known stereotype of another ethnic, religious, or national group that shares a salient feature with the local population. For example, Miller and Moskos (1995) noted that the stereotype of the Somali people expressed by many U.S. soldiers, particularly European American soldiers, was very similar to the cultural stereotype associated with African Americans. Peacekeepers, like any other individuals, have learned the stereotypes of the various social groups within their own countries. These stereotypes are acquired through early socialization, and by the time a person reaches adulthood these stereotypes are so overlearned that they become automatic. Even if a person does not believe the stereotype is accurate, the stereotype will be implicitly activated in memory whenever an environmental cue related to the stereotyped group is present (Devine, 1989). Furthermore, once activated, the stereotype may subtly influence people's social judgments without their awareness (Greenwald & Banaji, 1995).

Even if peacekeepers come to a region without a stereotype of the locals, it is unlikely that they will leave without one. Stereotypes form because of people's natural tendency to categorize and simplify their environment (Ashmore & DelBoca, 1981; Hamilton & Sherman, 1994). Once a social category is created in memory, a stereotype of that category is practically inevitable (Hamilton, 1981). Although stereotypes, by their nature, are overgeneralizations, they are not necessarily inaccurate and may be based on a "kernel of truth" (Levine & Campbell, 1972; Mackie, 1973; McCauley & Stitt, 1978). Real cultural differences between the peacekeepers and the local population will certainly become incorporated into the peacekeepers' stereotypes. However, the content of that stereotype may also be biased by several factors.

One factor is the salience of the outgroup and their actions. When two salient stimuli co-occur, they are more likely to be recalled. Because of the greater accessibility of the salient stimuli in memory, they are assumed to be related, even if they are not—what Chapman (1967) called an illusory correlation. Hamilton and Gifford (1976) showed that people are more likely to remember the negative behaviors of minorities because negative behaviors and minority members are salient. Thus negative stereotypes of minority groups may be illusory correlations. Similarly, during peacekeeping operations, the local people are salient to the peacekeepers because they are the focus of the mission. Thus, as in the Hamilton and Gifford research, when local citizens act negatively (e.g., stealing supplies, attacking peacekeepers or each other), these events are more easily recalled than incidents when local citizens acted positively. As a result, a negative stereotype of the local population may form.

Another factor that biases the stereotype that people form is the tendency, as we have already mentioned, to make dispositional attributions for the outgroup's negative behaviors. In fact, people generally make dispositional attributions for the behaviors of others, often ignoring the situational variables that constrain behavior—a phenomenon commonly known as the *fundamental attribution error* (Ross, 1977). Dispositional attributions are automatic. As soon as the perceiver identifies a behavior, the mind immediately and involuntarily furnishes a dispositional explanation (Gilbert, Pelham, & Krull, 1988). Thus when groups of Somalis threw rocks at peacekeepers stationed in Mogadishu (Miller & Moskos, 1995), peacekeepers would have quickly identified the behaviors as hostile acts and have automatically perceived the Somalis as hostile people. Furthermore, these dispositional attributions will likely generalize beyond just the individuals committing the behaviors and become associated with the salient social category to which the individuals belong. Because causation is found in whatever is the focus of our attention (Heider, 1958; Taylor & Fiske, 1975), when a person's group membership is salient, attributions may generalize to the disposition of the group. Thus some peacekeepers wondered why the Somali *people* were so angry and hostile, even though only a minority of Somalis attacked peacekeeping forces (Miller & Moskos, 1995). The potential for such inferences is present wherever peacekeepers encounter hostile acts from members of the local population, including peacekeeping operations in Bosnia (see Soeters & Rovers, 1997), Kosovo (Castro, Bienvenu, Huffman, & Adler, 2000), and Haiti (Halverson, Bliese, Moore, & Castro, 1995).

Only after the dispositional attribution is furnished do people correct the attribution by considering the situational constraints on the behavior (Quatrone, 1982). For example, some peacekeepers recognized that the Somali citizens were being manipulated by local warlords who distributed flyers urging women and children to attack the peacekeepers (Miller & Moskos, 1995). However, this correction process is effortful and requires sufficient cognitive capacity (Gilbert, Pelham, & Krull, 1988). When people are distracted, fatigued, or under stress, cognitive capacity diminishes (Cohen & Spacapan, 1978; Hasher & Zacks, 1979; Kahneman, 1973; Klein & Boals, 2001). Peacekeepers experience considerable fatigue and stress as a result of travel, heavy workloads, extreme working conditions, unexpected violence, traumatic events, and organizational conflicts (Kidwell & Langholtz, 1998). As a result, peacekeepers are likely to stick with their initial dispositional explanations for the behaviors of the local population.

Fatigue and stress not only bias stereotype formation but also influence whether or not people use their stereotypes to form impressions and make judgments about individual outgroup members. Stereotypes act as heuristics— mental shortcuts—that aid in the processing of information (Bodenhausen, 1993). Forming an impression of a person based solely on that person's evident characteristics requires considerable cognitive resources and time. Stereotypes help by providing a premade impression that can be applied to all members of the group. Although people can avoid using their stereotypes, they must have sufficient motivation and cognitive capacity to do so (Devine, 1989; Fiske & Neuberg, 1990). For example, people rely on their stereotypes more when they are cognitively engaged with another task (Gilbert & Hixon,1991) and during the low points of their circadian cycles when they are less alert (Bodenhausen, 1990). Thus the onerous demands of peacekeeping operations may strain the peacekeeper's ability to avoid using stereotypes. As noted in various chapters in this volume, the stress soldiers experience on various peacekeeping missions can be intense, resulting in increased fatigue and decreased cognitive capacity. Under this stress, peacekeepers' stereotypes, whether preexisting or newly formed, are likely to surface. Indeed, Miller and Moskos (1995) reported that many African American soldiers were surprised at the racist comments of European American soldiers while in Somalia; they had never suspected them of being prejudiced before the mission.

ANTECEDENT CONDITIONS

According to Stephan and Stephan (2000), a number of antecedent conditions influence feelings of threat. Perhaps one of the strongest factors is negative contact with members of the outgroup (Stephan et al., 2002). The more often peacekeepers are attacked or experience other unpleasant interactions with local individuals, the more likely the local population as a whole will be perceived as a threat. Another factor is a prior history of intergroup conflict. Peacekeepers are likely to feel threatened if their country of origin has had or continues to have an antagonistic relationship with the government or other factions within the target region. For example, U.S. soldiers being deployed to Afghanistan, Turkish soldiers being deployed to Greece, or African soldiers being deployed to regions that had previously been at war with their home territory might heighten feelings of threat and therefore exacerbate intergroup hostilities.

Perceived status differences between groups can also contribute to feelings of threat (Stephan et al., 2002; Stephan & Stephan, 2000). Groups perceived to have greater military, political, or economic power than one's own group are more threatening. Typically, peacekeepers come from higher status countries (i.e., countries with greater military, political, and economic resources); thus they are unlikely to feel threatened by the status of the local population. However, members of higher status groups may develop symbolic beliefs and negative stereotypes about lower status groups as a means of legitimizing the status difference (Sidanius, 1993). For example, peacekeepers may justify the greater economic well-being of their country relative to the target region by characterizing the local population as lazy.

Another contributor to feelings of threat is the degree to which people identify with the ingroup—that is, believe the ingroup is an important part of who they are (Stephan et al., 2002; Stephan & Stephan, 2000). In peacekeeping operations, ingroup identification is likely to be high, particularly among military personnel. Indeed, patriotism and loyalty to country are deemed admirable qualities as well as necessary job requirements for soldiers (see Franke, this volume). Unfortunately, ingroup identification is also related to greater prejudice toward other groups (Blanz, Mummendey, & Otten, 1995; Guimond, 2000; Pettigrew, 1997; Stephan et al., 2002). This relationship may exist because ingroup identification highlights intergroup boundaries. Thus, when encountering members of another group, interactions are likely to be intergroup rather than interpersonal. When these encounters are negative, the outgroup as a whole becomes a source of threat instead of a specific individual.

REDUCING PREJUDICE

Perhaps one of the earliest suggested strategies for reducing prejudice and intergroup conflict is the contact hypothesis (see Allport, 1954). According to this hypothesis, contact between various groups should increase knowledge about other groups, challenge the veracity of stereotypes, and ultimately eliminate prejudiced feelings. A number of studies support this idea. For example, increased contact as a result of desegregation in inner-city housing projects and in the army was associated with decreased racial prejudice (Deutch & Collins, 1951; Stouffer, Suchman, DeVinney, Star, & Williams, 1949). Also, the more contact European Americans had with African Americans, the less intergroup anxiety they reported feeling toward African Americans (Britt et al., 1996). In the context of peacekeeping missions, Britt, Adler, and Bartone (2001) found that, for soldiers deployed to Bosnia as part of Operation Joint Endeavor, those who reported getting outside of their base camp and having contact with the local population reported deriving more benefits from the deployment in comparison to soldiers who primarily spent the entire deployment in a circumscribed location. Greater contact may have benefited not only soldiers' views of the deployment but also their perceptions of the local population as well.

Of course, the nature of the contact is important. As we have noted, negative contact is likely to heighten intergroup anxiety and increase feelings of threat and prejudice. Thus merely bringing groups together will not necessarily reduce intergroup conflict. Indeed, considerable research on the contact hypothesis over the years has yielded mixed results; sometimes contact decreased prejudice, but just as often it increased prejudice (see Amir, 1969; Stephan, 1987). The consensus from this research indicates that, in order for contact to reduce prejudice, several conditions must be present, including equal status between groups, institutional support, interpersonal rather than intergroup interactions, similarity in beliefs and values, and contact across various group members and situations. Perhaps the most important condition, however, is the presence of superordinate goals. Superordinate goals are outcomes that can only be obtained through the cooperative efforts of both groups. In a now classic study, Sherif, Harvey, White, Hood, and Sherif (1961) created prejudice between two groups of boys attending summer camp, and then they attempted to eliminate the prejudice by initiating a series of cooperative tasks. As a result, Sherif et al. noticed a dramatic decrease in intergroup hostilities and an increase in cross-group friendships.

The presence of superordinate goals may partially explain the different experiences of peacekeepers stationed in rural areas of Somalia during Operation Restore Hope compared to those in urban areas such as Mogadishu (see Miller & Moskos, 1995). Peacekeepers in rural areas helped remove land mines and repair roads so relief workers could transport much needed food and medical supplies to the Somali countryside. Thus peacekeepers in these rural areas had generally positive experiences with Somalis because they both were combating a common enemy—famine and disease. In contrast, peacekeepers in the urban areas of Somalia were not allowed to aid the locals. Rather, the urban peacekeepers were stationed there as a "security" force, which essentially meant they were to defend themselves and their camps. Without clear superordinate goals, a competitive intergroup situation arose in which desperate Somalis would try to steal food, money, or other valuable items from peacekeepers. Therefore, the urban peacekeepers experienced more threats from the Somalis than did the rural peacekeepers.

Superordinate goals promote cooperative interdependence between groups, which leads to the recategorization of ingroup and outgroup members into a single superordinate ingroup (Gaertner, Mann, Dovidio, Murrell, & Pomare, 1990). As a result, interactions are no longer intergroup but intragroup and interpersonal, former outgroup members now benefit from people's tendency to favor the ingroup (Brewer, 1979; Tajfel, 1982), and former outgroup members are perceived to be more similar to the self. Furthermore, perceived similarity is one factor that promotes empathy—vicariously experiencing another's feeling and perceptions (Batson, Duncan, Ackerman, Buckley, & Birch, 1981), which has been considered a necessary quality for successful peacekeeping operations (Greenberg, 1992). Although we know of no research directly addressing this speculation, we propose that empathy may also work in the reverse causal direction. That is, in the absence of superordinate goals, increasing people's empathy for members of an outgroup (e.g., by having them imagine what it is like "to be in that person's shoes") may also subsequently increase the perceived similarity of the outgroup members to the self and reduce the salience of intergroup boundaries. Thus, by empathizing with the local population, peacekeepers may begin to see them, not as a separate group in need of aid, but as fellow members of humanity deserving of the same democratic freedoms that the peacekeepers themselves enjoy.

Prejudice can also be reduced by changing social norms and appealing to people's egalitarian values. In the United States, the civil rights movement of the 1950s and 1960s forced European Americans to confront what Myrdal (1944) termed the American dilemma—the contradiction of accepting the American creed of equality and opportunity for all while simultaneously excluding African Americans from those very rights. As a result, open expressions of racism became socially undesirable, and, in some cases—following the 1954 Supreme Court ruling that ended segregation and the Civil Rights Act of 1964—unlawful. Today, many Americans are motivated to control their prejudices because they fear public censure or because their prejudices conflict with their egalitarian values and nonprejudiced self-image (Plant & Devine, 1998). Thus one way of reducing prejudice on peacekeeping missions is to set clear egalitarian norms; peacekeepers should know that expressing prejudice toward the local population is unacceptable and is contrary to the goals of the mission. Peacekeepers need to recognize the importance of egalitarian norms for helping to ensure impartiality toward the former warring factions so the mission will succeed (Kidwell & Langholtz, 1998). If service members see a connection between the importance of such norms and mission success, they should be more likely to adopt egalitarian beliefs (Britt, 1998).

According to Devine and her colleagues (e.g., Devine & Monteith, 1993; Devine, Monteith, Zuwerink, & Elliot, 1991), when people perceive a discrepancy between their behaviors and their egalitarian beliefs, they experience negative, self-directed affect (e.g., guilt and shame). To eliminate the negative affect, people attempt to regulate their behavior and prevent future discrepancies. However, like trying to break a bad habit, the process of controlling one's prejudices requires attention and effort (Devine, 1989)—a luxury that many peacekeepers cannot afford when under attack or facing other high levels of stress. Under such adverse conditions, peacekeepers must act as cognitive misers, selectively expending cognitive resources on those goals that are most critical (c.f., Fiske & Taylor, 1991). Such a strategy is necessary for making split-second decisions that may save lives. Thus we do not advocate that peacekeepers carefully process all situations before deciding to react. Nonetheless, peacekeepers should be aware that while under stress, or when their attentional resources are distracted by potential dangers in the environment, they are more likely to use negative stereotypes and form prejudiced attitudes about the locals. When off duty, when they do not have to be cognitive misers, peacekeepers should take the time to reassess their views of the local population. For instance, when peacekeepers are off duty, superiors can open a dialogue that allows peacekeepers to reevaluate their recent encounters with the local population and provide them the opportunity to counter their automatic prejudiced reactions.

CONCLUSIONS AND DIRECTIONS FOR FUTURE RESEARCH

In the present chapter we have attempted to show how social psychological principles of prejudice and stereotyping are useful in understanding the experiences peacekeepers might have when engaging people of other nationalities. Given research showing how easily stereotypes and prejudice can be formed and elicited, and given the importance of maintaining impartiality for mission success, military planners need to consider steps that can be taken to reduce the impact of prejudice and stereotyping. We have attempted to illustrate some of the steps that may help decrease the impact of these processes (e.g., providing peacekeepers with accurate information about the local population, promoting superordinate goals and positive contact, increasing empathy, emphasizing the importance of egalitarian norms for mission success, and providing time for peacekeepers to process their experiences).

Although our analysis has focused on the prejudices of peacekeepers toward the local population, we do not want to give the impression that the impetus of intergroup conflict between peacekeepers and locals lies solely with the peacekeepers. Prejudice is an intergroup phenomenon, and it is typically the case that members of both groups feel prejudice toward the other. Indeed, we could easily write a chapter applying the same principles of prejudice to understanding the hostility of local populations toward peacekeepers on certain peacekeeping missions (e.g., Operation Restore Hope to Somalia). Certainly, when the local population expresses hostility toward peacekeepers, such reactions increase peacekeepers' feelings of threat, which promotes prejudiced reactions toward the local population. Prejudice begets prejudice. However, peacekeepers' prejudiced reactions would likewise threaten the local population, which would further promote prejudice, and so on. Thus prejudice on the part of both parties creates a vicious cycle that endangers the success of the operation. However, because it is the responsibility of the peacekeepers, not the local population, to ensure the success of the operation, peacekeepers must break the cycle and not return prejudice in kind.

As should be evident from our discussion, this chapter illustrates the need for future research designed to assess the presence of prejudice during peacekeeping operations, the predictors of such prejudice, the impact of prejudice on well-being and performance, and the empirical evaluation of attempts to decrease prejudice. For example, researchers could develop measures of prejudice and stereotyping suitable for surveys administered to peacekeepers, and they should also assess what factors are likely to predict prejudice and stereotyping. The present chapter highlights a variety of factors that should predict reports of prejudice (e.g., negative experiences with the local population, lack of contact or accurate information about the population, a high level of stress among the peacekeepers). If peacekeeping researchers can understand the predictors of prejudice and the impact of prejudice on performance, attempts to decrease the effects of prejudice on mission success can be developed and evaluated.

NOTE

1. Although not an official UN peacekeeping mission, Operation Desert Storm was carried out in part to prevent further Iraqi aggression into Kuwait and Saudi Arabia. Therefore, in a sense, the soldiers of Operation Desert Storm, like UN peacekeepers, were helping preserve the peace in the entire region.

REFERENCES

Allport, G. W. (1954). *The nature of prejudice.* Reading, MA: Addison-Wesley.

Amir, Y. (1969). Contact hypothesis in ethnic relations. *Psychological Bulletin, 71,* 319–342.

Ashmore, R. D., & DelBoca, F. K. (1981). Conceptual approaches to stereotypes and stereotyping. In D. L. Hamilton (Ed.), *Cognitive processes in stereotyping and intergroup behavior* (pp. 1–35). Hillsdale, NJ: Erlbaum.

Batson, C. D., Duncan, B., Ackerman, P., Buckley, T., & Birch, K. (1981). Is empathic emotion a source of altruistic motivation? *Journal of Personality and Social Psychology, 40,* 290–302.

Berkowitz, L. (1989). Frustration-aggression hypothesis: Examination and reformulation. *Psychological Bulletin, 106,* 59–73.

Biernat, M., Vescio, T. K., & Theno, S. A. (1996). Violating American values: A "value congruence" approach to understanding outgroup attitudes. *Journal of Experimental Social Psychology, 32,* 387–410.

Biernat, M., Vescio, T. K., Theno, S. A., & Crandall, C. S. (1996). Values and prejudice: Toward understanding the impact of American values on outgroup attitudes. In C. Seligman, J. M. Olson, & M. P. Zanna (Eds.), *The psychology of values: The Ontario symposium* (Vol. 8, pp. 153–189). Mahwah, NJ: Erlbaum.

Blanz, M., Mummendey, A., & Otten, S. (1995). Perceptions of relative group size and group status: Effects on intergroup discrimination in negative evaluations. *European Journal of Social Psychology, 25,* 231–247.

Bobo, L. (1983). Whites' opposition to busing: Symbolic racism or realistic group conflict? *Journal of Personality and Social Psychology, 45,* 1196–1210.

Bobocel, D. R., Hing, L. S. S., Davey, L. M., Stanley, D. J., & Zanna, M. P. (1998). Justice-based opposition to social policies: Is it genuine? *Journal of Personality and Social Psychology, 75,* 653–669.

Bodenhausen, G. V. (1990). Stereotypes as judgmental heuristics: Evidence of circadian variations in discrimination. *Psychological Science, 1,* 319–322.

Bodenhausen, G. V. (1993). Emotions, arousal, and stereotypic judgments: A heuristic model of affect and stereotyping. In D. M. Mackie & D. L. Hamilton (Eds.), *Affect, cognition, and stereotyping: Interactive processes in group perception* (pp. 13–37). San Diego: Academic Press.

Boniecki, K. A. (1997). The influence of prejudice on the formation of stereotypes about the outgroup (Doctoral dissertation, University of Florida, 1997). *Dissertation Abstracts International, 58,* 3964.

Brewer, M. B. (1979). In-group bias in the minimal intergroup situation: A cognitive-motivational analysis. *Psychological Bulletin, 86,* 307–324.

Britt, T. W. (1998). Psychological ambiguities in peacekeeping. In H. J. Langholtz (Ed.), *The psychology of peacekeeping* (pp. 111–128). Westport, CT: Praeger.

Britt, T. W., & Adler, A. B. (1999). Stress and health during medical humanitarian assistance missions. *Military Medicine, 164,* 275–279.

Britt, T. W., Adler, A. B., & Bartone, P. T. (2001). Deriving benefits from stressful events: The role of engagement in meaningful work and hardiness. *Journal of Occupational Health Psychology, 6,* 53–63.

Britt, T. W., Boniecki, K. A., Vescio, T. K., Biernat, M., & Brown, L. M. (1996). Intergroup anxiety: A Person × Situation approach. *Personality and Social Psychology Bulletin, 22,* 1177–1188.

Campbell, D. T. (1967). Stereotypes and the perception of group differences. *American Psychologist, 22,* 817–829.

Castro, C. A., Bienvenu, R., Huffman, A. H., & Adler, A. B. (2000). Soldier dimensions and operational readiness in U.S. Army forces deployed to Kosovo. *International Review of the Armed Forces Medical Services, 73,* 191–199.

Chapman, L. J. (1967). Illusory correlation in observational report. *Journal of Verbal Learning and Verbal Behavior, 6,* 151–155.

Cohen, S., & Spacapan, S. (1978). The aftereffects of stress: An attentional interpretation. *Environmental Psychology and Nonverbal Behavior, 3,* 43–57.

Deutsch, M., & Collins, M. E. (1951). *Interracial housing: A psychological evaluation of a social experiment.* Minneapolis: University of Minnesota Press.

Devine, P. G. (1989). Stereotypes and prejudice: Their automatic and controlled components. *Journal of Personality and Social Psychology, 56,* 5–18.

Devine, P. G., & Monteith, M. J. (1993). The role of discrepancy-associated affect in prejudice reduction. In D. M. Mackie & D. L. Hamilton (Eds.), *Affect, cognition, and stereotyping: Interactive processes in group perception* (pp. 317–344). San Diego: Academic Press.

Devine, P. G., Monteith, M. J., Zuwerink, J. R., & Elliot, A. J. (1991). Prejudice with and without compunction. *Journal of Personality and Social Psychology, 60,* 817–830.

Esses, V. M., Haddock, G., & Zanna, M. P. (1993). Values, stereotypes, and emotions as determinants of intergroup attitudes. In D. M. Mackie & D. L. Hamilton (Eds.), *Affect, cognition, and stereotyping: Interactive processes in group perception* (pp. 137–166). San Diego: Academic Press.

Fiske, S. T., & Neuberg, S. L. (1990). A continuum of impression formation, from category-based to individuating processes: Influences of information and motivation on attention and interpretation. In M. P. Zanna (Ed.), *Advances in experimental social psychology* (Vol. 23, pp. 1–74). San Diego: Academic Press.

Fiske, S. T., & Taylor, S. E. (1991). *Social cognition* (2nd ed.). New York: Random House.

Gaertner, S. L., Mann, J., Dovidio, J. F., Murrell, A., & Pomare, M. (1990). How does cooperation reduce intergroup bias? *Journal of Personality and Social Psychology, 59,* 692–704.

Gilbert, D. T., & Hixon, J. G. (1991). The trouble of thinking: Activation and application of stereotypic beliefs. *Journal of Personality and Social Psychology, 60,* 509–517.

Gilbert, D. T., Pelham, B. W., & Krull, D. S. (1988). On cognitive busyness: When person perceivers meet persons perceived. *Journal of Personality and Social Psychology, 59,* 601–613.

Greenberg, K. E. (1992). The essential art of empathy. *The Quarterly Journal of Military History, 5,* 64–69.

Greenwald, A. G., & Banaji, M. R. (1995). Implicit social cognition: Attitudes, self-esteem, and stereotypes. *Psychological Review, 102,* 4–27.

Guimond, S. (2000). Group socialization and prejudice: The social transmission of intergroup attitudes and beliefs. *European Journal of Social Psychology, 30,* 335–354.

Halverson, R. R., Bliese, P. D., Moore, R. E., & Castro, C. A. (1995). *Psychological well-being and physical health of soldiers deployed for Operation Uphold Democracy: A summary of human dimensions research in Haiti.* Alexandria, VA: Defense Technical Information Center (DTIC: # ADA298125).

Hamilton, D. L. (1981). Stereotyping and intergroup behavior: Some thoughts on the cognitive approach. In D. L. Hamilton (Ed.), *Cognitive processes in stereotyping and intergroup behavior* (pp. 333–353). Hillsdale, NJ: Erlbaum.

Hamilton, D. L., & Gifford, R. K. (1976). Illusory correlation in interpersonal perception: A cognitive basis for stereotypic judgments. *Journal of Experimental Social Psychology, 12,* 392–407.

Hamilton, D. L., & Sherman, J. W. (1994). Stereotypes. In R. S. Wyer, Jr. & T. K. Srull (Eds.), *Handbook of social cognition* (2nd ed., Vol. 2, pp. 1–68). Hillsdale, NJ: Erlbaum.

Hasher, L., & Zacks, R. T. (1979). Automatic and effortful processes in memory. *Journal of Experimental Psychology: General, 108,* 356–388.

Heider, F. (1958). *The psychology of interpersonal relations.* New York: Wiley.

Hovland, C. I., & Sears, R. (1940). Minor studies of aggression: Correlation of lynchings with economic indices. *Journal of Psychology, 9,* 301–310.

Islam, R. M., & Hewstone, M. (1993). Dimensions of contact as predictors of intergroup anxiety, perceived outgroup variability, and outgroup attitude: An integrative model. *Personality and Social Psychology Bulletin, 19,* 700–710.

Jackson, J. W. (1993). Realistic group conflict theory: A review and evaluation of the theoretical and empirical literature. *The Psychological Record, 43,* 395–414.

Kahneman, D. (1973). *Attention and effort.* Englewood Cliffs, NJ: Prentice-Hall.

Katz, I., & Hass, R. G. (1988). Racial ambivalence and American value conflict: Correlational and priming studies of dual cognitive structures. *Journal of Personality and Social Psychology, 55,* 893–905.

Katz, I., Wackenhut, J., & Hass, R. G. (1986). Racial ambivalence, value duality, and behavior. In J. F. Dovidio & S. L. Gaertner (Eds.), *Prejudice, discrimination, and racism* (pp. 35–60). New York: Academic Press.

Kidwell, B., & Langholtz, H. J. (1998). Personnel selection, preparation, and training for U.N. peacekeeping missions. In H. J. Langholtz (Ed.), *The psychology of peacekeeping* (pp. 89–100). Westport, CT: Praeger.

Kimmel, P. R. (1998). Cultural and ethnic issues of conflict and peacekeeping. In H. J. Langholtz (Ed.), *The psychology of peacekeeping* (pp. 57–71). Westport, CT: Praeger.

Kinder, D. R., & Sears, D. O. (1981). Symbolic racism versus racial threats to the good life. *Journal of Personality and Social Psychology, 40,* 414–431.

Klein, K., & Boals, A. (2001). The relationship of life event stress and working memory capacity. *Applied Cognitive Psychology, 15,* 565–579.

Latorre, A. V., Jr. (1984). Peacekeeping as a military mission. *The Marine Corps Gazette, 68,* 20–26.

Lerner, M. J. (1980). *The belief in a just world: A fundamental delusion.* New York: Plenum.

Levine, R. A., & Campbell, D. T. (1972). *Ethnocentrism: Theories of conflict, ethnic attitudes, and group behavior.* New York: Wiley.

Litz, B. T., King, L. A., King, D. W., Orsillo, S. M., & Friedman, M. J. (1997). Warriors as peacekeepers: Features of the Somalia experience and PTSD. *Journal of Consulting and Clinical Psychology, 65,* 1001–1010.

Mackie, M. (1973). Arriving at "truth" by definition, the case of stereotype inaccuracy. *Social Problems, 20,* 431–447.

McCauley, C., & Stitt, C. L. (1978). An individual and quantitative measure of stereotypes. *Journal of Personality and Social Psychology, 39,* 929–940.

McConahay, J. B. (1986). Modern racism, ambivalence, and the Modern Racism Scale. In J. Dovidio & S. L. Gaertner (Eds.), *Prejudice, discrimination, and racism* (pp. 91–125). San Diego: Academic Press.

Miller, L. L., & Moskos, C. (1995). Humanitarians or warriors?: Race, gender, and combat status in Operation Restore Hope. *Armed Forces and Society, 21,* 615–637.

Myrdal, G, (1944). *An American dilemma: The Negro problem and modern democracy.* New York: Harper.

Pettigrew, T. F. (1979). The ultimate attribution error: Extending Allport's cognitive analysis of prejudice. *Personality and Social Psychology Bulletin, 5,* 461–476.

Pettigrew, T. F. (1997). The affective component of prejudice: Empirical support for the new view. In S. A. Tuch & J. K. Martin (Eds.), *Racial attitudes in the 1990s: Continuity and change.* Westport, CT: Praeger.

Plant, E. A., & Devine, P. G. (1998). Internal and external motivation to respond without prejudice. *Journal of Personality & Social Psychology, 75,* 811–832.

Quatrone, G. A. (1982). Overattribution and unit formation: When behavior engulfs the person. *Journal of Personality and Social Psychology, 42,* 593–607.

Ross, L. (1977). The intuitive psychologist and his shortcomings: Distortions in the attribution process. In L. Berkowitz (Ed.), *Advances in experimental social psychology* (Vol. 10, pp. 174–221). New York: Academic Press.

Schlenker, B. R., & Leary, M. R. (1982). Social anxiety and self-presentation: A conceptualization and a model. *Psychological Bulletin, 92,* 641–699.

Sears, D. O. (1988). Symbolic racism. In P. A. Katz & D. A. Taylor (Eds.), *Eliminating racism: Profiles in controversy* (pp. 53–84). New York: Plenum.

Segal, D. R., & Gravino, K. S. (1985). Peacekeeping as a military mission. In C. D. Smith (Ed.), *The hundred percent challenge: Building a national institute of peace* (pp. 38–69). Cabin John, MD: Seven Locks Press.

Sherif, M. (1966). *In common predicament: Social psychology of intergroup conflict and cooperation.* Boston: Houghton Mifflin.

Sherif, M., Harvey, O. J., White, B. J., Hood, W. R., & Sherif, C. W. (1961). *Intergroup conflict and cooperation: The Robber's Cave experiment.* Norman, OK: University Book Exchange.

Sidanius, J. (1993). The psychology of group conflict and the dynamics of oppression: A social dominance perspective. In S. Iyengar & W. J. McGuire (Eds.), *Explorations in political psychology* (pp. 183–219). Durham, NC: Duke University Press.

Soeters, J. L., & Rovers, J. H. (1997). *Netherlands annual review of military studies 1997: The Bosnian experience.* Breda, The Netherlands: Royal Netherlands Military Academy.

Stephan, W. G. (1985). Intergroup relations. In G. Lindzey & E. Aronson (Eds.), *The handbook of social psychology* (3rd ed., Vol. 2, pp. 599–658). New York: Random House.

Stephan, W. G. (1987). The contact hypothesis in intergroup relations. In C. Hendrick (Ed.), *Group processes in intergroup relations: Review of personality and social psychology* (Vol. 9, pp. 13–40). Newbury Park, CA: Sage.

Stephan, W. G., Boniecki, K. A., Ybarra, O., Bettencourt, A., Ervin, K. S., Jackson, L. A., McNatt, P., & Renfro, C. C. (2002). The role of threats in racial attitudes of Blacks and Whites. *Personality and Social Psychology Bulletin, 28,* 1242–1254.

Stephan, W. G., Diaz-Loving, R., & Duran, A. (2000). Integrated threat theory and intercultural attitudes: Mexico and the United States. *Journal of Cross-Cultural Psychology, 31,* 240–249.

Stephan, W. G., & Stephan, C. W. (1985). Intergroup anxiety. *Journal of Social Issues, 41,* 157–175.

Stephan, W. G., & Stephan, C. W. (1996). Predicting prejudice. *International Journal of Intercultural Relations, 20,* 409–426.

Stephan, W. G., & Stephan, C. W. (2000). An integrated threat theory of prejudice. In S. Oskamp (Ed.), *Reducing prejudice and discrimination* (pp. 23–46). Hillsdale, NJ: Erlbaum.

Stephan, W. G., Ybarra, O., & Bachman, G. (1999). Prejudice toward immigrants: An integrated threat theory. *Journal of Applied Social Psychology, 29,* 2221–2237.

Stephan, W. G., Ybarra, O., Martinez, C., Schwarzwald, J., & Tur-Kaspa. (1998). Prejudice toward immigrants to Spain and Israel: An integrated threat theory analysis *Journal of Cross-Cultural Psychology, 29,* 559–576.

Stouffer, S. A., Suchman, E. A., DeVinney, L. C., Star, S. A., & Williams, R. M., Jr. (1949). *The American soldier: Adjustment during army life.* New York: Wiley.

Tajfel, H. (1982). Social psychology of intergroup relations. *Annual Review of Psychology, 33,* 1–39.

Taylor, S. E., & Fiske, S. T. (1975). Point-of-view and perceptions of causality. *Journal of Personality and Social Psychology, 32,* 439–445.

United Nations Department of Public Information. (2001). *United Nations peacekeeping: In the service of peace.* Retrieved January 28, 2002, from http://www.un.org/Depts/dpko/dpko/home_bottom.htm

Weisæth, L. (1990). Stress of U.N. military peacekeeping. *WISMIC Newsletter, 2*(2), 15–18.

Wright, K. M., Marlowe, D. H., Martin, J. A., Gifford, R. K., Belenky, G. L., & Manning, F. J. (1995). Operation Desert Shield/Desert Storm: A summary report. *Defense Technical Information Center ADA303327.* Alexandria, VA: DTIC.

5

Can Participation in Peacekeeping Missions Be Beneficial? The Importance of Meaning as a Function of Attitudes and Identity

Thomas W. Britt

Military personnel from countries all over the world are increasingly being called on to serve on missions where the goal is to either establish or preserve peace among nations or among warring factions within a nation (Breed, 1998). Many military personnel who serve on these missions have been trained to have a combat mentality, with the goal of using strategic force to attain a clearly defined objective. Furthermore, most personnel who serve on these missions encounter stressors and frustrations that they could not have anticipated prior to deploying, such as difficult living conditions, decreased ability to use force in the face of provocation, and a distrust of military personnel by the local community (Britt & Adler, 1999; Litz, 1996). These stressors are compounded by the fact that most military personnel are required or volunteer to serve on peacekeeping operations for at least six months or longer. Given the challenging and potentially stressful nature of peacekeeping operations, how do service members make sense of the mission? That is, how do they justify to themselves the time, effort, and sacrifices they are making by participating in the operation? Furthermore, is it possible that military personnel might derive some benefits from participating in a challenging operation where peace between warring nations or factions may or may not be preserved?

The present chapter addresses these questions through an analysis of how service members assign meaning to their participation in peacekeeping operations, and how the meaning they assign to their participation predicts the degree to which service members derive benefits from the operation. The underlying assumption is that service members benefit from participating in peacekeeping operations when they are able to construe the operation in a meaningful way. After presenting psychological models of how individuals perceive the meaning of different types of events, a large portion of the chapter will address those factors that predict whether or not service members will derive meaning from participation in a peacekeeping operation. After addressing the predictors of meaning for peacekeepers, psychological theory and research on deriving benefits from stressful events is reviewed and applied to an examination of the potential benefits service members might obtain from participation in peacekeeping operations. Finally, the last part of the chapter makes the explicit connection between meaning and deriving benefits from peacekeeping operations, using data from a study of U.S. soldiers deployed to Bosnia in order to illustrate the theoretical linkage.

THEORETICAL MODELS OF MEANING

Generally, models of meaning have addressed how an individual makes sense of an event, or how an individual "finds meaning" in an event. There has, however, been no consensus as to the definition of meaning. Previous authors have referred to meaning as a general orientation toward life, the personal significance of an event, and an analysis of causality for why an event occurred (Park & Folkman, 1997). Such definitions distinguish between situational meaning and global meaning. *Situational meaning* refers to the personal significance or relevance of a specific event, and *global meaning* refers an overall awareness of order, coherence, and a sense of purpose in one's life. Along similar lines, Tait and Silver (1989) have defined finding meaning in events as "construing their personal significance in cognitive and affective terms" (p. 355). These authors have argued that whenever individuals are placed in a stressful or unusual situation, that the search for some sort of meaningful perspective on the event is crucial for adjusting adequately to the event.

Another approach to meaning is that of Baumeister (1991), who has argued that four needs provide individuals with a sense of meaning: purpose (goals and intrinsic motivations that are fulfilled), value (that actions are right and justified), efficacy (that an individual has some control over events), and self-worth (that individuals feel they have positive value). Baumeister argues that key aspects of people's lives enable them to satisfy these four needs of meaning. For example, an individual's job might allow an individual to achieve important goals, express values such as self-determination and compassion, exercise control over his or her work product, and allow the individual to feel good about himself or herself as a function of praise and accomplishment. All four of these needs contribute to the meaning that an individual derives from his or her work.

Of particular relevance to a discussion of peacekeepers is Baumeister's analysis of how work is essential to life's meaning. He argues there are three "meanings" of work that are prevalent in today's society, including work as a job, work as a calling, and work as a career. An individual who operates according to a "work as job" is working simply for the paycheck, and the individual's job or occupation does not really reflect his or her identity or values.

However, Baumeister (1991) notes that even this level of orientation toward work can provide individuals with a basic sense of meaning, in terms of bringing home money to support one's family, and at least being able to define themselves as "employed," as opposed to unemployed.

Work as a calling occurs when individuals perform a job because of some sense of obligation, duty, or destiny. Baumeister notes that the sense of calling for an individual can be internal, when individuals feel called to a job that fits with their identity or self-concept, or external, when individuals feel called by something outside of themselves, such as an important group or higher order spiritual force. Baumeister notes that this orientation to work is exemplified by missionaries who feel called by God to help others and make them aware of certain beliefs, as well as by service members who feel called to military service by a sense of duty toward one's country.

Work as a career occurs when the individual engages in a job out of a desire for success and recognition. Baumeister argues that these individuals are primarily motivated by the desire to progress within an established organizational hierarchy, rather than by the joy of performing the job itself. Examples of this orientation to work would be an executive climbing the prototypical "company ladder," as well as a military service member who does his or her job primarily in order to get promoted to the next rank. Later in the chapter we will see that the orientation toward work adopted by peacekeepers has implications for the ability for the peacekeeper to find meaning in the operation.

DETERMINANTS OF MEANING DURING PEACEKEEPING OPERATIONS

When peacekeepers find themselves on operations in which the rules of engagement are less clear than in combat, and peacekeepers are required to act in ways that might be inconsistent with their combat identity, they undoubtedly will attempt to make sense of the situation (Britt, 1998; Segal & Segal, 1993). This analysis of the situation may be more or less conscious or deliberate, and peacekeepers will certainly differ in the extent to which they spend time pondering the meaning of the situation (see Cacioppo & Petty, 1982; Trapnell & Campbell, 1999). However, all peacekeepers will on some level attempt to make sense of their situation, and the extent to which peacekeepers derive meaning from their experience will determine how they ultimately adapt to the peacekeeping mission. Perhaps the clearest statement emphasizing the role of meaning for peacekeepers is from Segal and Segal (1993), who noted, "If a peacekeeping mission has a meaning that 'makes sense' to the soldiers, if families understand and share these meanings, and if society at large shares and reinforces them as well, then soldier motivation and performance will be high" (p. 46). Clearly, how service members make sense of peacekeeping missions should have relevance to their morale and performance.

Ultimately, a confluence of factors determines whether a soldier is able to "make sense" of his or her participation on peacekeeping operations. The conceptual framework for the predictors is provided in Figure 5.1. Note that the various factors associated with meaning are indicated in the figure as causal indicators (see Bollen & Lennox, 1991, for a discussion of causal indicators of latent variables). That is, the individual's positive attitude toward the operation, the individual's perception of the operation as relevant to his or her identity, the positive views expressed by military leaders toward peacekeeping missions, and public support of the operation are factors that contribute to a high level of meaning. Therefore, the more of these factors that are present, the more meaning service members will assign to the peacekeeping operation. I now discuss each of the variables identified in the model that predict the meaning service members assign to peacekeeping operations.

Attitudes

One traditional area of social psychology that has relevance to how peacekeepers assign meaning to their participation on peacekeeping operations is attitudes. An *attitude* can be defined as an evaluation of an object, person, or idea as either favorable or unfavorable (Eagly & Chaiken, 1993). Individuals hold attitudes toward a diversity of objects and concepts, and attitudes can range from the rather trivial (e.g., one's attitude toward vanilla ice cream) to extremely important concepts (e.g., attitude toward one's self or partner). The study of attitudes has a long history in military research. The most dramatic

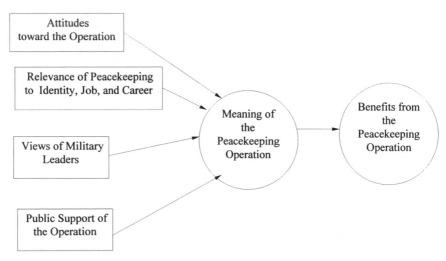

Figure 5.1 Theoretical Model of Predictors of Meaning and Deriving Benefits from Peacekeeping Operations

example of the implications of attitudes for service members was demonstrated by Stouffer et al. (1949). In their classic study of the American soldier in World War II, these authors found that attitudes toward equipment measured before participation in combat predicted a military unit's attrition during combat. That is, the mortality rate in combat was higher for units who had negative attitudes toward their equipment going into combat. Although it is difficult to determine whether the actual quality of the equipment or the motivational context induced by the attitude was the main determinant of mortality, it became clear that attitudes could be measured and are predictive of important outcomes.

In addition to the relevance of soldier attitudes to combat operations, soldier attitudes are also important to understanding the experience of military personnel on peacekeeping operations. Attitudes toward peacekeeping have the potential to provide an individual with a sense of meaning and understanding. Researchers have noted that attitudes can differ in the functions they serve for individuals, and in the level of their importance to the individual. Katz (1960) argued that attitudes can serve a value-expressive function, in which the attitude allows the individual to express important values that make up his or her self-concept. Katz (1960) also argued that attitudes serve a knowledge function, allowing individuals to make sense of their social world (see also Herek, 1987). Krosnick (1988) has also pointed out that attitudes differ in their importance to the individual. Whereas one's attitude toward conservation might not be very important to one individual, the attitude might be central to someone else's self-definition (see also Boninger, Krosnick, Berent, & Fabrigar, 1995). Therefore, attitudes have the potential to help an individual make sense of his or her environment, allow for self-expression, and provide a sense of importance to various life activities.

For an event to have meaning for an individual, the individual must construe the event as having some form of personal significance, or the event must satisfy one or more basic needs for meaning (Baumeister, 1991; Park & Folkman, 1997). An analysis of soldier attitudes toward a number of peacekeeping operations indicates that soldier support for peacekeeping operations is lukewarm, especially among service members from the United States (Britt, 1998; Halverson & Bliese, 1996; Miller & Moskos, 1995). Britt (1998) found that among U.S. service members deployed to Operation Joint Endeavor to Bosnia, where the mission was to enforce the Dayton Peace Accords agreed on by the Serbs, Croats, and Muslims, only 40% of service members agreed with the statement that the U.S. military serves an important role by participating in peacekeeping operations. Since Bosnia, U.S. soldiers appear to be increasingly positive about deploying as peacekeepers. In a 1999 survey of U.S. peacekeepers on the first rotation in Kosovo, 49% agreed with the statement that the U.S. military serves an important function by participating in peacekeeping missions (U.S. Army Medical Research Unit—Europe, 2000). Such numbers suggest that although the majority of U.S. soldiers are still reluctant to embrace the role of peacekeeper, this attitude has changed over the course of three years.

Similar findings were obtained by Halverson and Bliese (1996) in their study of U.S. peacekeepers during Operation Uphold Democracy in Haiti, where the mission was initially to be a forced insertion to overthrow the existing government, but turned out to be a peacekeeping mission, where the service members monitored the peaceful exchange of governments. During this mission, 49% of the service members did not believe the U.S. should be involved in the operation, 43% did not believe in the value of the operation, and 38% did not think the mission was important. Miller and Moskos (1995) studied U.S. service members who had deployed to Operation Restore Hope in Somalia, where service members were sent on a humanitarian mission to help end the starvation caused by interclan warfare. When asked if the United States was right to send forces into the region, 47% of the service members agreed, and 48% disagreed. In all, survey data indicate mixed support for the personal significance of peacekeeping operations among service members from the United States.

Such a relatively unenthusiastic attitude toward peacekeeping operations suggests that peacekeepers will be less likely to accept the reasons why they are enduring stressful conditions to help troubled factions or nations, and as a result will be unable to construe the operation in meaningful terms. As discussed earlier in the chapter, an individual is most likely to perceive meaning in an event when the event has a personal significance and relevance to the individual (Park & Folkman, 1997). If peacekeepers do not support the operation, they are unlikely to see the significance or relevance of the mission to their own lives or job.

Relevance of Peacekeeping Operations to Identity, Job, and Career

Attitudes can play an important role in an individual's identity, but an individual's identity is composed of more than attitudes. In the previous chapter, Franke noted the importance of social groups in how individuals' define themselves. Identity can be defined as an individual's unique constellation of demographic and physical attributes, personality traits, roles, attitudes, values, competencies, and social groups (Baumeister, 1998; Erikson, 1968). Many researchers have also noted the importance of an individual's job to his or her identity (Baumeister, 1991; Richardson, 1993). Although a thorough discussion of the determinants of an individual's identity is beyond the scope of the present chapter, it is worth noting that "making sense" of participation in a peacekeeping operation might be more likely when individuals possess identity images that are relevant to such operations. In the present section we examine the extent to which individuals identify with the "human side" of peacekeeping operations, whether their job is relevant to peacekeeping operations, and whether they see peacekeeping operations as relevant to their career. In general, when service members perceive peacekeeping operations as relevant to their job, identity, and career, they should become more personally engaged in the peacekeeping operation, and therefore derive more meaning from participation (see Britt, 1998, 1999; Schlenker, Britt, Pennington, Murphy, & Doherty 1994). Again, when individuals see the personal relevance and significance of an event, they will be more likely to construe the event as meaningful (Park & Folkman, 1997).

Aspects of Identity Relevant to Peacekeeping Operations

Britt and his colleagues (Britt, 1998; Britt, Adler, & Bartone, 2001) have developed a "Peacekeeping Identity" scale to assess whether peacekeeping missions are consistent with a soldier's identity. Sample items from this scale include "I like the human side associated with peacekeeping operations," and "I feel comfortable in the role of peacekeeper." Service members who score high on this scale see aspects of peacekeeping operations as personally relevant and important, whereas service members who score low on the scale do not identify as much with peacekeeping operations. As is discussed in more detail later in this chapter, peacekeeper identity contributes to the latent construction of meaning developed by peacekeepers (Britt et al., 2001), and this scale has also been found to predict feelings of responsibility and commitment during peacekeeping operations (Britt, 1998).

Researchers have also examined other aspects of identity that might contribute to individuals perceiving more meaning in peacekeeping operations. In particular, researchers have examined whether a soldier's ethnicity and gender might predict support for peacekeeping operations. Both Miller and Moskos (1995) and Halverson and Bliese (1996) found that service members from certain demographic groups were more likely to support the peacekeeping operation than were other service members. Significantly, in both Somalia and Haiti, U.S. peacekeepers were deployed to aid countries with a black majority. Miller and Moskos (1995) noted that black service members were less likely to dehumanize the Somalia natives than were nonblack service members. Halverson and Bliese (1996) also found that women were more likely than men to support the peacekeeping operation. These authors have noted that the skills and ethos of peacekeeping operations might be more relevant to the identity of women than men.

Relevance of Job and Career to Peacekeeping Operations

The theoretical models of meaning described earlier emphasize the personal significance of an event in determining whether an individual will find participation in an event meaningful (Park & Folkman, 1997; Tait & Silver, 1989). In addition, Baumeister (1991) emphasized the importance of one's job in providing individuals with a sense of meaning and purpose. Service members will find meaning in their participation in peacekeeping operations when they perceive the personal significance of participation, and when they believe participation in peacekeeping operations is relevant to their job and will be beneficial to their career. Although theorists have conceptualized personal significance and work identity as distinct constructs, these constructs combine into a powerful force in the case of peacekeepers: military professionals who find personal significance in the execution of their work.

Halverson and Bliese (1996) examined some of these issues in their study of U.S. soldiers who had deployed to Haiti as part of Operation Uphold Democracy. These authors found that two main predictors of soldier support for the operation were task significance (e.g., what the soldier is doing helps accomplish the mission) and being briefed about the mission and accomplishments of the unit. In terms of the theoretical framework of finding meaning in peacekeeping operations, this research suggests that soldiers are most likely to see the personal significance of a peacekeeping operation when their role on the mission is made clear, and when leaders communicate successes to the soldier. Communicating the unique role of the soldier in the mission and mission accomplishments also satisfies three of Baumeister's (1991) needs for meaning: providing the soldier with a sense of purpose, efficacy, and self-worth.

As a further indication of the relevance of a soldier's job to peacekeeping operations, 800 service members returning from deployment to Bosnia were asked to respond in their own words as to whether the Bosnia mission was important to them, and whether it was relevant to their role as a service member (Britt, 1997). After the open-ended responses were coded for content category, 39% of the sample used statements reflecting the mission was personally important, 54% wrote statements reflecting the mission was not important, and 8% gave ambivalent responses (e.g., "yes" and "no"). However, in response to the question of whether the mission was relevant to their role as a service member, 65% responded yes, 29% responded no, and 6% were ambivalent. These results seem to be consistent with the idea that although service members do not consider peacekeeping missions important, they nevertheless realize that such missions are increasingly becoming a part of their job as service members.

The perceived relevance of the operation is also in part a function of the particular job of the soldier during the operation (Britt, 1997). Like many peacekeeping operations, service members deployed in support of Operation Joint Endeavor to Bosnia came from many job specialties in the military, including the combat arms (e.g., armor, infantry), combat support (e.g., military police), and combat service support (e.g., medical personnel, supply). This distinction is significant because some jobs appear to be more appropriate for peacekeeping operations than others. For example, many military leaders feel that military police are especially suited for peacekeeping operations. Furthermore, the jobs for some service members are highly similar in peacekeeping and combat operations, whereas others are not. The job for a medical laboratory technician or vehicle mechanic will be similar whether the individual is participating in a peacekeeping or combat operation. However, the job of an armor crewman or infantry soldier will be radically different on a peacekeeping opera-tion. The individual may stand alert for months on end with no changes in the routine, whereas on a combat operation, there are more likely to be occasions when the individual is actively engaged. When the responses of the service members to the mission relevance question were examined as a function of their MOS (military occupational specialty), service members whose MOS was judged relevant to peacekeeping (e.g., medical laboratory technician, truck driver) were more likely to say the mission was relevant to their role as a service member (74%) than were service members (55%) whose MOS was judged to be irrelevant to peacekeeping (e.g., armor crewman, infantry; Britt, 1997). Halverson and Bliese (1996) also found that support units were more likely to be in favor of the peacekeeping operation than were combat units. These results suggest that when soldiers' jobs are relevant to the peacekeeping operation, they are more likely to see the meaning and purpose of the opera-tion, and perhaps the meaning of their own involvement (Park & Folkman, 1997). Peacekeepers should also be more likely to feel a sense of efficacy and purpose when the job they are performing is relevant to the operation (Bau-meister, 1991).

Finally, Segal and Meeker (1985) examined the importance of soldiers per-ceiving participation in a peacekeeping operation as relevant to their future career. These authors studied U.S. peacekeepers participating in the Sinai Multi-national Forces and Observers in support of the Camp David Accords. The authors found that soldiers who were more combat oriented were actually more likely to feel peacekeeping duty would be good for their career, and to agree with the statement that a good soldier does what he or she is trained to do, than were soldiers who were more oriented to service support (Segal & Meeker, 1985).

Military Leader Views on Peacekeeping

Service members' views are also likely to be influenced by the views of their leaders. Although I am aware of no research that has examined the impact of statements made by military leaders about the value of peacekeeping operations on soldier attitudes, findings from social psychology (e.g., Forsyth, 1990) sug-gest that group leaders play a defining role in establishing individual group member attitudes and morale. An analysis of the perspectives of military lead-ers is also important because the volume of commentary by military profes-sionals attests to the unique issues service members face on peacekeeping operations. Franke (this volume) provided many excellent quotes from service members and leaders regarding the ambiguities and concerns encountered dur-ing different types of peacekeeping operations. Perhaps the most often-quoted comment is by Dag Hammarskjold, who noted that "peacekeeping is not a soldier's job, but only a soldier can do it" (Cornell-D'Echert, 1994). This quote implies that although service members are perceived to have the only set of unique skills that can enable successful performance on peacekeeping missions, peacekeeping operations do not really fall under the purview of what should be expected from service members.

Hunt (1994) has noted that many aspects of peacekeeping operations prove to be difficult for service members to understand. He notes that such operations are often driven by diplomatic conditions that are beyond the soldier's control, and that it is often unclear what constitutes successful performance. Service members often hear that the "negotiations continue" upon returning from a peacekeeping deployment, therefore never being sure if they have accomplished their goal as a unit or made a lasting difference. Therefore, this uncertain outcome casts doubt on the purpose of the operation for the soldier, as well as limiting the soldier's belief in his or her ability to effect change in the conflict. Such a situation is unlikely to lead the service member to feel a sense of efficacy and purpose in his or her participation in the operation, which will lead to a lesser likelihood of the individual perceiving meaning in the operation (see Baumeister, 1991).

Adolph (1992) has echoed the view that service members are often ill at ease in a quasi-diplomatic role, in which there are no clear-cut objectives, no enemy, and no clear goal. Adolph argues that if peacekeeping operations continue to become a major component of the U.S. Armed Services activities, then service members need to be trained to see the relevance of such operations to the role of the United States as supporters of democracy (see also Britt, 1998). Abizaid (1993) and Greenberg (1992) have both noted the importance of training service members to engage in a major shift in mentality when participating in peacekeeping operations, where an emphasis is placed on keeping cool under provocative circumstances, and "walking in the shoes" of the local population. One of the main reasons these commentaries and viewpoints are important is that they are likely to reflect some of the dominant themes among military officers and planners, and these beliefs, as well as the beliefs of the general public, will undoubtedly influence the beliefs of service members participating in such operations.

Public Support for Peacekeeping Operations

In addition to the influence of military leaders on service members' perceptions of peacekeeping, attitudes expressed by the public also play a role in how service members construe events. Such perceptions may shape how service members themselves perceive the mission, and ultimately influence service members' perception of the significance and purpose of the operation. In one of the few studies specifically designed to examine soldier perceptions of public support for a peacekeeping operation, Halverson and Bliese (1996) found 50% of the soldiers reported being unsure about whether the U.S. society supported Operation Uphold Democracy to Haiti. More importantly, soldier perceptions of public support were one of the important predictors of their own level of support for the operation.

Eyre, Segal, and Segal (1993) have argued that U.S. society is still in the process of determining the importance of peacekeeping operations relative to other military activities. That is, although many people in the United States see the importance of peacekeeping operations, there is widespread variability in how individuals rank the importance of peacekeeping operations relative to the more central mission of national defense. Such ambivalence regarding the importance of peacekeeping operations apparently also underlies German society's views of peacekeeping (Kornhuber, 1994).

Public support and understanding of peacekeeping operations might be one of the reasons why many service members from other nations generally view peacekeeping missions in a more favorable light. It is worth noting that in comparison to countries such as Norway and Sweden, the United States has a relatively small amount of experience in peacekeeping operations (see Breed, 1998). In a retrospective study of Norwegian peacekeepers who participated in UNIFIL (United Nations Interim Force in Lebanon) from 1978 to 1991, Weiseth, Aaraug, Mehlum, and Larsen (1993) found that 90% of the service members were contented or very contented with their work, and 55% felt their contribution was important to establishing peace in the region. In a retrospective study of Swedish peacekeepers who were deployed to Bosnia as part of the United Nations Protection Force (UNPROFOR), Johansson (1997) found that 70% of the peacekeepers believed they had "quite a lot" or "a great extent" of success in alleviating civilian suffering during their involvement in the peacekeeping mission. Part of the reason for these positive appraisals might be that peacekeepers are aware of the support and understanding shown by their society in the conduct of such operations.

Deriving Benefits from Stressful Events: Applications to the Peacekeeper

Individual, leader, and public attitudes affect the meaning that military personnel assign to their involvement in peacekeeping operations. One of the main arguments of this chapter is that the meaning peacekeepers perceive will affect the degree to which they can feel satisfied with their participation in the mission and the degree to which they can derive benefits from that participation. Recently, both theory and research findings have converged to demonstrate that stressful events can not only have negative consequences, but positive effects as well.

Theory and Research on Benefits from Stressful Events

The idea that people may derive some benefits from dealing with stressful events has been around for some time (e.g., Murphy & Moriarity, 1976). Evidence for this theory has been documented in more recent studies. In a review of people with major physical illnesses, Affleck and Tennen (1996) found that people reported several positive outcomes of dealing with the illness, including feeling closer to family members, an increased appreciation for life, and an increased ability to deal with stress (see also Aldwin, Sutton, & Lachman, 1996). Holahan and Moos (1994) also proposed similar classes of benefits that might result from confronting different traumas in life, including increased personal resources (e.g., self-reliance, increased empathy), social resources (e.g., better relationships with family), and new coping skills (e.g., ability to regulate and control affect). Tedeschi and Calhoun (1996) developed a structured instrument labeled the "Post-Traumatic Growth Inventory" in order to measure more systematically the benefits that people report from dealing with stressful life events, and the questionnaire assesses such benefits as developing new possibilities, relating to others, personal strength, spiritual change, and appreciation for life.

Davis, Nolen-Hoeksema, and Larson (1998) made an important distinction that has relevance to the present chapter. These authors noted a difference between making sense of an event and finding benefits in a stressful experience. Davis et al. (1998) argued that whereas making sense of an event allows the individual to perceive the world as predictable and orderly, finding benefits in a stressful event allows individuals to have a feeling of purpose and value.

Understanding when and how individuals derive benefits from stressful events is important not only because of the benefits themselves, but also because research shows that perceiving benefits from a stressful experience is associated with an improvement in psychological and physical health (Davis, Nolen-Hoeksema, & Larson, 1998; Park & Folkman, 1997; Tennen, Affleck, Urrows, Higgins, & Mendola, 1992; Upton & Thompson, 1992). This suggests that finding benefits in a stressful event might have implications not only for dealing with the event in question, but also for adjustment to future life stressors.

Potential Benefits of Participation in Peacekeeping Operations

Few researchers have explicitly emphasized the potential psychological benefits of serving on peacekeeping missions. In an examination of the benefits Norwegian service members reported after serving in UNIFIL, Mehlum (1995) found that a majority of the service members reported their experience in the operation had increased their self-confidence, expanded their political understanding, increased their stress tolerance, and improved their military qualifications. Similarly, some military leaders have noted that peacekeeping missions, when performed well, can lead to feelings of pride and efficacy among the service members participating in the operation. An example of such a mission was given by Abizaid (1993), who described Operation Provide Comfort in Iraq, the mission to aid Kurdish refugees in the area. Soldiers trained hard for the mission, and they left knowing they had helped the local population. The local population was also impressed by the friendly nature and goodwill of the soldiers.

In an attempt to provide a broad-based view of how peacekeeping operations affect service members, U.S. military personnel returning from Operation Joint Endeavor to Bosnia were asked an open-ended question about the impact of the mission on their lives as part of the same open-ended survey of 800 soldiers mentioned earlier (Britt, 1997). Expecting a cataloguing of negative effects, I was surprised to find that many service members remarked that they had benefited from the operation. When the responses to the open-ended question were coded into various content areas, 33% of the service members indicated some benefit to the self as a result of the operation (e.g., "I am a stronger person," "I can deal with stress better now"), 8% indicated a positive effect on work (e.g., "I got a chance to do my MOS"), and 5% even indicated a positive effect of the deployment on one's family (e.g., "I realized the importance of family"). An important question is, What causes some service members to derive benefits from participation in peacekeeping operations, whereas other service members may experience a host of negative consequences? The answer to this question is the meaning that service members assign to their participation in the peacekeeping operation.

MEANING, PSYCHOLOGICAL GROWTH, AND ADJUSTMENT AMONG PEACEKEEPERS

The benefits service members derive from peacekeeping are both theoretically and practically linked to the meaning they assign their experiences. Past researchers have noted that finding meaning in a stressful event is an important step in adjusting to, and potentially benefiting from, the stressful event (Park, Cohen, & Murch, 1996). Of course, in order to answer the question of whether meaning is associated with deriving benefits from a peacekeeping mission after it has been completed, it would be preferable to conduct a longitudinal study, where meaning assigned to the deployment is assessed during the deployment, and deriving benefits is assessed some time following the deployment.

In general, there is a dearth of longitudinal research on service members participating in any type of military operation. First of all, it is often difficult to assess service members once they have been notified they will be participating in a peacekeeping operation, because the unit immediately shifts into a high level of activity, with little time for service members to respond to questionnaires. Assuming service members are assessed prior to deployment, it may be even more difficult to travel to the location of the deployed unit and conduct surveys and interviews in an operational setting. Finally, assuming one is able to survey service members during the deployment, it may be difficult to track down the service members after the operation to complete a follow-up survey or interview. Service members may have moved to a different duty station or may have left the army altogether.

As part of a larger longitudinal project of U.S. soldiers participating in the peacekeeping mission Operation Joint Endeavor to Bosnia, we examined how soldiers' experiences and perceptions during their deployment predicted whether they derived benefits from the deployment months after it was over (Britt et al., 2001). The operation is interesting to examine in the context of soldiers deriving meaning from their participation, because prior to their deployment all soldiers were required to participate in predeployment training, and part of this training was a presentation of the reason for the conflict and the likely prognosis for peace among the nations. In addition, all U.S. soldiers watched a video made by British soldiers who had served in the region, illustrating the devastation caused by the prior conflict and activities engaged in by the soldiers, including aiding the local population. Therefore, an attempt was made to provide soldiers with a meaningful rationale for the conflict prior to the deployment. Of course, despite such efforts, we expected soldiers to differ in the extent to which they found meaning in the operation.

In terms of the empirical data we collected, I focus on the relationship between measures of meaning soldiers assigned to their experiences during the deployment (at approximately the 6th month of a 10-month deployment), and the benefits soldiers reported receiving from participation in the peacekeeping mission three to four months after it was over. I also examine some cross-sectional results from the postdeployment survey that assessed how much soldiers had experienced the destruction of the former war and the civilians they were supposed to be helping.

To assess the meaning peacekeepers were assigning to their work during the deployment, we tapped many of the dimensions discussed earlier in the chapter. To assess the personal significance of what soldiers were doing on the mission, we first asked questions regarding how important their job was to them personally, as well as how important their job was to accomplishing the unit's mission (see Baumeister, 1991; Britt, 1998; Richardson, 1993). In order to assess how engaged soldiers were in their job, soldiers were asked how much their performance mattered to them and how responsible for and committed to their job performance they felt (Britt, 1999). We also examined their overall attitude toward peacekeeping operations with questions assessing how comfortable they felt in the peacekeeper role, the importance of peacekeeping operations in general, and whether they liked the "human side" associated with peacekeeping missions.

To assess the benefits soldiers might have reported following the operation, we developed a "Perceived Benefits" scale based on soldiers' responses to the open-ended question described earlier on the impact of the mission. The items comprising the scale tapped dimensions mentioned by nonmilitary researchers on the benefits of other types of stressful events (e.g., becoming a stronger person, dealing with stress better, recognizing the importance of family, and gaining knowledge about the world; Holahan & Moos, 1994; Tedeschi & Calhoun, 1996). The postdeployment survey also assessed experiences soldiers may have had during the deployment that may have helped them understand the meaning behind the operation. Such experiences included seeing the destruction caused by the former war, having contact with local civilians, and having contact with other NATO forces.

In the longitudinal sample, 161 soldiers provided information on both the mid-deployment and postdeployment surveys. Using structural equation modeling, Britt et al. (2001) found that perceiving meaning during the deployment strongly predicted deriving benefits from the deployment after it was over. Those soldiers who felt they were personally engaged in an important and relevant mission at mid-deployment were much more likely to report deriving benefits from participating in the operation at postdeployment. Furthermore, this relationship was not a function of the personality variable hardiness (see Bartone, 1999). Although hardiness did predict the tendency to derive meaning during the operation, hardiness did not predict the tendency to derive benefits from the deployment, and the relationship between perceived meaning during the deployment and benefits following the deployment was obtained after controlling for the effects of personality hardiness.

Another interesting finding relevant to the issue of the meaning of peacekeeping operation participation concerned experiences soldiers reported having during the operation. Specifically, the more soldiers reported such events as seeing the destruction caused by the war and contact with local civilians, the more likely they were to report deriving benefits from the deployment. Furthermore, soldiers deployed to Bosnia or Croatia (where the effects of the former war were more salient) were more likely to report benefits from the operation than were soldiers who were deployed to Hungary (a logistical support area far removed from the main conflict). However, the effects of deployment location on benefits were reduced to nonsignificance when meaningful experiences were controlled. This suggests that the differences in benefits between those soldiers deployed to Hungary as opposed to Bosnia or Croatia were a result of the fact that soldiers deployed to Bosnia and Croatia were more likely to experience events that helped place the deployment in a meaningful context. This suggests that the effects of location on benefits were a function of the different levels of meaningful experiences reported by the soldiers, not just the location of their deployment.

SUMMARY

When service members from different nations are tasked with enforcing or promoting peace among former warring nations or factions, they inevitably try to make sense of their task. The meaning service members assign to the peacekeeping mission varies depending on demographic characteristics, the nature of their specific job on the mission, and their overall attitudes toward the peacekeeping mission. Service members can interpret and understand peace-keeping operations in different ways, and such interpretations have implications for whether or not they can actually turn a stressful experience into a source of positive outcomes. The implications of the relationship between meaning and deriving benefits suggests that military leaders should pursue efforts to enable service members to understand that peacekeeping missions serve an important and relevant purpose. Such efforts can focus on making sure service members understand that participation in peacekeeping missions will be rewarded in terms of consideration in promotion, as well as helping service members see the purpose behind why they are being sent to the troubled region. If service members believe they are being deployed to help preserve an important peace that will prevent further bloodshed and destruction, they may be more motivated to perform well on the mission and perceive the experience as a benefit in both professional and personal terms.

REFERENCES

Abizaid, J. P. (1993). Lessons for peacekeepers. *Military Review, 73*, 11–19.

Adolph, R. B. (1992, July-Sept.). Peacekeeping: Our least understood mission. *Military Intelligence,* , pp. 17–19.

Affleck, G., & Tennen, H. (1996). Construing benefit from adversity: Adaptational significance and dispositional underpinnings. *Journal of Personality, 64*, 898–922.

Aldwin, C. M., Sutton, K. J., & Lachman, M. (1996). The development of coping resources in adulthood. *Journal of Personality, 64*, 837–871.

Bartone, P. T. (1999). Hardiness protects against war-related stress. *Consulting Psychology Journal: Practice and Research, 51*, 72–82.

Baumeister, R. F. (1991). *Meanings of life.* New York: Guilford.

Baumeister, R. F. (1998). The self. In D. T. Gilbert, S. T. Fiske, & G. Lindzey (Eds.), *The handbook of social psychology* (4th ed., Vol. 1, pp. 680–740). New York: McGraw-Hill.

Bollen, K., & Lennox, R. (1991). Conventional wisdom on measurement: A structural equation perspective. *Psychological Bulletin, 110*, 305–314.

Boninger, D. S., Krosnick, J. A., Berent, M. K., & Fabrigar, L. R. (1995). The causes and consequences of attitude importance. In. R. E. Petty & J. A. Krosnick (Eds.), *Attitude strength: Antecedents and consequences* (pp. 159–190). Hillsdale, NJ: Erlbaum.

Breed, H. (1998). Treating the new world disorder. In H. J. Langholtz (Ed.), *The psychology of peacekeeping* (pp. 239–254). Westport, CT: Praeger.

Britt, T. W. (1997). *The psychological experience of soldiers during Operation Joint Endeavor.* Paper presented to the Army Medical Department Training Conference, Weillingen, Germany.

Britt, T. W. (1998). Psychological ambiguities in peacekeeping. In H. J. Langholtz (Ed.), *The psychology of peacekeeping* (pp. 111–128). Westport, CT: Praeger.

Britt, T. W. (1999). Engaging the self in the field: Testing the Triangle Model of Responsibility. *Personality and Social Psychology Bulletin, 25*, 696–706.

Britt, T. W., & Adler, A. B. (1999). Stress and health during medical humanitarian assistance missions. *Military Medicine, 164,* 275–279.

Britt, T. W., Adler, A. B., & Bartone, P. T. (2001). Deriving benefits from stressful events: The role of engagement in meaningful work and hardiness. *Journal of Occupational Health Psychology, 6,* 53–63.

Cacioppo, J. T., & Petty, R. E. (1982). The need for cognition. *Journal of Personality and Social Psychology, 42,* 116–131.

Cornell-D'Echert, B. (1994). We need a peacekeeping MTP [Mission Training Plan]. *Infantry, 84,* 34–35.

Davis, C. G., Nolen-Hoeksema, S., & Larson, J. (1998). Making sense of loss and benefiting from the experience: Two construals of meaning. *Journal of Personality and Social Psychology, 75,* 561–574.

Eagly, A. H., & Chaiken, S. (1993). *The psychology of attitudes.* Fort Worth, TX: Harcourt Brace Jovanovich.

Erikson, E. H. (1968). *Identity, youth, and crisis.* New York: Norton.

Eyre, D. P., Segal, D. R., & Segal, M. W. (1993). The social construction of peacekeeping. In D. R. Segal & M. W. Segal (Eds.), *Peacekeepers and their wives* (pp. 42–55). Westport, CT: Greenwood Press.

Forsyth, D. R. (1990). *Group dynamics* (2nd ed.). Pacific Grove, CA: Brooks/Cole.

Greenberg, K. E. (1992). The essential art of empathy. *MHQ: The Quarterly Journal of Military History, 5,* 64–69.

Halverson, R. R., & Bliese, P. D. (1996). Determinants of soldiers' support for Operation Uphold Democracy. *Armed Forces & Society, 23,* 81–96.

Herek, G. M. (1987). Can functions be measured? A new perspective on the functional approach to attitudes. *Social Psychology Quarterly, 50,* 285–303.

Holahan, C. J., & Moos, R. H. (1994). Life stressors and mental health. In W. R. Avison & I. H. Gotlib (Eds.), *Stress and mental health: Contemporary issues and prospects for the future* (pp. 213–238). New York: Plenum.

Hunt, J. B. (1994). Thoughts on peace support operations. *Military Review, 74,* 76–85.

Johansson, E. (1997). The role of peacekeepers in the 1990s: Swedish experience in UNPROFOR. *Armed Forces and Society, 23,* 451–466.

Katz, D. (1960). The functional approach to the study of attitudes. *Public Opinion Quarterly, 24,* 163–204.

Kornhuber, A. W. (1994, June). *Personal experience from GECOMFORSUM/UNSOSOM II: Both neurology and psychiatry are required.* Paper presented to the International Congress on Military Medicine, Augsburg, Germany.

Krosnick, J. A. (1988). The role of attitude importance in social evaluation: A study of policy preferences, presidential candidate evaluations, and voting behavior. *Journal of Personality and Social Psychology, 55,* 196–210.

Litz, B. T. (1996). The psychological demands of peacekeeping for military personnel. *NCP Clinical Quarterly, 6,* 1–8.

Mehlum, L. (1995). Positive and negative consequences of serving in a UN peacekeeping mission. A follow-up study. *International Review of Armed Forces Medical Services, 68,* 289–295.

Miller, L. L., & Moskos, C. C. (1995). Humanitarians or warriors? Race, gender, and combat status in Operation Restore Hope. *Armed Forces & Society, 21,* 615–637.

Murphy, L. B., & Moriarity, D. (1976). *Vulnerability, coping, and growth*. New Haven, CT: Yale University Press.

Park, C. L., Cohen, L. H., & Murch, R. L. (1996). Assessment and prediction of stress-related growth. *Journal of Personality, 64,* 71–105.

Park, C. L., & Folkman, S. (1997). Meaning in the context of stress and coping. *Review of General Psychology, 2,* 115–144.

Richardson, M. S. (1993). Work in people's lives: A location for counseling psychologists. *Journal of Counseling Psychology, 40,* 425–433.

Schlenker, B. R., Britt, T. W., Pennington, J., Murphy, R., & Doherty, K. (1994). The Triangle Model of Responsibility. *Psychological Review, 101,* 632–652.

Segal, D. R., & Meeker, B. F. (1985). Peacekeeping, warfighting, and professionalism: Attitude organization and change among combat soldiers on constabulary duty. *Journal of Political and Military Sociology, 13,* 167–181.

Segal, D. R., & Segal, M. W. (Eds.). (1993). *Peacekeepers and their wives.* Westport, CT: Greenwood Press.

Stouffer, S. A., Lumsdaine, A. A., Williams, R. B., Smith, M. B., Janis, I. L., Star, S. A., & Cottrell, L. S. (1949). *The American soldier: Combat and its aftermath* (Vol. 2). Princeton, NJ: Princeton University Press.

Tait, R., & Silver, R. C. (1989). Coming to terms with major negative life events. In J. S. Uleman & J. A. Bargh (Eds.), *Unintended thought* (pp. 351–382). New York: Guilford.

Tedeschi, R. G., & Calhoun, L. G. (1996). The Posttraumatic Growth Inventory: Measuring the positive legacy of trauma. *Journal of Traumatic Stress, 9,* 455–471.

Tennen, H., Affleck, G., Urrows, S., Higgins, P., & Mendola, R. (1992). Perceiving control, construing benefits, and daily processes in rheumatoid arthritis. *Canadian Journal of Behavioral Science, 24,* 186–203.

Trapnell, P. D., & Campbell, J. D. (1999). Private self-consciousness and the five-factor model of personality: Distinguishing rumination from reflection. *Journal of Personality and Social Psychology, 76,* 284–304.

Upton, D., & Thompson, P. J. (1992). Effectiveness of coping strategies employed by people with chronic epilepsy. *Journal of Epilepsy, 5,* 119–127.

U.S. Army Medical Research Unit-Europe. (2000). *USAREUR Soldier Study II: Kosovo Mid-Deployment Codebook.* Unpublished report. Heidelberg, Germany: Author.

Weisæth, L., Aaraug, P., Mehlum, L., & Larsen, S. (1993). *The UNIFIL study (1991–1992). Report I: Results and recommendations.* Headquarters Defence Command Norway—The Joint Medical Service.

III
Industrial-Organizational Psychology Issues in Peacekeeping

6

Task Identification and Skill Deterioration in Peacekeeping Operations

Robert A. Wisher

As with any military operation, peacekeeping requires a force well prepared for the mission. Personnel not acquainted with the tasks and demands of peacekeeping, however, can impact a contributing nation's ability to sustain peace (Durch, 1993). For a unit assigned temporary peacekeeping duty, an investment in learning and sustaining new peacekeeping skills must be made, but perhaps at the cost of not maintaining war-fighting skills. This introduces a dilemma: to what extent should peacekeeping skills be learned, and how often should they be refreshed as opposed to what extent can a deterioration in war-fighting skills be accepted? Furthermore, what are the characteristics of typical peacekeeping tasks, and how well are they remembered if they are not sustained?

This chapter examines several facets of these issues. In particular, how are peacekeeping tasks identified, and what are the underlying characteristics of learning and remembering them? Also, what do we know about predicting the decay of skills related to these tasks, and what are the tendencies of units in prioritizing tasks for sustainment training during a peacekeeping assignment? To address these questions, three applied studies are reported, associated with two peacekeeping missions involving U.S. troops. The first concerns identifying peacekeeping tasks and predicting their decay based on an empirically derived analytic model. Here, the tasks relate to a peacekeeping mission to Bosnia. The second study concerns the identification of tasks and the predeployment training patterns of two units assigned during separate rotations to the Multinational Force and Observers mission in the Sinai. One unit was drawn from the regular army and represented the active component of the U.S. Army, whereas the other was composed primarily of reserve-component soldiers. The third study, which further examined the same two units, concerns the comparative behavior of these units in sustaining proficiency on both peacekeeping and war-fighting tasks during their deployments.

Throughout the chapter, the construct of skill decay, or deterioration, is used. *Skill decay* refers simply to the natural forgetting of tasks over periods of nonuse or nonpractice. The capacity to retain skills, or skill retention, is the complementary effect. *Tasks* are the descriptors that identify the behavior linked to an established performance standard. An example is "Determining Grid Coordinates" to a specified degree of accuracy within a certain time period. *Skill* refers to an individual's (or team's) capacity to execute a task to a standard. The study of skill decay has a long history as an area of study in experimental psychology (Ebbinghaus, 1885) with implications for education, training, and human factors design. Here it is linked to the skills of the peacekeeper.

The training of peacekeeping skills is central to this chapter. *Training* refers to "the systematic acquisition of skills, rules, concepts, or attitudes that result in improved performance in another environment" as identified by Goldstein (1993, p. 3). Traditionally, training is linked to organizational objectives and correcting deficiencies in the workforce (Kraiger & Jung, 1997). Here, training is related to a successful peacekeeping mission and the identification and development of specific skills underpinning a successful mission.

TRAINING FOR PEACEKEEPING OPERATIONS

The literature on peacekeeping operations relegates training to a decidedly secondary role. Most work focuses on geopolitical issues, internationalism, military strategy, and economics. Some authors (e.g., Diehl, 1988; Kutter, 1986) contend that deploying highly trained combat soldiers for peacekeeping operations places our troops in a paradoxical situation. Successful peacekeeping soldiers must function well in environments where only minimal force is usually required. Under these circumstances, their strength lies not in their lethality but rather in their ability to negotiate and make compromises. The guidelines for conduct may change, the rules of engagement may be modified, and the individual's role as a soldier becomes less certain. This can lead to psychological ambiguities for highly trained war-fighters (Britt, 1998).

According to Kutter (1986), previous behavioral research has established that careful predeployment training can succeed in preparing soldiers and leaders psychologically for peacekeeping. During preparation for a peacekeeping deployment, training focuses more on mission-relevant rather than basic soldiering or war-fighting tasks. Upon completion of the assignment, the focus of training reverts to war-fighting performance because a reconstruction of deteriorated skills and competencies is essential for readiness. Of course, much of this depends on the status of the unit prior to a peacekeeping assignment. Certain units from some nations specialize in peacekeeping, whereas others must be trained on peacekeeping skills during a predeployment preparation phase. Before examining the decay of these skills, I present a review of how tasks are selected for a peacekeeping mission.

Identification of Tasks and Peacekeeping Courses

Let us first turn to peacekeeping on a broader scale. Within the UN, there is no single unified training system. The UN Department of Peacekeeping Operations coordinates and standardizes training among member states contributing to peacekeeping operations (Kidwell & Langholtz, 1998). This department develops training manuals, provides expert training assistance, and conducts train-the-trainer and senior management seminars. Each nation, however, is responsible for the screening, training, and evaluation of the personnel it sends as part of its national commitment. The UN Institute for Training and Research, Programme of Correspondence Instruction provides self-paced training courses on various aspects of UN peacekeeping, with titles such as Principles for the Conduct of Peace Support Operations or Methods and Techniques for Peacekeeping on the Ground.

Within the North Atlantic Treaty Organization (NATO), an examination of training practices reveals the broad scope of peacekeeping tasks. Faced with new challenges and missions, NATO has changed its organization and strategy, opening itself to new members and recently emerged nations. The Partnership for Peace (PfP) and Combined Joint Task Forces are examples of initiatives to increase security and stability in Europe (NATO, 1998). The introduction of the PfP initiative in 1994 added a new dimension to relationships between countries and a call for training and cooperation for peacekeeping and related areas, such as humanitarian aid and dealing with refugees. Thus far, eight countries have established PfP training centers to provide qualitative education and training support to military and civilian personnel and to reach interoperability objectives and PfP goals. The course offerings are open to civilians and military personnel of PfP and NATO countries.

Courses cover areas concerning operational and military-political considerations as well as technical-tactical courses and a variety of seminars. The PfP training center in Turkey, for example, offers 24 courses, including Civilian Military Cooperation, Military Observer in Peace Support Operations (PSO), and Mine Counter Measures. Many of the specific tasks in these courses relate to NATO interoperability objectives, such as command and control procedures, maps and symbologies, and land operations. Another example is the PfP training center in Slovenia, which specializes in language training, in particular courses to meet interoperability objectives for peace support operations, such as language requirements for air traffic control or CNN/BBC listening skills. A third example is the PfP training center in Austria, which offers courses such as Staff Officers Course for PSO and Military Police Course for PSO.

The selection of tasks is naturally driven by the demands of the assignment. Training is usually clustered into modules, and the modules are coupled to learning objectives. The courses are typically between one to three weeks in length, although some can require several months. The participants are assumed to possess adequate soldiering skills acquired in their home country, so the training focus is on the mission-specific tasks. As with nearly all skills, however, once acquired they are subject to deterioration unless they are exercised shortly after the training.

Skill Decay. Regardless of the mission, soldiers and peacekeepers alike rely on three abilities as they attempt to perform their military tasks: (1) ability to retrieve from memory previously learned knowledge (job-related facts, rules, terminology, etc.); (2) ability to combine incoming information, evaluate a situation, and decide among alternative courses of action; and (3) ability to execute the chosen action or procedural step in a sufficiently skilled manner (Sabol & Wisher, 2001). Skill decay refers to the degradation in performance over time due to a lack of practice. It has been studied extensively, showing that large amounts of forgetting can occur naturally over periods as short as several hours or as long as many years (Wisher, Sabol, & Ellis, 1999). Models have been developed and empirically validated to predict skill decay of procedural, or step-by-step tasks (Hagman & Rose, 1983). Related to skill decay is the notion of knowledge decay, though the two are often, and erroneously, interchanged. Knowledge decay is surprisingly more stable, with an expected relative loss of approximately 15% to 20% during a full year (Conway, Cohen, & Stanhope, 1991; Semb & Ellis, 1994). The decay rates of procedural tasks, as illustrated in the study later, varies greatly. Such procedural tasks are commonly used in peacekeeping assignments.

AN APPLIED STUDY ON PREDICTING SKILL RETENTION

The U.S. Army Research Institute for the Behavioral and Social Sciences (ARI) examined the 27 tasks selected for training prior to deployment to Bosnia or Hungary as part of Operation Joint Endeavor (Wisher, Sabol, & Ozkaptan, 1996). The training was conducted at the U.S. Army 7th Training Command in Germany. The tasks were individual in nature. Each soldier needed to score a "Go" on the task (indicating successful performance) in order to proceed to the operation. The tasks were identified by the command as those being of highest importance to soldiers deploying to this particular peacekeeping operation.

All newly learned skills are subject to forgetting unless they are practiced periodically. There is thus a normal tendency over time for a decrease in the percentage of soldiers able to perform unpracticed tasks at the "Go" level. The rapidity of the decline in proficiency is dependent on use (or practice) after the original learning and on certain characteristics of the task itself. That is, the time course of forgetting for different tasks during periods of nonuse is predictable. The purpose of the analysis of the 27 tasks, then, was to offer predictions of skill decay. These predictions could then serve as the basis for scheduling sustainment training during the deployment, especially for tasks that are critical and easily forgotten.

The source of the predictions is an empirically based model developed by ARI researchers and endorsed by the Army Training Board. The basis for the model, derived from numerous field studies, is described by Hagman and Rose (1983). Essentially, predictions can be derived through structured interviews with subject matter experts who rate 10 key characteristics of each task as described here.

Data Collection Methodology

Data were collected through structured interviews with eight instructors from the 7th Army Training Center. Each instructor was responsible for a particular task area, and each task area had between two and seven tasks. The instructors were very familiar with the tasks, having taught them daily for more than a month. Each interview took between 20 and 45 minutes, depending on the number of tasks examined.

Tasks were first discussed in general terms, and then a series of 10 questions were asked for each. The questions concerned these characteristics: (1) availability of a job/memory aid while performing the task; (2) quality of the job aid (if available); (3) number of steps to execute the task; (4) requirements for sequencing the steps; (5) built-in feedback for each step; (6) time limits; (7) mental processing demands; (8) number of facts, terms, and rules a soldier must know to perform the task; (9) difficulty of remembering these facts, terms, and rules; and (10) motor control demands (precision of finger, hand, and arm movements). A point-scoring system, derived from the model, was applied to the responses. The aggregate score yielded a basis for computing a task retention curve. (Note: The higher the level of task retention, the lower the degree of skill decay.) Examples of the predicted retention curves for a highly perishable task, "Extraction from Minefield," and a moderately perishable task, "Working in the Cold," are presented in Figure 6.1.

An instructive manner in which to present the findings is in terms of predicted retention after a two-month interval of nonuse. This interval is relative to the time a soldier last performed the task to standard, either during initial training, sustainment training, or actual field use. A two-month interval was selected because it is here that the divergence of retention rates between tasks begins to become pronounced. The predicted retention for each task, measured in terms of the percentage of soldiers who would perform the task successfully, is presented in Table 6.1. A *job aid* refers to a means to facilitate performance by minimizing the need for recall from memory, such as a label with start-up instructions attached to equipment.

Recommendations for Application

Several factors must be considered when applying these findings to the scheduling of refresher training. Obviously, the criticality of a task for a particular unit must be the primary consideration. If, for example, the "React to

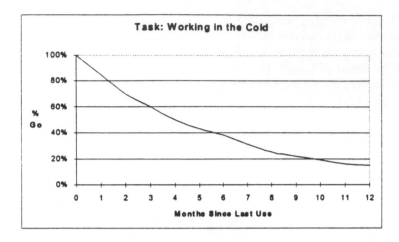

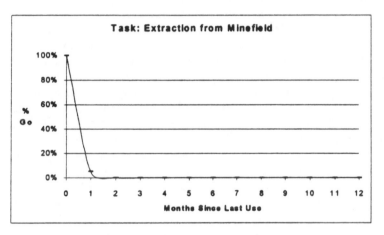

Figure 6.1 Predicted Decay of Two Tasks

Mines" task is judged as highly critical, it should be included in a sustainment-training schedule, even though it is predicted to be well retained. However, if a task such as "React to Media" is judged not to be highly critical for a unit, perhaps because of the unit's remote location, it may be a low priority for training, even though it is predicted to be only moderately retained.

Another consideration is frequency of use. Task retention becomes an issue after periods of nonuse. If, for example, tasks are being executed properly in the field regularly, there is little opportunity for them to decay. Patterns of field use vary across units and even within a particular unit, so the frequency-of-use factor must be determined cautiously. As the data suggest, retention of tasks can vary greatly after a period as short as two months. Also, because a

Table 6.1
Predicted Retention of Peacekeeping Tasks

RANKING OF TASK RETENTION
(Task ranked 1 is hardest to remember.)
%Go = percentage of soldiers predicted to perform the task at 'Go' level
after two months of nonuse

Rank	Task	%Go
1	Extraction from Minefield	0%
2	React to Civilian on Battlefield	8%
3	React to Sniper	9%
4	Prevent Shock	18%
5	Carbon Monoxide Inhalation	28%
6	Apply Tourniquet	29%
7	React to Indirect Fire	30%
7	Winter Driving	30%
9	Vehicle Search	34%
10	Negotiation	36%
11	Rules of Engagement	42% (27%)
12	React to Media	54%
13	V Corps Convoy Mine Strike Drill	56%
14	Living in the Cold	62% (48%)
15	Identify/Detect Trip Wires	68%
17	Driving Postcheck	71% (44%)
17	Working in the Cold	71%
17	Identify/Detect Booby Traps	71%
19	Sleeping in the Cold	73%
20	Recognize/React to UXO	75%
21	Mine Detection	76%
21	Locate a Mine by Probing	76%
23	Driving Precheck	89% (62%)
24	Personal Search	90% (62%)
25	React to Mines	96% (68%)
26	Field Dressing/Pressure Dressing	98%
27	Indications of Mines/Body Traps	99% (84%)

Note: Tasks with two "Go" percentages have job aids; percentages in parentheses apply when job
aids are not available.

task is predicted to be performed well does not guarantee a soldier will remember under what conditions or when it should be performed. The context of task performance also needs refreshing during sustainment training.

The recommendations summarized here and the predictions of skill retention from Figure 6.1 were captured onto a 4-by-6-inch laminated card and referred to as the "Trainer's Guide for Refresher Training—Operation Joint Endeavor." These were distributed to units in the field of operation in Bosnia and Hungary.

AN APPLIED STUDY ON PREDEPLOYMENT TRAINING

Tasks related to peacekeeping operations are generally not the sole focus of predeployment training. Training on established combat and basic tasks continues, to a degree, throughout the predeployment period. Because many facets of normal military operations apply to peacekeeping operations, training to enhance the skills of a unit's primary mission should be a continuing feature of predeployment training. The following study illustrates several points: first, the identification of mission-specific peacekeeping tasks; second, details on the blending of these new tasks with soldiering tasks during a predeployment training; and third, the contrasting behavior of small units in the field in prioritizing their sustainment training activities in view of their differing follow-on missions. This applied study concerns the Multinational Force and Observers (MFO) for the Sinai peninsula.

The MFO was created as a neutral organization to observe and report violations to the Egyptian-Israeli Treaty of Peace, 1979. As part of its contribution to the MFO, the United States has deployed an infantry battalion for six-month rotations to the Sinai continuously since 1982 (Segal, Furukawa, & Lindh, 1990). This battalion has the peacekeeping responsibility for an area of operation in the southern third of the Sinai, bordering the strategic Gulf of Aqaba and the Strait of Tiran. In 1995, for the first time, a rotation composed mostly of volunteers from the reserve component assumed the mission. Hereafter, this unit, comprising 80% reservists, is referred to as the *composite unit*.

The singular mission of this composite unit was the Sinai assignment. Unlike units rotating from the active component (AC) that were assigned the MFO mission, the composite unit did not need to adjust from a war-fighting mission to a peacekeeping operation because it was drawn from a multitude of units across the country. Nor did it need to reorient to a war-fighting mission afterward, because the unit was immediately deactivated. Deploying a newly formed composite unit to a stable peacekeeping operation has this attractive feature: no need to regear to a collective war-fighting capacity.

The expected degradation of war-fighting skills, those that are not applied or trained during a peacekeeping mission, has been recognized as a drawback to deploying active component units to such missions (Taws & Peters, 1995). The drawback comes from an immediate reduction in readiness to the battalion's parent division. The time needed to prepare (about three months), execute (six months), and then reorient to war fighting afterward (at least three months) adds up to at least a year of reduced readiness for the parent division. In contrast, a unit derived largely from reserve volunteers has much less of a negative impact on overall readiness. Because of its unique characteristics and lack of drawdown to overall readiness, it is instructive to contrast the predeployment training activities of a composite unit to the predeployment phase of an AC unit rotation to the MFO mission. Note that there is no principled reason to expect that a concentration on executing peacekeeping skills will interfere with the execution of war-fighting skills. Rather, it is the lack of time to sustain war-fighting skills that leads to skill degradation, though this point may be debatable regarding tasks related to the restraint of force (e.g., shoot to miss).

Training Requirement

The composite unit was formed from reserve volunteers and regular army soldiers solely for peacekeeping operations in the Sinai (Phelps & Farr, 1996). The predeployment training activities spanned a period of 11 months. The training encompassed a variety of topics that included soldiering tasks and tasks unique to the demands of peacekeeping operations, such as the history and culture of the Sinai region, making detailed observations and reports, and becoming familiar with new and explicitly defined rules of engagement.

A key element of the MFO mission was to observe and report violations of the Egypt-Israel peace treaty. The soldiers were required not only to be able to recognize aircraft, ships, vehicles, license plates, and uniforms, but they also needed to be knowledgeable about standard reporting formats for the mission. Learning the individual tasks unique to the mission was critical in the predeployment training phase. A program to develop unit cohesion and sharpen leadership skills was another component of the predeployment preparation. Training on small-unit collective tasks—mainly squad level—was also conducted, in part to develop cohesion.

Predeployment Training Phases

The training concept called for dividing the predeployment training into three phases. These phases were geared to the formation of the unit in three stages, beginning with key leaders and staff personnel, adding the leadership cadre, and finally the bulk of the junior enlisted personnel. A key document, the MFO Pre-Deployment Training Management Plan, assisted the unit's leadership in identifying the essential predeployment training requirements. It also advised the inclusion of some senior trainers in the reconnaissance to the Sinai, enabling them to better direct the predeployment training.

The plan identified 18 lessons, each specifying objectives, conditions, and standards for the training, as well as required equipment and a suggested conduct of training. Table 6.2 lists the 18 lesson names.

Throughout the predeployment training, the commander sought opportunities for team-building activities. Training on the mission-essential tasks was to be conducted primarily by squad leaders. One purpose for this was the early development of small unit cohesion, which would presumably promote performance of the units during their deployment to the Sinai.

Training Phase 1

The goal of the initial phase was planning by the first five members to join the staff. The mission analysis was performed during this phase, and a mission-essential task list was established with associated collective and individual tasks. The primary outcome was the predeployment training guidance issued after 90 days.

Among the early objectives was a compilation of soldiering tasks, many considered common tasks, that would be trained to the leadership during Phase 2 and to the bulk of the unit during Phase 3. These tasks were segmented into three tiers. Each tier is further divided into blocks, most blocks comprising tasks from a common area, such as first aid. A tier comprises approximately 45 tasks. A sample of some of the soldiering tasks identified as critical to this particular peacekeeping mission is presented in Table 6.3.

Training Phase 2

This phase occurred over a 150-day period. The emphasis during this phase was to train the trainer on both soldiering tasks, which are commonly referred

Table 6.2
Predeployment Training Lessons

1. Introduction to the MFO	10. Use of force and firearms
2. Introduction to the Sinai	11. Survival
3. Field sites	12. Hygiene
4. Patrols	13. First aid
5. Observation	14. Vehicle drills
6. Recognition	15. Explosive ordnance disposal
7. Reporting procedures	16. Helicopter operations
8. Communications	17. Cooking
9. Threat assessment and defense measures	18. Generators

Table 6.3
Sample of Soldiering Tasks Trained during Predeployment

Determine grid coordinates	Identify terrain features on a map
Identify topographical symbols on a map	Locate an unknown point by resection
Prevent shock	Put on field dressing
Put on a tourniquet	Give first aid for burns
Guide a helicopter	Search and scan
Locate mines by visual means	Move under direct fire

to as *common tasks* in the U.S. Army, and MFO-specific tasks. During this phase, 213 soldiers were added to the unit, bringing the unit strength to 218.

The train-the-trainer process was conducted on the Tier 1 and Tier 2 tasks. Because the trainers were NCOs familiar with many of these tasks, the training was more a refresher course. In addition to the critical training areas, soldiers were also trained on topics such as guard duty, land navigation, radio-telephone operator procedures, civil disturbance, water safety, counterterrorism, military justice, and alcohol and drug abuse. The common task training, along with the land navigation course, was integrated into a four-day field training exercise.

Training Phase 3

The final phase occurred over a 99-day period. This final phase served as the bulk training period for the unit, because the majority of soldiers (an additional 352) joined the unit at the beginning of this phase, raising the unit strength to 570. This phase covered rifle marksmanship, common task training, squad training and patrolling, and MFO-specific tasks (e.g., Arabic phrases, aircraft identification) and MFO specialized tasks (field sanitation, generator operations, cooking). The third phase included an MFO site field training exercise. The culmination of the third phase was a certification exercise, followed by two weeks of block leave.

The training of soldiering tasks reflected in Table 6.3 required six weeks. Training was accomplished primarily at the squad level. A "crawl-walk-run" approach to training, that is, a level of instruction starting at an elementary level and progressing to a level of task performance conforming to the required conditions and standards, was adopted. Included in this six-week period were two weeks of squad training on collective tasks. Also included was a four-day patrolling exercise. The goal here was to train fire teams and squads in dismounted patrolling, such as conducting a local security patrol, and establishing temporary observation posts, activities that would be performed at the remote sites in the Sinai. Afterward, the concentrated training of MFO tasks (tasks 1–14 in Table 6.2) was conducted over a 10-day period, introducing the soldiers to the Sinai mission.

Sector Training and Certification

Squad sector training was conducted as a battalion-level field training exercise. The goal was for the battalion to execute the mission in the local training area as it would be executed in the Sinai. Posts were assembled to resemble the layouts of a remote site in the Sinai, either an observation post, a checkpoint, or a sector control center. During the occupation of sites, the squads trained for four days on specific MFO tasks that would be tested during the certification exercise the following week.

Eight critical MFO-specific tasks were evaluated during the certification exercise. Altogether, 535 soldiers were evaluated and certified. There was no set limit on the number of attempts a soldier could make on a particular task, but the evaluators maintained established conditions and standards in qualifying a soldier as a "Go" for any particular task. Overall, soldiers performed extremely well, with 98% of the tasks being performed successfully on the first attempt.

Comparison to Active Component Unit

Predeployment Phase. An active component battalion assigned the Sinai mission on an earlier rotation was tracked in order to contrast its predeployment training with that of the composite unit. Because the AC unit was already intact, its predeployment training clearly differed from a composite unit. No personnel build-up phase was required, other than accessing some specialists into the unit, such as linguists. Rather, an abrupt shift from a war-fighting mission to a peacekeeping operation occurred. The MFO-specific skills described earlier obviously needed to be learned, so, of necessity, there was a period of intense training during the predeployment phase. Predeployment training began in earnest 111 days before departure (D-111) to the Sinai.

The initial week of MFO training consisted of blocks of leader and individual training, on tasks such as Arab customs and courtesies, rules of engagement, survival skills, and reporting procedures. The second week of training focused on squad leader training and validation, squad specialty training, and an exercise conducted at the simulation center on post. The overall goal was to provide squad leaders and the task force chain of command with the bigger picture of observing and reporting to either a sector control center or the tactical operations center.

A physical mock-up of an MFO site was completed on D-97. Predeployment training for squads continued through D-66. A field training exercise, during which squad validation was internally conducted, started on D-61. Squad validation was completed on D-46. General preparation and block leave for the advance party took place next. Final preparations were underway during this period, with the first main body departing on D day.

Soldiers' Assessment of Predeployment Training

Ratings of the adequacy of the predeployment training, from the soldiers' viewpoint, was accomplished through a pair of questions included in an ARI questionnaire related to leadership, motivation, and cohesion. Soldiers from the line squads of the composite unit and an active component unit rated the adequacy of their training for both MFO and soldiering tasks. The ratings were provided toward the end of their Sinai deployment, when they would best be able to reflect on the adequacy of training in light of their peacekeeping experiences. As shown in Figure 6.2, about half of each group thought there had been too much MFO task training, and only around 15% thought there had

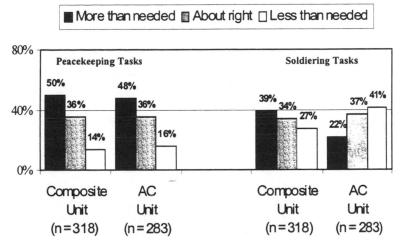

Figure 6.2 Soldier Rating of Predeployment Training

been less MFO training than needed. The pattern of ratings on training adequacy for MFO tasks, then, shows no difference between groups (chi square test for independence, $\chi^2 = 0.43$, ns).

A much different story emerges for the soldiering tasks, as shown in the right half of Figure 6.2. Here, there is a distinct difference in the rating patterns between the two groups ($\chi^2 = 23.2$, p < .001). For the composite unit, 39% believed the training on soldiering tasks was more than needed, compared to only 22% of the AC unit. One explanation for the difference can be the conventional orientation by the AC unit on their usual war-fighting mission, which certainly demands a high level of proficiency in soldiering skills. Even a temporary departure from this orientation while serving as peacekeepers may have induced a perception of inadequacy by these soldiers. It should be noted that upon return from the Sinai, an AC unit normally requires six months of reorientation training on soldiering and war-fighting skills to be considered mission ready.

AN APPLIED STUDY ON TRAINING WHILE DEPLOYED TO A PEACEKEEPING MISSION

Maintaining skills during a Sinai tour is important for members of all rotations, regardless of their follow-on assignments. It is useful, then, to examine the daily patterns of training that occurred during the execution of the MFO mission. Composite units are unlikely to have follow-on missions, simply because the personnel disperse to many separate units upon redeployment. This can prove advantageous in peacekeeping operations. For example, a composite unit can, without later penalty, emphasize the maintenance of peacekeeping skills throughout the mission. Certain skills would be susceptible to significant decay unless used or retrained, as illustrated earlier in the predictions of skill decay for the Bosnia mission (see Figure 6.1). In contrast, an AC unit may, in anticipation of its follow-on mission, shift emphasis from peacekeeping tasks toward soldiering tasks at some point during the rotation. Balancing the training needs of the immediate mission against the need to maintain selected soldier skills is a significant judgment call for trainers at all levels, but especially at the squad level, where responsibility rests in the day-to-day training at remote sites. Here, the daily training patterns may reveal how this balance is managed.

During a unit's deployment to the Sinai, training continues on both peacekeeping and soldiering tasks. This training occurs at the remote sites during a typical three-week rotation and is generally conducted by the squad leader. The amount of training directed at collective war-fighting skills is restricted. Although there is limited training available for squad- and platoon-level tasks with access to a small arms range, the lack of an adequate maneuver area, the lack of time, the demands of other duties, and the treaty's requirement not to appear aggressive prohibits any significant training of collective tasks.

Training Patterns at Remote Sites

One consideration in deploying an active unit to a peacekeeping mission is the degree to which the individual soldiers' and overall unit's performance on essential war-fighting tasks degrade after a period of little or no use. In anticipation of this skill deterioration, an AC unit may increase the frequency of soldiering tasks in the training schedule at some point during the rotation. The situation may be different for a composite unit. Such units could concentrate equally on peacekeeping and soldiering tasks, because upon redeployment they would not regroup as a unit, let alone prepare as a unit for a war-fighting mission.

Squads rotated to remote sites have the continuing requirement to train on individual tasks, both MFO-specific and soldiering tasks, generally at the call of the squad leader. Squad leaders are required to schedule daily training activities, which typically involve three or four individual tasks. A clear-cut way to document any differences is by tracking the daily training activities of squads while at the remote sites. These activities reflect both training guidance from the unit's leadership and the squad leader's sense of the tasks on which training is needed. By categorizing the tasks selected for training as either peacekeeping or soldiering, the cumulative patterns of training can be analyzed for trends within a rotation and between rotations from different units.

Methodology

Special squad training booklets were developed by ARI and distributed to all squad leaders. Instructions on their use were given on the front page of the booklet. Six weeks into the rotation, ARI researchers met with each squad leader to encourage the accurate recording of daily training schedules.

For the AC unit, the analyses were derived from the recording of 4,622 tasks trained at remote sites during the first 20 weeks of training. Interestingly, the number of times that peacekeeping (or MFO) tasks were trained, 2,301, nearly equaled the number of times soldiering tasks were trained: 2,321. Figure 6.3 charts these data in terms of tasks trained per day, beginning with D day (arrival in the Sinai) and incremented by seven-day intervals, so the "D" point on the abscissa represents training during the first week, "D + 7" represents training during the second week, and so on. Each point represents the average number of peacekeeping or soldiering tasks trained during that week. Clearly, there is an emphasis on training MFO tasks during the first four weeks, then a convergence through D + 105 (week 16), then a divergence toward soldiering tasks out to week D + 133 (week 20), when data collection discontinued. Apparently, the active component unit was concentrating training time on the peacekeeping tasks early and then gradually shifted to soldiering tasks as they neared their redeployment date.

Comparison to the Composite Unit

The same squad training booklets were provided to the squad leaders of the composite unit. Data could be recorded only from D + 35 through D + 126, so the between-rotation comparison is restricted to this period. The data obtained were sampled from the remote sites in about the same proportion from the three types of remote sites—sector control, observation post, and check point—allowing an acceptable comparison to be made between the composite and AC units.

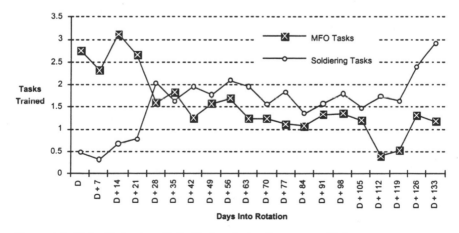

Figure 6.3 Tasks Trained on Daily Basis—Active Component Unit

The comparison data are presented in Figure 6.4. To illustrate an effect we believe is revealing, the AC unit data from Figure 6.3 have been replotted in the following manner: rather than charting the number of MFO or soldiering tasks, we have combined those measures into a single measure. Specifically, we computed and plotted the proportion of tasks trained that were MFO, so if 20 soldiering and 80 MFO tasks were taught during a week, the value 80% was plotted. All available data points are plotted in Figure 6.4. A linear trend line (depicted as a dashed line) is superimposed over the data points for both the reserved unit and the AC unit. The statistical analysis of these trends, however, was restricted to the D + 35 through D + 126 time period, because both units furnished data for comparison during this period.

These data (D + 35 through D + 120) were analyzed through a moderated regression analysis with two variables (time and unit) and an interaction (time by unit). The first step of the regression shows that as time increases, there is not a significant relationship of the ratio of MFO tasks taken together (t = 0.35, p = 0.73). Step 2 of the regression shows a significant difference in the ratio of MFO tasks trained between the two units (t = 7.26, p<.001). Finally, the third step shows the interaction of time and unit to be significant (t = 2.57, p = 0.02), indicating that the slopes of patterns in training differ between the two units. This is graphically illustrated with the divergence of the linear trend lines (depicted as dashed lines in Figure 6.4). This then establishes that the training patterns at the remote sites do differ between the two units, with the active component favoring soldiering tasks as the six-month mission progresses to completion.

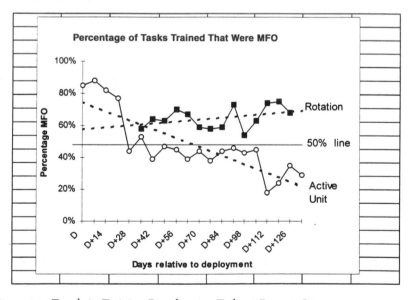

Figure 6.4 Trends in Training Peacekeeping Tasks at Remote Sites

SUMMARY AND FUTURE CONSIDERATIONS

At the request of the Deputy Assistant Secretary of Defense for Peacekeeping and Peace-Enforcement Policy, the DOD Inspector General formed a study team to review specialized training for peacekeeping operations (DOD Inspector General, 1994). The study concluded that peace operations had a different requirement for knowledge, skills, attitude, and environmental considerations than war fighting. At the same time, the study also concluded that a well-trained, disciplined force was a fundamental prerequisite for conducting peacekeeping operations.

The identification of specialized tasks for peacekeeping operations has been reviewed. As one would expect, it is clearly driven by the requirements of the mission. For example, the "Working in the Cold" task included in the predeployment training for Bosnia is inappropriate for the predeployment training for the Sinai mission. The majority of specialized peacekeeping tasks examined here are procedural (step by step) in nature. Thus the predicted deterioration of peacekeeping skills can be derived from an existing analytic model, and recommendations can be provided to trainers for selecting tasks for sustainment training.

The AC unit had a clear trend toward favoring soldiering tasks for refresher training during the peacekeeping mission. The concentrated training of peacekeeping tasks for the first four weeks of the rotation coupled with the soldiers' perceptions that the MFO training during the predeployment phase was more than adequate may have been sufficient preparation for the AC unit to execute the mission. Although they continued to sustain peacekeeping tasks, through training and of course through practice on the job, the unit favored training soldiering tasks toward the end of the rotation. What is important here is the relative pattern: as time progressed, the contrasting trend of the composite unit was a steady ratio of peacekeeping to soldiering tasks.

As described in the introduction to this chapter, an inherent drawback to deploying an AC unit to any peacekeeping environment is the reduction in readiness of the parent division. For the Sinai mission, this reduction extends for at least one year. Our data indicate that not only does an AC unit view their predeployment training of soldiering tasks as being less than needed (41% vs. 27%; see Figure 6.2), they also gear toward soldiering tasks as the mission progresses. Perhaps the unit leadership is sympathetic to their primary mission as war-fighters rather than their temporary mission as peacekeepers. This argument would not extend to a specially formed unit of reserve volunteers, who disperse to many units upon redeployment. Another possibility is perhaps the AC unit perceives the peacekeeping mission as being more threatening than the composite unit, thus needing to stay sharp on soldiering skills. Whatever the reasons, there is a clear difference between units in both their perceptions and their within-mission training preferences.

Although both peacekeeping and soldiering skills, as defined in this chapter, appear to deteriorate because of lack of training, there are other ways in which soldier skills may in fact be enhanced by the deployment experience. Specifically, decision making and leadership may be developed in ways unique to the deployment experience because of the independence and responsibility frequently required of small teams on peacekeeping deployments in sector. These kinds of skills may not be assessed by the kind of metric developed in the training environment, but they remain, nevertheless, a key component of military performance.

Peacekeeping is a multifaceted mission that requires a balance of soldiering tasks and mission-specific peacekeeping tasks. Not only must these tasks be identified during a planning process and trained during a predeployment phase, they must also be maintained during the mission. The natural deterioration of these tasks needs to be recognized, and refresher training that takes into account the criticality, recency of use, and predicted retention of these tasks can underpin optimal performance. To add to the claim of Kutter (1986) regarding the importance of predeployment training, skills must continue to be maintained throughout a peacekeeping operation.

NOTE

The views and opinions expressed are those of the author and do not necessarily reflect the views or opinions of the Department of Army or the U.S. Army Research Institute for the Behavioral and Social Sciences.

REFERENCES

Britt, T. W. (1998). Psychological ambiguities in peacekeeping. In H. J. Langholtz (Ed.), *The psychology of peacekeeping* (pp. 111–128). Westport, CT: Praeger.

Conway, M., Cohen, G., & Stanhope, N. (1991). On the very long-term retention of knowledge acquired through formal education: Twelve years of cognitive psychology. *Journal of Experimental Psychology: General, 120,* 395–409.

Diehl, P. E. (1988). Avoiding another Beirut disaster: Strategies for deployment of U.S. troops in peacekeeping roles. *Conflict, 8,* 261–270.

DOD Inspector General. (1994, September 1). *Specialized military training for peace operations, Program Evaluation.*

Durch, W. J. (1993). Running the show: Planning and implementation. In W. J. Durch (Ed.), *The Evolution of UN Peacekeeping* (pp. 59–75). New York: St. Martin's Press.

Ebbinghaus, H. (1885). *Uber das Gedachtnis.* Leipzig: Dunker. H. Ruyer & C. Bussenius (Trans.), *Memory.* New York: Teachers College, Columbia University, 1913.

Goldstein, I. L. (1993) *Training in organizations* (3rd ed.). Pacific Grove, CA: Brooks/Cole.

Hagman, J., & Rose, A. (1983). Retention of military tasks: A review. *Human Factors, 25,* 199–213.

Kidwell, B., & Langholtz, H. J. (1998). Personnel selection, preparation, and training for U.N. peacekeeping missions. In H. J. Langholtz (Ed.), *The psychology of peacekeeping* (pp. 89–100). Westport, CT: Praeger.

Kraiger, K., & Jung, K. (1997). Linking training objectives to evaluation criteria. In M. A. Quiñones and A. Ehrenstein (Eds.), *Training for a rapidly changing workplace: Applications of psychological research* (pp. 137–155). Washington, DC: American Psychological Association.

Kutter, W. D. (1986). *Operational guidelines for U.S. peacekeeping commanders.* Carlyle Barracks, PA: U.S. Army War College.

NATO. (1998). *The NATO handbook.* Brussels: NATO Office of Information and Press.

Phelps, R. H., & Farr, B. J. (1996). *Reserve component soldiers as peacekeepers.* Alexandria, VA: U.S. Army Research Institute for the Behavioral and Social Sciences.

Sabol, M. A., & Wisher, R. A. (2001). Retention and reacquisition of military skills. *Military Operations Research, 6,* 59–80.

Segal, D. R., Furukawa, T. P., & Lindh, J. C. (1990). Light infantry as peacekeepers in the Sinai. *Armed Forces & Society, 16,* 385–403.

Semb, G., & Ellis, J. (1994). Knowledge taught in school: What is remembered? *Review of Educational Research, 64*(3), 253–286.

Taws, J. M. & Peters, J. E. (1995). *Operations other than war: Implications for the U.S. Army.* Santa Monica, CA: RAND.

Wisher, R., Sabol, M., & Ellis, J. (1999). *Staying sharp: The retention and reacquisition of military skills and knowledge* (Special Report 39). Alexandria, VA: U.S. Army Research Institute for the Behavioral and Social Sciences.

Wisher, R., Sabol, M., & Ozkaptan, H. (1996). *Retention of "peace support operations" tasks during Bosnia deployment: A basis for refresher training* (Special Report). Alexandria, VA: U.S. Army Research Institute for the Behavioral and Social Sciences.

7

Work Motivation and the Peacekeeper

Maria Grazia Galantino

The growth of work motivation theories and research in the last decades has undoubtedly enhanced our knowledge of organizational behavior and offered useful tools to managers and practitioners working in this field. However, researchers have argued that the different approaches to work motivation are often conflicting and, though a trend toward the consolidation and integration of extant theories has been noted (Kanfer, 1990), the state of the literature is still far from offering a general unifying conceptual framework (Locke & Henne, 1986).

The transposition of work motivation theories to a particular work organization, such as the military, is even more complex. Although there is a growing realization of the advantages of implementing approaches and tools developed in organizational and managerial studies, a strong emphasis on the uniqueness of the military work environment persists in the literature. To what extent can the military profession be compared to other professions? Is the military diverse just as any organization is—considering its history, culture, and environment—or is being a soldier "more than just a job"? How do the new tasks and the new organizational goals, which emerged in the last decade, affect the motivational processes of soldiers?

The present chapter addresses these issues through an analysis of the main motivational sources that might drive soldiers' attitudes and behavior in peace-keeping operations. After a review of the main research and studies on motivational issues concerning the military profession, the chapter elaborates a model of work motivation for peacekeeping. Finally, a study designed to test this model is presented, using data from Italian soldiers deployed in Bosnia.

MOTIVATIONAL ISSUES AND THE UNIQUENESS OF SOLDIERS' JOBS

Traditionally, discussion of soldiers' motivation has focused primarily on combat motivation in an attempt to answer some old and uneasy questions: why do men fight? why are they willing to kill? and—especially—why are they ready to sacrifice their lives? Writers, historians, and social scientists have advanced explanations based on a combination of individual and collective attributes: the personal value of the heroic fighter and a set of collective values, idealistic and altruistic in their nature, such as patriotism or nationalism.

Since World War II, efforts have been made in order to identify and operationalize the main motivational sources among military personnel. Empirical research, aimed at a better understanding of what motivates individuals in combat and—generally—to serve as soldiers, have gone hand in hand with the development of social psychology and behavioral theories and their application to work organizations. In the debate on work motivation in the military, three main approaches can be identified, based either on social, rational-economic, or self-actualization needs of individuals.[1]

The social approach emerged with the monumental research on *The American Soldier*, carried out during World War II, which emphasized the importance of the workplace for the satisfaction of social needs in the form of communication, affiliation, and social interaction. In a chapter that specifically addressed motivational issues, Smith (1949) suggested that soldiers attached little importance to patriotism, to what the war is fought for or other idealistic concerns, while underscoring the role of the primary group and face-to-face relationships in motivating men in combat. Despite some criticisms, this approach was a big step toward a better understanding of relations and behavior of men in combat, and it continues to represent a paradigmatic theory for military personnel management today.

The so-called rational-economic approach is based on the assumption that a reward system is the most influential human relations (HR) tool regarding employee behavior enabling to create a self-motivated workforce (Lawler, 1973). With the transition from a draft system to professional armed forces in the beginning of the 1970s, such ideas flourished within U.S. military research and policies (Burk, 1984). The fact that the military profession henceforth had to compete for recruits in the "normal" labor market led to a "bureaucratic rationalism": the stress of research and policies was put on managerial effectiveness and on financial rewards as the best way of attracting qualified recruits (Faris, 1988). Simultaneously, in the context of a general societal secularization process aimed at substituting traditional values and beliefs with rationality, the emphasis on traditional military values, that is, patriotism or honor, was also reduced.

In the following years, new trends became increasingly evident. Society as a whole moved from materialistic to postmaterialistic values (Inglehart, 1977; 1997) and new, less calculative, issues related to quality of life became more and more relevant to the behavior of persons and organizations. The marginal effectiveness of additional financial benefits decreased; people began to consider nonfinancial aspects of work (e.g., whether the work is interesting and can contribute to one's self-fulfillment and to the development of one's potentialities). In this respect, the debate in military research was not as late as perhaps resulting policies. Already in 1976, Bowers showed that although "the traditional American values of independence and material success still are important and are likely to remain so for the immediate future" (p. 95), a generation gap is already visible among higher educated navy men in terms of "adherence to autocratic beliefs" and higher concerns about having a challenging job (pp. 111–114).

All these different approaches acknowledge the diminishing motivational importance of commitment to the institutional goals expressed by patriotic and political values for military personnel. Instead, economic and social needs are deemed to drive individual behavior in the military organization. However, this generally accepted notion has been challenged. Even during the Vietnam War, Moskos (1971) proposed that "latent ideology" also played a role in soldier motivation. Even if American soldiers do not openly express ideological opinions and are reluctant to express patriotic feelings, they have elementary nationalistic feelings, latent beliefs about the legitimacy and superiority of the American way of life. Groups are important in sustaining men in combat as long as they share the common values of the society they are fighting for (Moskos, 1971). In research on the motivation of junior enlisted personnel, the conclusion of Brown and Moskos (1997) was that "primary group determinants will be less salient in explaining combat performance in the future than was the case in the past. [. . .] The volunteer soldier is more likely to reflect an internalized value system rather than relying primarily on group opinion in his unit" (p. 6).

In other words, the explanation of soldier motivation requires a comprehensive motivational model that not only considers the already cited self-oriented sources but also includes other motivation sources, which are specific or particularly amplified in the military profession. As Böene (1990, 2000) points out, different logics of action coexist in the military organization: one is cooperative and "does not in any way deviate from industrial forms of sociability" (Böene, 2000, p. 10); the other is conflictual in nature and oriented toward the enemy. While recognizing a process of convergence between civilian and military organizations, the conflictual logic is peculiar for the military, requiring "a unique motivational structure in which self-interest, while not absent, is radically insufficient and has to be supplemented by factors enabling agents to endure and cherish a communitarian, hierarchical environment expecting heroic behavior on their part in the face of danger and uncertainty in battle or operations, inspiring the will to conquer or subdue opposing parties, and imposing powerful norms on service members: open-ended terms of service, obedience and commitment to organizational goals" (Böene, 2000, p. 9).

Hence, from the uniqueness of the conflictual logic, descends the uniqueness of the psychological contract, the set of expectations between the employee and the organization. Using the framework of a "contractual continuum" advanced by Rousseau and Parks (1993), the case of the military represents one extreme:

the relational contract. It requires high investment by both employees and employers, involving a high degree of emotional commitment and mutual interdependence (Rousseau & Wade-Benzoni, 1994).

An interesting contribution to the discussion on motivation in the military, accounting for a variety of motivational sources, has been advanced by Battistelli (1996, 1997). On the basis of survey findings collected among Italian soldiers deployed in Operazione Pellicano in Albania (1993), Restore Hope in Somalia (1994), and the SFOR missions in Bosnia (1996), the author developed a three-dimensional typology of motivations: paleomodern, modern, and postmodern. Paleomodern motivations are immaterial and other oriented, based on an affective belonging to the organization; they include motivation related to traditional values of the military like the altruistic ideal to serve the country and promote its image. Hence they are based on internalization of institutional goals. Modern motivations are instrumental and self-oriented, primarily based on economic and occupational considerations. Postmodern motivations are self-oriented but more expressive, based on self-actualizing needs, including the desire of adventure or the desire to have a meaningful experience.

The validity of this typology was tested using Bosnia data (Battistelli, Ammendola, & Galantino, 2000). The results of a principal component analysis show quite clearly that three main dimensions (with eigenvalues >1) can be found, which explain cumulatively 60% of the total variance (Table 7.1).

The distribution of frequencies shows it is possible to find prevalent types more than pure types (Table 7.2). Yet modern motivation appears to be invoked less frequently, whereas the paleomodern and postmodern motivations are on

Table 7.1
Principal Components Analysis of Enlistment Motivations

	FACTOR 1 Paleomodern motivations	FACTOR 2 Modern motivations	FACTOR 3 Postmodern motivations
To promote my country's international image	0,811		
To be part of a close-knit community	0,808		
To serve my country	0,75		
To get a steady job		0,836	
To enter the world of work		0,799	
To improve my social position		0,646	
To put myself to the test			0,779
To visit new places			0,691
Out of desire for adventure			0,677

Table 7.2
Motivations for Enlisting by Rank (% of interviewees who deemed each
item to be important)

	Privates	NCOs	Officers	ALL
Paleomodern motivations				
To promote my country's international image	50,6	59,3	59,0	**59,3**
To be part of a close-knit community	55,5	63,5	60,0	**57,6**
To serve my own country	72,7	87,4	85,0	**77,6**
Modern motivations				
To get a steady job	55,9	45,1	25,0	**49,4**
To enter the world of work	32,4	28,0	17,0	**29,3**
To improve my social position	47,4	40,3	40,0	**44,8**
Postmodern motivations				
To put myself to the test	71,4	47,1	54,1	**63,9**
To visit new places	65,1	62,4	50,0	**63,0**
Out of desire for adventure	76,1	70,3	68,0	**74,4**

average more frequent. Paleomodern motivations are more relevant to officers; the postmodern are more relevant to privates. This pattern shows a cleavage based on the double effect of generational change and socialization. Privates (youngsters) are more likely to have postmodern motivation because of a diffuse change in society, but also because they have undergone a shorter period of institutional socialization, based on loyalty to the service and on patriotic values.

TOWARD A MODEL OF WORK MOTIVATION FOR PEACEKEEPERS

It is evident that some progress in understanding motivational processes influencing soldiers' attitudes and behavior has been made. Yet more research on motivation that is both theory driven and empirically based is increasingly needed, in the midst of an ever-changing world security system that imposes new tasks and important organizational changes on the armed forces worldwide.

In the last decade, soldiers have been deployed primarily in peacekeeping operations, taking place in a structurally different environment from traditional war-fighting, which they were accustomed and trained for. The arena for peacekeeping operations is crowded, but "although at the tactical level the arena for peace operations may be full of 'bad guys' (i.e., people who shoot at the peace operation force), it lacks strategic enemies. [. . .] In addition, the arena for peace operations is full of other people (innocents, unknowns, neutral and third parties) and is generally a place where even the military needs a program to tell the players apart" (Segal & Eyre, 1996, p. 28). In this new, multivalent, and complex context, the binary friend/foe logic, which represented the cognitive horizon for individuals in classic war-fighting, can no longer provide the orientation for action. The conflictual and the cooperative logic are mixed in confusing ways, making it hard to say which one "is dominant, as local contexts are apt to change without much notice" (Böene, 2000, p. 24). The peacekeeping environment, in fact, is based on a blurred, friend/foe/nonfoe logic where the actors shift continuously from one position to the other, a logic that can be defined as "fuzzy"[2] (Battistelli, Ammendola, & Galantino, 2000).

How and whether such new issues and the changed environment can affect soldiers' motivation is still a controversial issue. In the last decade, the experience gained from peacekeeping missions seems to be strongly context dependent, and several factors contribute to the ad hoc character of each mission. Primarily, each mission is taking place in a different political and strategic scenario with different rules of engagement for the forces deployed. Moreover, the impact of peacekeeping operations on the military is different in each national context, being strongly related to the culture and the history of each national armed force and the particular pattern of relations it established with its society. Most research based on American experiences illustrates the resistance of soldiers to adapt to the changing character of military missions. Peacekeeping is seen as antagonistic with the traditional identity of the war fighter and often perceived as diverting soldiers from their primary goal of fighting and winning wars. At the same time, no dominant view but ambivalent attitudes emerge from case studies: soldiers do not consider themselves suitable for the mission, or they think peacekeeping "is not a soldier's job but only soldiers can do it," because it requires discipline and obedience (Miller, 1997; Moskos, 2000; Segal & Segal, 1993). Cases of mid-powers, where soldiers are less likely to be involved in a "real" war for geo-strategic reasons, show different patterns and reveal a high level of professional satisfaction among soldiers (Ammendola, 1999, Carreiras, 1999; Battistelli, 1996). However, peacekeeping operations have led to an increased social recognition of the military in most countries. Opinion polls in several countries—including the United States—show a substantial increase in public support for military missions, the objectives of which are depicted as noble and humanitarian (Everts & Isernia, 2001; van der Meulen, 1997).

All these new issues might influence—in diverse directions—soldier motivation. Thus any theoretical model aimed at understanding the factors and the processes that energize, direct, and sustain behavior needs to be put in context, taking into account multiple aspects, including not only individuals' achievement needs and moral involvement in the organization, but also situational variables related to the specific tasks soldiers are asked to perform.

A theoretical model of motivation, which can be very useful to account for some of these aspects, suggests a dichotomy, based on the different locus of causality: intrinsic versus extrinsic motivation (de Charmes, 1968, Deci, 1975). According to this model, intrinsically motivated behavior has internal causality and occurs in the absence of external control; hence it is related to the work itself, whereas extrinsically motivated behavior is induced by external forces and external rewards. Elaborating on this theory, Etzioni (1975) developed a model based on three main types of involvement in organizations: alienative, calculative, and moral. The first two refer to motivation related to external rewards, entailing the assumption that behavior is determined by the aim of personal utility maximization. Moral involvement, by contrast, has internal causality and can derive from an internalized system of values and norms (pure morale) or from the social pressures of the primary groups (social morale). The main motivational sources identified in the literature on the military can be easily classified according to these motivational types. It is likely, though, that these sources do not just preexist to a specific work situation: Peacekeepers already have a set of expectations and moral values before their deployment, but they are interpreted, developed, and changed while peacekeeping work is being carried out. In fact, more recent research has made clear that extrinsic events, such as a pay rise, can interact with intrinsic motives, reinforcing or reducing them according to situational properties of the event and how it is interpreted by the individual (Bandura, 1986; Deci, 1975).

Hence the motivation-behavior link remains difficult to identify using this model alone. Locke and Henne (1986) suggest that the most predictive models of work motivation are those aimed at a proximal construct, based on purposive action, rather than those focusing on dispositional and motive approaches (distal constructs) such as intrinsic motivation models. Accordingly, Kanfer (1992) argues that motives theories can be considered predictors of intention rather than behavior per se. Moreover, "individual differences in knowledge, skills, and abilities, as well as dynamic changes in situational demands, further influence the extent to which an intrinsic motivational orientation will influence behavior" (Kanfer, 1992, p. 23).

Locke's goal-setting model and its recent elaborations well address these limitations and offer an additional framework useful to a discussion of work motivation in a peacekeeping environment. Locke (1968) focuses on the goal-performance relationship, suggesting that specific goal assignments produce better performance than vague and nonspecific goal assignments. Moreover, of particular relevance here is the concept of goal commitment: goal assignments will influence performance only if the individual accepts them. On this premise, most research and managerial implementations focused on the importance of participative procedures of goal setting for enhancing goal commitment, and therefore performance. However, recent research findings show no difference on goal commitment and performance between participatively set and assigned goal procedures when individuals were provided with a rationale for the goal assignment (Latham, Erez, & Locke, 1988).

Building on the theoretical framework outlined in the previous pages, we hypothesize that peacekeeper motivation can be seen as a function of a set of variables, which can be grouped according to the three main sources of motivation: instrumental motivation, intrinsic motivation, and motivation based on goal commitment. These sources of motivation are described in Table 7.3. Each of the three groups includes enlistment motivation, which exists prior to the peacekeeping deployment, and context-related attitudes, which are constructed while performing the mission. The first set of variables includes instrumental-external-directed motivations, such as modern-instrumental motivations for enlisting and the perceived equity of the pay received. The second group includes sources of motivation coming directly from the content and the attributes of the task performed. Postmodern motivations for enlisting are reported here together with opinions on organizational issues: the relations with fellow soldiers' and the confidence in leaders' abilities, the professional satisfaction achieved during the deployment, and the relative boredom experienced. The last dimension is related to goal commitment and includes both paleomodern motivations for enlisting and attitudes toward the mission's aims, its rightness/wrongness, and its perceived utility.

MOTIVATION AND THE ITALIAN PEACEKEEPER

Attempting to test our model, we used data collected from Italian soldiers deployed to Bosnia[3] using a multiple regression analysis aimed at understanding the role of the previously discussed motivational dimensions in shaping soldiers' choice of volunteering for a peacekeeping operation. Some method-

Table 7.3
Sources of Motivation in Peacekeeping Military Operations

Instrumental motivation	Intrinsic motivation	Goal commitment motivation
Modern enlistment motivations	Postmodern enlistment motivations	Paleomodern enlistment motivations
Perceived equity of the salary	Relative boredom of the mission	Support for the mission goals
	Relation with peers	Perceived utility of the mission
	Confidence in superiors' HR management competence	
	Confidence in superiors' technical competence	

ological caveats require clarification. First, lacking measures of individual behavior and performance and having personnel commanded for deployment, we used the nearest proxy of volunteering available: "If you could choose, would you have voluntarily participated in this mission?"[4] Obviously, the question wording of our outcome measure requires an emotional response to a hypothetical situation that might never occur; hence the answer might not represent the real attitude nor predict the actual behavior. Then, we should recognize that the predictor variables selected are probably not exhaustive of the variety of drives that may influence the choice of participating in peacekeeping missions.[5] The variability of such a choice is strongly related to individual and contingent situations that cannot be assessed or foreseen before the actual choice is made. Furthermore, a diachronical perspective is missing here. As motivations are constructed in time according to previous and current experience, it would be interesting to examine how the evaluation of previous deployments (if any) could affect the decision of further involvement. Overall, the complexity of the issues necessitates caution in establishing any causal relations among variables. Nevertheless, results of the regression model summarized in Table 7.4[6] show that our model has explanatory value and may shed some light on the blurred issue of motivation in peacekeeping.

In our analysis, just five of the variables originally selected were predictive of the desire to participate in the peacekeeping operation, and they explain approximately 22% of the variance in our outcome variable.[7] At first glance, it is evident that instrumental-external considerations do not appear to be significant in determining the willingness to voluntarily participate in peacekeep-

Table 7.4
Multiple Regression of Variables Predicting Willingness to Participate in Peacekeeping

| | Unstandardized Coeeficients | | Standardized Coefficients | | |
	B	Std. Error	Beta	t	Significance
(Constant)	1,936	0,142		13,655	0,000
Support for the mission goals	0,370	0,037	0,332	9,894	0,000
Postmodern enlistment motivations	0,110	0,023	0,154	4,761	0,000
Confidence in superiors' technical competence	0,091	0,026	0,119	3,530	0,000
Paleomodern enlistment motivations	0,072	0,024	0,099	3,004	0,003
Rank	0,073	0,033	0,071	2,215	0,027

ing missions, and the outcome variable seems to be driven from motivation based on goal commitment and intrinsic sources. Although occupational motivations are still relevant for the decision to enlist—especially in marginal sectors of the society and/or in societies with a high unemployment rate, for example Italy—they are probably not sufficient alone to explain active involvement in a relatively risky environment and to perform complex tasks.

In contrast, motivation based on goal commitment plays an important role. In fact, looking at the beta coefficients, the most important predictor is the support for the mission's goal (Table 7.4). Two different components can be identified at this level: commitment to institutional goals *tout court* (represented by the paleomodern motivation index) and commitment to the mission's goals (represented by the support for the mission aims and the perceived utility of the mission for obtaining them). The perception of doing a job consistent with the internalized military values is a strong source of motivation in itself and not related to the satisfaction of needs: "the consequence of acting in line with one's internalized values is not a sense of pleasure or need fulfillment, but rather a sense of affirmation attained when the person abides by his or her moral commitment or espoused values" (Leonard, Beauvais, & Scholl, 1999, p. 971).

However, values are not espoused once and for all. Apart from the core values, the "fundamental ideology" that shapes the military culture, other, sometimes conflicting, values can intervene in operational situations (Galantino & Ricotta, 1999). Although there is widespread awareness that real-time information renders military actions much more accountable to the public, we should not forget that the peacekeeping environment is much more open to external information than any traditional war situation. Soldiers are exposed to various inputs coming from different sources: the media at home and in the operation country, the opinion of the host population, and so on. Thus soldiers' mission behavior needs to be sustained by the conviction of the "rightness" of the political reasons that underlay the decision to deploy troops abroad. Our results show that when soldiers support the decision of their government to deploy troops in a peacekeeping mission, they are more likely to be motivated to participate. As other research has pointed out, legitimacy is a crucial issue in peacekeeping, not just at societal level, but even within the military organization (Dandeker & Gow, 2000).

Practical reasons render the ideological dimension of peace operations even more important. Soldiers in peacekeeping missions do not experience the "absolute deprivation" that distinguishes life in combat, where the decisions of the state that made them deploy are largely meaningless to them, because their main concern is keeping themselves alive (Moskos, 1971). Therefore, we can agree to a certain extent with Mackewitsch, Biehl, and vom Hagen (2000), who argue that the dominance of political attitudes and opinions is due to the relative calm of life during peacekeeping missions, though it is likely the specific peacekeeping context and social changes in the society may play a major role.

Postmodern motivations related to the job itself are also relevant, indicating the importance of both intrinsic sources related to the traditional values of the military institution and to the military profession as a means for self-expression and self-fulfillment. Peacekeeping suits soldiers who enlisted because they wanted a challenging job and the opportunity to enjoy adventurous situations and travel to new places. Although these sources of motivation have been considered too far from the traditional military ethos, because they are oriented to the "immediate gratification of self-interest" (Burk, 1984), motivational theories show how crucial and persistent intrinsic motivation based on the need for self-expression can be in directing and reinforcing behaviors (Katz & Kahn, 1978).

Leadership plays a role in shaping soldiers' motivation as well: confidence in superiors' professional competence seems to be very relevant in the choice of participating in peacekeeping. Studies have shown that leadership has a strong impact on unit cohesion (Bartone & Adler, 1999). As leaders manage to prove their technical competence and skills, soldiers are more likely to develop ties to the unit. Clearly, the relatively new profile of peacekeeping missions, with a high level of uncertainty and ambiguity, renders leadership skills more visible (Britt, 1998).

As for individual-structural variables related to private or organizational life, rank proved to be the only predictor of soldiers' intention to be involved in a peacekeeping operation. This finding indicates that socialization and organizational learning still have an influence in motivating soldiers, regardless of their individual work-related attitudes. Note here that this higher propensity of higher ranks to be involved in peacekeeping operations probably offsets the importance of other variables, such as marital status. Leaving constant all the other variables, being married does not seem to have an influence on the choice of participating in peacekeeping missions for Italian soldiers, though the family distance turned out to be the major source of concern for married personnel. It seems realistic to say, then, that as married personnel are concentrated among noncommissioned officers (NCOs) and officers, the internalization of goals and the commitment to work that they develop through education and socialization within the institution counterbalance other factors that can deter them from deployment in operations abroad.

Summing up, we can say there are two main components to soldier motivation in peacekeeping. One is prominently cultural and related to the institutional values of the military and also includes political considerations and opinions on issues specifically related to the situation in which peacekeepers are asked to intervene. The other dimension is more variable and based on the evaluation of the inner character of the job. Situational variables are also important and demonstrate how motivation is changeable and continuously reconstructed on the basis of day-to-day experiences in the organization.

Overall, we should add that attitudes toward any kind of task are constructed also in comparison with role expectations. In the case of Italian soldiers—and perhaps of other so-called middle power countries—peacekeeping represents "the best—if not the only—*succedaneum* of combat" (Isernia & Lanzieri, 1999, p. 232), or at least one chance to perform a proper military task. Hence it is not surprising that soldiers with stronger organizational and goal commitment are more motivated to participate.

SUMMARY

This chapter has explored motivational issues in a relatively unique work setting: the military in peacekeeping. Soldier motivation was examined through a theoretical framework—based on organizational and military studies—including sources based on intrinsic motivation, goal commitment, and instrumental considerations. By analyzing the case of Italian soldiers we found out that the most important predictors of motivation in peacekeeping were related to intrinsic motivation and considerations related to the specific experience of the mission, particularly individuals' goal commitment.

Thus we can conclude that new, more self-oriented attitudes are important among soldiers. They are not necessarily conflicting with the institutional goals; on the contrary, they can play an essential role in motivating participation in more active and challenging tasks in peacekeeping operations. However, the importance of paleomodern attitudes and the persistence of a rank-based cleavage suggests that socialization to the normative military system and the internalization of institutional values is still essential to reinforce and sustain individual motivation and behavior.

Furthermore, the importance of political considerations supporting the decision to deploy troops in the mission reveals that motivation is not determined once and for all but is constructed in a strongly context-related process. Soldiers need to be further socialized to the meaning of peacekeeping operations and provided with a rationale for their goal assignment in order to be motivated and committed to the mission's specific goals and therefore to perform better. At the same time, through effective performances they might also contribute to the legitimacy of peacekeeping in the broader public.

NOTES

1. Schein (1980) suggests a similar typology for the entire realm of work motivation theory and research.

2. An interesting application of fuzzy sets to social science can be found in Ragin (2000).

3. We studied a representative sample of the Italian military personnel deployed in Bosnia, stratified by rank and corps. Data collection began in July 1996 in Sarajevo with 52 interviews of military personnel deployed in Bosnia, opinion leaders, and NGO's representatives working in the field. The survey (n = 902) was conducted in November 1996 at the Italian base in Bosnia (n = 603) and from February to April 1997 in Italy,

on recently returned soldiers (n = 299). Two main areas of interest were addressed: (1) the characteristics and the evaluation of the mission and (2) the attitudes toward the role of the military and the peacekeeping mission. See Ammendola (1999). I thank Fabrizio Battistelli (research director) and my colleagues at Archivio Disarmo who allowed me to use common data and provided with useful remarks and suggestions on this chapter.

4. Respondents rated their answer on a scale from 1 (*certainly yes*) to 4 (*certainly not*).

5. Several predictor variables have been included: paleomodern, modern, and postmodern enlistment motivation indexes, relative boredom of the mission, relation with peers, confidence in superiors' HR management competence, confidence in superiors' technical competence, support for the mission goals, and perceived utility of the mission. Other variables have been added in order to explore whether structural variables, either individual (age, education, marital status) or organizational (rank, corps) also play a role.

6. Multiple regression with stepwise variable selection method, which evaluates at each step which variables are eligible for inclusion or removal on the basis of the probability of F, has been used.

7. $R = .474$; $R^2 = .224$.

REFERENCES

Ammendola, T. (1999). (Ed.). *Missione in Bosnia. Le caratteristiche sociologiche dei militari italiani*. Milan: Franco Angeli.

Bandura, A. (1986). *Social foundations of thought and action: a social cognitive theory*. Eaglewood Cliffs, NJ: Prentice-Hall.

Bartone, P. T., & Adler, A. B. (1999). Cohesion over time in a peacekeeping medical task force. *Military Psychology, 11*, 85–107.

Battistelli, F. (1996). *Soldati*. Milan: Franco Angeli.

Battistelli, F. (1997). Peacekeeping and the postmodern soldier. *Armed Forces & Society, 23*, 469–484.

Battistelli, F., Ammendola, T., & Galantino, M. G. (2000). The fuzzy environment and postmodern soldiers: The motivations of the Italian soldiers in Bosnia. In E. A. Schmidl (Ed.), *Peace operation between war and peace*. London: Frank Cass.

Böene, B. (1990). How "unique" should the military be? *Archives Européennes de Sociologie, 31*, 3–59.

Böene, B. (2000). How unique is the military today? How unique should it be? In B. Böene, C. Dandeker, J. Kuhlmann, & J. van der Meulen (Eds.), *Facing uncertainty*, Report No 2 (pp. 7–39). Karlstad: National Defense College.

Bowers, D. G. (1976). Work-related attitudes of military personnel. In N. L. Goldman & D. R. Segal (Eds.), *The social psychology of military service* (pp. 89–115). Beverly Hills, London: Sage.

Britt, T. W. (1998). Psychological ambiguities in peacekeeping. In H. J. Langholtz (Ed.), *The psychology of peacekeeping* (pp. 111–128). Westport, CT: Praeger.

Brown, C., & Moskos, C. C. (1997). The American volunteer soldier: Will he fight? *Military Review, 77*(1), 30–36.

Burk, J. (1984, Fall). Patriotism and the all-volunteer force. *Journal of Political and Military Sociology, 12,* 229–241.

Carreiras, H. (1999). O que Pensam os Militares Portugueses do Peacekeeping? *Estratégia, 14,* 65–95.

Dandeker, C., & Gow, J. (2000). Military culture and strategic peacekeeping. In E. A. Schmidl (Ed.), *Peace operation between war and peace.* London: Frank Cass.

de Charmes, R. (1968). *Personal causation: The internal affective determinants of behavior.* New York: Academic Press.

Deci, E. L. (1975). *Intrinsic motivation.* New York: Plenum Press.

Etzioni, A. (1975). *Comparative analysis of complex organizations.* New York: Macmillan.

Everts, P., & Isernia, P. (2001). *Public opinion and the international use of force.* London: Routledge.

Faris, J. H. (1988). The social psychology of the military service and the influence of bureaucratic rationalism. In C. C. Moskos & F. R. Wood (Eds.), *The military. More than just a job?* (pp. 57–65). New York: Pergamon-Brassey's.

Galantino, M. G., & Ricotta, G. (1999). Guerrieri e centristi, sedentari e umanitari. L'ideologia del Militare e la sfida del peacekeeping. In T. Ammendola (Ed.), *Missione in Bosnia. Le caratteristiche sociologiche dei militari italiani* (pp. 151–190). Milan: Franco Angeli.

Inglehart, R. (1977). *The silent revolution. Changing values and political styles among Western publics.* Princeton, NJ: Princeton University Press.

Inglehart, R. (1997). *Modernization and postmodernization. Cultural, economic and political change in 43 societies.* Princeton, NJ: Princeton University Press.

Isernia, P., & Lanzieri, G. (1999). I soldati italiani amano il peacekeeping? Un modello delle deteminanti della soddisfazione per le missioni di pace. In T. Ammendola (Ed.), *Missione in Bosnia* (pp. 191–237). Le caratteristiche sociologiche dei militari italiani. Milan: Franco Angeli.

Kanfer, R. (1990). Motivation theory and industrial/organizational psychology. In M. D. Dunnette and L. M. Hough (Eds.), *Handbook of industrial and organizational psychology* (2nd ed., pp. 75–170). Palo Alto, CA: Consulting Psychologists Press.

Kanfer, R. (1992). Work motivation: New directions in theory and research. In C. L. Cooper & I. T. Robertson (Eds.), *International Review of Industrial and Organizational Psychology* (Vol. 7, pp. 1–53). London: Wiley and Sons.

Katz, D., & Kahn, R. L. (1978). *The social psychology of organizations.* New York: Wiley.

Latham, G. P., Erez, M., & Locke, E. A. (1988). Resolving scientific disputes by the joint design of crucial experiments by the antagonists: Application to the Erez-Latham dispute regarding participation in goal setting. *Journal of Applied Psychology, 73,* 753–772.

Lawler, E. E. (1973). *Motivations in work organizations.* Monterrey, CA: Brooks.

Leonard, N. H., Beauvais, L. L., & Scholl, R. W. (1999). Work motivation: The incorporation of self-concept-based processes? *Human Relations, 52*(8), 969–998.

Locke, E. A. (1968). Toward a theory of task motivation and incentives. *Organizational Behavior and Human Performance, 3,* 157–189.

Locke E. A., & Henne, D. (1986). Work motivation theories. In C. L. Cooper & I. T. Robertson (Eds.), *International review of industrial and organizational psychology* (pp. 1–35). Chichester: Wiley and Sons.

Mackewitsch, R., Biehl, H., & vom Hagen, U. (2000, December 6–10). *Motivation of soldiers during assignment abroad.* Paper presented at the ERGOMAS VII Biennial Conference, Prague.

Moskos, C. C. (1971). Vietnam: Why men fight. In E. Z. Friedenberg (Ed.), *The anti-American generation* (pp. 217–237). New York: Transaction.

Moskos, C. C. (2000). *Report on task force falcon.* Unpublished paper.

Miller, L. (1997). Do soldiers hate peacekeeping? The case of preventive diplomacy operations in Macedonia. *Armed Forces & Society, 23*(3), 415–449.

Ragin, C. C. (2000). *Fuzzy-set social science.* Chicago, London: University of Chicago Press.

Rousseau, D. M., & Parks, J. M. (1993). The contracts of individuals and organizations. In L. L. Cummings and B. M. Staw (Eds.), *Research in organizational behavior, 15* (pp. 1–43). Greenwich, CT: JAI Press.

Rousseau, D. M., & Wade-Benzoni, K. A. (1994). Psychological contracts and human resources practice? *Human Resource Management, 33*(3), 385–402.

Schein, E. H. (1980). *Organizational psychology.* Englewood Cliffs, NJ: Prentice-Hall.

Segal, D. R., & Eyre, D. P. (1996). *U.S. Army in peace operations at the dawning of the twenty-first century.* Alexandria, VA: U.S. Army Research Institute for the Behavioral and Social Sciences.

Segal, D. R., & Segal, M. W. (1993). *Peacekeepers and their wives.* Westport, CT: Greenwood Press.

Smith, M. B. (1949). Combat motivations among ground forces. In Stouffer Lumsdaine, A. A., Williams, R. B., Smith, M. B., Janis, I. L., Star, S. A., & Cottrell, L. S. (Eds.), *The American soldier: Combat and its aftermath* (Vol. 2). Princeton: Princeton University Press.

van der Meulen, J. (1997). Post-modern societies and future support for military missions. In G. C. de Nooy (Ed.), *The Clausewitzian dictum and the future of Western military strategy* (pp. 59–74). The Hague: Kluwer Law International.

8

Organizational Behavior and the U.S. Peacekeeper

Jeffrey L. Thomas and Carl Andrew Castro

INTRODUCTION

The principal role of a military psychologist is to promote and maintain the health and well-being of soldiers. Military psychologists perform this role in many ways, ranging from clinical treatment and care to the application of research findings to organizational policies and procedures. In short, military psychologists work where they are needed, or said differently, where soldiers are located. Today, this has meant a focus on peacekeeping missions. Peacekeeping missions are certainly not new (see Langholtz, 1998). However, the sheer number, and intensity, of peacekeeping missions has resulted in military psychologists focusing their research efforts on these types of deployments with the goal of applying psychological, sociological, and even psychiatric principles to the stressors faced by peacekeepers. The central question has been, "How do peacekeeping deployments affect soldier and unit well-being?"

In this chapter we focus on the role of the organization in promoting and maintaining the well-being of the peacekeeper. We argue that the organization engages in numerous behaviors, through its policies and procedures, which can either attenuate or exacerbate the impact of the stressors that the peacekeeper must adapt to and overcome. Over the past few years, researchers have identified a number of these peacekeeping stressors that directly impact on the psychological well-being of the peacekeeper. However, because the nature of these stressors, which can run the gamut from boredom to the fear of injury or death, is critical to our discussion of the value of organizational behavior in maintaining the well-being of peacekeepers, we begin our discussion here.

PEACEKEEPING STRESSORS

It is important to place the stressors encountered by peacekeepers in the appropriate context. Although some have suggested that the peacekeeping environment introduces soldiers to "unique" stressors, our contention is that all peacekeeping stressors can also be found in combat environments. Indeed, all known humanitarian, training, and even garrison stressors can be found in combat environments. Moreover, stressors that occur in peacekeeping environments might well overlap to some extent with the other environments as well, that is, with humanitarian, training, and garrison environments. See Figure 8.1 for a schematic representation of these relationships. Notice that, according to our view, all military stressors can be found in combat, and peacekeeping stressors, indeed all other environmentally related stressors, represent a subset of them. Furthermore, we propose, for example, that all peacekeeping or humanitarian stressors will be found in combat, but that not all combat stressors will be found in peacekeeping or humanitarian environments.

Certainly, peacekeeping missions do differ from combat. What distinguishes peacekeeping missions from combat is not the presence of unique stressors, but the different "constellation of stressors" present in each environment. For example, the most important stressors in combat certainly are fear of being killed or maimed, fear of displaying cowardice in front of your comrades, or anxiety over killing another human being (Stouffer et al., 1949). For peacekeeping missions, the constellation of stressors is quite different. For peacekeeping, the most prevalent stressors are boredom, isolation, cultural deprivation, separation from family and friends, and perhaps unclear or unachievable missions or objectives. All of these peacekeeping stressors, however, are also present in combat, and some of them are also present during training exercises and hu-

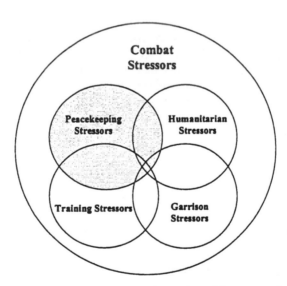

Figure 8.1 Venn Diagram Illustrating the Relationship of the Major Classes of Military Stressors

manitarian missions, as well as in a garrison environment. And although there are certainly other peacekeeping stressors than the ones just listed, the point we are making is they are not unique to peacekeeping. Rather, we believe peacekeeping stressors are best viewed as representing a constellation of stressors with multiple sources with varying levels of intensity that are subsumed under the broader construct of military-related stressors.

Failure to appropriately identify the correct type of military deployment with its concomitant stressors can lead to confusion when interpreting research findings. An example of such confusion can be seen in a study describing the psychiatric symptomatology of U.S. soldiers who participated in Operation Restore Hope in Somalia (Orsillo, Roemer, Litz, Ehlich, & Friedman, 1998). These investigators wrote, "although the military operation in Somalia was considered to be a *humanitarian* mission, a significant proportion of soldiers were exposed to significant, *war-zone* [combat] related stressors . . . symptoms of hostility, psychoticism, depression, and paranoid ideation appeared to be the most common psychiatric reactions to the *peacekeeping* mission in Somalia" (italics added; Orsillo et al., 1998, pp. 621–622). Notice that these researchers are unsure whether the mission to Somalia was a humanitarian mission or combat mission, and end up referring to it as a peacekeeping mission. In point of fact, the mission to Somalia did begin as a humanitarian aid mission, the mission being to guard the truck convoys delivering food to the starving Somalis. The local "warlords," however, did not approve of this and began attacking the U.S. forces guarding the convoys. Thus the mission to Somalia began as a humanitarian mission and ended in a combat operation; that is why all the U.S. soldiers who served in Somalia wear the right shoulder combat patch. The mission to Somalia was never a peacekeeping mission; therefore any reference to the psychological effects of the Somalia mission properly belong to that of combat and not that of peacekeeping missions, or even humanitarian missions for that matter.

The mission in Somalia highlights the shifting nature inherent in all military operations. As seen in Somalia, missions can begin as humanitarian and end in combat. In the case of Operation Restore Democracy in Haiti, quite the opposite was true. The mission began as a combat mission, and while the soldiers were in the air on their way to Haiti preparing to attack the governmental forces, a peace initiative was agreed to and the soldiers landed in Haiti as peacekeepers as part of Operation Uphold Democracy (see Halverson & Bliese, 1996). Therefore, a key challenge faced by researchers, clinicians, and military planners in preparing soldiers for peacekeeping deployments is that they must realize the nature of the mission can change suddenly and without warning. Thus the stressors faced by "peacekeepers" can range widely from monotony and boredom to the traditional stressors encountered in combat. Understanding the stressors therefore during these critical transitions becomes extremely important.

ORGANIZATIONAL BEHAVIOR

Having briefly discussed a general framework of deployment stressors, we now turn to the central focus of the chapter, the role of the military organization in the interplay between the peacekeeper and their overall well-being and functioning. In our discussion of this topic, we borrow from theory and literature in organizational psychology. Specifically, we focus on organizational behavior (see Stroh, Northcraft, & Neale, 2001, for an excellent introduction) and how organizational behavior plays a critical role for peacekeepers and units deployed on peacekeeping missions. What part does the military organization play in facilitating peacekeeper attitudes, well-being, mission legitimacy, and performance of duty? How do peacekeeper perceptions of organizational and leader behavior affect their commitment to their unit and leaders, and their intent to stay in the military? What should military planners and leaders be aware of during a peacekeeping deployment? These are the questions we address in the remainder of this chapter.

We must first, however, offer one caveat. The data reported here were collected with U.S. Army soldiers serving in Kosovo. Although we offer other evidence that military organizational behavior can have an impact on soldier well-being and functioning, our focus is on the Kosovo deployment. It serves as our point of reference. Nevertheless, the heart of the matter remains the same for any military deployment and certainly applies to other national militaries as well. Does the military organization mitigate or exacerbate soldier well-being and functioning when on a peacekeeping mission? It is our hope that our analysis will provide some insight for all military organizations planning for or taking part in a peacekeeping deployment.

We begin our discussion by presenting a brief description of what we believe is the most germane aspect of organizational behavior to apply: social exchange theory. Then we note two particular aspects of social exchange theory that are apropos in the understanding of how peacekeeping stressors can be mitigated or exacerbated by the organization: perceived organizational support (POS) and perceived organizational justice (POJ). We then present a peacekeeping adjustment model highlighting how organizational behavior impacts peacekeeper well-being. Next, we provide specific examples of how military organizational behavior influences soldier well-being based on our study of U.S. soldiers deployed to Kosovo. Lastly, we discuss the implications of these findings followed by some recommendations in the form of key issues that military planners and leaders need to be aware of when engaged in or planning peacekeeping operations.

The Application of Social Exchange Theory

We base our assertions regarding how military organizations may have a substantial impact on soldier and unit well-being and functioning on the norm of reciprocity (Gouldner, 1960) that is pervasive in social exchange theory (Blau, 1964). Simply put, it is the golden rule applied to how employees and organizations interact. When an employee is treated well by the organization, and vice versa, the norm of reciprocity necessitates that favorable treatment is returned to the donor—the employee or organization—in order to achieve a balanced relationship. It is in precisely these simple terms that many researchers of organizational behavior use to describe the intricate relationship between employee attitudes, motivation, and behavior within their organization (e.g., Levinson, 1965). Thus there is an obligation on the part of the recipient to compensate favorable treatment by acting in ways that are valued and reinforced by the organization. For instance, an employee may be strongly motivated to maintain a positive image in the organization as a future means to obtain more favorable treatment. In this way, the reciprocity norm lays a conceptual basis to describe how the interpersonal relationships between employees and organizations are mutually reinforced, and, in the case of the perception of inequitable treatment, how it may be mutually disintegrated. Moreover, Levinson maintains (as cited in Eisenberger, Cummings, Armeli, & Lynch, 1997, p. 812) that, "employees view their employment as a reciprocal-exchange relationship, one that may encourage the attribution of benevolent or malevolent intent of the organization. When the organization is personified through attributions, leaders and organizational planners may be perceived as agents of the organization in terms of its policies, norms, culture, and the power each exerts." Under Blau's social exchange theory and the norm of reciprocity, Eisenberger, Huntington, Hutchison, and Sowa (1986) proposed that perceived organizational support provides a theoretical framework for how military organizations' behavior in a peacekeeping deployment may be related to soldier and unit well-being and functioning.

Perceived Organizational Support

In contrast to researchers who examine the commitment of employees to an organization (e.g., Meyer & Allen, 1991), perceived organizational support (POS) researchers are interested in understanding the organization's commitment to the employee (e.g., Shore & Wayne, 1993). POS is an extension of social exchange theory built on reciprocity between the employee and the employer. Eisenberger et al. (1986) coined the phrase POS, which refers to employees' general perception about how much their contributions and well-being are valued by the organization. Specifically, employees form general perceptions about how much they are valued by the organization based on whether the organization meets their needs for approval, affiliation, and esteem. In addition, employees also ascertain the organization's willingness to recognize greater individual employee effort with more individual recognition and rewards. The notion here is that feeling valued by the organization leads to a reciprocal feeling toward the organization through employee self-identity, and consequently, to positive outcomes for both.

Indeed, a good deal of research exists demonstrating significant links between POS and many positive performance outcomes: attendance (Eisenberger, Fasolo, & Davis-LaMastro, 1990); job performance appraisals (Wayne & Ferris, 1990); organizational citizenship behaviors (Shore & Wayne, 1993); turnover intentions (Guzzo, Noonan, & Elron, 1994); organizational commitment (Robinson, Kraatz, & Rousseau, 1994); and low role conflict and ambiguity (Jones, Flynn, & Kelloway, 1995). Thus POS taps into an employee's willingness to repay the organization in terms of positive regard, and in many instances, as cited earlier, tangible performance outcomes.

In terms of relevance for the peacekeeper, we suggest that perceived organizational support is the best conceptual way to characterize organizational military behavior, one that is based on reciprocal social exchange with the individual peacekeeper. Generally speaking, POS is a commitment measure, but it is distinct in that it assesses the organization's commitment to the employee. This can be of particular importance for the peacekeepers who find themselves in a stressful environment with ambiguities, which is often the case (see Britt, 1998). Any perception that the organization is not reciprocating in its commitment to the peacekeeper can result in adverse peacekeeper functioning, cohesion, morale, and overall well-being, which, in turn, can lead to decrements in performance.

Of course, the literature just cited provides examples where employees perceive *high* organizational support. What about situations where employees perceive *low* organizational support? Under the stress experienced in peacekeeping, innocuous organizational behavior may be perceived as malicious. Levinson (1965) notes that employees may view their employment as an exchange relationship that takes shape through the attributions the employee makes about the benevolent or malevolent intent of the organization. The policies, norms, and culture of an organization can serve to reinforce either benevolent or malevolent intent depending on whether they reflect the organization's value of the employees. Peacekeepers who repeatedly feel undercompensated or undervalued by the organizational unit may choose to lessen their investment in their duty. Similarly, the organizational unit may be placed in a difficult situation by constraining actions and policies that are seen as misguided and not in the best interest of peacekeepers. Whether from the peacekeeper or unit perspective, this can breed a cycle of reciprocal wariness (Lynch, Eisenberger, & Armeli, 1999) that can engulf an organizational unit and result in dysfunction. To the extent to which higher echelon units are perceived as valuing individual peacekeeper contributions and well-being, the more resilient peacekeepers will be in the face of adversity experienced in peacekeeping environments.

Perceived Organizational Justice

Another important aspect of social exchange relevant at the organizational level in the military is perceived organizational justice (POJ). Justice research in organizational psychology treats fairness as a socially constructed variable, one that is based on individual perceptions of the fairness of allocation of rewards and/or policies and processes. For an excellent review of organizational justice research, see Colquitt, Conlon, Wesson, Porter, and Ng (2001). We briefly describe the three most often researched areas of organizational justice: distributive justice (Homans, 1961), procedural justice (Thibaut & Walker, 1975; Leventhal, 1980), and interactional justice (Bies & Moag, 1986). We believe that POJ, like POS, can either mitigate or exacerbate soldier stress appraisal and, subsequently, important soldier outcomes (e.g., well-being, organizational commitment).

Distributive Justice

In short, distributive justice can be thought of as the end outcome or payoff. Distributive justice was the first work in the psychology of justice and grew out of Homans's (1961) equity theory. Equity theory states that people engage in a comparison process wherein they compare ratios of their own perceived outcomes given their own perceived inputs to the corresponding ratios of comparison others. When there is an inequality between one's own ratio and comparison others, individuals with the higher ratio may feel guilt and modify their outputs/inputs to restore equity. Likewise, individuals with lower ratios will feel anger and frustration and attempt to reduce this by modifying their own output/input ratio. Thus people restore equity via psychological and/or behavioral means.

Leventhal (1980) built on Homan's work and offered his Justice Judgment Model. In it, he explains conditions under which people employ justice norms. He makes a key distinction in how these norms are applied by noting the difference between maintaining social harmony and maximizing employee performance. That is, in a social harmony setting, equal allocation is the best norm, whereas, in maximizing performance, equity is the best norm. This model made organizational behavior researchers aware that employee perceptions of distributive justice hinged not only on the allocation decisions, but also on the justice norm implemented.

Procedural Justice

Whereas distributive justice concerns the ends, procedural justice concerns the "means to that end." The earliest work in procedural justice was done by Thibaut and Walker (1975). In a study examining reactions to simulated dispute-resolution procedures, these investigators found that dispute-resolution decisions made allowing people control of the processes were perceived more fairly than decisions not allowing people control. Thibaut and

Walker's work quickly spawned a large interest in understanding fairness as seen as regarding to processes and policies. Leventhal (1980) proposed a set of rules that people use in order to determine the fairness of processes, procedures, and policies. His criteria states that procedures must be unbiased, create consistent allocation across individuals, rely on accurate information, be correctible, represent concerns of all recipients, and be perceived as moral and ethical. Procedural justice's relevance in predicting important work outcomes has been highlighted by researchers such as Greenberg (fairness of performance appraisals, 1986), Folger and Konovosky (organizational commitment and trust in supervision, 1989), Lind and Tyler (attitudes about institutions and authorities, 1988), and Schappe (job satisfaction, 1996), to name a few.

Interactional Justice

Centering on how people are treated interpersonally when policies and procedures are being implemented, interactional justice (Bies & Moag, 1986) is closely linked to procedural justice. Greenberg (1990) has suggested that interactional justice consists of two dimensions of interpersonal treatment: interpersonal justice and informational justice. Interpersonal justice reflects the degree to which authorities or third parties implementing processes or procedures treat individuals respectfully. Informational justice is concerned with the communications and explanations provided to people regarding the implementation of policies and procedures and distribution of the outcomes.

As with perceived organizational support reviewed here, we present data on how perceptions of organizational justice may provide insight into key military organizational behaviors in the U.S. Kosovo peacekeeping mission. However, before turning to these specific organizational behaviors, we need to present a framework to organize our thoughts on why and how POS and POJ are important. In Figure 8.2, we present a peacekeeping adjustment model that includes both individual-level and organizational-level behaviors and characteristics.

PEACEKEEPING ADJUSTMENT MODEL OF ORGANIZATIONAL BEHAVIOR

Whether it is stated a priori or interpreted post priori, all research is guided by working models. In terms of research that investigates soldier reactions to stressors (physical, psychological, environmental) and how these reactions lead to various outcomes, military researchers (e.g., Thomas & Ritzer, 2000) have been strongly influenced by two sources: the work of Lazarus (e.g., Lazarus & Folkman, 1984) and variations of the work stress model developed by Katz and Kahn (1978). Figure 8.2 is our Peacekeeping Adjustment Model that we present as a means of understanding how organizational behavior can influence the

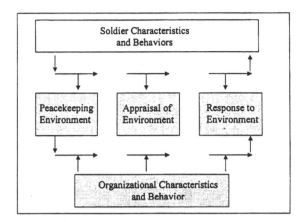

Figure 8.2 Peacekeeping Adjustment Model for Organizational and Soldier Behavior

health and well-being of a peacekeeping deployed force. We have highlighted the model components we discuss later. The key addition to the model proposed by Katz and Kahn (1978) is the examination of organizational behavior as a higher level construct that can influence the stressor-appraisal-response process.

One of the key strengths of our model is that it explicitly differentiates between the objective environment, the peacekeeper's appraisal of the environment, and the peacekeeper's response to that environment. Our model also distinguishes between soldier (or peacekeeper) characteristics and organizational behavior and characteristics, and how these factors are related to other components in the model. This model will serve as a reference point for our discussion of the peacekeeping stress effects on soldiers apropos for examining the health and well-being of soldiers and units in peacekeeping environments.

In our model we also note the difference between the objective environment and the psychological environment. The peacekeeping environment is the objective environment experienced as the same for all soldiers, whereas the appraisal of the environment (the psychological environment) will vary from peacekeeper to peacekeeper. That is, the psychological environment is what is construed in an individual's stress appraisal of the objective environment. For example, peacekeeping soldiers will have varying perceptions of their unit having an uncertain date of return from the peacekeeping deployment. To varying degrees this uncertainty may be stressful to peacekeepers, perhaps for some it will not be stressful at all.

Responses to the environment can manifest themselves in any combination of physiological, behavioral, or affective patterns. These can be thought of as strains placed on individuals who perceive stress from some event in their objective environment. Sticking with the same example provided earlier, a peacekeeper might express lower job satisfaction and commitment as an affective response to having an uncertain return date from the peacekeeping deployment. This, in turn, can covary with changes in reports of mental or physical health (e.g., listlessness, psychosomatic complaints), a problem that any organization strives to avoid in its workforce. Moreover, behaviorally a peacekeeper's duty performance can succumb to stress reactions through poor motivation, causing a peacekeeper to be late for a shift, leave early, or malinger. This would be classified as a behavioral response that could stem from lower motivation due to an uncertain return date or some other perceived stressor of the peacekeeping mission.

The next two features of our peacekeeping model point to potential buffers of stressful appraisals of the environment and their effect on individuals. These are peacekeeper characteristics and behaviors and organizational characteristics and behaviors. These elements play the mitigating role in the model and are best conceptualized as moderators and/or mediators. Peacekeeper characteristics are clearly individual difference variables such as personality, experience, past traumas, and psychosocial history. As an illustration, a peacekeeper who has more deployment experience or is hardier (e.g., Kobasa, 1979) may not be as adversely affected by appraising stress from the peacekeeping mission as a soldier who has less deployment experience or is less hardy. Thought of in this way, individual difference variables like hardiness and experience may inhibit stress responses and bolster peacekeepers' resiliency. Similarly, peacekeepers' behaviors can buffer or exacerbate responses to an environment perceived as stressful. The degree to which peacekeepers take advantage of services offered by the military while on deployment (e.g., morale, welfare and recreation services) will help lessen the impact of peacekeeping stressors.

The final component of the model, organizational characteristics and behavior, is the most appropriate in understanding how a military organization's behavior can impact a peacekeeping deployed unit. Organizational characteristics allow for such things as organizational culture, formal and informal social norms, quality of social interactions, the level of cooperation between organization members, and leadership. Our main focus, however, is on organizational behaviors. We briefly discussed earlier how social exchange theory could offer insight into how organizational behavior can influence peacekeeper functioning and well-being. We propose that the role of perceived organizational support and perceived organizational justice on critical peacekeeper outcomes ranging from military commitment to health and morale is a moderating and/or mediating one. That is, perceived support and justice are group-level constructs that can mitigate responses to stressors in the following form: when both perceptions of support and justice are high, peacekeepers' adverse responses to the peacekeeping deployment stressors will be significantly less than when perceptions of support and justice are low. Later we present examples of military organizational behavior that may act as buffers or conduits of peacekeeping-related stress.

KOSOVO AND ORGANIZATIONAL BEHAVIOR

The data presented here were gathered using both quantitative and qualitative methodologies. Survey and interview data were collected from two studies. The first study was conducted with soldiers deployed from the U.S. Army, Europe as part of the first six-month rotation into Kosovo by American forces in 1999 (see Castro, Bienvenu, Huffman, & Adler, 2000). The second study was conducted with U.S. Army, Europe soldiers deployed to Kosovo in 1999 and 2000 in support of a research protocol examining the effects of operations tempo in the U.S. Army (see Castro, Adler, Bienvenu, Huffman, Dolan, & Thomas, 1998).

To the extent that the organization engages in behaviors that reduce the danger and ambiguity of the situation, for example, POS and POJ will be high. Conversely, to the extent that the organization engages in behaviors that fail to minimize the danger or uncertainty of the situation, POS and POJ will be low. In this section we provide several examples of organizational behaviors for the U.S. peacekeeping mission to Kosovo. In our discussion of these behaviors, we present results from field studies in Kosovo that illustrate how each of these behaviors can affect individual peacekeepers' outcomes. This discussion is by no means intended to be exhaustive, as many other examples of organizational behaviors could be provided. Instead, our goal here is to demonstrate the importance of organizational behavior and how it can impact the well-being and performance of peacekeepers.

The United States has participated in many peacekeeping missions; however, the mission in Kosovo is unique in many ways. First, it is the first peacekeeping mission that the United States has participated in that has followed combat operations in which the nation was a major participant. U.S. forces entered Kosovo immediately following the Kosovo Air War against Yugoslavia while negotiations with the Kosovo Liberation Army (KLA) were still in progress and while the Yugoslavian military were still withdrawing from the Kosovo province. Second, both warring factions, the remaining Serbians and the Albanian Kosovars, were still actively engaged in hostilities, most of which took the form of attacks of retaliation and revenge to include grenade and mortar attacks, daily shootings and bombings, and criminal acts to include arson, murder, and rape. Although U.S. forces were never the direct targets of these attacks, they were constantly exposed to the aftermath of such attacks and participated in the investigation and apprehension of the instigators. Finally, many U.S. soldiers were stationed outside the base camps within the cities at various locations of high visibility such as fire stations, farmhouses, and gymnasiums, thus placing U.S. forces at potential flash points where the remaining Serbians and Albanian Kosovars were most likely to come into conflict.

For these reasons, certainly Kosovo was an extremely dangerous environment for U.S. peacekeepers. In fact, one could argue that the peacekeeping mission in Kosovo was the most potentially dangerous peacekeeping mission that U.S. forces have participated in to date. And as we noted earlier, in such highly stressful situations individuals interpret all organizational behaviors such as policies, procedures, and even statements as direct indicators of the organization's commitment and concern for them. Next we provide three examples of organizational behavior that either directly or indirectly affected the well-being of U.S. peacekeepers deployed to Kosovo.

K + 90

The K + 90 agreement was the most complex and one of the most important of all of the organizational behaviors that the United States engaged in. It directly affected the safety and security of U.S. peacekeepers. At the end of the Kosovo Air War, as agreed to in the Dayton Peace Accords, the Yugoslavian military (composed primarily of Serbians) was to withdraw entirely from the province of Kosovo, and the KLA (comprised primarily of Albanian Kosovars) was to turn in all of their weapons. The time frame for the Yugoslavian military withdrawal was K + 0, meaning that the United States would end its bombing campaign against Yugoslavia only after it completely evacuated its military from Kosovo. The time frame for the KLA to turn in their weapons was 90 days after the Yugoslavian military left Kosovo, or K + 90.

These two measures were important for several reasons. First, it would end the Yugoslavians' military campaign of terror against the civilian Kosovar Albanians by forcing them to leave the region. Second, forcing the Yugoslavian military to withdraw from Kosovo would also end the hostilities of the two warring factions by forcing them apart. Third, requiring the KLA to turn in their weapons would reduce their means for initiating retaliation against the remaining Serbs in Kosovo. Finally, and perhaps most important from the peacekeepers' perspective, requiring the KLA to lay down their weapons would also serve to create a relatively safe environment in Kosovo because there would be no other armed group in Kosovo other than peacekeepers.

Although the Yugoslavian military did fulfill their obligation of the terms of this agreement by withdrawing from Kosovo, the KLA did not. The KLA changed their minds about disarming and insisted on retaining their weapons in order to protect themselves should the Yugoslavian military return. Although this reneging of the KLA to lay down their weapons led to further negotiations between NATO and KLA leaders, the U.S. soldiers in Kosovo were confident that ultimately the KLA would be required to turn in all of their weapons by K + 90. After all, the Yugoslavian military did withdraw from Kosovo as promised, and there was no need for the KLA to retain their weapons because a well-armed peacekeeping force was in Kosovo to protect them against the Yugoslavian military if necessary.

The U.S. peacekeepers, however, were soon disappointed. The K + 90 deadline was extended not once but multiple times, with the KLA still remaining armed. Clearly, the U.S. peacekeepers in Kosovo were beginning to perceive that an important shift in policy had occurred, one they felt was making their job in Kosovo more dangerous. The U.S. peacekeepers did not remain silent. The soldiers and leaders at the company level began to voice their objections to these continued K + 90 extensions. As one company commander stated, KLA members were allowed "to freely roam the province armed to the teeth" and there was "nothing we could do about it." When armed KLA members were stopped, the U.S. peacekeepers were prohibited from confiscating either their weapons or their munitions. Indeed, the U.S. peacekeepers had no means of determining whether a stopped individual was or was not a member of the KLA. As a result, very few arms were ever confiscated, and basically anyone who wanted to go around Kosovo armed could. This led to Kosovo being described as "the Wild West," an analogy to the western U.S. in the nineteenth century when carrying six-shooters and Winchesters was commonplace.

Through continued negotiations, it was eventually agreed that approximately 10,000 former KLA members could retain and carry small arms weapons, primarily pistols and rifles. The U.S. peacekeepers were shocked and outraged. In interviews and discussions with soldiers and leaders in Kosovo shortly after the agreement was announced, it was clear that nearly everyone was angry at the decision. In a postdeployment survey of U.S. peacekeepers deployed to Kosovo, nearly half of the officers (45.1%) and over one third of the noncommissioned officers (NCOs, 34.7%) felt betrayed by the senior military leadership for allowing former KLA members to remain armed. In the this same postdeployment survey, over two thirds (67.1%) of the officers and nearly two thirds of the NCOs (60%) believed that allowing former KLA members to keep their weapons made their job more difficult. As one staff sergeant whom we interviewed in Kosovo noted, "It was about the safety of our soldiers and politics, and politics won." Eventually, dissatisfaction with this new agreement reached a point where soldiers were prohibited from even mentioning the original K + 90 agreement.

It is extremely important to note that those NCOs who were concerned about these policies reported lower morale and well-being than NCOs who did not have policy concerns. Similarly, NCOs who had concerns about the policy in Kosovo were less likely to state they intended to stay in the military (29.4%) compared to those NCOs who did not have any policy concerns (70.6%). These findings provide a clear demonstration that organizational behavior is related to the well-being and retention of peacekeepers.

Officer Rotations

Another aspect of the Kosovo peacekeeping mission that many junior enlisted soldiers and NCOs found difficult to understand was the officer rotation policy. During the deployment, platoon leaders and company commanders were changed or rotated to new positions. These changes occurred not because the current officers were doing a bad job; on the contrary, in most instances their performances had been outstanding in every respect. Instead, the changes were mandated simply to give other officers a chance to perform in these leadership positions. In many respects, this policy was similar to that followed in Vietnam, where officers were also changed frequently in order to enhance or broaden their experiences.

In general, most officers understood and agreed these changes were necessary, with over one half (53.9%) agreeing with the rotation policy. In contrast, neither the junior-enlisted soldiers nor the NCOs agreed with the policy. Only about one quarter (25.1%) of the NCOs agreed with the rotation policy and less than 20% (18.3%) of the junior enlisted did. In numerous interviews, both NCOs and junior-enlisted soldiers felt that officers should have been stabilized in their current positions at least until after the deployment was over. One soldier noted that because the deployment was only for six months it certainly should have been possible to stabilize the officers in their current position if the "powers to be" wanted it to happen. Another soldier rhetorically inquired, "We trained with them, we deployed with them, we know them. Why change now?" The message was clear: many junior-enlisted soldiers and NCOs felt the rotation of officers created unnecessary tumult in units because everyone had to adjust to the leadership style of the new officer.

Again, in a postdeployment survey of soldiers deployed to Kosovo, soldiers who disagreed with the rotation policy were more likely to state that they intended to leave the military than those who agreed with the policy. Surprisingly, soldiers who disagreed with the officer rotation policy were also more likely to score higher on a self-report measure of depression. Although we cannot infer causation, this linkage between policy and health should be followed up in future peacekeeping missions. This is a further demonstration that organizational behavior during a peacekeeping mission may have important links to soldier reports of their well-being and career intentions.

Soldier Recognition

U.S. soldiers are usually recognized for their performance by receiving official military awards. U.S. military awards fall into two general classes: achievement and service. On peacekeeping missions such as Kosovo, all soldiers receive the NATO medal and the Kosovo Campaign medal. The eligibility requirements for those who received these service awards are pretty cut and dried because the requirements are determined by written military policy. The much more difficult issue concerns the eligibility requirements for those who receive achievement medals. Inevitably, there is always the perception on the part of the soldiers that the awarding of achievement medals was handled unfairly.

For instance, in interviews with soldiers following their deployment to Kosovo, many believed there was a quota on the number of achievement medals that could be awarded, thus preventing all deserving soldiers from being recognized. Further, many soldiers felt that those soldiers who did receive an achievement medal were no more deserving than those who did not. Achievement medals are important to soldiers, not because, as Napoleon would say, it is "a bit of ribbon" for soldiers to show off with, but because they count toward promotion points. The paradox here is that what was intended to have a positive effect on soldier morale and motivation instead created hurt feelings, animosity, and a sense of unfairness as these sentiments were expressed during soldier interviews. Surprisingly, in most cases, the senior leadership within the organization was generally unaware of this negative perception on the part of the soldiers.

When U.S. soldiers are in a deployed environment, they receive special pay incentives. Specifically, they receive hazardous duty pay and are placed in a tax-exempt status so they pay no federal taxes while serving in a deployed environment. In addition, if soldiers reenlist while deployed, their reenlistment bonus is tax exempt. In total, these special pays are relatively modest; without a doubt, however, they do convey to soldiers a sense of commitment and appreciation on the part of the military and the country for their service in Kosovo. This is especially important given that U.S. peacekeepers are not motivated by money in order to serve. This does not mean that such incentives are unimportant or unappreciated; it is simply that the value of special pay is to be found in its secondary effects on soldiers, such as giving them a sense of feeling appreciated for their service and sacrifices rather than the amount of money itself. This is true because the amounts of these special pays are not sufficient to alter the lifestyle of the deployed peacekeepers once they return from the deployment.

CONSIDERATIONS FOR MILITARY PLANNERS AND SENIOR STAFFERS

The discussion thus far has focused on the conceptual and theoretical aspects of how peacekeepers are affected by various organizational behaviors, such as policies and procedures. We provided several examples from the Kosovo peacekeeping mission to demonstrate in very concrete terms how such organizational behavior can directly affect the peacekeeper. In this final section we highlight the implications of our analysis for the operational planners and commanders as they prepare for and deploy to peacekeeping environments. It is important to appreciate that operational planners and commanders engage in behaviors through the development of policies, plans, procedures, and various other mechanisms that provide the peacekeepers with the necessary guidance, means, and acknowledgments for performing the peacekeeping mission (see Table 8.1). One may think of these three categories of organization support as precursors to organizational justice (or perhaps more appropriately, fairness). Let us consider each of these three important types of organizational supports in turn.

Table 8.1
The Three Major Categories of Organizational Support for Military Operations with Key Examples

---

Guidance
- Rules of engagement (ROE)
- Treaties, accords (e.g., K + 90)
- Commander's intent (expectations, definition of mission success, end state)
- Freedom of movement
- Autonomy
- Departure date/Return date

Means
- Training
- Equipment
- Leadership
- Order of battle
- Location of forces
- Work environment
- Quality of life indicators (e.g., housing, food, latrines, etc.)
- Interaction with local civilians

Acknowledgments
- Special pay
- Awards/Recognition
- Leave/Pass policy (i.e., R&R)
- Extra duties
- Recovery period

Guidance

Peacekeepers require clear, unambiguous guidance in order to accomplish their peacekeeping duties. Guidance can occur in many forms and includes such things as the unit mission statement, the objectives of the peacekeeping mission, the commander's intent, the rules of engagement (ROE), and the stipulation of any treaties, agreements, or accords that prescribe the rules of conduct that the peacekeepers must follow (Britt, 1998). Our discussion of the K + 90 agreement clearly belongs to the last category. Guidance maps directly onto the concept of interactional justice or fairness, and it is useful to think of guidance as a precursor to interactional fairness. In the K + 90 example, the U.S. peacekeepers felt the leadership ignored their safety and personal concerns by allowing former KLA members to retain their small-arms weapons. This perceived lack of concern on the part of the U.S. peacekeepers was further viewed as an assault on their dignity and respect as soldier peacekeepers. Again, we found correlational relationships between soldier views of K + 90 and self-reported health and military commitment following the Kosovo deployment.

Means

Policymakers, commanders, and operational planners must ensure that the peacekeepers have the necessary means to accomplish the mission assigned to them. Means includes such things as providing the peacekeepers with the necessary equipment to conduct the peacekeeping mission, the appropriate training, adequate housing, food, and other quality of life items, as well as the best leaders available. Means is the precursor that is related to the concept of procedural fairness or justice. Here procedures must be consistent, accurate, without bias, and justifiable. In the example we provided for the Kosovo peacekeeping mission, the soldiers and NCOs believed they were initially provided the best leaders. However, the officer rotation policy took proven leaders out of key leadership positions and replaced them with unproven leaders. Unfortunately, the reasons given for this decision were viewed by soldiers as capricious and unnecessary. In this case, rotating officers before the end of the deployment resulted in perceived procedural injustice. And, as noted, this too was linked with the self-reported health and well-being of the U.S. peacekeepers.

Acknowledgments

Of all the support that peacekeepers need in order to conduct their mission successfully, one would think that acknowledgment would be the easiest to provide. After all, special pays, military awards, and numerous recognition programs have already been established for such purposes. Nevertheless, time and again, a majority of the soldiers we talk to report dissatisfaction with how these programs are implemented, and as just discussed, the peacekeepers deployed to Kosovo were no exception. Acknowledgment might be viewed as a precursor to distributive justice or fairness. When peacekeepers feel their contributions are not appropriately acknowledged and rewarded, or that others are undeservingly recognized, cynicism sets in, or distributive injustice occurs. As predicted by social exchange theory, this may lead to a reciprocal lack of commitment on the part of the peacekeeper to either remain in the military or to perform at his or her highest level.

Deployment Stressors and Organizational Behavior

These three concepts regarding organizational support—guidance, means, and acknowledgments—should never be viewed in isolation because all are without doubt interrelated, as a change in one certainly affects the status of another. Moreover, the stressors that the peacekeepers encounter should also be kept in mind because all organizational support provided to the peacekeeper should be directed at addressing these stressors, which in turn will directly enhance the likelihood of mission success. Thus, as the nature of the peacekeeping mission changes, the guidance, means, and acknowledgments should also change to reflect the new and/or emerging dynamics of the mission. This then requires that commanders, operational planners, and policymakers continuously reevaluate existing procedures and policies in light of the current deployment environment. As the peacekeeping environment changes, there should be concomitant changes in the guidance, means, and acknowledgments. Of course, it is ultimately the responsibility of the commander to ensure that such analyses of the peacekeeping environment take place and that necessary changes in organizational support occur. This way, organizational support will align with the existing peacekeeping stressors, further enhancing the well-being and performance of the peacekeepers.

FINAL COMMENT

Organizational behavior matters to the well-being of peacekeepers. Policies, procedures, and all the other mechanisms that prescribe the conduct of the peacekeeper can and do affect the peacekeepers' health and well-being, and ultimately their performance. This fact should never be forgotten or minimized because it is the peacekeeper, the son or daughter, mother or father, who ultimately determines whether the peacekeeping mission will succeed or fail.

NOTE

The views expressed in this paper are those of the authors and do not necessarily represent the official policy or position of the Department of Defense or the U.S. Army Medical Command. The Kosovo findings described in this paper were collected under WRAIR Research Protocol 700, "A Human Dimensions Assessment of the Impact of OPTEMPO on the Forward-Deployed Soldier," Castro, C. A., Adler, A. B., Bienvenu, R. V., Huffman, A. H., Dolan, C. A., and Thomas, J. L., which was funded by the Research Area Directorate for Military Operational Medicine, U.S. Army Medical Research and Materiel Command, Fort Detrick, Maryland.

REFERENCES

Bies, R. J., & Moag, J. F. (1986). Interactional justice: Communication criteria of fairness. In R. J. Lewicki, B. H. Sheppard, & M. H. Bazerman (Eds.), *Research on negotiations in organizations* (Vol. 1, pp. 43–55). Greenwich, CT: JAI Press.

Blau, P. M. (1964). *Exchange and power in social life*. New York: Wiley.

Britt, T. W. (1998). Psychological ambiguities in peacekeeping. In H. J. Langholtz (Ed.), *The psychology of peacekeeping* (pp. 111–128). Westport, CT: Praeger.

Castro, C. A., Adler, A. B., Bienvenu, R. V., Huffman, A. H., Dolan, C. A., & Thomas, J. L. (1998). *Walter Reed Army Institute of Research Protocol #700: A human dimensions assessment of the impact of OPTEMPO on the forward-deployed soldier*.

Colquitt, J. A., Conlon, D. E., Wesson, M. J., Porter, C. O. L. H., & Ng, K. Y. (2001). Justice at the millennium: A meta-analytic review of 25 years of organizational justice research. *Journal of Applied Psychology, 86*, 425–445.

Eisenberger, R., Cummings, J., Armeli, S., & Lynch, P. (1997). Perceived organizational support, discretionary treatment, and job satisfaction. *Journal of Applied Psychology, 8,* 812–820.

Eisenberger, R., Fasolo, P., & Davis-LaMastro, V. (1990). Perceived organizational support and employee diligence, commitment, and innovation. *Journal of Applied Psychology, 75,* 51–59.

Eisenberger, R., Huntington, R., Hutchison, S., & Sowa, D. (1986). Perceived organizational support. *Journal of Applied Psychology, 71,* 500–507.

Folger, R., & Konovosky, M. (1989). Effects of procedural and distributive justice on reactions to pay raise decisions. *Academy of Management Journal, 32,* 115–130.

Gouldner, A. W. (1960). The norm of reciprocity: A preliminary statement. *American Sociological Review, 25,* 161–178.

Greenberg, J. (1986). Determinants of perceived fairness of performance evaluations. *Journal of Applied Psychology, 71,* 340–342.

Greenberg, J. (1990). Organizational justice: Yesterday, today, and tomorrow. *Journal of Management, 16,* 399–432.

Guzzo, R. A., Noonan, K. A., & Elron, E. (1994). Expatriate managers and the psychological contract. *Journal of Applied Psychology, 79,* 617–626.

Halverson, R. R., & Bliese, P. D. (1996). Determinants of soldiers' support for Operation Uphold Democracy. *Armed Forces & Society, 23,* 81–96.

Homans, G. (1961). *Social behaviour: Its elementary forms.* London: Routledge & Keegan Paul.

Jones, B., Flynn, D. M., & Kelloway, E. K. (1995). Perception of support from the organization in relation to work stress, satisfaction, and commitment. In S. L. Sauter and L. R. Murphy (Eds.), *Organizational risk factors for job stress* (pp. 41–52). Washington, DC: American Psychological Association.

Katz, D., & Kahn, R. L. (1978). *The social psychology of organizations* (2nd ed.). New York: Wiley.

Kobasa, S. C. (1979). Stressful life events, personality, and health: An inquiry into hardiness. *Journal of Personality and Social Psychology, 37,* 1–11.

Langholtz, H. J. (1998). The evolving psychology of peacekeeping. In H. J. Langholtz (Ed.), *The psychology of peacekeeping* (pp. 3–15). Westport, CT: Praeger.

Lazarus, R. S., & Folkman, S. (1984). *Stress, appraisal, and coping.* New York: Springer.

Leventhal, G. S. (1980). What should be done with equity theory? New approaches to the study of fairness in social relationships. In K. Gergen, M. Greenberg, & R. Willis (Eds.), *Social exchange: Advances in theory and research* (pp. 27–55). New York: Plenum.

Levinson, H. (1965). Reciprocation: The relationship between man and organization. *Administrative Science Quarterly, 9,* 370–390.

Lind, E. A., & Tyler, T. R. (1988). *The social psychology of procedural justice.* New York: Plenum Press.

Lynch, P. D., Eisenberger, R., & Armeli, S. (1999). Perceived organizational support: Inferior-versus-superior performance by wary employees. *Journal of Applied Psychology, 84,* 467–483.

Meyer, J. P., & Allen, N. J. (1991). A three-component conceptualization of organizational commitment. *Human Resource Management Review, 1,* 61–89.

Orsillo, S. M., Roemer, L., Litz, B. T., Ehlich, P., & Friedman, M. J. (1998). Psychiatric symptomatology associated with contemporary peacekeeping: An examination of post-mission functioning among peacekeepers in Somalia. *Journal of Trau-matic Stress, 11,* 611–625.

Robinson, S. L., Kraatz, M. S., & Rousseau, D. M. (1994). Changing obligations and the psychological contract: A longitudinal study. *Academy of Management Journal, 37,* 137–152.

Schappe, S. P. (1996). Bridging the gap between procedural knowledge and positive employee attitudes. *Group & Organization Management, 21,* 337–364.

Shore, L. M., & Wayne, S. J. (1993). Commitment and employee behavior: Comparison of affective organizational commitment and continuance commitment with per-ceived organizational support. *Journal of Applied Psychology, 78,* 774–780.

Stroh, L. K., Northcraft, G. B., & Neale, M. A. (2001). *Organizational behavior: A man-agement change* (3rd ed.). Hillsdale, NJ: Erlbaum.

Stouffer, S. A., Lumsdaine, A. A., Lumsdaine, M. H., Williams, R. M., Jr., Smith, M. B., Janis, I. L., Star, S. A., & Cottrell, L. S. (1949). *The American soldier: Combat and its aftermath.* Princeton, NJ: Princeton University Press.

Thomas, J. L., & Ritzer, D. R. (2000). Leader information moderating strains associated with work unpredictability in the U.S. Army. *Proceedings from the 41st Annual International Military Testing Association Conference, 229–234.* Edinburgh, Scotland.

Thibaut, J., & Walker, L. (1975). *Procedural justice: A psychological analysis.* Hillsdale, NJ: Erlbaum.

Wayne, S. J., & Ferris, G. R. (1990). Influence tactics, affect, and exchange quality in supervisor-subordinate interactions: A laboratory experiment and field study. *Journal of Applied Psychology, 75,* 487–499.

IV
Health Psychology in Peacekeeping

9

The Nature of Peacekeeping Stressors

Amy B. Adler, Brett T. Litz, and Paul T. Bartone

Peacekeeping duty can be highly stressful and can lead to a range of negative health and performance consequences. Organizations that participate in peacekeeping operations seek to prevent or minimize related ill effects among their members, typically through enhanced training programs. But in order for training and prevention programs to be effective, the nature of the stressors encountered on peacekeeping missions must be much better understood than they are currently. This chapter seeks to clarify the nature of peacekeeping stressors and how best to conceptualize them.

When military members deploy on a peacekeeping mission, they are confronted with three basic challenges. First, they experience a separation from home or garrison life. Second, they assume the duties of peacekeeping. Third, they must live for a time in the deployed environment. These combinations of stressors can be characterized in several different ways. Generally, the stressors of peacekeeping encompass occupation-related stressors found in other kinds of work environments, including war-zone-related stressors, minor hassles and inconveniences, role strain or stress, and often, a combination of all of these types of stressors. This chapter explores (1) how stress theory informs the structuring of the construct of peacekeeping stressors, (2) how peacekeeping stressors encompass both potentially traumatic and nontraumatic stressors, and (3) how peacekeeping stressors can be best conceptualized for future research.

WHAT IS STRESS?

A stressor is some event external to the individual that the individual perceives as demanding, frustrating, or in some way exceeding his or her available coping resources. According to Lazarus and Folkman (1984), an event or situation is considered stressful when it is perceived by the individual as taxing or exceeding coping resources, competencies, values, or self-concept. Individuals appraise external events through two basic processes: *primary appraisal* determines the degree to which a threat is present, and *secondary appraisal* determines the options for coping with that external event. Some stress theories emphasize the subjective evaluation of stress in determining the presence of a stressor; others define stressors in terms of their negative impact on functioning or health (Dohrenwend & Dohrenwend, 1980). Regardless of the relative emphasis placed on the stressor-response connection, the stress response includes the person's psychological and physiological activation (e.g., arousal of the central and peripheral nervous systems) that helps manage the threat or demand. This activation of the stress response can vary in intensity and duration.

Exposure to extreme stressors can lead to posttraumatic stress disorder (PTSD) and other forms of psychopathology (McFarlane & de Girolamo, 1996). However, stress reactions can also be fleeting and coped with effectively. Therefore, the relationship between exposure to stressful conditions or stressors and stress reactions is not isomorphic. Exposure to severe and catastrophic stressors leads to PTSD only in a relatively small percentage of those exposed, reinforcing the importance of mediating variables such as cognitive appraisal and construction, temperament, personality, coping styles and skills, and social context. Furthermore, a stress reaction is not in and of itself indicative of abnormal behavior or psychopathology. Indeed, stressor exposure and stress reactions can lead to personal growth (see Britt, this volume).

In the case of peacekeepers, there is the potential for exposure to both chronic and acute stressors, and for responses reflecting the activation of a coping response and/or some impairment in functioning. In order to understand the impact of deploying on peacekeepers, and before the role of variables that moderate the impact of deployment stressors on peacekeepers can be fully explored, we need to delineate the nature of peacekeeping stressors.

WHAT MAKES PEACEKEEPING STRESSFUL?

According to Lazarus and Folkman (1984), there are aspects of situations, contexts, and environments that are associated with risk for stress. These are the components of situations that, when coupled with individual differences in personality and coping, determine their stressfulness. As defined by Lazarus and Folkman, these components include (1) novelty, (2) predictability, (3) temporal factors including imminence, duration, and temporal uncertainty, and (4) ambiguity. All of these components can be found in peacekeeping deployments, especially predictability, ambiguity, and novelty (Litz, 1996).

Several of these situational factors have already been examined in peacekeeping stress research. In the case of novelty, for example, some evidence indicates that soldiers who have already been deployed on a peacekeeping mission have less difficulty adapting than soldiers for whom the mission is their first deployment (Martinez, Huffman, Adler, & Castro, 1999). Novelty can be operationalized in several different ways, however, and includes prior experience with particular events that occur during peacekeeping as well as experience with particular emotions associated with peacekeeping (e.g., frustration, help-lessness). Lazarus and Folkman (1984) propose that novelty contributes to the stressful nature of a situation particularly when there is potential for harm or danger, both of which exist in a peacekeeping environment.

Another key variable, predictability, has been identified as an important con-struct for military personnel in a series of studies examining the impact of operations tempo on U.S. soldiers stationed in Germany (Castro & Adler, 2001). In the case of peacekeeping, predictability is relevant across several domains including the basic parameters of the deployment: What will the job actually consist of? And how will the former warring factions behave? Lazarus and Folkman (1984) describe lack of predictability as particularly problematic if individuals cannot control the situation and if there are expectations that the situation should have been predictable. In the case of peacekeeping, it is unclear whether or not these two conditions exist—peacekeepers will certainly try to exert control over their environment, consistent with their military training, but their expectations will vary across individuals and specific peacekeeping missions.

Temporal factors consist of three basic characteristics that can alter the degree to which an event is perceived as stressful. The first temporal factor, imminence, refers to the degree to which an event is anticipated. In the case of peacekeeping stressors, the degree to which a peacekeeper can anticipate a difficult stressor varies depending on the event. Some events (such as guarding mass grave sites) can be anticipated (e.g., McCarroll et al., 1993), and thus evoke the complex psychological response that accompanies the anticipation of delayed events. The lack of anticipation, however, can also be stressful when soldiers do not have the opportunity to marshal their coping resources in dealing with certain stress-ors, such as rejection by the local population.

The second temporal characteristic, duration, suggests that the longer the stressor lasts, the more difficult it is for the individual because he or she may become exhausted. However, longer duration does not necessarily result in greater stress if the individual habituates to that stressor. In the case of peace-keeping stressors, both of these aspects of duration, exhaustion and habituation, may occur. Peacekeeping deployments can wear on the soldier, as evidenced by the link between the length of a peacekeeping deployment and psychological symptomatology described by Huffman, Adler, and Castro (1999), but peace-keepers can also develop new coping strategies and adjust to life on a deploy-ment (Dolan, Crouch, West, & Castro, 2001).

The third temporal component involves temporal uncertainty. This situation has been a critical issue for peacekeeping deployments in the past. Bartone, Adler, and Vaitkus (1998) describe this exact difficulty faced by soldiers prior to their deployment to Croatia as part of Operation Provide Promise, the UN mission in the former Yugoslavia. At that time, there was great uncertainty not just about who exactly would be deploying but also when the deployment would actually occur and when soldiers would be returning. As such deployments become more routinized, the stress around the departure and return dates is likely to diminish.

The final aspect of a situation that can intensify stress is the degree to which there is ambiguity. Ambiguity is considered present when "the information necessary for appraisal is unclear or insufficient" (Lazarus & Folkman, 1984, p. 103). In the case of peacekeeping, lack of clear information can be a challenge in formal ways (e.g., the chain of command for specially constituted international task forces) and informal ways (e.g., applying rules of engagement in the midst of a chaotic encounter with the local population; see Britt, 1998).

The framework provided by Lazarus and Folkman (1984) suggests the mechanisms that account for why certain experiences are considered stressful. We propose that threats to physical, psychological, and spiritual integrity are also important characteristics of stressful events needed to account comprehensively for the stress response mechanism. At the basic physical level, exposure to discomfort, pain, and injury result in these experiences being catalogued as a stressor. At the psychological level, threats to one's sense of coherence, to one's sense of self in the world, are also components of situations that can result in stress. These existential concerns, when operationalized in a peacekeeping environment, include not being able to intervene to alleviate suffering despite one's identity as a peacekeeper or to punish perpetrators despite one's identity as a soldier. Such a stressor may be identified as role conflict (see Britt, 1998), but is worth explicitly introducing in any detailed discussion of peacekeeping stressors. Finally, atrocities that represent the most inhumane of acts, such as mass killings and other activities associated with "ethnic cleansing," are capable of stressing observers at a fundamental level. This fundamental level, whether characterized as psychological or spiritual, entails a qualitatively different kind of stress that is an important factor to consider in understanding stressors associated with peacekeeping operations or other deployments. Such physical, psychological, and spiritual loads can result in more or less stress, depending on their novelty, predictability, imminence and duration, individual coping styles, and primary and secondary appraisals.

Such factors help identify situations, contexts, or events that are stressful for individuals. Based on the Lazarus and Folkman framework, Gal and Jones (1995) developed a model of soldier behavior in combat stress situations and used it to clarify what it is about combat that is stressful for soldiers, and how it gets to be that way. In applying such a framework to peacekeepers, the mechanisms proposed by Lazarus and Folkman can also be used to explain why events are stressful and how they might share characteristics with other types of stressful events. However, these mechanisms do not identify the specific challenges faced by peacekeepers. Every individual, occupational group, or context may have factors in common that underlie stressors (such as novelty or threat), and also specific stressors unique to that particular individual or circumstance. Identifying these specific stressors is critical in order to train peacekeepers with the goal of reducing the novelty of the stressors and to develop policies when possible that minimize ambiguities and uncertainties and increase predictability. Similar to Gal and Jones's (1995) approach, we are guided by a conceptual framework that derives from the Lazarus and Folkman perspective on stress and coping, but we draw on a range of field studies in order to identify the specific potentially stressful situations encountered on peacekeeping operations.

Conceptualizing and Measuring Peacekeeping Stressors

Several studies have assessed stressors and demands unique to peacekeeping roles. Typically, a set of rationally derived stressors is presented in a survey to peacekeepers in the middle or at the end of a deployment. There are usually two rating schemes for these lists. Soldiers are asked to rate the occurrence of such stressors either on a response option for frequency or dichotomously (i.e., experienced or not). Alternatively, peacekeepers rate the degree to which the experience has caused subjective distress. These studies then typically report the frequency with which peacekeepers endorse particular stressor items.

To date, research on peacekeeping stressors has been less than comprehensive. Beyond the way in which stressors are rated by peacekeepers, the strategy for identifying what is stressful is not particularly methodical. The lists of stressors may be restricted to potentially traumatic events, or just to the mundane stressors of living in a deployed environment. At times both of these areas may be assessed by a particular stressor scale, but the topics included are often organized into major areas like low versus high magnitude events, without a careful review of the possible dimensions that comprise the peacekeeping stressors. This occurs perhaps because researchers are asked to respond quickly to a particular deployment or because researchers are attempting to adapt combat scales to the peacekeeping arena.

Given the subjective nature of stress, and the wide variety of demands of various peacekeeping operations, what is required is a systematic bottom-up approach to the assessment of stressors on a peacekeeping operation (Litz, 1996). In planning a comprehensive assessment of peacekeeping stressors, certain issues need to be considered. For example, note that within the two major classes of stressors identified by Lazarus and Folkman (1984), low magnitude daily hassles and potentially traumatic events, there are other categories and gradations of intensity within and between them. For the purpose of organizing the research on peacekeeping stressors, the two major classes (daily hassles and high magnitude stressors) provide a useful heuristic, but such classification is not intended to discount the complexity and gradations of stressful experiences associated with peacekeeping. The level of intensity, the type of stressor, and the various possible responses (i.e., not just PTSD) all need to be taken into account in order to develop a comprehensive understanding of the challenges faced by peacekeepers.

Some peacekeeping deployments entail a high level of threat and exposure to potential trauma, akin to a war zone. However, peacekeeping operations can be fluid, with changing levels of threat. In fact, one of the uniquely stressful aspects of peacekeeping is the unexpected nature of the demands (Litz, 1996), as theorized by Lazarus and Folkman (1984). McFarlane and de Girolamo (1996) developed a model of deployment stressors that emphasizes not only the importance of operational context and individual difference variables but also operationalizes the definitions of high and low intensity stressors with examples. Comprehensive discussions of peacekeeping stressors must take into account that some peacekeeping operations are very stable and relatively safe, whereas others blur the boundary of combat.

PEACEKEEPING STRESSORS

Deployed soldiers, whether in combat or in peacekeeping, may be exposed to both traumatic events and daily hassles. Although beyond the scope of this chapter, much of the research with combat deployments emphasizes potentially traumatic stressors (e.g., engagement in firefights; Fontana, Rosenheck, & Brett, 1992). The degree to which the stressor-related experiences are similar in combat and peacekeeping deployments ranges from highly similar to highly dissimilar. This range exists, in part, because of the varied nature of peace support operations (see Langholtz, 1998, for a review). Some of these stressors tend to be particular to certain peacekeeping deployments (e.g., particular policies, level of physical threat); others overlap across deployments (e.g., boredom, family separation).

Generally, when peacekeeping stressors are assessed, there is a tendency to derive a total stressor score that is then correlated with outcomes (e.g., Schade & Schuffel, 1995) or the specific hassles or stressors involved are not identified (e.g., MacDonald, Chamberlain, Long, Pereira-Laird, & Murfin, 1998). There are, however, some exceptions to this tendency to treat peacekeeping stressors as a single construct. Bache and Hommelgaard (1994) studied Danish soldiers deployed with UNPROFOR in Croatia in 1993 and found that when soldiers reported stress from feelings of powerlessness, they were more likely to report avoidance symptoms from a scale assessing post-traumatic stress symptoms. When soldiers reported stress from having been threatened, they reported high rates of reliving symptoms. The PTSD symptom of hyperalertness was linked to both feeling powerless and threatened.

Consideration of the different types of peacekeeping stressors and their specific impact on military personnel is relatively rare. More typically, studies on peacekeeping have attempted to organize the list of peacekeeping stressors into a conceptual framework (e.g., Bartone et al., 1998). Other researchers have used factor analysis to identify major areas of concern (e.g., Adler, Dolan, & Castro, 2000; Farley, 1996), whereas others have listed out the most frequently endorsed items (e.g., Ritzer, Campbell, & Valentine, 1999). Whereas each of these approaches has its merits both pragmatically and procedurally, one goal of this chapter is to identify the major areas of stress encountered by peacekeepers in order to develop a more comprehensive basis from which to assess stressors. The framework presented in Table 9.1 is a heuristic designed to identify major categories of concern to peacekeepers that summarizes published reports on peacekeeping from a wide range of operations. The items are considered descriptive and overlapping.

Table 9.1
Major Stressor Categories and Examples of Stressors Encountered by Peacekeepers on Deployment

Stressor	Example
Deployed Environment	
Separation from Home	Missing family
	Difficulty communicating home
	Unfamiliar surroundings
Work-Related Stressors	Leadership issues
	Differences in pay
	Lack of meaningful work
	Boredom
Physical Conditions	Climate
	Food
	Privacy
	Latrines
	Hygiene
	Protection from heat or cold
Peacekeeping Duty	
Potentially Traumatic	Snipers
	Mines
	Assault
	Accidents
	Mass graves
	Body handling
	Being taken hostage
Nontraumatic	Uncontrolled mobs
	Conflict at checkpoints
	Witnessing effects of conflict
	Contact with child victims of conflict
	Rejecton by local population
	Teasing/Taunting

A detailed review of the literature on peacekeeping stressors reveals two basic categories of these stressors: the chronic, daily hassles of deployed life and the peacekeeping duty itself. Within the chronic hassles of deployed life there are three basic stressor categories: (1) separation from home, (2) work-related problems, and (3) physical conditions. The second major category, peacekeeping duty, encompasses two areas: (1) potentially traumatic stressors, and (2) non-traumatic stressors. Both of these variables, the deployment life hassles and the peacekeeping duty, comprise the domain of peacekeeping stressors. Personal backgrounds, skills, coping styles, and cognitive appraisals combine with these stressors to produce stress responses unique to each interaction between individuals and the environment. Furthermore, these stressors contain a combination of novelty, unpredictability, and ambiguity that is unique for each particular circumstance and individual.

Deployment Environment

Regardless of what a member of the peacekeeping force is tasked with accomplishing, the mere act of being in a deployed environment means the individual confronts a unique set of deployment-related stressors. The degree to which any one of these may be subjectively experienced as stressful will, of course, vary with individual differences in background, personality, and coping strategy as well as with the actual intensity of the stressors themselves. Peacekeepers bring with them stressors from home (e.g., relationship problems, family members or friends with health problems, financial problems, previous traumatic stress history). Individuals with stressors from home might also be more vulnerable to the impact of stressors during the peacekeeping deployment (e.g., Macdonough, 1991).

Separation from Home

As Bartone and colleagues (1998) describe in their five-dimension model of peacekeeping stressors, isolation, both from family, one's home, and from what is familiar presents a significant challenge to peacekeepers. These challenges range from practical constraints, such as difficulty communicating back home or getting access to news, to the psychological isolation that comes from living in a foreign environment. Some peacekeepers live on military compounds, in tent cities or deteriorated, formerly abandoned buildings, far from familiar homelike settings. The stress of family separation is identified in several studies (e.g., Litz, Orsillo, Friedman, Ehlich, & Batres, 1997; MacDonald et al., 1998; Miller & Moskos, 1995). Farley (1996) also found that family concerns emerged as an important stress factor for Canadian soldiers deployed in support of the UN mission in the former Yugoslavia. Evidence suggests such a stressor is relatively constant across peacekeeping operations. In a comparison of U.S. soldiers deployed in support of Operation Joint Endeavor (OJE) and Operation

Joint Guard (OJG) in the Bosnia theater of operations, for example, 74% and 65%, respectively, of U.S. peacekeepers in the former Yugoslavia reported family separation as a moderate to extreme stressor, respectively (Ritzer et al., 1999).

Work-Related Problems

Any work environment presents challenges regarding core job dimensions (Hackman & Oldham, 1975). Skill variety can be a major stressor for military personnel deployed on relatively stable peacekeeping missions. As Harris and Segal (1985) established in one of the first published studies of peacekeepers, U.S. soldiers deployed on the Multinational Force and Observer (MFO) mission to keep watch at the Egyptian-Israeli border in the Sinai, were profoundly bored during their six-month deployment. The stress of boredom was also evident among the U.S. soldiers in an assessment of U.S. medical personnel assigned to the UNPROFOR mission in Croatia (Bartone et al., 1998) and U.S. Army personnel deployed as part of the first NATO force in Bosnia (Bartone, 1997). Although more than half (53%) of U.S. peacekeepers in Bosnia reported high levels of concern about boredom and repetitive work, only 41% of U.S. soldiers deployed to Kosovo reported the same stressor (Bienvenu, Huffman, Castro, & Adler, 1999).

Other core job dimensions are reflected in work-related stressors faced by peacekeepers. Bartone (1997) described peacekeepers in Bosnia as experiencing heavy workload, little recognition, poor communication, and micromanagement during the early phases of the first NATO mission into Bosnia. Indeed, Canadian peacekeepers in the former Yugoslavia rated work stressors as the most stressful events they experienced, including double standards among military ranks in applying rules, superiors overreacting to situations, and being treated "like kids" (Farley, 1996). Each of these work-related stressors can be found in garrison and civilian work environments as well.

Physical Conditions

The physical conditions of a peacekeeping deployment vary dramatically based on the maturity of the theater of operations. For example, Ritzer et al. (1999) noted that 63% of soldiers surveyed who had deployed in support of the second year of the NATO mission in Bosnia (Operation Joint Guard; OJG) reported no or little concern about living conditions, whereas 49% of those deployed in the first year of the NATO mission (Operation Joint Endeavor; OJE) were unconcerned. Other issues associated with physical conditions that were reported included desire to escape from the environment (e.g., cold, mud, wet), beds, showers, and lack of privacy (reported by 72% of OJE peacekeepers and 60% of OJG peacekeepers).

In their assessment of U.S. soldiers in Somalia, Miller and Moskos (1995) also identified problems with logistical infrastructure as creating significant stress for soldiers. These items included lack of privacy, the looting of food supplies, and having to endure the climate (see also Litz, King, King, Orsillo, & Friedman, 1997). Note that not all peacekeepers experience the same type of environmental stressors. For example, U.S. soldiers deployed on both OJE and OJG to the Balkans did not report significant stress from food or water problems (Ritzer et al., 1999).

U.S. researchers examining stressors faced by peacekeepers in Somalia termed these stressors "low magnitude" (Litz et al., 1997). Although some of these conditions are what military personnel expect from a deployed environment, the presence of these low-level chronic stressors may serve as a backdrop, exacerbating the effects of other more difficult stressors. These stressors have some overlap with what has been characterized as the malevolent environment that permeates a war zone (King, King, Gudanowski, & Vreven, 1995), but also include mundane yet essential components of daily life on a deployment. Such apparently low-magnitude characteristics of the deployed environment range from the type of latrine facilities, the access to toiletry supplies (including toilet paper), hot food, and bedding to protection from cold and wet weather. These kinds of physical stressors may not immediately exhaust or threaten military personnel, but the duration of these stressors can potentially wear down the physical and psychological resilience of deployed personnel.

Peacekeeping Duty or Deployment Incidents

Beyond the challenge of trying to adapt physically and psychologically to living in a deployed environment, peacekeepers face the challenge of the actual work of peacekeeping. Again, the tasks of a peacekeeper vary widely both across deployments and within the context of one deployment. Some personnel go on patrols and deal with former warring factions; others are involved only indirectly by, for example, providing medical or personnel services. Most of the peacekeeping research to date has focused on the stressors experienced by those individuals actively engaged in contacts with former warring factions and local civilians. It must be noted, however, that for some countries like the United States, a sizable portion of their peacekeepers has minimal direct contact with the world outside of the base on which they operate (Britt, Adler, & Bartone, 2001; Caniglia, 2001).

Potentially Traumatic Stressors

In recent years, many peacekeepers have been confronted with direct threats to their physical well-being. The many countries supporting the UN mission in Bosnia and the U.S. experience in Somalia are the prototypes for this kind of direct physical challenge. Many researchers have documented the level of direct threat to life experienced by peacekeepers across many different peacekeeping missions including the Australians in Rwanda (Hodson, Ward, & Rapee, 2001), the Danish in the former Yugoslavia (Elklit & Knudsen, cited in

Elklit, 1998), the Norwegian in South Lebanon (Mehlum, 1999), Canadian soldiers in Croatia and Bosnia (Farley, 1996), and the United States in Somalia (Orsillo, Roemer, Litz, Ehlich, & Friedman,1998). Hodson et al. (2001) reported that 79% of Australian soldiers deployed to Rwanda believed they were in danger of being killed. Elklit and Knudsen (cited in Elklit, 1998) surveyed Danish soldiers who had been deployed to the former Yugoslavia. The majority (54%) of these peacekeepers reported that their worst experience was when they felt their life was threatened. Larsson, Michel, and Lundin (2000) found that 35% of Swedish soldiers deployed to the UN peacekeeping mission in the former Yugoslavia had experienced something traumatic during the mission. Typical life-threatening stressors include being fired upon and being held hostage. Mehlum (1995) reported that 44% of Norwegian soldiers in South Lebanon experienced bombardment; Litz and colleagues (1997) found that 76% of U.S. soldiers in Somalia reported that their unit came under fire at least 15 times.

Peacekeepers also report being held hostage. In a survey of Norwegian peacekeepers in South Lebanon, 9% reported having been held hostage (Mehlum, 1995). Similarly, 8% of Dutch peacekeepers deployed to Bosnia reported having been held hostage (Flaach & Zijlmans, 1997), although of these 326 soldiers, 25% of them did not consider having been held hostage to be a traumatic experience. There was, however, a positive relationship between having perceived the experience as traumatic and having symptoms of posttraumatic stress disorder. Thirty percent of Australian peacekeepers in Rwanda (Hodson et al., 2001) reported witnessing a hostage situation, and 19% reported being involved in one.

Other significant stressors, although not perhaps as imminently life threatening, included exposure to minefields, unruly crowds or mobs, and witnessing killing and other violence. During the first year of the U.S. deployment in support of the NATO mission in Bosnia, for example, 11% reported handling unexploded ordnance (Castro, Bartone, Britt, & Adler, 1998). On the Somalia mission, the majority of U.S. soldiers (57%) on peacekeeping duty surveyed by Orsillo et al. (1998) reported going on patrols or other dangerous duties at least 13 times, and 25% reported managing Somalis in chaotic or unpredictable circumstances equally as often. Mehlum (1995) also reported that of the Norwegian peacekeepers in Lebanon he surveyed, 33% witnessed violence, 19% witnessed people being killed, and 20% reported intervening to protect civilians from violence.

In a comparison of stressful events experienced by Dutch soldiers deployed in support of the Implementation Force (IFOR), the first year of the peacekeeping force in Bosnia after the Dayton Accords, and Swedish UNPROFOR soldiers in Bosnia prior to IFOR, Vogelaar, Soetters, and Born (1997) found that Swedish soldiers experienced stressful events much more frequently than did their counterparts with the NATO operation. This research is particularly informative because it used the same items and thus allows for direct comparison between the two missions. In addition, the study demonstrates the importance of characterizing peacekeeping stressors as time and context dependent, based on the nature of the operational environment. For example, although 49% of Dutch IFOR and 44% of Swedish UNPROFOR soldiers reported frequently crossing a "Mine Danger" area, 27% of Swedish soldiers experienced shelling of their camp or near their camp on an almost daily basis compared to only 3% of Dutch soldiers.

Other potentially traumatic stressors include exposure to psychologically or spiritually threatening events. These psychological threats included exposure to death, severe injury, mass graves, and body parts. In an assessment of U.S. peacekeepers in Kosovo, 45% of soldiers reported smelling the stench of decomposing bodies, and 38% reported handling or uncovering dead bodies (Adler et al., 2000). Schade and Schuffel (1995) also included exposure to death as one of four major types of stressors in their assessment of German peacekeepers in Cambodia. In their study of U.S. military personnel, Litz, Orsillo, and colleagues (1997) included witnessing Somalis dying as one of the major stressors, and found that 31% of soldiers reported experiencing this more than 15 times. Similarly, 45% of Danish soldiers deployed to Croatia as part of the UN peacekeeping mission reported seeing wounded or killed individuals, and 18% participated in the exchange of dead bodies (Bache & Hommelgaard, 1994). Almost all (93%) of the Australian soldiers surveyed about their experiences on a humanitarian mission in Rwanda reported witnessing human degradation and misery on a large scale (Hodson et al., 2001). These kinds of experiences can threaten an individual's sense of coherence, or sense of order in the world. Indeed, exposure to particular groups of victims, especially children, can place a strain on belief systems and one's sense of injustice and create tension between the desire for action and the rules of engagement limiting military personnel to certain kinds of responses.

One area that has not been documented in the peacekeeping literature on stressors is the degree to which peacekeepers have been involved in perpetrating acts of violence themselves. Based on press reports (e.g., "Army to Report," 2000), this is an area that needs to be addressed in any comprehensive assessment of stressors. In a study of Danish soldiers deployed to Croatia as part of the UN peacekeeping mission, 25% reported having fired their own weapons during the course of the deployment. Johansson (1997) reported that 30% of Swedish soldiers deployed to Bosnia for peacekeeping as part of the UN mission had witnessed cruelty to the civilian population; 25% had witnessed it "seldom," and 5% had witnessed it "almost daily." When asked specifically about mistreatment of the local population by NATO peacekeepers, only 2% of U.S. soldiers deployed during the first year of the NATO mission in Bosnia reported witnessing mistreatment of the local population, and 6% of U.S. soldiers deployed during the first peacekeeping rotation into Kosovo reported witnessing such behavior (Bienvenu et al., 1999). Involvement in the perpetration of violence or mistreatment also has the potential to strain an individual's psychological and spiritual sense of self.

Nontraumatic Stressors

Beyond the more obvious stressors just outlined are other peacekeeping related events that may cause significant levels of stress. These stressors are based on the fundamental nature of a peacekeeping assignment—there will be confrontations with the local population, there will be exposure to the suffering of the local population, and the mission itself may not be appreciated, neither by the local population nor by the nation served by the peacekeeper.

Patrolling duties themselves can be a stressor even without exposure to the dramatic or violent. The sheer uncertainty of the patrol, the lack of mission clarity, the lack of understanding of the rules of engagement, and the potential threat of land mines, snipers, and other dangers are important stressors faced by soldiers on a peacekeeping mission. In addition, exposure to the suffering of the local population can be a stressor for soldiers even in the absence of mass graves or dead bodies. For example, 66% of Danish soldiers deployed to Croatia as part of the UN peacekeeping force (Bache & Hommelgaard, cited in Elklit, 1998) reported seeing hunger and distress.

Mehlum (1995) also reported that the kinds of stressors to which Norwegian peacekeepers in Lebanon were exposed were not primarily combat-related stressors. The kinds of incidents were attempts by the former warring factions to provoke a response from the peacekeepers that would jeopardize the peace by insulting them (reported by 23% of peacekeepers) or placing them under extreme duress, such as through hostage taking mentioned earlier. Mehlum reported that these soldiers felt like a "punching ball" (1995, p. 291) in their attempts to provide a buffer between the various warring factions. The majority of Danish soldiers (61%) deployed on the UN peacekeeping mission in Croatia also reported being scorned by the local population (Bache & Hommelgaard, cited in Elklit, 1998). Dutch researchers also noted that rejection by the local population was experienced by over a quarter of the peacekeepers in the former Yugoslavia, although at a decreasing rate following implementation of the Dayton Accords (47% during the early missions prior to 1996 and about 28% after; cited in Weerts et al., 2001). Similarly, 26% of U.S. soldiers deployed during the first year of the NATO mission in Bosnia reported experiencing rejection by the local population (Castro et al., 1998).

Peacekeeping missions have the potential to provide positive experiences to soldiers through giving them a real-world opportunity to utilize their soldier skills, to engage in relevant work that has meaning, and to make a difference in the lives of others (Britt et al., 2001). The reverse of these positive aspects, however, is also true, as delineated by the ambiguity dimension of peacekeeping stressors described by Bartone and colleagues (1998). Soldiers may feel underutilized or wrongly employed if their job specialty is a significant mismatch for their peacekeeper role. They may feel as if their work is meaningless, and they may feel the mission is not appropriate or effective. Such concerns are reflected in a report of Danish peacekeepers in Croatia (Bache & Hommelgaard, 1994): 77% experienced the mission as hopeless. In all, positive and negative experiences work together to affect the way in which deployment stressors are experienced and appraised by peacekeepers.

COMBAT VERSUS PEACEKEEPING

To what extent are the stressors described in the peacekeeping literature distinct from those found in a combat environment? In reviewing each of the broad categories listed under the peacekeeping stressor model, it is evident that most are also applicable to a combat context. There are however, two differences: (1) the relative emphasis placed on soldier well-being during what should be a relatively peaceful deployment in a noncombat context, and (2) the psychological expectations of peacekeeping deployment (the divergence from the "warrior" identity, the types of patrol-related stressors, and the expectations—often unmet—of gratitude). Several areas of overlap naturally exist. Chief among them are the daily hassles associated with a deployed environment. Family separation and stressors related to the work environment are not unique to peacekeeping. The maturity of the theater and the creature comforts of home, however, are more expected on a peacekeeping deployment that has been established for some time.

In terms of the deployment events, it is indeed possible for each of these stressors to also be present in a combat situation. The specific constellation of stressors and their relative likelihood and intensity are more likely to differ, however, between combat and peacekeeping operations. In addition, certain peacekeeping operations are likely to share more in common with combat than others. In the case of Somalia, for example, soldiers deployed expecting a peace support operation and wound up in a combat environment.

Furthermore, even though traditional combat events may occur on a peacekeeping mission, other kinds of confrontations may characterize that peacekeeping deployment. For example, Mehlum (1995) found that 22% of Norwegian peacekeepers in Lebanon reported they had been involved in regular combat. Far more frequent, however, were experiences designed to provoke a response that would compromise the mission. Mehlum notes that this method of destabilization is what differentiates combat-related missions from peacekeeping.

DEPLOYMENT CYCLE

Although this chapter has focused on stressors that occur during the peacekeeping deployment, we note that the types of stressors that peacekeepers experience will change depending on the phase of the deployment cycle. Stressors at predeployment include preparation in terms of training, taking care of personal business, and anticipation of the deployment (Bartone et al., 1998) and family separation (Pavia, Cerdeira, Rodrigues, & Ferro, 1997). Stressors during the deployment also vary in content and effect depending on whether the experience is assessed early, mid, or late in the deployment (e.g., Bartone & Adler, 1999; Miller & Moskos, 1995). Stressors at postdeployment are primarily reintegration with job, family, and coming to terms with difficult deployment-related experiences.

A frequently overlooked issue with respect to the stressors associated with the deployment cycle is the stress that comes with transitions. The transition to the deployment can be a difficult period because of the uncertainty facing military personnel, the amount of work that goes into preparing one's personal life for an extended absence, job-related packing for the deployment, and forming new units in the case of some task forces or specially configured units. Once the military personnel reach the deployed environment, there can be stress associated with the adjustment both to the job and to the living environment, learning the new environment, feeling the impact of culture shock or cultural isolation for the first time, and adjusting to the work itself. The transition back to home station also presents a series of stresses, which include packing up, preparing the new group to take over, receiving task assignments to be performed back at home station even before the redeployment occurs, and preparing for reintegration into the family. These stresses can be both positive and negative, but during the frantic pace that often accompanies these transition points, the awareness of transitions as a special period of stress can be lost.

FUTURE RESEARCH

Research designed to assess the impact of peacekeeping deployment on military personnel needs, at its core, a comprehensive assessment of the stressors experienced by peacekeepers. Such an assessment needs to take into account the stressors associated with the daily hassles of deployed life and those found in any work environment, as well as the stressors associated with the actual conduct of peacekeeping duties. This description of stressors needs to recognize the diversity of demands placed on peacekeepers and the possibility of stressors shifting during a mission, and to allow for comparisons with other deployments. When experiences are novel, unpredictable, ambiguous, imminent, unyielding, and uncertain, they are likely to be experienced as placing a greater load on the resources of the individual. When these events tax physical, psychological, and spiritual resources, they are also likely to be experienced as stressors. How any one individual experiences these events, however, will depend on that individual's personal history, coping, appraisals, and external supports.

Although beyond the scope of this chapter, these individual difference variables may be the key to developing interventions and training models in order to optimize the ability of military personnel to withstand the stress associated with peace support operations. The identification of the stressors confronting peacekeepers is still, however, a necessary first step in understanding the relationship of peacekeeper experience with performance and adjustment. By first specifying a clear set of possible stressors, the field of peacekeeping research will continue to develop into an applied science with implications for both peacekeeping deployments and the understanding of the stress and coping process.

NOTE

The views expressed in the article are those of the author and do not reflect the official policy or position of the Department of the Army, Department of Defense, or the U.S. government. This research is funded by the U.S. Army Medical Research and Materiel Command, Fort Detrick, Maryland.

REFERENCES

Adler, A. B., Dolan, C. A., & Castro, C. A. (2000, September). U.S. soldier peacekeeping experiences and well-being after returning from deployment to Kosovo. *Proceedings of the 36th International Applied Military Psychology Symposium,* Split, Croatia.

Army to report on beatings by G.I.'s in Kosovo. (2000, September 16). *New York Times,* p. A5.

Bache, M., & Hommelgaard, B. (1994). *Danish UN soldiers: Experiences and stress reactions.* Copenhagen, Denmark: Defense Center for Leadership.

Bartone, P. T. (1997). American IFOR experience: Psychological stressors in the early deployment period. In J. L. Soetters and J. H. Rovers (Eds.), *NL Arms—Netherlands Annual Review of Military Studies. The Bosnian Experience* (pp. 87–97). Breda, The Netherlands: Royal Military Academy.

Bartone, P. T., & Adler, A. B. (1999). Cohesion over time in a peacekeeping medical task force. *Military Psychology, 11*(1), 85–108.

Bartone, P. T., Adler, A. B., & Vaitkus, M. A. (1998). Dimensions of psychological stress in peacekeeping operations. *Military Medicine, 163,* 587–593.

Bienvenu, R. V., Huffman, A. H., Castro, C. A., & Adler, A. B. (1999). *USAREUR Soldier Study II: Kosovo mid-deployment.* U.S. Army Medical Research Unit-Europe Technical Brief (TB 99–04). Heidelberg, Germany: USAMRU-E.

Britt, T. W. (1998). Psychological ambiguities in peacekeeping. In H. J. Langholtz (Ed.), *The psychology of peacekeeping* (pp. 111–128). Westport, CT: Praeger.

Britt, T. W., Adler, A. B., & Bartone, P. T. (2001). Deriving benefits from stressful events: The role of engagement in meaningful work and hardiness. *Journal of Occupational Health Psychology, 6*(1), 53–63.

Caniglia, R. R. (2001, July-August). U.S. and British approaches to force protection. *Military Review,* pp. 73–81.

Castro, C. A., & Adler, A. B. (2001). The impact of operations tempo: Issues in measurement. In S. Truscott & S. Flemming (Eds.), *Human dimensions of deployments among TTCP nations* (pp. 29–25). Ottawa, Ontario: National Defense Headquarters.

Castro, C. A., Bartone, P. T., Britt, T. W., & Adler, A. B. (1998). *Operation Joint Endeavor (OJE): Lessons learned for improving psychological readiness.* USAMRU-E Technical Brief #98–04. Heidelberg, Germany: U.S. Army Medical Research Unit–Europe.

Dohrenwend, B. S., & Dohrenwend, B. P. (1980). What is a stressful event? In H. Selye (Ed.), *Selye's guide to stress research* (Vol. 1, pp. 1–20). New York: Van Nostrand Reinhold.

Dolan, C. A., Crouch, C. L., West, P., & Castro, C. A. (2001, September). *Sources of stress and coping strategies among U.S. soldiers and their leaders.* Paper presented at the European Health Psychology Conference, St. Andrews, Scotland.

Elklit, A. (1998). UN-soldiers serving in peacekeeping missions: A review of the psychological after-effects. *International Review of the Armed Forces Medical Services, 71,* 7/8/9, 197–208.

Farley, K. M. (1996). *Stress in military operations.* Paper presented at the 104th Annual convention of the American Psychological Association, Toronto.

Flaach, A., & Zijlmans, A. (1997). Psychological consequences of being taken hostage during peace operations. In J. L. Soetters & J. H. Rovers (Eds.), *NL Arms— Netherlands Annual Review of Military Studies. The Bosnian Experience* (pp. 141–152). Breda, The Netherlands: Royal Military Academy.

Fontana, A., Rosenheck, R., & Brett, E. (1992). War zone traumas and posttraumatic stress disorder symptomatology. *The Journal of Nervous and Mental Disease, 180,* 748–759.

Gal, R., & Jones, F. D. (1995). A psychological model of combat stress. In F. D. Jones, L. R. Sparacino, V. L. Wilcox, J. M. Rothberg, & J. W. Stokes (Eds.), *War Psychiatry* (Textbook of Military Medicine: Part I, Warfare, Weaponry, and the Casualty) (pp. 133–148). Washington, DC: Office of the Surgeon General/Borden Institute, Walter Reed Army Medical Center.

Hackman, J. R., & Oldham, G. R. (1975). Development of the Job Diagnostic Survey. *Journal of Applied Psychology, 60,* 159–170.

Harris, J. J., & Segal, D. R. (1985). Observations from the Sinai: The boredom factor. *Armed Forces & Society, 11,* 235–248.

Hodson, S. E., Ward, D., & Rapee, R. (2001). Post deployment predictors of traumatic stress—Rwanda a case study. In G. E. Kearney, M. Creamer, & R. P. Marshall (Eds.), *The Fire Within: Military stress and performance—The experience of the Australian Defence Forces.* Melbourne, Australia: Melbourne University Press. [www.psy.mq.edu.au/MUARU/ptsdresults.htm on 12/19/01].

Huffman, A. H., Adler, A. B., & Castro, C. A. (1999). *The impact of deployment history on the well-being of military personnel.* Defense Technical Information Center Report # ADA3611109. Alexandria, VA: DTIC.

Johansson, E. (1997). *In a blue beret: Four Swedish UN battalions in Bosnia.* Karlstad, Sweden: National Defence College.

King, D. W., King, L. A., Gudanowski, D. M., & Vreven, D. L. (1995). Alternative representations of war zone stressors: Relationships to posttraumatic stress disorder in male and female Vietnam veterans. *Journal of Abnormal Psychology, 104,* 184–196.

Langholtz, H. J. (Ed.). (1998). *The psychology of peacekeeping.* Westport, CT: Praeger.

Larsson, G., Michel, P., & Lundin, T. (2000). Systematic assessment of mental health following various types of posttrauma support. *Military Psychology, 12,* 121–135.

Lazarus, R. S., & Folkman, S. (1984). *Stress, appraisal, and coping.* New York: Springer.

Litz, B. T. (1996). The psychological demands of peacekeeping for military personnel. *PTSD Clinical Quarterly, 6,* 1–8.

Litz, B. T., King, L. A., King, D. W., Orsillo, S. M., & Friedman, M. J. (1997). Warriors as peacekeepers: Features of the Somalia experience and PTSD. *Journal of Consulting and Clinical Psychology, 65,* 1001–1010.

Litz, B. T., Orsillo, S. M., Friedman, M., Ehlich, P., & Batres, A. (1997). Post-traumatic stress disorder associated with peacekeeping duty in Somalia for U.S. military personnel. *American Journal of Psychiatry, 154,* 178–184.

MacDonald, C., Chamberlain, K., Long, N., Pereira-Laird, J., & Mirfin, K. (1998). Mental health, physical health, and stressors reported by New Zealand Defence Force peacekeepers: A longitudinal study. *Military Medicine, 163,* 477–481.

Macdonough, T. (1991). Noncombat stress in soldiers: How it is manifested, how to measure it, and how to cope with it. In R. Gal and A. D. Mangelsdorff (Eds.), *Handbook of military psychology* (pp. 531–558). New York: Wiley.

Martinez, J. A., Huffman, A. H., Adler, A. B., & Castro, C. A. (1999). Assessing psychological readiness in U.S. soldiers following NATO operations. *International Review of the Armed Forces Medical Services, 73,* 139–142.

McCarroll, J. E., Ursano, R. J., Ventis, W. L., Fullerton, C. S., Oates, G. L, Friedman, H., Shean, G. L., & Wright, K. M. (1993). Anticipation of handling the dead: Effects of gender and experience. *British Journal of Clinical Psychology, 32,* 466–468.

McFarlane, A. C., & de Girolamo, G. (1996). The nature of traumatic stressors and the epidemiology of posttraumatic reactions. In B. A. van der Kolk, A. C. McFarlane, and L. Weisæth (Eds.), *Traumatic stress: The effects of overwhelming experience on mind, body, and society* (pp. 129–154). New York: Guilford Press.

Mehlum, L. (1995). Positive and negative consequences of serving in a UN peacekeeping mission: A follow-up study. *International Review of the Armed Forces Medical Services, 68,* 289–295.

Mehlum, L. (1999). Alcohol and stress in Norwegian United Nations peacekeepers. *Military Medicine, 164,* 720–724.

Miller, L. L., & Moskos, C. (1995). Humanitarians or warriors? Race, gender, and combat status in Operation Restore Hope. *Armed Forces & Society, 21,* 615–637.

Orsillo, S. M., Roemer, L., Litz, B. T., Ehlich, P., & Friedman, M. (1998). Increases in retrospective accounts of war-zone exposure over time: The role of PTSD symptom severity. *Journal of Traumatic Stress, 11,* 597–607.

Pavia, T., Cerdeira, E., Rodrigues, L., & Ferro, S. (1997). *Portuguese military in peacekeeping missions: Human factors in pre- and post-deployment.* Proceedings from the Partnership for Peace Workshop on Psychological Readiness for Multinational Operations: Directions for the 21st Century [CD-ROM]. Heidelberg: U.S. Army Medical Research Unit–Europe.

Ritzer, D. R., Campbell, S. J., & Valentine, J. N. (1999). Human dimensions research during Operation Joint Guard, Bosnia. *Army Medical Department Journal, 8,* 5–16.

Schade & Schuffel (1995, May). *Medical service personnel in the United Nations peace-keeping forces: An empirical study on the strains and stress of German medical personnel in Cambodia.* Presented at the Fourth European Conference on Traumatic Stress, Paris.

Vogelaar, A. L. W., Soetters, J. L, & Born, J. B. G. A. (1997). Psychological consequences of being taken hostage during peace operations. In J. L. Soetters and J. H. Rovers (Eds.), *NL Arms—Netherlands annual review of military studies. The Bosnian experience* (pp. 113–132). Breda, The Netherlands: Royal Military Academy.

Weerts, J. M. P., White, W., Adler, A. B., Castro, C. A., Algra, G., Bramsen, I., Dirk-zwager, A. J. E., van der Ploeg, H. M., de Vries, M., & Zijlmans, A. (2001). Studies on peacekeepers. In Y. Danieli (Ed.), *Sharing the front line and the back hills* (pp. 31–48). Amityville, NY: Baywood.

10

Coping with Peacekeeping Stress

Christian Moldjord, Lars Kristian Fossum, and Are Holen

Several contemporary international conflicts have rather complex and tangled causes; some may be rooted in history, others in ethnic mistrust, and some in the absence of future prospects for the populations. Nondemocratic leaders often exploit such problems by arousing people's fears. Protracted internal conflicts or wars may be the unfortunate outcome. In many cases, the conflicts are not solved by shifting borders or by establishing buffer zones guarded by peacekeepers. Comprehensive efforts by the international community are often warranted and may involve preventive measures, developmental programs, democratization, and the implementation of human rights. Ideally, peacekeeping operations will restore peace and security in countries or regions. When the UN or other supranational alliances decide to intervene in conflicts, the goals are to change the situations that led to the eruptions and to establish new self-sustained societies in which peace and security will prevail. Nevertheless, such honorable goals may at times entail direct confrontations and involvement with frustrated civilians, aggressive local police and paramilitary groups. One of the most important tasks of the peacekeepers is to avoid the escalation of conflicts and, ideally, to calm the bellicose parties.

In this chapter, we explore some of the stressors and the psychological challenges encountering peacekeepers, theories on coping, and other stress-modifying factors. Throughout, we draw on our research from the Norwegian helicopter wing, NORAIR, to illustrate stress and coping on a peacekeeping deployment.

STRESSORS AND CHALLENGES OF THE PEACEKEEPER

Stressors in Peacekeeping Missions

A commonly held view is that peacekeeping missions consist of fewer risks and less strain than traditional warfare. As a rule, this is probably true. Nevertheless, peacekeeping missions vary a lot, and in some cases, peacekeepers find themselves in situations not very different from traditional warfare. Studies and reports from Lebanon, Bosnia, and Somalia have documented major risks and life-threatening situations for peacekeeping personnel (Fossum & Moldjord, 1999; Johansson, 1997; Solberg, 1997). Several of the studies also report posttraumatic stress disorder (PTSD) and related symptoms in the wake of missions (Litz, Orsillo, Friedman, Ehlich, & Batres, 1997; Mehlum & Weisæth, 2002).

In a study of Polish peacekeepers in the UN Protection Force (UNPROFOR 1992–1995), in the former Yugoslavia, 72% found themselves in a life-threatening situation at least once. Fifty-seven percent reported that someone in their company was wounded; 91% saw civilians or others injured as a result of war operations (Ilnicki, 2000). In a study from the same operation, 71% of Swedish peacekeepers (UNPROFOR 1992–1995) reported having been shot at (Johansson, 1997). In NORAIR, several of the helicopter personnel were shot at during flight missions; other personnel reported isolation, insecurity, grotesque scenes, "close shaves" and major threats to life and health (Moldjord & Fossum, 1999). The most frequently reported stressors were "Witnessing wounded and dead people"; "Witnessing firing over and into towns"; "Witnessing destroyed buildings and infrastructure"; "Passing through areas of war"; "Passing through areas of mine danger"; "Being precluded from fulfilling U.N. missions"; "Negotiations and conflicts at checkpoints"; and "Being shot at" (Fossum & Moldjord, 1999; Johansson, 1997; Solberg, 1997; Statens Helsetilsyn, 1998).

Such findings indicate that peacekeeping operations can be replete with risky and threatening situations. Similar stressors are also likely to be part of future peacekeeping missions. Accordingly, the prevention of psychological after-effects is an appropriate goal for modern military forces that originate in democratic nations and are built on the respect and concern for the welfare of the individual.

Challenges in Peacekeeping Service

Although in general peacekeeping operations may be less dangerous than traditional warfare, they present new challenges as well. The peacekeeper is not supposed to fight the enemy with all available means. The peacekeeper is not supposed to engage in combat, but to act as a buffer between hostile parties. In certain respects, peacekeepers have more complex psychological tasks than soldiers trained for "traditional" warfare. Peacekeepers are equipped for self-defense, and they have to comply with strict rules of engagement (ROE) to prevent unwanted use of weapons in threatening situations. When repeatedly exposed to dangerous, provocative, or humiliating situations, the peacekeeper has few options for letting go of anger and frustration (The Norwegian Armed Forces Joint Medical Service University of Oslo, 1993).

Almost daily, peacekeepers talk with civilians, establish contacts and build trust with the local population. Occasionally, the peacekeeper must also get involved in controversies, intense and unpleasant negotiations, or showdowns between warring parties. At times, the life of the peacekeeper may even be in danger. Figure 10.1 illustrates the environment of the peacekeeper. On the "continuum of power," the peacekeeper must be prepared to move toward the "violent end," that is, into situations in which combat or self-defense and the use of weapons may be authorized by the ROE. In such cases, the risk of making a mistake that can escalate the situation may be quite taxing. The peacekeeper may feel a tremendous responsibility; one erroneous step, and the situation might get out of hand with devastating consequences. A relevant question may be "How well are peacekeepers psychologically prepared for moments of these kinds?"

Several studies have underscored that one of the most demanding challenges for peacekeepers is to control their aggression (Litz, 1996; Wallenius, 1997; Weisæth, 1982). Being the neutral party limits the options for action. Usually, peacekeepers are not allowed to attack; nor do they usually have the possibility to flee. Accordingly, they are precluded from acting on their basic survival impulses, the propensity toward fight or flight, which may have its costs. The notion of a "Peacekeepers' stress syndrome" has been introduced to capture the core symptoms of soldiers overwhelmed by fears of losing control over their aggression (Egge, Mortensen, & Weisæth, 1996). Peacekeeping services provide plenty of opportunities to accumulate, but few possibilities to discharge, aggressive tensions. Litz (1996) noted that exercise of restraint in the face of danger is quite troubling for combat-trained soldiers and may contribute to feelings of helplessness and increased anxiety. This is especially so whenever uncertainty or ambiguity about the rules of engagement may exist. Although in a study of U.S. soldiers in Somalia, restraint was not associated with PTSD, Litz, King, King, Orsillo, & Friedman (1997) did not rule out other maladaptive responses stemming from restraint. Traditionally trained soldiers in peace-

Figure 10.1 Continuum of Power for the Peacekeeper

keeping missions may be at risk of acting out their aggression both during the mission, but also later, on their return home (Litz, Orsillo, et al., 1997).

The following example from Bosnia illustrates the relief that is felt when soldiers let go of their aggressive impulses. Soldiers in a Swedish UN platoon (NORBAT 2, Bosnia 1993–1995) came under repeated fire without being able to defend themselves. Aggressive tensions built up, exemplified by a quote from one soldier: "If they shoot back, I thought, I'll pay back the same way." Later on, the situation allowed for self-defense. Many felt relieved whenever they could retaliate. Some even reported that they fired back, just because they felt like it: "We started firing rapidly and forcefully. . . . It was one of the most wonderful moments of my life, just to retaliate, have the opportunity to shoot that much. It may sound rather sick, but in that situation. . . . It was an unbelievable feeling to fire back at them; not to be at the receiving end all the time. Just being able to act, . . . it was wonderful!" (Wallenius, 1997).

Given such challenges, this question naturally arises: What can be done to enhance coping with such peacekeeping stress? In our attempt to address this question, we first review some of the relevant conceptualizations on coping and related topics.

THEORIES OF COPING AND RELATED TOPICS

Coping consists of cognitive and behavioral efforts to manage specific external and/or internal demands that are appraised as taxing or exceeding the resources of the person (Monat & Lazarus, 1991). Thus coping has been defined in terms of strategies and processes that individuals use to modify adverse aspects of their environment, as well as to minimize internal distress induced by environmental demands.

Lazarus and Folkman (1984) have also argued that stress consists of three processes. Primary appraisal is the process of perceiving a threat to oneself, secondary appraisal is the process of bringing to mind a potential response to the threat, and coping is the process of executing that response. There are several ways in which coping may alter emotions: cognitive activity may influence the deployment of attention, cognitive activity may alter the subjective meaning or significance of an encounter with regard to well-being, and actions may alter the actual person-environment relationship (Monat & Lazarus, 1991).

In operationalizing coping theories and related topics, we identified four relevant coping categories: (1) practical handling of a stressor, (2) cognitive or internal strategies, (3) stress diminution by situation and environment, and (4) personal approaches. This categorization is used in the discussion of coping theories presented later.

Practical Handling of Stressor

Problem-Focused Coping

The concept of problem-focused coping deals with the practical and physical handling of a stressor. Problem-focused coping may involve activities like planning, direct action, seeking assistance, and screening out other activities. The process of taking steps to try to remove or circumvent the stressor or to ameliorate its effects is defined as the active part of problem-focused coping. Activities like planning action strategies and thinking about steps to take and how to handle the problems are clearly problem focused, yet they do not directly involve problem-focused action. Planning activities, as a part of secondary appraisal, bring to mind potential responses to the threat, such as soldiers seeking shelter, firing weaponry, or scanning or scouting the terrain (Gal & Jones, 1995).

Restraint

Peacekeepers often have to exercise restraint. Carver, Scheier, and Weintraub (1989) defined restraint as a problem-focused coping strategy: "Restraint coping is waiting until an appropriate opportunity to act presents itself, holding oneself back, and not acting prematurely" (Carver et al., 1989, p. 269). In threatening situations, the challenge of the peacekeeper is not to escalate, but rather to calm the opponent. Then restraint serves as an active coping strategy; the peacekeepers are focused on effectively dealing with the stressor. In contrast, restraint may also be seen as a passive strategy as the use of restraint means not to act (Carver et al., 1989). In the Norwegian UNIFIL study, 22% reported having struggled with doubts about what to do in life-threatening situations. This doubt underscores the inherent psychological challenge involved in handling conflicting impulses such as applying force and exercising restraint when one's life is in danger. Peacekeeping missions may create a sense of vulnerability unique to these kinds of situations (Litz, 1996).

Cognitive or Internal Strategies

Emotion-Focused Coping

Emotion-focused coping is used to maintain hope and optimism, sometimes by denying facts and their implications, or by engaging in activities that minimize the focus on the threat (Lazarus & Folkman, 1984). According to Lazarus and Folkman, emotion-focused coping may be divided into cognitive and behavioral processes. Cognitive processes are directed at lessening emotional distress and include strategies such as avoidance, minimization, distancing, and finding positive values in negative events; behavioral strategies are directed at distracting the individual from emotional distress.

Problem-focused coping tends to predominate when people find that something constructive can be done, whereas emotion-focused coping tends to predominate when people find the stressor has to be endured (Carver et al., 1989; Solomon, Mikulincer, & Benbenishty, 1989). A wide range of additional emotion-focused coping strategies have been described in the literature (Kobasa, Maddi, & Kahn, 1982; Kobasa, Maddi, Puccetti, & Zola, 1985; Monat & Lazarus, 1991).

Distraction, Avoidance and Denial

Several studies have defined distractions as cognitive coping strategies (Olff, Brosschot, & Godaert, 1993; Schreurs, Tellegen, van de Willige, & Brosschot, 1988). According to Gal and Jones (1995), the active mode of coping may take various forms for military personnel such as checking gear or last-minute details. Stress-reducing activities need not be related to threats and may include card playing, book reading, letter writing, and so on. Other distractions include seeking entertaining company, drinking, smoking, eating, or physical training (Eriksen, Olff, & Ursin, 1997). Some of these activities might promote successful coping; the individual is distracted from preoccupation with death or wounding, which may promote resolve and cohesion within the soldiers (Gal & Jones, 1995). These behaviors may also strengthen the soldiers' feelings of mastery and diminish anxiety, especially when preparing for combat (Gal & Lazarus, 1975).

Psychological avoidance may also be defined as mental strategies that parry negative emotional responses by bending aspects of reality (Olff et al., 1993). Lazarus and Folkman (1984) defined avoidance as a specific coping behavior. Others have seen coping and defense as opposites (Haan, 1977). Distinctions have been made between denial as an inadequate way of distorting reality and coping as positive thinking, or minimization that enables the person to uphold morale and cope constructively (Monat & Lazarus, 1991). For example, Solberg (1997) found that for UN observers, denial as a method for coping with grotesque scenes of dead and wounded people was associated with more favorable outcomes. People using denial in this positive sense may experience greater emotional ease in the first place, but are likely to turn out more vulnerable on subsequent exposures to similar situations. Similarly, people facing threats will be more distressed at the outset, but are probably better prepared to handle the demands of similar situations later on (Monat & Lazarus, 1991). For example, in a study of young recruits, soldiers using avoidance strategies were at greater risk for developing mental health problems (Johnsen, Laberg, & Eid, 1998).

STRESS DIMINUTION BY SITUATION OR ENVIRONMENT

Social Support

Social support is a psychosocial stress moderator that frequently has been addressed in the literature (Bartone, 1997; Kobasa et al., 1985; Lazarus & Folkman, 1984; Noy, 1991; Olff et al., 1993). Social support refers to comradeship in units and groups, loyalty to the unit, and unit morale (Marlowe, 1986; Milgram, Orensten, & Zafrir, 1989). Group comradeship has been identified as the most important factor in reducing the effects of strong stressors (Milgram et al., 1989). A military unit with strong comradeship is characterized by confidence, trust, and respect between both soldiers and officers. High levels of social support tend to make groups function well during times of crisis; emotional support, information, comradeship, and practical help make individuals assess the situation more adequately (Milgram et al., 1989).

Several studies have found that social support and comradeship are most relevant to coping under stress (Cobb, 1976; Glass, 1973; Kobasa et al., 1985; Lefcourt, Martin, & Selah, 1984). When individuals are exposed to alarming incidents, their stress usually decreases when they feel their emotions and behaviors are understood and supported. Similarly, stress can be diminished when persons are spared from having to make difficult decisions alone (Kobasa et al., 1985). Some studies report group cohesion as the most important factor in reducing stress responses (Glass, 1973; Grinker & Spiegel, 1945). In Norwegian peacekeepers deployed in Lebanon, Weisæth (1982) found that good leadership, strong group feelings, and high motivation increased soldier tolerance of stress.

Personal Approaches

In this section, we briefly review two personal approaches relevant to handling major stress. Rotter (1954, 1966) was one of the first to hold that coping with stress was explained by a person's cognitive orientation. An individual's locus of control has been found to predict how well a person handles difficult situations, including warfare (Hobfoll, 1985; Lefcourt, 1976). Kobasa's concept of *hardiness,* a measure of a person's emotional resilience, has also been linked to peacekeepers being engaged in meaningful work during deployment, and the ability to derive benefits from military service (Britt, Adler, & Bartone, 2001).

Another cognitive style, Antonovsky's *sense of coherence* (SOC), is based on what he calls the salutogenic orientation (Antonovky, 1979, 1987). With strong SOC, the person seeks a balance between rules and strategies, between known and potential information. The world is seen as a challenge, not as a threat, and the individual is open to feedback. Antonovsky emphasizes that a strong SOC is not a coping strategy, but rather a predisposition for coping with stress. Sense of coherence, along with the various coping strategies already discussed, form the basis for approaches that may affect the impact of peacekeeping stressors on soldiers. What follows is an application of these principles in one study of Norwegian Air Force personnel deployed to Bosnia.

THE NORAIR STUDY

The NORAIR study, described elsewhere in more detail (Moldjord, Fossum, & Holen, 2001), was conducted in part to identify factors that reduced stress in peacekeepers following critical events. Study participants were air force personnel assigned to the Norwegian helicopter wing NORAIR, deployed in support of the UN peacemaking forces (UNPROFOR) in Tuzla, Bosnia, from October 1993 until fall 1995. The primary mission of this unit was medical evacuation of wounded personnel as well as search and rescue. In addition, NORAIR was involved in medical supply and in the transportation of spare parts, mail, money, and VIP and UN personnel.

There were three main categories of personnel: (1) flight personnel, (2) convoy drivers, and (3) ground and support personnel. Several missions were quite risky and special procedures were established for high-risk flying. Secret rescue missions were conducted after dark, without radar cover and in areas without clearance. Tank truck drivers supplied fuel to the helicopters primarily by driving from Tuzla in Bosnia to Split in Croatia. Civilians were engaged as convoy drivers and given the rank of sergeant. Road standards were generally poor. During transportation, the risk of sniper attacks, mines, and threats from local militia at checkpoints were commonplace. Ground and support personnel spent most of their time on the base. They were in charge of maintenance and repair, administration and supply. Sporadically, they also served as relief personnel on helicopters and as passengers on the fuel convoys.

Five Ways of Coping with Major Stressors

After returning to Norway, 134 NORAIR personnel (71% of the entire unit) were asked to rate how helpful certain behaviors had been in coping with stress after the most adverse events during the deployment. The degree of help was specified on a scale from 0 to 9. The list of behaviors was derived from qualitative interviews with nine NORAIR soldiers; some items were also derived from the literature. In the factor analysis of the items, 65.8% of the total variance was explained by five extracted factors: seeking safety, diversion through stimuli, seeking changes of scene, diversion by thinking about other things, and seeking social support.

Overall, "seeking safety" and "seeking social support" obtained the highest mean scores. The NORAIR personnel generally saw these two as the most helpful ways of handling adverse stress. The remaining three factors may also be subsumed under the rubric of "cognitive or internal strategies." "Diversion through thinking about other things" was the third most endorsed factor, and "Diversion through stimuli" and "Seeking changes of scene" were the least endorsed.

Seeking Safety

The first factor was labeled "seeking safety" (M = 5.1, SD 1.9, alpha = 0.88) and included having work to do all the time, talking confidentially with the commander, knowing there was shelter in the base, knowing the base area was guarded, having access to medical personnel and physicians, knowing the weapons of the belligerent parties, knowing the developments between the belligerents parties, knowing the location of the fighting, and thinking of positive aspects of NORAIR service. The items deal with conditions contributing to safety through assurance and control. Some items emphasize the need for protection; others imply situational awareness through information about the war situation around the base. The item that loaded highest on the factor was "knowing the base area was guarded."

Seeking safety may be categorized under the rubric "cognitive or internal strategies." The factor emphasizes the importance of protection, safety, and adequate information. The behaviors facilitate rational thinking and planning, orient the peacekeepers toward possible hazards or volatile conditions, and thus contribute toward situational awareness. In a sense, the factor provides the foundation for internal locus of control. Peacekeepers know their options and challenges, may take necessary steps for preparation, and feel better prepared to deal with unpredictable circumstances. This approach is likely to reinforce positive expectations of the outcome in dangerous situations.

Diversion through Stimuli

The second factor, "diversion through stimuli" (M = 2.6, SD 2.0, alpha = 0.76), included having access to alcohol, having access to cigarettes or snuff, being able to party in the bar, and having the opportunity to get drunk. The factor emphasized diversions through substances or stimuli. The item that loaded highest on this factor was "having the opportunity to get drunk."

Of the NORAIR personnel surveyed, 65% reported higher consumption of alcohol in Bosnia than in Norway, and 7.5% acknowledged that they drank "a lot more." Tendencies toward more alcohol use and alcohol-related behaviors following alarming incidents were more pronounced among convoy drivers than among those with higher military education (i.e., the flight, ground, and support personnel; Moldjord & Fossum, 1999).

In spite of anecdotal reports to the contrary, substance use and nonsocial behaviors were evidently not helpful in the reduction of major stress. Alcohol, however, served two functions—as an escape and also as a social outlet. NORAIR had its own bar at the base, which sold alcohol, cigarettes, and snuff. As a location, the bar served several purposes. It was a meeting point, an arena for social exchange, and, at times, the place for parties. In interviews with NORAIR veterans, the bar was described by some as the natural place for getting together after missions. Having a beer was the regular context for gathering, particularly for the flight personnel and the fuel drivers. They carried out the toughest missions. Thus socializing and limiting the use of stimuli or substances were interpreted as the constructive direction of these coping behaviors or strategies.

It may be that when deployed military personnel drink alcohol, they may not get the same beneficial effects from their social interactions. In a survey of health-related behaviors in the U.S. military, heavy users of alcohol had more problems with stress and mental health and were more likely to exhibit depressive symptoms than those who did not drink (Bray, 1998). In a longitudinal study of Norwegian soldiers, higher alcohol consumption, drinking behaviors, and alcohol-related behaviors was more prevalent in soldiers with avoidance-focused coping than in those with problem-focused and emotion-focused coping strategies (Johnsen et al., 1998). Our results are consistent with these findings.

Seeking Changes of Scene

The third factor was labeled "seeking changes of scene" (M = 3.1, SD 2.0, alpha = 0.69). Factor items included wearing civilian clothes outside of the base area, going on welfare trips out of the war zone, being able to party with the locals, and using civilian clothes off duty. The items indicate that the diminution of stress was felt by shifting gear, activities, or locations away from the base or the war zone. The item that loaded most highly on this factor was "wearing civilian clothes outside of the base area."

The factor *seeking changes of scene* implies the need for a break from the peacekeeper role through changes in clothes and recreation. To enjoy weekends, NORAIR personnel flew to Split on the Croatian coastline. Wearing civilian clothes out of the base area in calm periods was also seen as a positive alteration in the daily life of the deployment. Both "diversion through stimuli" and "diversion through thinking about other things" had inherent elements of escapism, and may be classified as avoidance coping strategies.

The fourth factor, labeled "diversion by thinking about other things" (M = 3.9, SD 1.8, alpha = 0.66), encompassed two main items, being completely alone and thinking of other things, the item that loaded most highly on the factor. Thus both elements of escape and social withdrawal comprised the factor.

Seeking Social Support

The fifth factor was labeled "seeking social support" (M = 5.0, SD 1.9, alpha = 0.64) and included speaking of an (adverse) incident with as many as possible, being together with others in the unit, and having a friend or colleague to talk openly with. These items express the need for sharing and socializing after adverse events. The first two items loaded highest on the factor.

Seeking social support may belong to the category of coping strategies called "stress diminution by situation or environment" but also to "cognitive or internal strategies." The factor expresses attempts to have someone listen and to understand the nature of an ordeal, a typical need after critical episodes. The absence of organized debriefings probably made informal social interaction and support particularly important. The salience of social relationships in NORAIR was further emphasized by the fact that the item "having a friend or colleague to talk openly with" received the most endorsements (16.8%). The question was examined further and demonstrated decreasing importance with increasing age. Younger peacekeepers were more likely to use this strategy than were older ones. The next two most endorsed items also involved social interaction and support. Together, the three top items covered 43.2% of the participants. This underscores the relevance of social support in relation to adverse events as seen by Scandinavian peacekeepers.

Similarly, other research has indicated that lack of social support may have negative effects on reactions after intense episodes (Noy, 1991; Solomon & Mikulincer, 1987). Close social relationships in groups have also been found crucial for resisting the stresses of war (Hobfoll, 1991). The quality of the social infrastructure that is formed determines the strength of the buffer capacity ascribed to social networks. Organizers of peacekeeping missions have major challenges in assisting the progress of healthy social environments—both on formal and informal levels—but the importance of supporting efforts and developing a healthy social environment is evident.

CLOSER EXAMINATION OF THE FIVE COPING FACTORS

The five behavioral factors reflect coping strategies. Nevertheless, we assumed that just some of them would positively correlate with psychiatric stress symptoms, and the rest would reduce normal expressions of arousal. When looking at the interplay between the five factors and the measure of posttraumatic stress symptoms (PTSS-12) in bivariate analyses, "seeking distractions through stimuli" ($r = 0.21$, $p < 0.05$) and "thinking about something else" ($r = 0.24$, $p < 0.01$) both had positive and significant correlations while the peacekeepers still were in Bosnia. After two to three years at home, however, only "seeking distractions through stimuli" maintained a positive and significant correlation. These findings indicate that using these coping strategies is associated with more symptoms of PTSD. The same relationship between distress and escapism applied to the factor *"diversion through thinking about other things"* when the peacekeepers still were in Bosnia, implying that social withdrawal and mental escapism are expressions of stress reactions.

Practical handling of stressor. None of the items in the NORAIR study were directly aimed at exploring problem-focused coping during critical incidents. The respondents were instead asked about what helped the most *after* such episodes. Accordingly, our study did not shed light on these issues, and we do not mean to convey that practical problem solving in moments of major stress is irrelevant.

Convoy drivers and flight personnel had limited opportunities to influence life-threatening situations by problem-solving activities. Often they depended on narrow escapes from the high-risk incidents. For example, when passing through checkpoints, NORAIR personnel had to negotiate and use bribes and defensive dialogue. These kinds of problems tested their ability to control frustrations, anger, and aggression.

Problem-focused strategies may be used to prevent or resolve stressful events, but they may also lead to stress reactions in unalterable situations (Sandal, Endresen, Vaernes, & Ursin, 1999). Accordingly, problem-focused strategies were not always preferable when peacekeepers were exposed to inescapable and uncontrollable stressors. Peacekeeping operations under life-threatening conditions and with restrictive rules of engagement and poor defense represent potentially traumatizing events. To cope with many of these challenges, peacekeepers had to withhold their feelings of fear, aggression, and frustration. In a study of U.S. veterans from the mission in Somalia, 25% reported clinically significant distress, particularly hostility and anger problems (Litz, 1996). The Somalia study found that frustration over restrictive ROE was predictive of PTSD (Litz, 1996).

Personal Approaches

In a multiple regression model with the symptom measures (PTSS-12) as the dependent variable, sense of coherence was tested together with the five behavioral factors. Sense of coherence showed the highest explanatory value ($B = -0.41$, $t = 4.53$, $p < .001$). The model was significant ($p < 0.001$) and explained 52% of total variance of stress reactions 2.5 to 3 years after termination of service in Bosnia. The negative B-value ($B = -0.41$) indicated that the higher scores on sense of coherence were associated with lower symptom levels. This was in accordance with the general theories reviewed earlier. In the regression model, sense of coherence outweighed the five behavioral factors. A finding of this study was that the personal resources had the strongest explanatory power in accounting for the reported stress symptoms.

A high total score on SOC has been postulated to enhance the coping capacity of a person (Antonovsky, 1987; Friedman, 1992). This was confirmed by our study. Antonovsky (1987) has further claimed that individuals with a strong SOC have a greater tendency to define incidents as nonstressors or as being irrelevant or unimportant. We found that flight personnel had significantly higher scores on SOC than fuel drivers. This difference in SOC scores may be because flight personnel were less exposed to stressors or that flight personnel assessed stressors as less dangerous and risky than fuel drivers.

CONCLUSION

In this chapter, we have explored aspects of the psychological challenges involved in modern peacekeeping operations. The stressors of such missions may imply less direct exposure to battle, but peacekeepers will probably instead have to utilize more psychological skills. One major characteristic of modern peacekeeping is embodied in the pressure to uphold restraint and to avoid escalation of conflicts. Likewise, negotiations without use of force or threats may at times be intimidating and taxing. To enhance peacekeepers' ability to tolerate and to maneuver well when faced with major stressors, these hardships have to be kept in mind when we recruit, train, and organize. A problem for the peacekeepers is to find constructive activities or ways to let go of frustrations and aggressions (Carlstrøm, Lundin, & Otto, 1990; Wallenius, 1997; Weisæth & Dittmann, 1997). The venting of anger and aggression to avoid various posttraumatic aftereffects seems essential, but is perhaps neither the only, nor the biggest psychological challenge associated with these operations.

The resources developed in the organization, in the personal and in the social environment, are also important. In this chapter, we have in particular focused on factors that advance coping. We have discussed the practical handling of major stressors and the cognitive and emotional coping strategies. We have also explored the implications of personal approaches and the diminution prompted by the situation and environment. From the NORAIR study, peacekeepers used seeking safety through protection and situational awareness and social support. Together, the two coping strategies obtained the highest ratings. In addition, no or moderate consumption of alcohol and other substances and the avoidance of escapisms also were significant coping mechanisms. Balancing between the negative effects of alcohol-based escapism and the benefits of social support often found in an informal barlike setting may maximize peacekeeping coping effectiveness.

Peacekeeping requires both offensive and defensive strategies. When situations are controllable, active coping strategies tend to predominate. When situations seem less controllable, however, alternative strategies dominate (Lazarus & Folkman, 1984). Despite tenuous and dangerous conditions, peacekeeping presupposes impartiality, neutrality, patience, and restraint. These are qualities not typically underscored by the doctrines of military affairs. Nevertheless, they need further attention for our conjoint efforts to succeed in creating a better and safer world through international peacekeeping operations.

REFERENCES

Antonovsky, A. (1979). *Health, stress and coping: New perspective on mental health and physical well-being.* San Francisco: Jossey-Bass.

Antonovsky, A. (1987) *Unraveling the mysteries of health: How people manage stress and stay well.* San Francisco: Jossey-Bass.

Bartone, P. T. (1997). American IFOR experience: Psychological stressors in the early deployment period. In J. L. Soetters and J. H. Rovers (Eds.), *NL Arms—Netherlands Annual Review of Military Studies. The Bosnian Experience* (pp. 87–97). Breda, The Netherlands: Royal Military Academy.

Bray, R. M. (1998). *The 1998 Department of Defense Survey of Health Related Be-haviors Among Military Personnel.* Cooperative Agreement No. DAMD 17–96–2-6021, Research Triangle Institute, North Carolina.

Britt, T. W., Adler, A. B., & Bartone, P. T. (2001). Deriving benefits from stressful events: The role of engagement in meaningful work and hardiness. *Journal of Occupational Health Psychology, 6,* 53–63.

Carlstrøm, A., Lundin, T., & Otto, U. (1990). Mental adjustment of Swedish U.N. soldiers in South Lebanon in 1988. *Stress Medicine, 6,* 305–310.

Carver, C. S., Scheier, M. F., & Weintraub, J. K. (1989). Assessing coping strategies: A theoretically based approach. *Journal of Personality and Social Psychology, 56*(2), 267–283.

Cobb, J. (1976). Social support as a moderator of life stress. *Psychosomatic Medicine, 38,* 300–314.

Egge, B., Mortensen, M. S., & Weisæth, L. (1996). Armed conflicts. Soldiers for peace: Ordeals and stress. The contributions of the United Nations peacekeeping forces. In Y. Danieli, N. S. Rodley, & L. Weisæth (Eds.), *International responses to traumatic stress* (pp. 257–282). New York: Baywood.

Eriksen, H. R., Olff, M., & Ursin, H. (1997). The Code: A revised battery for coping and defence and its relations to subjective health. *Scandinavian Journal of Psychology, 38,* 175–182.

Fossum, L. K., & Moldjord, C. (1999). *Stress and coping in NORAIR/Bosnia 1993–1996.* Trondheim: Psychological Institute, Norwegian University of Science and Technology.

Friedman, H. S. (1992). *Personality and disease.* New York: Wiley.

Gal, R., & Jones, F. D. (1995). A psychological model of combat stress. In F. D. Jones, L. R. Sparacino, J. M. Rothberg, and J. W. Stokes (Eds.), *War psychiatry* (pp. 133–148). Washington, DC: Office of Surgeon General, Borden Institute, Walter Reed Army Medical Center.

Gal, R., & Lazarus, R. S. (1975). The role of activity in anticipating and confronting stressful situations. *Journal of Human Stress [now Behavioral Medicine], 1,* 4–20.

Glass, D. C. (1973). Stress, behavior patterns and coronary disease. *American Scientist, 65,* 177–187.

Grinker, R. R., & Spiegel, J. P. (1945). *Men under stress.* Philadelphia: Blakiston.

Haan, N. (1977). *Coping and defending processes of self-environment organization.* New York: Academic Press.

Hobfoll, S. E. (1985). The limitations of social support in the stress process. In G. Sarason & B. R. Sarason (Eds.), *Social support: Theory, research and application* (pp. 391–414). The Hague, Marinus Niijhogg.

Hobfoll, S. E. (1991). Traumatic stress: A theory based on rapid loss of resources. *Anxiety Research, 4,* 187–197.

Ilnicki, S. (2000). *Polish participation in U.N. Peacekeeping missions and researches in PTSD.* Warszawa, Poland: Department of Psychiatry, Central Clinical Hospital Military Medical School.

Johansson, E. (1997). *In a blue beret: Four Swedish UN battalions in Bosnia.* Karlstad, Sweden: National Defence College.

Johansson, E. (1997, Spring). The role of peacekeepers in the 1990's Swedish experience in U.N.PROFOR. *Armed Forces & Society, 23*(3), 451–466.

Johnsen, B. H., Laberg, J. C., & Eid, J. (1998). Coping strategies and mental health problems in a military unit. *Military Medicine, 163*(9), 599–602

Kobasa, S. C., Maddi, S. R., & Kahn, S. (1982). Hardiness and health: A prospective study. *Journal of Personality and Social Psychology, 42*(1), 168–177.

Kobasa, S. C., Maddi, R. S., Puccetti, M. C., & Zola, M. A. (1985). Effectiveness of hardiness: Exercise and social support as resources against illness. *Journal of Psychosomatic Research, 29*(5), 525–533.

Lazarus, R., & Folkman, S. (1984). *Stress, coping and appraisal.* New York: Springer.

Lefcourt, H. M. (1976). *Locus of control: Current trends in theory and research.* Hillsdale, NJ: Erlbaum.

Lefcourt, H. M., Martin, R. A., & Selah, W. E. (1984). Locus of control and social support: Interactive moderators of stress. *Journal of Personality and Social Psychology, 47*(2), 378–389.

Litz, B. T. (1996). The psychological demands of peacekeeping for military personnel. *PTSD Clinical Quarterly, 6,* 1–8.

Litz, B. T., King, L. A., King, D. W., Orsillo, S. M., & Friedman, M. J. (1997). Warriors as peacekeepers: Features of the Somalia experience and PTSD. *Journal of Consulting and Clinical Psychology, 65*(6), 1001–1010.

Litz, B. T, Orsillo, S. M., Friedman, M. J., Ehlich, P., & Batres, A. (1997). Posttraumatic stress disorder associated with peacekeeping duty in Somalia for U.S. military personnel. *American Journal of Psychiatry, 154,* 178–184.

Marlowe, D. H. (1986). The human dimension of battle and combat breakdown. In R. Gabriel (Ed.), *Military psychiatry: A comparative perspective* (pp. 7–24). Westport, CT: Greenwood Press.

Mehlum, L., & Weiseath, L. (2002, February). Predictors of posttraumatic stress reactions in Norwegian U.N. peacekeepers seven years after service. *Journal of Traumatic Stress, 15*(1), 17–26.

Milgram, N. A., Orensten, R., & Zafrir, E. (1989). Stressors, personal resources and social support in military performance during war. *Military Psychology, 1,* 185–199.

Moldjord, C., & Fossum, L. K. (1999). *Stress and coping in NORAIR/Bosnia 1993–1995,* Trondheim, Norway: Psychological Institute, Norwegian University of Science and Technology.

Moldjord, C., Fossum, L. K., & Holen, A. (2001). Stress and coping in the Norwegian Helicopter Wing in Bosnia—Leadership challenges. In P. Essens, A. Vogelaar, E. Tanercan, & D. Winslow (Eds.), *The human in command: Peace Support Operations.* Amsterdam: Mets & Scilt.

Monat, A., & Lazarus, R. S. (1991). *Stress and coping, an anthology.* New York: Columbia University Press.

Noy, S. (1991). Combat stress reaction. In R. Gal & D. Mangelsdorf (Eds.), *The handbook of military psychology* (pp. 507–530). New York: Wiley.

Olff, M., Brosschot, J. F., & Godaert, G. (1993). Coping styles and health. *Personality and Individual Differences, 15*(1), 81–90.

Rotter, J. B. (1954). *Social learning and clinical psychology.* New York: Prentice-Hall.

Rotter, J. B. (1966). Generalized expectancies for internal control of reinforcement. *Psychological Monographs, 80,* 609.

Sandal, G. M, Endresen, I. M., Vaernes, R., & Ursin, H. (1999). Personality and coping strategies during submarine mission. *Military Psychology, 11*(4), 381–404.

Schreurs, P. J., Tellegen, B., van de Willige, G., & Brosschot, J. F. (1988). *De Utrechtse Coping Lijst: Handleiding.* Lisse: Swets en Zeitlinger.

Solberg, O. A. (1997). *The U.N.-observer—stressors and reactions among Norwegian U.N.-observers in the former Yugoslavia.* Trondheim: Psychological Institute, Norwegian University of Science and Technology.

Solomon, Z., & Mikulincer, M. (1987). Family characteristics and posttraumatic stress disorder: A follow-up of Israeli combat stress reaction casualties. *Family Process, 26,* 383–394.

Solomon, Z., Mikulincer, M., & Benbenishty, R. (1989). Locus of control and combat-related post-traumatic stress disorder: The intervening role of battle intensity, threat appraisal and coping. *British Journal of Clinical Psychology, 28,* 131–144.

Statens, Helsetilysn (1998). A longitudinal study of Norwegian personnel in international operations. Report Nr: 7–98. The Norwegian Ministry of Social Affairs and Health, Oslo.

The Norwegian Armed Forces Joint Medical Service University of Oslo. (1993). *The Unifil study 1991–1992.* Oslo, Norway: Division of Disaster Psychiatry, University of Oslo.

Wallenius, C. (1997). *Reactions and performance when in life-threatening danger; Interview study with Swedish UN-soldiers.* Department of Leadership, Scientific Report Nr 8, 1997. Swedish National Defence College, Karlstad.

Weisæth, A. S. (1982). Psychiatric problems of UNIFIL and the U.N.-soldiers' stress syndrome. *International Review of the Army, Navy, and the Air Force Medical Services, 55,* 109–116.

Weisæth, A. S., & Dittmann, S. E. (1997). Aggression control can prevent UN-soldier encroachment. *Norwegian Military Magazine, 81*(5), 34–40. Oslo.

11

The Soldier Adaptation Model (SAM): Applications to Peacekeeping Research

Paul D. Bliese and Carl Andrew Castro

Since the mid-1980s, the U.S. Army has been involved in a number of research projects involving soldiers deployed on peacekeeping missions. Guiding this research has been a meta-theoretical framework that we refer to as the soldier adaptation model (SAM). This chapter describes our conceptualization of the soldier adaptation model and reviews peacekeeping and humanitarian work from this perspective. There are two goals associated with this chapter. The first is to provide an integrative review of peacekeeping research conducted by the U.S. Army in terms of the SAM. This review is centered on data collected from U.S. Army troops deployed on peacekeeping missions to Haiti in 1994, Bosnia in 1996 and 1997, and Kosovo in 2000; however, it will be augmented with results from garrison-focused research conducted during the same time periods. The second goal of the chapter is to suggest areas for future work.

In our review and discussion of the soldier adaptation framework, we go beyond what is published and thereby accessible in the peer-reviewed scientific literature (though this work is referenced extensively). Many of the observations that we make are *not* part of the public record because the observations represent the trial-and-error efforts of behavioral scientists attempting to study inherently complicated phenomena. Nonetheless, we believe going beyond the published record and including historical observations will make the chapter more informative and allow us greater latitude in suggesting areas for future research.

The outline of the chapter is as follows. We begin by discussing the three components (stressors, moderators, and outcomes) of the soldier adaptation model (SAM), and we discuss the idea of a meta-theoretical framework as a tool for organizing occupational stress research. In discussing the moderator component of the SAM, we introduce the concept of levels-of-analysis, because the identification and modeling of moderators requires careful attention to multilevel issues (Bliese & Jex, in press). Next, we examine stressors and moderators as they relate to peacekeeping operations. Specifically, we identify the types of stressors that have been found to be significant in peacekeeping missions and suggest research areas that appear promising for future stressor-related research. Finally, we discuss key moderators and identify those that appear particularly important in peacekeeping missions.

THE SOLDIER ADAPTATION MODEL AS A META-THEORY

Before describing the soldier adaptation model and reviewing work directly relevant to peacekeeping, it is worth considering the role of the SAM as a framework for hypothesis generation. We view the SAM as a meta-theory. By this we mean that the SAM provides a broad conceptual scheme that can be used to organize constructs or phenomena within the domain of military stress research. That is, the SAM provides an explanation for the phenomena under its domain and a framework from which new phenomena can be assimilated. For us, the soldier adaptation model provides the necessary conceptual background from which particular substantive theories originate and develop, but it does not lead to the deduction of substantive theories. In many ways, the SAM is similar to the theoretical model of occupational stress that emerged out of the University of Michigan's Institute for Social Research (see French & Kahn, 1962; Katz & Kahn, 1978).

All the particular substantive theories developed are then embedded within the meta-theoretical framework. For instance, the components of Karasek's (1979) demands-control theory are embedded within the SAM meta-theoretical framework. That is, data collected within the soldier adaptation framework (either via survey or archival methods) typically contain measures of demands, measures of control, and various outcome measures that allow for replications of the demands-control model. Clearly, the generation of specific hypotheses comes from theories embedded within the broader soldier adaptation framework.

One advantage associated with embedding theories, such as the demands-control theory, into the SAM is that it sets the stage for examining the boundary conditions of theories such as the demands-control model. In a typical study, one could examine the generalizability of the demands-control model by examining how control moderates different types of demands and/or how it relates to various strains. One might find, for instance, that control moderates demands when examining health-related outcomes, but that it does not show a moderating effect for attitudinal or performance-related outcomes. The examination of boundary conditions for theories such as the demands-control model is an exciting area of occupational health research (see Schaubroeck & Merritt, 1997).

Keep in mind that most theoretical examinations of relationships among constructs involve a relatively small number of variables. For example, the demands-control model involves three constructs (a measure of demand, a measure of control, and a measure of strain), and the demands-control-support model (a boundary condition model proposed by Johnson & Hall, 1988) involves four. In terms of analysis, the examination of three variables in a boundary condition model involves two-way interactions, and the examination of four variables involves testing for and interpreting three-way interactions (e.g., Bliese & Castro, 2000; Jex, Bliese, Buzzell, & Primeau, 2001). Sets of interactions more complex than three-way interactions are very difficult to interpret, so this in turn tends to limit the number of variables examined in tests of hypotheses.

Military operational stress research conducted within the U.S. Army typically involves assessing a wide range of variables to ensure that all pertinent issues are addressed. Within this context, the SAM provides (1) a way to categorize the variables collected on surveys and via archival sources and (2) a way to conceptualize the broad relationships among variables. However, the specific hypothesis generation and testing tends to be based on more micro-oriented theories such as demands-control theory (Karasek, 1979), stress efficacy theory (Chen & Bliese, in press; Jex & Bliese, 1999), or the triangle model of responsibility (Britt, 1999). That said, the SAM does make some very specific predictions as well, which we point out in our discussion of the various components of the model. We believe that attention to both macro and micro theories are important in advancing occupational stress research in peacekeeping.

Components of the Soldier Adaptation Model

Implicitly or explicitly, theoretical models guide all research. In military operational research, in particular, it is critical to delineate clearly the components of the theoretical model. In so doing, one can then articulate the expected relationships among variables and thereby facilitate theory advancement. One of the reasons why it is important to delineate the components of the theoretical model in military stress research is to avoid confusion about terminology (see Castro & Adler, 2000; Jex, Beehr, & Roberts, 1992). Thus, for military stress research to advance, it is important for researchers to adopt a common linguistic terminology. Once this terminology is accepted and there is general consensus about where constructs fit within the framework, progress can be made in terms of articulating and testing interrelationships among the various constructs.

The SAM represents an explicit attempt to categorize constructs into one of three major categories—a stressor, a moderator/buffer, or a strain. Placing constructs into this framework sets the stage for systematically exploring relationships among variables. As an aside, the adaptation of the SAM was particularly important for researchers in the U.S. Army because the need for shared terminology was heightened by the fact that behavioral science researchers in the program come from a number of diverse backgrounds to include anthropology, psychiatry, psychology, social work, and sociology, and each of these disciplines have important differences in terminology.

Figure 11.1 is a representation of the SAM with examples of constructs in each of the major categories. Following is a description of the model components and the fundamental assumptions we make that guide this research.

Stressors

The first component of the SAM is military stressors. Stressors are aspects of the environment that place a load or demand on the soldier (Jex et al., 1992). If one applies the terminology of stressors to Karasek's (1979) demands-control model, we would consider job demands to be the stressor.

The first fundamental assumption that the SAM makes is that measurable stressors exist in all environments. Conceptually, we can think of the key soldier environments as consisting of the garrison, training, and deployment. Both the types of stressors present and the relative importance of the existing stressors distinguish these environments (Castro & Adler, 1999). Thus the SAM predicts that the stressors and/or the constellation of stressors should differ depending on the military environment. If the constellation of stressors in the environments were not different, the SAM would consider the environments functionally (and theoretically) the same. This distinction also holds when comparing different peacekeeping missions. If the constellation of stressors for the peacekeeping missions is the same, then the peacekeeping missions too can be viewed as being similar. For instance, in garrison work, hours and job conflict

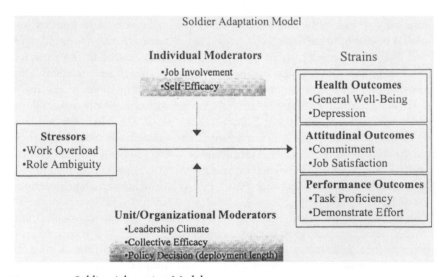

Figure 11.1 Soldier Adaptation Model

might be the predominant stressors of interest, whereas on a peacekeeping deployment, mission ambiguity and social isolation might be the most important stressors present (Bartone, Vaitkus, & Adler, 1998; Harris & Segal, 1985; Mehlum, 1995).

Despite the importance of stressors, relatively few stressors have been routinely examined in the military and occupational stress literature. In occupational stress research, role conflict, role ambiguity, and work overload tend to be the dominant stressors even though there are potentially a large number of stressors present in the work environment (e.g., Abramis, 1994; Jackson & Schuler, 1985). The identification and measurement of additional measures of stressors is an important topic area in military and occupational stress research (see Spector & Jex, 1998). As we note later, this need for reliable measures of stressors is important in peacekeeping research.

Moderators

Moderators are the second component of the SAM. Moderators represent constructs that ameliorate or attenuate the relationship between stressors and strains. Within the domain of moderators, we postulate three levels where effective moderation (or intervention) might occur. These levels include the individual, the group or local leader, and the organization. The second fundamental assumption of the SAM is that moderating constructs for each of these levels can be identified and measured. If this is indeed the case, we should be able to test the postulate that there exist three distinct levels of intervention or moderation.

Moderators are arguably the most critical component of the SAM because they are the constructs on which most interventions are based, and they represent the constructs underlying soldier adaptation. This is because interventions aimed at reducing strain require either (1) a reduction in the levels of the stressor or (2) an increase in factors that enhance resiliency in the face of stressors (i.e., enhanced moderators). However, in many situations (including peacekeeping) the stressors are likely to be immutable: mission accomplishment requires soldiers to endure difficult living conditions, heavy workloads, ambiguity, and so on. Thus it is simply not always feasible (or necessarily desirable) to reduce strain by reducing stressors. In contrast, it is theoretically and often practically feasible to reduce strain by affecting the moderating variables. For instance, if unit cohesion serves as a moderating effect akin to social support and protects soldiers from the severe stressors of combat (see Manning, 1991; Shils & Janowitz, 1948), there may be practically feasible interventions that can be designed to help foster cohesion during garrison training. Parenthetically, we believe that soldier well-being and performance is at its peak when moderation at each of the three levels, the individual, the group, and the organization, is maximal.

Statistically, moderators are identified as interactive effects. For instance, in the demands-control model (Karasek, 1979), the construct of "control" is a moderator because high demands are assumed to lead to negative outcomes *only* in combination with low job control. That is, it is the multiplicative (non-additive) combination of high demands and low control that result in high strain. In addition to control, evidence indicates that social support, coping skills, job engagement, job control, self-efficacy, and leadership have moderating effects (Bliese & Castro, 2000;; Britt & Bliese, 2003; Cohen & Wills, 1985; Jex & Bliese, 1999; Jex et al., 2001).

Individual-level moderators reflect properties of individual soldiers. For instance, self-efficacy, job engagement, and coping styles are all attributes of an individual that have been shown to have moderating effects. Generally speaking, interventions based on individual-level moderators would require direct contact with individual soldiers through information or training. Individual-level moderators might be used as the basis for selecting soldiers with specific characteristics, or individual moderators might serve as the basis for identifying individuals at risk and providing them with specialized skill development (e.g., enhanced coping skills).

In contrast, unit and organizational level moderators are attributes of a broader social network such as the immediate work group or the larger organization. Unit and organizational moderation is based on the premise that individual behavior is at least partially influenced by larger contextual factors—it is, in essence, a move away from models that implicitly conceptualize the stress and health processes as an entirely individual phenomenon (see Bliese, 2002; Bliese & Jex, in press; Diez-Roux, 1998). Leadership climate and collective efficacy (group members' confidence that the group can perform its mission) are examples of unit-level moderators (Bliese & Castro, 2000; Bliese & Halverson, 2002; Jex & Bliese, 1999). Broad policy decisions such as the length of time soldiers should deploy on peacekeeping missions are examples of organizational moderators.

Unit and organizational-level moderators are particularly interesting from a pragmatic perspective because they provide a mechanism by which relatively minor interventions can be leveraged to impact a large number of individuals. For instance, leadership training and development targeted to five or six key company-level leaders may have a large impact on levels of strain within an entire company because leadership appears to impact levels of strain directly, in addition to serving as a moderating effect when stressors are present (Bliese & Castro, 2000). Pragmatically, it may be easier to work with a struggling company commander (group-level intervention) to develop the necessary skills to lead effectively than to teach all members of a company how to cope effectively with stressors caused by poor leadership (individual-level intervention).

Strains

Strains are the final component of the SAM. Strains represent outcomes. In the SAM we have classified strains into one of three broad categories: health, attitudes, or performance. The final assumption of the SAM, then, is that health, attitudes, and performance can be measured and these categories reflect the existence of strain.

Health-related outcomes represent variables that assess some aspect of individual well-being. Typical health-related strains assessed via survey are (1) general well-being, (2) depression, and (3) physical health symptoms (Castro, Bienvenu, Huffman, & Adler, 2000; Stuart & Halverson, 1997). Clearly, a number of additional health-related measures could be assessed either via survey or through physiological monitoring. Promising areas for future research on strains center on developing and field-testing nonintrusive devices that would assess well-being–related strain over extended periods of time.

In the SAM, attitudinal outcomes represent individuals' perceptions of their job and/or organization. Typical outcomes are (1) job satisfaction and (2) commitment. Widespread attitudinal strains such as low job satisfaction and low commitment may reveal a great deal about the status of a group such as a company or platoon. In other words, these strains may be more sensitive to differences among groups than health and well-being strains.

Performance-related strains in the SAM center on a wide variety of job performance dimensions. Within the model, the definition of performance-related strains has been heavily influenced by Campbell's (1999) taxonomy of performance components. These components include (1) job-specific task proficiency, (2) nonjob-specific task proficiency, (3) written and oral communication proficiency, (4) demonstration of effort, (5) maintenance of personal discipline, (6) facilitation of peer and team performance, (7) supervision and leadership, and (8) management and administration proficiency.

Campbell's taxonomy is important because it emphasizes the multifaceted nature of performance. This, in turn, has encouraged researchers to consider collecting both archival performance measures (when available) in addition to survey-based measures. Clearly, no study in either peacekeeping or garrison environments has been able to assess each of these performance components; nonetheless, we are currently attempting to incorporate as many performance dimensions as possible and to investigate how stressors and moderators are related to performance (Jex & Thomas, 2002; Thomas & Jex, 2002). This work is critical for understanding how work stress impacts performance.

The other area of strain-related research that is currently receiving attention is the interrelationships among strains. In the SAM depicted in Figure 11.1, the classes of strains are represented as distinct groups; in reality, however, strains (this is true for stressors and moderators as well) have complex interrelationships. For instance, it is possible that well-being strains play a key mediation role in terms of performance outcomes. That is, stressors may directly impact well-being, which in turn directly impacts performance (Bliese, Thomas, & Jex, 2002). Assessing how the various constructs interact within each component of the SAM certainly deserves future study.

Applying the SAM to Peacekeeping Work

In this section, we focus on some of the specific findings from peacekeeping studies within the context of the soldier adaptation framework. As noted, the goal of this work is to consolidate what has been done and to suggest areas for future research and focus.

Stressors in Peacekeeping

In the SAM, one's selection of stressors is generally directly linked to one's selection of strains. For instance, if the focus of a peacekeeping study is on identifying individuals who are likely to develop posttraumatic stress disorder (PTSD), the stressors assessed should focus on traumatic events that theoretically precipitate PTSD. That is, the selection of the stressors and strains under study should be theoretically congruent. In contrast, if the focus of a study is to enhance individual well-being and organizational performance, the focus will be on relatively common stressors, such as intragroup conflict and work overload, in order for the stressor-strain link to be congruent.

In garrison research, strains such as well-being and performance are generally of most interest to commanders and researchers. In peacekeeping research, however, it is not always clear whether the focus of the research should be on the small subsample of respondents likely to develop syndromes such as PTSD or whether the focus should be on the well-being and performance of the larger sample. Essentially, researchers must decide whether to direct resources at attempting to model the small number of individuals who develop syndromes such as PTSD, or whether they should direct resources towards improving the well-being and performance of the population as a whole.

One's answer to the question just posed will dictate whether one develops a model for a particular study that (1) focuses on stressors that are typically found in garrison; (2) focuses on stressors commonly found in combat, or (3) focuses on a combination of garrison and combat type stressors. Clearly the decisions to emphasize traumatic stressors versus common stressors must be made with some judgment about the nature of the deployment. That said, based on observation from several U.S. peacekeeping operations, it is our impression that few soldiers have developed PTSD-type syndromes. Thus our research group has tended to deemphasize traumatic events and model nontraumatic stressors such as work overload, intragroup conflict, and task insignificance. It should be noted, however, that the SAM easily accommodates both approaches. It should also be noted that military units deployed to other countries (such as the Canadians in Rwanda) were definitely exposed to conditions that could be expected to lead to PTSD-type symptoms. Thus one cannot make very broad generalizations about whether or not conditions will be ripe for PTSD-type outcomes.

Although it is our impression that many of the stressors encountered by U.S. peacekeepers appear to be similar to those found in garrison, analyses of peacekeeping data have revealed several unique nontraumatic stressors. These stressors are generally associated with living conditions. Data reveal that soldiers fairly consistently report concern about privacy and living conditions during deployments. Furthermore, these concerns appear to be related to well-being. For instance, both Bliese and Britt (2001) and Britt and Bliese (2003) found these two stressors to be important in analyses of peacekeepers deployed to Haiti and Bosnia, respectively. Parenthetically, one cannot help but wonder whether these stressors are culturally specific. A highly materialistic and individualistic culture such as the United States would be expected to report concern about privacy and living conditions when deployed; however, it is unclear whether the militaries from other nations would focus in on these "stressors" as did the U.S. military.

Our perception that untraumatic stressors such as work overload, intragroup conflict, and lack of privacy tend to dominate peacekeeping deployments has been an evolutionary process. When U.S. soldiers were deployed to Haiti in 1994, we struggled to identify the unique and potentially traumatic stressors that would be associated with the deployment. A number of stressors were identified, including exposure to extreme poverty, fear of injury and death, concern about potential attacks, fear of contracting disease, and feelings of helplessness. Subsequent analyses, however, suggested these stressors tended to be relatively inconsequential compared to more mundane stressors such as work overload and task (in)significance (Halverson, Bliese, Moore, & Castro, 1995).

This was somewhat ironic because the research staff largely dismissed work overload as a key stressor when developing the survey instrument. Thus there were only a bare minimum number of work overload measures. The basis for largely excluding work overload measures was the erroneous belief that because personnel were deployed, they were therefore working 24 hours a day, 7 days a week. Nonetheless, interviews in theatre clearly revealed that work overload and work hours were a key source of stress for a large number of soldiers. In retrospect, it seems obvious that even during deployments soldiers have a clear sense of time on and time off duty, and that soldiers highly value personal time when deployed. Thus the lesson to be learned from this was that the exotic and potentially traumatic stressors such as "fear of injury and death" were not very important in understanding strains for most soldiers. In contrast, the ordinary stressor of work hours commonly examined in occupational research was quite important (see Sparks, Cooper, Fried, & Shirom, 1997).

The Haiti deployment also highlighted the importance of task (in)-significance as a stressor—task significance reflects a soldier's beliefs that the tasks assigned are meaningful (Bliese, Halverson, & Schriesheim, 2002). This stressor is present in garrison as well in the form of soldiers complaining about having to perform seemingly meaningless tasks; however, the task significance stressor seemed particularly salient for soldiers deployed to Haiti. It was almost as though soldiers felt it was particularly difficult to endure family separation and austere living conditions to perform insignificant tasks.

On a speculative basis, one interesting aspect of nontraumatic stressors in peacekeeping missions is that the stressors may very well show *more* variability in a deployed peacekeeping sample than in a garrison sample. This can have important implications for subsequent modeling because the increased variability may be associated with increases in predictive power. Stated another way, certain stressors in garrison may suffer from range restriction, thereby showing weaker relationships with criterion variables, whereas stressors in peacekeeping may have less range restriction and thus display a stronger relationship with criterion variables. There are at least two reasons why nontraumatic stressors may show increased variability in peacekeeping environments. First, deployments are characterized by a wide variety of units performing a wide variety of missions. Thus it is common for stressors to be unevenly spread out across units as a function of the mission. Some groups may have high workloads, whereas other groups may have low workloads simply as a function of the unit's mission. For instance, units in Haiti involved in transporting logistical equipment from the shipping docks experienced very heavy workloads; those involved in medical care did not. Interestingly, even with the same unit, changes in levels of stressors are likely to vary on a temporal basis, as shown by Bartone and colleagues (1998). That is, there is likely to be a discernible pattern of stressors over time for individual units.

The second reason why there may be more variability in stressors is that many of the common stressors are a product of interpersonal interaction, and deployments increase the interaction potential. If unit relationships are positive, this may result in strong bonding and supportive relationships; however, if unit relationships are strained, stressors such as intragroup conflict may escalate. In garrison, the ability to remove oneself from one's peers at the end of the day may serve to dissipate intragroup tension, whereas in deployments this outlet valve is not present. Research that examined both the variability and mean ratings of stressors such as work overload, intragroup conflict, and role ambiguity across garrison and peacekeeping settings would shed light on the nature of stressors in peacekeeping.

In concluding this discussion of stressors in the soldier adaptation model, we reiterate that the findings noted here stem from modeling well-being and performance-related stains. If the research above had focused on modeling PTSD-type syndromes, it is likely a different set of stressors would have been identified as being important (see Orsillo, Roemer, Litz, Ehlich, & Friedman, 1998). Although PTSD syndrome responses and exposure to traumatic events appear rare in peacekeeping, it does not mean this type of research is without merit. For instance, one interesting finding is that within any deployed population one is likely to have a fairly large number of soldiers who have previously been exposed to traumatic events (see Bolton, Litz, Britt, Adler, & Roemer, 2001). Furthermore, current research suggests that individuals with previous trauma experiences may be at heightened risk for a number of health-related outcomes (Felitti et al., 1998). Thus there may be considerable value in considering past trauma exposure as a moderator even if low trauma exposure is the norm in peacekeeping settings. It is also possible that "semi" traumatic peacekeeping stressors may trigger negative reactions in individuals with a history of past exposure to traumatic events.

The important point about looking at stressors in the context of the SAM is simply that this model helps ensure congruency between stressors and strains. If a SAM is developed to investigate PTSD-type syndromes, it needs to include trauma-based stressors. In contrast, if the SAM is intended to assess well-being and performance in the broad population, stressors should center on factors such as work overload that impact a large percentage of the population. The act of putting constructs into the soldier adaptation framework helps ensure consistency among constructs.

Moderators and Outcomes in Peacekeeping

Within the soldier adaptation framework, the moderators that are identified as important also tend to depend partially on the specific stressors and strains examined in the research. For example, the moderators likely to act as a buffer between traumatic stressors and PTSD are likely to differ from moderators identified as important in examinations of nontraumatic stressors and performance-related strains. Given our interest in well-being and performance, it will come as no surprise that the moderators we view as important in peacekeeping research are moderators related to nontraumatic stressors.

Although moderators play a key role in peacekeeping research and in occupational stress research in general, their detection tends to be particularly difficult in nonexperimental data (see McClelland & Judd, 1993). Therefore, the following review is based on only three published findings. Two of these studies found unit-level moderators in data collected from Haiti; and the remaining study detected an important individual-level moderator among soldiers deployed to Bosnia. To augment the relative paucity of moderator research, we also discuss some promising individual-level moderator work that has been conducted on soldiers in garrison. Recall that, from a pragmatic perspective, unit-level moderators are important because they directly lend themselves to interventions directed at units (or key individuals in units); consequently, they provide the opportunity to effect maximum impact with relatively little cost.

Despite the theoretical and practical impetus to find unit-level moderators, their detection remains difficult. Perhaps the main reason why it is difficult to detect unit-level moderators is that the appropriate level-of-analysis for unit-level studies is typically the company. Unpublished findings conducted by our research group, for instance, have decomposed the variance of key outcomes into individual, platoon, and company-level portions. These analyses fairly consistently reveal that most of the variance resides at the individual and company levels—relatively little variance appears to reside at the platoon level.

For instance, it would be common to find that 95% of the variability in well-being was a function of individual differences, and the remaining 5% was a function of company membership, with squad and platoon membership contributing negligible amounts of variance. This implies that many of the group processes impacting individuals are company-level processes. Unfortunately, because companies tend to be rather large (50–150 soldiers), one needs thousands of soldiers to complete surveys to get a sufficient number of units (30 or more) to perform unit-level moderator analyses with sufficient power to detect interactions.

The Haiti data was one sample that had both a sufficient number of units and individuals to support tests of unit-level moderation. The complete sample had over 3,205 respondents from over 50 units. From this sample, two unit-level moderators were identified: (1) unit leadership climate and (2) consensus about leadership. In both cases, the unit-level moderators were modeled as shared attributes among group members. That is, both the leadership rating and the consensus about leadership rating were identical for all members within the same group (see Bliese & Britt, 2001; Bliese & Halverson, 2002; Gavin & Hofmann, 2002).

Theoretically, it is not surprising that leadership climate serves as a moderator, given that leadership can be considered a form of social support (see Leather, Lawrence, Beale, Cox, & Dickson, 1998). However, few studies have examined the buffering effects of leadership when leadership has been modeled as a shared attribute among group members (i.e., leadership climate). In Haiti, leadership climate played an important role in the relationship between task significance and hostility. In general, soldiers who reported low task significance also reported high levels of psychological hostility. As noted earlier, soldiers appeared particularly loath to endure hardships in cases where they felt the tasks they were asked to perform had little significance (Bliese et al., 2002).

Interestingly, however, the strength of the relationship between task (in)significance and hostility varied depending on the leadership climate within the company. Companies that had positive leadership climates tended to have low hostility regardless of whether soldiers had high or low task significance. In contrast, when leadership climate was poor, the link between task significance and hostility was very strong. Specifically, hostility was low in poor leadership climate groups as long as individuals reported high task significance; however, hostility was extremely high when soldiers in units with poor leadership reported low task significance. Thus it was the interactive effect of both low task significance coupled with poor leadership climate that resulted in high levels of hostility (see Bliese & Halverson, 2002; Gavin & Hofmann, 2002; Markham & Halverson, 2002). It was as though soldiers could accept being deployed and having low task significance as long as the unit's leadership was good.

As noted previously, the second study that identified unit-level buffering effects was also conducted using data from Haiti (Bliese & Britt, 2001). This study also involved leadership; however, in this case we were interested in consensus about leadership as a moderator. That is, we had a theoretical basis to believe units that "agreed" about the quality of unit leadership would have a more positive social climate than would units that disagreed about the quality of the leadership in the unit (see also Bliese & Halverson, 1998).

The consensus study examined whether consensus about leadership (as a group-level attribute) moderated the relationship between (1) work stressors and morale and (2) work stressors and depression. The work stressor variable included concern about living conditions, privacy, lack of time off, and type of work. The results of the study showed that the relationship between (1) work stressors and morale and (2) work stressors and depression was stronger for members of groups with low consensus about leadership. That is, individuals in groups with low consensus about leadership were more strongly impacted by work stressors in terms of reporting high strain.

These results are interesting because they suggest that both the mean and the variance of soldiers' perceptions of leadership reveal important insights about the group's social environment. Bliese and Britt (2001) argued that the mean-variance relationship could be divided into four quadrants ranging from the most positive to the least positive social environments. The most positive quadrant consisted of groups that had positive mean ratings of leadership and low variance (high consensus). The least positive quadrant consisted of groups that had moderate to low leadership ratings and high variance (low consensus). Groups in this quadrant apparently had highly divergent factions within the group regarding perceptions of leadership.

The remaining two quadrants imply neither particularly positive nor particularly negative social environments. The third quadrant is characterized by relatively high leadership ratings coupled with low consensus. Groups in this quadrant might be ones with new leaders. Finally, relatively low leadership ratings, but high consensus suggests agreement about poor leadership indicates that group members are not splintered (i.e., it suggests the group is intact).

In short, consensus about leadership appears to play a moderating role between stressors and strains in peacekeeping environments. We are currently pursuing research to determine whether consensus about leadership plays a moderating role in other peacekeeping settings and in garrison settings. We are confident, however, that consensus about leadership tells something important about unit functioning and that it is related to a variety of strains. Thus we would encourage other researchers to examine consensus about leadership in ongoing peacekeeping research.

The final moderator that has been found to be important in peacekeeping research by WRAIR researchers is job engagement. Not surprisingly, job engagement has a direct relationship with a number of strains—individuals who are highly engaged in their jobs tend to have high satisfaction and high well-being. However, Britt and Bliese (2003) found that individual engagement acted as a moderator between work stressors and several well-being–related strains.

The basic finding was that individuals who had high job engagement tended to be less influenced by work stressors. That is, individuals with high job engagement would report low strain even when exposed to work stressors.

Although somewhat speculative, we believe the moderating effect of high job engagement probably depends on the nature of the stressor. In the Britt and Bliese study, the stressors centered on concerns about living conditions, privacy, and lack of time off (nearly identical to stressors used by Bliese and Britt, 2001). One can argue that the stressors thus identified tend to be tangential to the job, even if they are common in peacekeeping environments. That is, the stressors were distracters that did not directly impede job performance.

In contrast, consider a stressor that is strongly related to task accomplishment. For instance, the stressor of inadequate resources presumably directly impedes task accomplishment. With this stressor one might actually expect job engagement to act in an "antibuffering" role (see Britt, 1999). Individuals with low job engagement might be relatively unaffected by inadequate resources, whereas those with high job engagement might be intensely impacted by inadequate resources.

Thus it appears that job engagement plays an important role in buffering individuals from many of the common stressors encountered in peacekeeping, but researchers should keep in mind that these buffering effects are almost certainly dependent on the type of stressors that soldiers encounter during peacekeeping missions.

In this final section on moderators, we briefly discuss two moderators that have been found to be important in garrison studies. These moderators have not been examined in peacekeeping settings (to the best of our knowledge); nonetheless, we expect they would serve important buffering roles in peacekeeping. The moderators are general self-efficacy and collective efficacy. General self-efficacy is an individual-level variable that reflects an individual's confidence in his or her ability to perform job-related tasks. Collective efficacy represents group members' perceptions of the ability of the group to perform job-related tasks.

Recent research using garrison samples suggests that both self- and collective efficacy serve to moderate stressor-strain relationships. Specifically, individuals with high self-efficacy appear more resilient in the face of garrison stressors such as work overload than do individuals with low self-efficacy. In addition, limited evidence suggests that individuals who are members of groups with high collective efficacy are also protected from work stressors such as work overload (Jex & Bliese, 1999).

One of the reasons why efficacy is interesting from a pragmatic perspective is that differences in efficacy may be strongly related to levels of training. That is, one would expect that high levels of training would lead to high efficacy in both individuals and groups. Because both individual and group training are integral parts of army preparation, it is interesting to consider that training not only helps prepare soldiers for the mission, but it may also buffer soldiers from the negative effects of stressors. Unfortunately, we did not ask self-efficacy questions on either the Haiti or Bosnia data, so we have no evidence to suggest that efficacy plays an important moderating role in peacekeeping missions. Work of this nature remains to be done.

CONCLUSION

From our discussion, it should be clear that the SAM model allows one to organize various components of peacekeeping research into a comprehensive framework. As such, it has considerable value as a tool to integrate research efforts. In practice, we have found that researchers have little difficultly in classifying variables as being stressors, moderators, or outcomes. In cases where variables defy classification we have generally found (1) the construct to be ill defined or (2) researchers to have very different ideas about how the construct operates in the context of the SAM model. One example is work-family conflict. Debate still continues about whether this is a stressor that leads to negative outcomes or an outcome that is the product of work stressors. This type of debate, however, is a healthy part of scientific inquiry.

In thinking about peacekeeping research within the SAM framework, keep in mind that second-order models that emerge from the SAM framework are also important research areas. For instance, constructs such as hardiness or self-efficacy are moderators in the SAM model because they ameliorate the relationship between stressors and outcomes. However, once these factors have been established as important moderators, they may become targets for subsequent modeling. For example, recall that Jex and Bliese (1999) showed that self-efficacy was a moderator in stressor-strain relationships. Individuals with high self-efficacy were less impacted by work stressors than those with low self-efficacy. This initial work clearly fell in the SAM framework. Follow-on work, however, has built off this research by using self-efficacy as an outcome in an attempt to identify leadership attributes that lead to self-efficacy (Chen & Bliese, in press). Thus one can think of the Chen and Bliese (in press) work as providing further elaboration of an important mediator in the SAM model.

In a similar vein, Britt and Bliese (1999) studied leadership factors that lead to job engagement in a study that concurrently showed engagement was an important moderator of stressor-outcome relationships. In this study of soldiers deployed to Bosnia, Britt and Bliese (1999) found out that initiating behaviors (directive behaviors) by leaders led to role clarity. Role clarity, in turn, led to job engagement. The study also revealed that consideration behaviors by leaders were relatively unimportant in that peacekeeping setting. The point we are making is simply that once one identifies a moderator in the SAM model, it can be very valuable to attempt to model the factors that predict the moderator. In this way, researchers provide organizations with rich information designed to help enhance soldier performance and well-being in peacekeeping operations.

In this chapter, we have introduced the soldier adaptation model (SAM) and reviewed current research within this framework. It should be clear that peace-keeping research is an interesting and dynamic area of research. It is, however, also in need of systematic integration efforts. Although no two deployments are exactly alike, we hope to have convincingly conveyed our belief that most of the stressors, moderators, and outcomes encountered in peacekeeping missions can be viewed within a larger meta-theoretical framework (SAM).

NOTE

The views expressed in this paper are those of the authors and do not necessarily represent the official policy or position of the Department of Defense or the U.S. Army Medical Command. During the writing of this manuscript the authors were funded by the Research Area Directorate for Military Operational Medicine (Karl E. Friedl, director), U.S. Army Medical Research and Materiel Command, Fort Detrick, Maryland.

REFERENCES

Abramis, D. J. (1994). Work role ambiguity, job satisfaction, and job performance: Meta-analysis and review. *Psychological Reports, 75,* 1411–1433.

Bartone, P. T., Vaitkus, M. A., & Adler, A. B. (1998). Dimensions of psychological stress in peacekeeping operations. *Military Medicine, 163,* 587–593.

Bliese, P. D. (2002). Multilevel random coefficient modeling in organizational research: Examples using SAS and S-PLUS. In F. Drasgow & N. Schmitt (Eds.), *Measuring and analyzing behavior in organizations: Advances in measurement and data analysis.* San Francisco: Jossey-Bass.

Bliese, P. D., & Britt, T. W. (2001). Social support, group consensus and stressor-strain relationships: Social context matters. *Journal of Organizational Behavior, 22,* 425–436.

Bliese, P. D., & Castro, C. A. (2000). Role clarity, work overload and organizational support: Multilevel evidence of the importance of support. *Work and Stress, 14,* 65–73.

Bliese, P. D., & Halverson, R. R. (1998). Group consensus and psychological well-being: A large field study. *Journal of Applied Social Psychology, 28,* 563–580.

Bliese, P. D., & Halverson, R. R. (2002). Using random group resampling in multilevel research: An example of the buffering effects of leadership climate. *Leadership Quarterly, 13,* 53–68.

Bliese, P. D., Halverson, R. R., & Schriesheim, C. A. (2002). Benchmarking multilevel methods in leadership: The articles, the model, and the data set. *Leadership Quarterly, 13,* 3–14.

Bliese, P. D., & Jex, S. M. (in press). Incorporating a multi-level perspective into occupational stress research: Theoretical, methodological, and practical implications. *Journal of Occupational Health Psychology.*

Bliese, P. D., Thomas, J., & Jex, S. M. (2002, April). *Job strain as a mediator between stressors and performance: Evidence from the field.* Paper presented at the 17th

Annual Conference for Industrial and Organizational Psychology, Toronto, Canada.

Bolton, E. E., Litz, B. T., Britt, T. W., Adler, A., & Roemer, L. (2001). Reports of prior exposure to potentially traumatic events and PTSD in troops poised for deployment. *Journal of Traumatic Stress, 14,* 249–256.

Britt, T. W. (1999). Engaging the self in the field: Testing the triangle model of responsibility. *Personality and Social Psychology Bulletin, 25,* 696–706.

Britt, T. W., & Bliese, P. D. (1999, August). *Leadership, work environment and the stress-buffering effects of job engagement.* Paper presented at the 59th Academy of Management meeting, Chicago, IL.

Britt, T. W., & Bliese, P. D. (2003). Testing the stress-buffering effects of self engagement among soldiers on a military operation. *Journal of Personality, 72,* 245–265.

Campbell, J. P. (1999). The definition and measurement of performance in the new age. In D. R. IlgenD. Pulakos (Eds.), *The changing nature of performance: Implications for staffing, motivation, and development* (pp. 399–429). San Francisco: Jossey-Bass.

Castro, C. A., & Adler, A. B. (1999, Autumn). OPTEMPO: Effects on soldier and unit readiness. *Parameters,* pp. 86–95.

Castro, C. A., & Adler, A. B. (2000). The impact of operations tempo: Issues in measurement. *Proceedings of the 42nd International Military Testing Association,* Edinburgh, UK.

Castro, C. A., Bienvenu, R. V., Huffman, A. H., & Adler, A. B. (2000). Soldier dimensions and operational readiness in U.S. Army forces deployed to Kosovo. *International Review of the Armed Forces Medical Services, 73,* 191–200.

Chen, G., & Bliese, P. D. (in press). The role of different levels of leadership in predicting self and collective efficacy: Evidence for discontinuity. *Journal of Applied Psychology.*

Cohen, S., & Wills, T. A. (1985). Stress, social support, and the buffering hypothesis. *Psychological Bulletin, 98,* 310–357.

Diez-Roux, A. V. (1998). Bringing context back into epidemiology: Variables and fallacies in multilevel analyses. *American Journal of Public Health, 88,* 216–222.

Felitti, V. J., Anda, R. F., Nordenberg, D., Williamson, D. F., Spitz, A. M., Edwards, V., Koss, M. P., & Marks, J. S. (1998). Relationship of childhood abuse and household dysfunction to many of the leading causes of death in adults: The adverse childhood experiences (ACE) study. *American Journal of Preventive Medicine, 14,* 245–258.

French, J. R. P., Jr., & Kahn, R. L. (1962). A programmatic approach to studying the industrial environment and mental health. *Journal of Social Issues, 18,* 1–47.

Gavin, M. B., & Hofmann, D. A. (2002). Using hierarchical linear modeling to investigate the moderating influence of leadership climate. *Leadership Quarterly, 13,* 15–34.

Halverson, R. R., Bliese, P. D., Moore, R. E., & Castro, C. A. (1995). *Psychological well-being and physical health of soldiers deployed for Operation Uphold Democracy: A summary of human dimensions research in Haiti.* Alexandria, VA: Defense Technical Information Center (DTIC: # ADA298125).

Harris, J. J., & Segal, D. R. (1985). Observations from the Sinai: The boredom factor. *Armed Forces & Society, 11,* 235–248.

Jackson, S. E, & Schuler, R. S. (1985). A meta-analysis and conceptual critique of research on role ambiguity and role conflict in work settings. *Organizational Behavior and Human Decision Processes, 36,* 16–78.

Jex, S. M., Beehr, T. A., & Roberts, C. K. (1992). The meaning of occupational stress
items to survey respondents. *Journal of Applied Psychology, 77,* 623–628.

Jex, S. M., & Bliese, P. D. (1999). Efficacy beliefs as a moderator of the impact of work-
related stressors: A multi-level study. *Journal of Applied Psychology, 84,* 349–
361.

Jex, S. M., Bliese, P. D., Buzzell, S., & Primeau, J. (2001). The impact of self-efficacy on
stressor-strain relations: Coping style as an explanatory mechanism. *Journal of
Applied Psychology, 86,* 401–409.

Jex, S. M., & Thomas, J. L. (2002). *Relations between stressors and perceptions of group
process: Job satisfaction and well-being as mediators.* Manuscript submitted for
publication.

Johnson, J. V., & Hall, E. M. (1988). Job strain, work place social support, and cardio-
vascular disease: A cross-sectional study of a random sample of the Swedish
working population. *American Journal of Public Health, 78,* 1336–1342.

Karasek, R. A, Jr. (1979). Job demands, job decision latitude, and mental strain: Implications for job redesign. *Administrative Science Quarterly, 24,* 285–308.

Katz, D., & Kahn, R. L. (1978). *The social psychology of organizations* (2nd ed.). New
York: Wiley.

Leather, P., Lawrence, C., Beale, D., Cox, T., & Dickson, R. (1998). Exposure to occupational violence and the buffering effects of intra-organizational support. *Work
and Stress, 12,* 161–178.

Manning, F. J. (1991). Morale, cohesion, and esprit de corps. In R. Gal & A. D. Mangelsdorff (Eds.), *Handbook of military psychology* (pp. 453–470). New York:
Wiley.

Markham, S. E., & Halverson, R. R. (2002). Within- and between-entity analyses in
multilevel research: A leadership example using single level analyses (SLA) and
boundary conditions (MRA). *Leadership Quarterly, 13,* 35–52.

McClelland, G. H., & Judd, C. M. (1993). Statistical difficulties of detecting interactions
and moderator effects. *Psychological Bulletin, 114,* 376–390.

Mehlum, L. (1995). Positive and negative consequences of serving in a UN peacekeeping mission. A follow-up study. *International Review of Armed Forces
Medical Services, 68,* 289–295.

Orsillo, S. M., Roemer, L., Litz, B. T., Ehlich, P., & Friedman, M. J. (1998). Psychiatric
symptomatology associated with contemporary peacekeeping: An examination
of post-mission functioning among peacekeepers in Somalia. *Journal of Traumatic Stress, 11,* 611–625.

Schaubroeck, J., & Merritt, D. E. (1997). Divergent effects of job control on coping with
work stressors: The key role of self-efficacy. *Academy of Management Journal,
40,* 738–754.

Shils, E., & Janowitz, M. (1948). Cohesion and disintegration in the Wermacht in World
War II. *Public Opinion Quarterly, 12,* 280–315.

Sparks, K., Cooper, C., Fried, Y., & Shirom, A. (1997). The effects of hours of work on
health: A meta-analytic review. *Journal of Occupational and Organizational
Psychology, 70,* 391–408.

Spector, P. E., & Jex, S. M. (1998). Development of four self-report measures of job stressors and strain: Interpersonal conflict at work scale, organizational constraints scale, quantitative workload inventory, and physical symptoms inventory. *Journal of Occupational Health Psychology, 3,* 356–367.

Stuart, J. A., & Halverson, R. R. (1997). The psychological status of U.S. Army soldiers during recent military operations. *Military Medicine, 162,* 737–743.

Thomas, J., & Jex, S. M. (2002, April). *Relations between stressors and job performance: An aggregate-level investigation using multiple criterion measures.* Paper presented at the 17th Annual Conference for Industrial and Organizational Psychology, Toronto, Canada.

V
Clinical Psychology in Peacekeeping

12

The Psychological Challenge of Peacekeeping Operations

Lars Weisæth

"It is like offering first aid to a rattle-snake."
—Ralph Bunche, UN vice secretary general, looking down from his plane on the warring factions in the Congo conflict (1960–1964)

A perusal of the history of military psychiatry shows that in the past veterans have suffered from a variety of combat and postcombat syndromes (Weisæth, 2002). In spite of the rapid developments in new weapons technology, the core stressors for combat soldiers have remained much the same at all times: risk of mutilation and lethal injuries, of witnessing death both when they kill and when their companions are killed, of having to reconcile the conflict between self-preservation instincts and loyalty to the unit. The ways in which combat stress reactions have been interpreted and how they have been expressed have also varied throughout the ages because the psychological injury in the individual soldier reflects the context of a particular place, circumstance, and period. As for postcombat syndromes, the last couple of decades have been the time of posttraumatic stress disorder. Recent experiences with new postcombat syndromes, such as the Gulf War illness, indicate we are entering the era of multiple ill-defined unexplained symptoms (Wessely, 2001).

If new types of symptom clusters and syndromes tend to emerge in soldiers who have been exposed to nontraditional stressors, what is to be expected of military personnel deployed on peacekeeping missions? Are there unique aspects of stressful events associated with peacekeeping that make it differ from all other types of active military service? The premise of this chapter is yes, peacekeeping presents a nontraditional stressor to military personnel at least when the combination of stressors is considered. This kind of stressful service experience is decisively different from everything else military operations may bring about.

Until recently, remarkably little research was focused on the problems of peacekeeping service even though they have been experienced for more than 50 years. The scarcity of research may be a reflection of the temporary and improvised nature that most peacekeeping missions have had from the outset. Another possible explanation may be the ambivalence toward these types of problems often demonstrated by traditional military officers. A third explanation for the delay in directly researching these problems may be that until the mid-1990s, nations traditionally responsible for most research in military psychology and psychiatry were only engaged in peacekeeping in a limited way.

This shift during the 1990s mirrored a shift in peace missions themselves. "Blue beret missions," designed to keep the peace in a particular region, were gradually transformed into peace enforcement operations under NATO command. The research has reflected this change by recognizing the need to address two major types of peacekeeping experiences: traditional nonvolatile peacekeeping missions, fast-changing peace enforcement operations, and the range of operational experiences in between.

Following a review of peacekeeping and peace enforcement operations, this chapter continues with a discussion of particular stressors and service-related stress reactions among peacekeepers. A pertinent question is whether very special situations imposed on peacekeeping soldiers combine to create specific harmful effects on their health and performance. The contrast between stress factors in peacekeeping missions, in which the conflicting parties consented to bring in the UN, the "blue beret missions," with the "green helmet missions" serves as a cornerstone for understanding the possible development of a unique set of symptoms consistent with nontraditional deployment stressors.

"As a peacekeeper you sometimes have to turn the other cheek. If a soldier does that, his nation is no longer a super-power."

—G. Hägglund, 1991

FROM BLUE BERET TO GREEN HELMET

One of the most important effects of the Second World War was the concerted attempt to create a world order in which military aggression could be avoided. The founding fathers of the UN established a new world order whereby the member nations solemnly declared to refrain from the threat or use of force against the territorial integrity or political independence of any state.

The Western democracies had been taught a lesson: they had to be willing to engage in aggressive campaigns in order to stop a dictator in time. The smaller nations, according to their own security interests, were then and still are, particularly in favor of a strong and vital UN playing an active role, even including military responses. The establishment of a permanent, individually recruited military unit at the disposal of the UN Security Council, has, however, proved to be a utopian dream.

Defining Missions

Two distinctly different approaches could, according to the UN Charter, be applied to resolve disputes between nations; a nonviolent and a violent approach. The following main categories came into practice: (1) UN presence, (2) observer missions, (3) peacekeeping missions, and (4) enforcement operations.

The Nonviolent Approach

Chapter VI of the UN Charter, entitled "Pacific Settlement of Disputes," commits member nations first of all to seek a negotiated settlement of their differences. Article 33 of that chapter gives the methods to be used in seeking a peaceful solution: "A solution by negotiation, enquiry, mediation, conciliation, arbitration, judicial settlement, resort to regional agencies or arrangements, or other peaceful means of their own choice."

The Enforcement Approach

Chapter VII of the UN Charter deals with threats to peace, breach of the peace, or acts of aggression. According to this chapter, the member states are obliged to take measures to maintain or restore international peace and security, including the use of force if necessary, in other words, willingness to fight a war, employing a traditional military force consisting of contingents from member states.

Historical Transitions

Whereas the UN Charter perceived interstate conflicts as the main peace problem, later history has proved otherwise. Boutros Boutros-Ghali (1992, 1995), secretary-general of the UN, pointed out that an increasing proportion of the problems creating the need for peacekeeping operations was intrastate in nature, in effect, civil wars. This contributed to a considerable number of new complications compared to the former international type of conflict. This new complexity—including the collapse of state institutions, breakdown of law and order, and general banditry and chaos—carries increased risk to the peacekeepers in the form of new stressors that could result in traumatic stress reactions.

The limited success of many Chapter VI operations, "the blue beret" missions, has led to an increase in Chapter VII operations. The development of these "green helmet" missions has been made possible by multinational forces consisting of national contingents at the disposal of the UN for a limited mission—and the use of the NATO Command System. The lightly armed soldier with a blue beret who monitored a cease-fire sandwiched between two parties has been replaced with a more combatlike soldier caught up in a conflict with no or sporadic consent from the conflicting parties.

When it comes to the difference between blue beret and green helmet missions, the findings are very clear. The change during the Balkan conflict in the 1990s from UN- to NATO-led missions provides us with an opportunity to compare soldiers' perception of these two forms of peace operations. Johansson (2001) compared 3,448 Swedish UN peacekeepers who had served in Bosnia from 1993 to 1995 with 2,298 Swedish soldiers who served in the NATO-led operation in Bosnia from 1995 to 1998. Sweden had rather extensive experience with UN operations, but considerably less regarding NATO, because Sweden is not a member. The needs regarding preparation and training were grouped into four themes: the need to understand the conflict in the region, the need to be able to handle new situations, the need to master military/technical matters, and the need for leadership and stress management. For all four themes, the UN-led operation was viewed as requiring more training than the NATO-led operation. For example, 42% of the soldiers in the UN operation reported needing training in negotiation techniques, whereas 26% of soldiers in the NATO operation did. Similarly, 45% of the soldiers in the UN operation reported needing training in the ability to counter threats and provocations, whereas 29% of soldiers in the NATO operation did. There were also differences between soldiers in the UN and NATO operations in terms of needing training in recognizing stress in others (45% vs. 29%, respectively). Overall, Johanssen concluded that the progression to a NATO-led operation meant the tasks and functions were closer to the role for which soldiers are traditionally trained.

The Nordic countries, with massive and varied experience with blue beret missions since 1947, had gradually come to recognize the unique training requirements for blue beret operations. Peacekeeping soldiers, and more specifically their commanders, needed special training in addition to their basic military training for war before they were deployed (Egge, Mortensen, & Weisæth, 1996).

The difference between the blue beret peacekeeping and the green helmet peace enforcement operations is also reflected in different attitudes that military personnel have about these missions. In difficult UN peacekeeping operations, such as in Southern Lebanon (UNIFIL) and Croatia and Bosnia (UNPROFOR), an increase in negative views among the soldiers of the different population groups has been documented (Weisæth, Aarhaug, Mehlum, & Larsen, 1993). When NATO took over for UNPROFOR, fewer expressed negative views (Johansson, 2001). Families of soldiers were also more supportive toward the NATO operation (56%) than the UN operation (39%).

The evidence thus far indicates that "blue beret missions" create more need for special training and more stress than "green helmet missions" because the demands and stressors of these missions are relatively unique

SERVICE-RELATED STRESSORS OF PEACEKEEPING
AND PEACE ENFORCEMENT

UN peacekeeping as a concept was not foreseen by the founding fathers of the UN Charter. The idea grew out of a necessity to introduce a third-party element in conflicts. The underlying philosophy was similar to that of a police force in a civilized democratic society: Police officers represent the law. The police officers do not take sides in the struggle between two persons or two gangs fighting in the street. Their job is to end the fighting and to bring the parties of the conflict to court where the dispute can receive a fair hearing.

This neutrality is not always easy for the individual peacekeeper to maintain, but he or she must make strong efforts to behave neutrally. The concept of "perceived neutrality," that the conflicting parties see and experience the UN as neutral, is of paramount importance. In several peacekeeping operations the UN has succeeded in stopping the bloodshed, but the basic dispute has remained unsettled (Egge et al., 1996). This has resulted in many peacekeeping missions being perpetuated without reaching a negotiated solution. This state of affairs is often frustrating to the participants in a peacekeeping operation.

The peacekeeper works at the intersection between political, humanitarian, and military objectives. The peacekeeper's family members' view of the absence and mission of the peacekeeper is significant to the morale and motivation of military personnel (Johansson, 2001). Daily media coverage of significant incidents in the field may scare the family, whereas the day-to-day routine work is not considered "news." Prior to the introduction of NATO into peace operations, there were sometimes several weaknesses in the composition of the force (Hägglund, 1991). Because UN peacekeeping forces have often been composed of contingents from many predominantly small countries, the military efficiency of the force has been hampered by differences in weaponry and equipment, military traditions and skills, and languages and cultural backgrounds. Furthermore, contingents from many small nations have not been able to use sophisticated equipment, even if it is provided by the UN. Some of the deficiencies have been overcome by appropriate divisions of labor and tasks and by directing necessary resources to the weakest contingents. Still, a multinational force composed of battalions from small countries from different parts of the world can never be expected to reach the level of military professionalism of a single nation force.

Another complicating factor in UN-led operations is the lack of unified military terminology and communication procedures, in contrast to NATO, which is tied together by strict standards. The military deficiency of the UN peacekeeping system has included, for example, inadequate public relations, liaison and reporting, and lack of intelligence information necessary for operation in the field.

What divides peacekeeping from peace enforcement is not the level of violence, but consent from the conflicting parties to bring in the UN. Consent is supported by the principles of impartiality, minimum force, legitimacy, credibility, mutual respect, and transparency. The rules of engagement for the operation are tied to a set of regulations closely in line with the standards of fundamental human rights. This may bring the responsible UN commander into a difficult position because the adversary may not always observe the same standards.

A variety of stress factors operate in the field. Among these are many stressors common to all deployments on foreign soil such as climate, cultural differences, language, boredom associated with the military routine, and so on. I will, however, limit exploration to those factors considered specific to the peacekeeper role.

Studies of soldiers on operations in Gaza, Congo (Galtung & Hveem, 1976) and Cyprus (Moskos, 1976) in the 1960s and 1970s revealed some lack of instrumental knowledge about the type of task soldiers faced. Research has also indicated that peacekeeping under conditions in which there is established peace (e.g., Sinai) is associated with frustration, boredom, and role conflict, particularly for soldiers specifically trained for active combat duty (Rikhye, Harbottle, & Egge, 1974; Segal, Furukawa & Lindh, 1990). Intraforce frustrations, often arising from cultural differences in a multinational force, can also add significantly to the general stress level.

For peacekeeping deployments in which the peace is not stable or established, other critical stressors emerge. These stressors may be categorized into three types of exposures each likely to initiate particular courses of stress symptoms: the single potential traumatic event followed by acute reactions; serial stressful events that may have a gradual cumulative effect over time; and the prolonged exposure to continuous threat that may, particularly when combined with low control and high uncertainty, be more likely to cause delayed posttraumatic reactions (Giller & Weisæth, 1996). Furthermore, the typical stressors reported by UN personnel may be categorized as (1) personal exposure to danger, (2) witnessing very stressful events involving civilians, (3) experiencing humiliation by the former warring factions, and (4) frustration in the operational tasks.

Exposure to Danger

Military personnel deployed on peace operations are at risk for exposure to physical danger. During the UN operation in the Congo, which started as a peacekeeping operation but developed into actual combat, 0.5% of the Swedish soldiers were killed and 2% wounded (Kettner, 1972). In a retrospective study of the 26 Norwegian UNIFIL contingents from 1978 to 1991, 50% of the veterans reported they had at least occasionally been exposed to severe threats; 38.8% had at least occasionally been exposed to gunfire; and 22.4% had been involved in combat (Weisæth et al., 1993). Among the infantry battalions of the first three Norwegian UNIFIL contingents, 80% reported an "exchange of fire" situation, and 7% had been taken hostage.

In the UN-led deployment to the Balkans, a sizable proportion of peace-keepers were also exposed to danger. Among Swedish soldiers in UNPROFOR (1993–1995), 27% had experienced shelling almost daily, whereas 17% had been exposed to direct fire (Johansson, 2001). In the Danish battalion on mission in Croatia in 1993, 65% had been threatened with arms, 38% had been in crossfire, and 25% had fired their own weapon (Bache & Hommelgaard, 1994).

Exposure to the danger of mined areas was rated as the most important stressor by more than 60% of military nurses serving in the former Yugoslavia (Knudsen, 1999). Passing through areas almost daily where there was a danger of mines was also reported by 44% in the Swedish study of UNPROFOR military personnel (Johansson, 2001).

Witnessing Experiences

Military personnel deployed on peacekeeping missions also report witnessing the suffering of others often in a context in which they are not allowed or able to intervene. Among Norwegian military personnel in the UNIFIL study and Swedish personnel in the UNPROFOR study, 3.2% and 16%, respectively, reported often or occasionally witnessing death. Seven percent of the Swedish battalion mentioned exposure to dead or wounded people daily or quite often, and 5% witnessed assault on civilians daily or quite often.

Among the most severe events typical for the peacekeeper was the witnessing of atrocities against civilians without being able to help them; what we have termed "double helplessness"—being a helpless spectator to helpless victims. Mandates that permitted use of force only in self-defense when exposed to severe danger to life made for such inescapable and shocking situations. The psychological effect was a threat to self-esteem and the questioning of the mission's meaning. In the event a soldier witnessed this kind of violence, the only official response open to soldiers was to write a report on the incident that would pass through the UN system, eventually end up in the UN Headquarters in New York, and possibly have an effect down the line. This kind of reporting was not enough, however, to secure the experience of manageability and meaningfulness, two factors that may help in coping with extreme events (Antonovsky, 1987).

Humiliations

The attitude of the civilian population may make a big difference. In South Lebanon the civilian population welcomed the UN troops as liberators from an occupation and as protectors. Whereas the conflicting parties, among them Palestinian and Israeli forces, obviously intended to humiliate. Verbal harassment was frequent, and name-calling included being told the "UN" stood for "United Nothing." In the UNIFIL study, 9.1% reported being humiliated often or very often, and 24% reported being humiliated occasionally. Before the NATO bombing in Bosnia, the verbal taunt was that NATO stood for "No Action, Talk Only."

Direct aggression from the civilian population, from verbal abuse to rock throwing and other violent acts, is dangerous, humiliating, and frustrating. In Somalia, what was originally a humanitarian mission that developed into combat, the situation became quite intense. U.S. soldiers reported stressors that included "rocks thrown at unit" (76%), "unit fired upon" (65%), and "rejected by Somalis when trying to help" (56%; Litz, Orsillo, Friedman, Ehlich, & Batres, 1997). Even one single incident may humiliate and enrage an entire nation, as was the case when the body of a U.S. serviceman was pulled through the dusty streets of Mogadishu and the incident was televised worldwide.

Frustrations

Another frequent stressor is when external factors hinder the fulfillment of duties. Local factions representing such obstacles were a daily experience reported by 56% in the Swedish study of UNPROFOR personnel. Nearly as many experienced negotiations and confrontations at checkpoints. Theft of personal or UN property was another problem. More dramatically, "human roadblocks" by women and children that prevented emergency transports and food deliveries to suffering civilian minorities made for confrontations that were reported as Catch-22 situations.

It may seem a modest figure that 13% of the Swedish soldiers reported that almost daily or quite often the rules of engagement prevented them from returning fire. For those who experienced this restriction, however, it represents a very particular type of stress. The tension inherent in controlling retaliatory impulses converges with the other deployment stressors. The impact of these stressors is discussed next.

The Spectrum of Peacekeeping Operations

The description of peacekeeping stressors just described is mainly based on data from UN peacekeeping operations. What is the comparable situation in the green helmet peace-enforcing operations? Quite a few of the soldiers with experience from both blue beret and green helmet missions reported that severe stress is less prevalent in NATO operations than in traditional UN peacekeeping. This difference is also reflected in the degree to which the military operation was able to carry out its mission: whereas only 47% of military personnel stated that their battalion succeeded in protecting civilians against attack/assault during the UN period in Bosnia, 86% did during the NATO period. Similarly, whereas a modest 43% during the UN period reported they had been able to mollify the conflicting parties, an impressive 94% reported this during the NATO period (Johansson, 2001).

Results from the Johansson (2001) and other studies suggest that the unique constellations of stressors and outcomes that have been found with military personnel on traditional blue helmet operations may not apply to NATO-led operations. Thus two key points must be established. First, to what extent has there been a specific cluster of stressors and symptoms associated with traditional peacekeeping? Second, to what extent may these stressors and symptoms emerge in NATO-led peace enforcement operations?

Stressors and Stress Reactions in Traditional Peacekeeping

How service-related stressors found on traditional peacekeeping missions such as those just described converge to create a stress reaction in peacekeeping soldiers depends on several factors. Next is an example of how one soldier deployed on a peacekeeping mission developed a traumatic stress reaction in response to the kinds of stressors that can be found during unstable blue helmet operations. The case study is an attempt to identify and generate a full picture of the potentially unique stressors and symptoms associated with traditional peacekeeping.

Following his compulsory military service, Peter, a 22-year-old single Norwegian soldier, volunteered for UN service and was trained as a rifleman in an army battalion that was part of Norway's Stand-by Forces in UN Service. Peter had good preservice functioning, and the only significant event in the months prior to his entering service was minor low back pain due to a parachute jump. A few weeks after volunteering, Peter was mobilized and within days was deployed to South Lebanon in the immediate aftermath of the civil war (United Nation Interim Force in Lebanon; UNIFIL). He adjusted well to the field conditions, quickly learning to discriminate among the different signs of external danger (e.g., type of gun or artillery fire).

When his tent was torn apart by grenade shrapnel while he was asleep, he experienced a strong, but normal fear response. The first days following this potentially traumatic event, he developed a somewhat generalized startle response that had to be controlled during periods of heavy fire. Before he was fully recovered from the tent incident, he was fired at from behind, which further taxed his resources. Before he had recuperated from this second stressor, an extremely severe event occurred. Approached by a PLO soldier who gestured for a cigarette lighter, Peter was suddenly seized by the soldier, who pulled out a hidden hand grenade. Peter was unable to escape or defend himself, although he did manage to pull the trigger of his rifle, which was on safety. The PLO soldier, intoxicated by cannabis, hung the hand grenade around Peter's neck while holding the release mechanism and threatening to blow Peter up by pulling a string tied to the trigger. Thinking coolly and unaware of emotions at the time, Peter was able to get the PLO soldier to move toward the UN platoon, which was in hiding nearby. UN soldiers quickly overpowered the

PLO soldier before he could do any harm. He was disarmed and then released according to the rules of engagement.

After this close escape and profound threat to his life, Peter had a defusing session with the battalion doctor, which involved expression of affect and the opportunity to relax in safer surroundings. Peter calmed down somewhat, but experienced generally increased muscular tension with sudden loss of tonus when he was exposed to strong acoustic stimuli. He also experienced nightmares about the incident and fear of being alone and of darkness. He was very irritable and had intense anxiety about losing control over his violent retaliatory impulses. In spite of his efforts to control his anger, he was considered too labile to be returned to frontline duty.

In terms of psychophysiological symptoms, Peter developed dyspepsia with hyperacidity and gradually developed low back pain irradiating down his leg. He was eventually admitted to the UNIFIL hospital for these somatic conditions where he came to the attention of a psychiatrist [LW]. He was repatriated for reasons related to his somatic condition, and after returning home recovered within 10 weeks from his sciatic symptoms. At a one-year follow-up he still had posttraumatic stress disorder (PTSD) with repetitive nightmares of being executed by hand grenades or being shot in his recovered leg. His main symptoms were easily provoked aggression with associated guilt and fear of loss of control. After psychotherapy for PTSD, he gradually became free of symptoms.

Five years later he phoned LW late at night in a drunk and suicidal state. He described symptoms of depression, fear of losing control over his aggressive impulses, and feeling constant tension and hyperalertness. The examination that followed this emergency call for help revealed severe PTSD and comorbid depression. Despite these symptoms, he had not been incapacitated in the years since his repatriation. He also had practiced a contraphobic coping strategy that gave him temporary relief from his symptoms: driving his motorcycle at double the speed limit. Eventually, he returned to therapy and sold his motorcycle.

The case illustrates several issues that confront soldiers deployed on peacekeeping operations. First, the peacekeeper's failure to balance between trust building and deterrence, in this case, led him into a dangerous trap. The breach in trust added much to the psychological injury. Second, the UN force had to let the perpetrator go because the UN mandate did not include the right to make arrests. Setting free the PLO soldier was an insult to the peacekeeper's sense of justice. Third, the principles of frontline treatment could not be followed. Because of the soldier's high level of arousal and his strong retaliatory impulses, his mental balance was seen as too unstable for a holding policy to be practiced, he had to be removed from contact with the parties, and he was separated from his unit. The importance of adhering to the PIE principles of early intervention (proximity, immediacy, and expectancy) is well documented (Shepard, 2000). The repatriation compounded the peacekeeper's sense of failure and sense of having let down his comrades that his removal from the front line had created in the first place.

To what degree do UN peacekeepers suffer from stress reactions that make them unfit for further service during the mission? A number of studies have described psychological reactions to peacekeeping stress. During the UN operation in the Congo, which started as a peacekeeping operation but developed into actual combat, 3.5% of the Swedish soldiers experienced such severe psychological combat reactions that they became unfit for further active service. Kettner's study (1972) of these troops indicated that these soldiers differed somewhat from controls, but not on a statistically significant level. The trend in this Swedish study indicated that soldiers under the age of 21 were more prone to develop combat stress reactions. This led to the conclusion that applicants for UN service should be enrolled only after the age of 21. Personality factors seemed to play a lesser role in mental breakdowns during combat than under less dangerous military conditions. The soldiers were, however, highly selected. Kettner's follow-up study (1972) of the same Swedish cases four years later showed that soldiers with combat reactions performed just as well as the controls in civilian life except they had a somewhat higher accident rate. This study exemplifies two fundamental points in research on the unique pattern of outcomes associated with traditional peacekeeping. First, the operation itself is fluid, and part of the difficulty was likely the shift from traditional peacekeeping to combat. The question as to whether the impact on the soldiers was based on the peacekeeping experience, the combat experiences, or the unmet expectation that the deployment would be a peacekeeping mission remain unresolved. Second, the shift in policy that resulted from this study's tentative conclusions demonstrates the military's interest in and need for greater understanding in predicting psychological adjustment following exposure to deployment stressors.

A study of the first two years of the UN Interim Force in Lebanon (UNIFIL) operation showed that the level of psychiatric morbidity, only 1.6% of the total force, was relatively low, but it still comprised the diagnosis that most frequently led to repatriation. Two thirds of the 34 soldiers who were repatriated due to mental problems in the first Norwegian battalion in UNIFIL had severe psychic traumas, and 80% of these individuals had normal pretrauma personality functioning. Psychiatric morbidity was also higher among volunteer conscript soldiers from industrialized countries than developing countries. The higher rates may have been partly due to different medical resources, more effective informal social supports, and attitudes such as less stigma attached to psychic problems and lower thresholds for sickness and patient roles. In terms of symptom rates, rather than diagnostic rates, 17% of the first Norwegian UNIFIL contingent reported having experienced significant psychic problems, compared to 6.3%, 7%, and 4.9% in contingents II, III, and IV (Weisæth, 1979; Weisæth & Sund, 1982). Such a contrast is evidence of how stress levels even within one operation can change dramatically depending on the time period and the rotation.

As illustrated by the case presentation, the demands for a well-balanced psyche and for complete control over angry impulses in this kind (and really any kind) of military service have to be strict. Because the soldiers had to be removed from their units in order to avoid contact with the former warring factions, a policy based on preferred early intervention was not possible. This has probably increased the numbers who were unable to return to duty and had to be repatriated, possibly also increasing their risk for PTSD several years after (Weisæth et al., 1993).

Other studies demonstrate psychological stress reactions that stem from peacekeeping stressors related to danger. For example, French studies (Doutheau, Lebigot, Moraud, Crocq, Fabre, & Favre, 1994) of 40 psychiatric cases (38 from ex-Yugoslavia and 2 from Somalia) recorded anxiety disorders related to the experience of sniper fire and with the insecurity of being a living target.

The prevalence of posttraumatic stress disorder (measured by the Posttraumatic Symptom Scale, PTSS-10) was 5% overall, but 16% in the subgroup of personnel having been prematurely repatriated from UNIFIL (Mehlum, 1995; Mehlum & Weisæth, 2002). Multiple regression analyses showed that the following variables made separate and significant contributions to the explained variance of the PTSS-10: service stress exposure, perceived lack of meaningfulness with respect to the military mission, and stressful life events in life after service. These factors explained 25% and 37% of the variation in the score on the PTSS-10, for the overall sample and the repatriated sample, respectively.

The hypothesis that peacekeeping stress reactions are exacerbated, if not caused, by the pressure of self-restraint under conditions of frustrating policies and experiences is supported in part by data from noncombat arms units. Swedish studies of medical and logistics units in UNIFIL (Carlström, Lundin, & Otto, 1990; Lundin & Otto, 1989) found that stress reactions among those personnel were not prominent. During service in UNFICYP, only 0.5 % of the Swedish contingent suffered from nervous breakdowns, (Lundin & Otto, 1992). Such findings suggest that the task of peacekeeping is most psychologically challenging to those soldiers in the combat arms—whether because they are exposed to more extreme events, because their specialized training leads them to experience these events as more stressful, or some combination of the two.

"Of all manifestations of power, restraint impresses men most."
(Thucydides, quoted by Colin Powell when he retired as
Chairman of the Joint Chiefs of Staff in 1993)

Peacekeeper's Stress Syndrome?

A cluster of posttraumatic stress symptoms was observed in many soldiers that might be tentatively termed "peacekeeper's stress syndrome" (Weisæth, 1979; Weisæth & Sund, 1982). In addition to the typical posttraumatic stress symptoms, a major symptom was fear of losing control over one's aggression, rather than fear of external threats. The essence of the underlying problem is a conflict between strong aggressive impulses seeking an outlet and the inability to express them in action and even verbally. As illustrated in the case study, the UNIFIL soldier had to control both fight and flight impulses and struggle to maintain his neutrality. Soldiers carry a heavy responsibility: if they return fire when the specific criteria for use of weapons are not present, the political and military conflict may escalate, and the UN position can be weakened.

This cognitive, emotional, and behavioral conflict, with its intra- and extrapsychic consequences, seemed to be an important problem for UN soldiers on traditional peacekeeping missions. Exposure to physical danger, provocations and humiliations, and being a passive witness to helpless victims of violence attacked by the feuding factions are significant stressors that provoke strong anger, which has to be mastered at almost any cost. In addition, uncertainty, lack of information, enforced passivity, low control, rapid changes, time pressure, high risk of failure, conflicting options, and high levels of responsibility compound the stressfulness of the situation. The effects of stress on perceptual, cognitive, affective, and behavioral functions have the potential to reduce severely the soldier's ability to solve complex problems.

Anger control is necessary; to abstain from retaliation when threatened or harassed demands a special type of courage and developed sense of self. In a follow-up study of Danish UN soldiers two years after their end of service in ex-Yugoslavia in 1995, Andersen (1998) found a very strong correlation between aggression and arousal. Twelve percent of all the veterans had problems controlling their temper, and 9% had become very angry. This rate of anger is consistent with the contention that anger problems are a fundamental component of the proposed constellation of symptoms that comprise a peacekeeper's stress syndrome and that soldiers confronted with the particular frustrations of peacekeeping can be at risk for developing problems with anger. Ironically, in ordinary warfare, lack of aggression among combat troops makes a high proportion of them unable to fire their weapon (Marshall, 1947). In peacekeeping, the problem seems to be the opposite—aggression associated with not to be allowed to use one's weapon.

Another peacekeeping stressor that may lead to the development of a particular kind of peacekeeping stress reaction is the need to maintain neutrality. Maintaining neutrality between two or more warring parties taxes the mental apparatus of the individual peacekeeper, thereby also possibly increasing the risk of psychiatric effects. As in the case of other military tasks, training and mental preparation of personnel are expected to lead to increased task-solving efficiency and reduced risk of severe traumatic effects. Thorough internalization of the mission's purpose with clear and detailed reference to specific paragraphs in the UN Declaration of Human Rights might be a possible method to bolster the soldier's mental strength.

In an article on military stress syndromes, Pearn (2000) describes diagnostic features and summary of the nosological evolution for five acute operational stress disorders. Peacekeeper's acute stress syndrome is listed along with acute combat stress disorder, conversion reactions, the counterdisaster syndrome, and the Stockholm syndrome. Pearn describes this peacekeeper's acute stress syndrome as a role-identity conflict compounded by the long-term effects of frustration, outrage, guilt, and mortal fear. It has been reported from several UN peacekeeping deployments.

The traditional options for a soldier in combat are either fight, flight, surrender, be wounded, or escape into some illness. However, given that in traditional peacekeeping operations, peacekeepers have been allowed to use their own weapon only in self-defense, they have been forced to endure the grueling experience of being the target of "firing close" while not being permitted to return fire (Egge et al., 1996). There are scores of other examples of life-threatening experiences and types of harassment that peacekeepers are expected to endure without losing their temper or retaliating in kind. In some cases, peacekeepers have been taken hostage and held for days with hand grenades tied to their body. Or they have had to observe cruel treatment of civilians in situations where they were either unable or not permitted to defend and protect the victims. Thus the traditional methods of response will not necessarily serve soldiers deployed on peacekeeping missions, particularly missions with restrictive rules of engagement and hostile environments. Soldiers in these circumstances may be more at risk for developing problems that can evolve into an operational stress reaction.

In order to understand whether there is indeed a unique syndrome associated with traditional peacekeeping, a comprehensive and systematic study needs to be conducted in which alternative diagnoses are considered using standard interview techniques or other formal methods of assessment. This research is important because simply adding a new label to an already established set of diagnoses reduces their clarity and precision and creates unnecessary confusion. Nevertheless, the goals of identifying a unique syndrome associated with peacekeepers would be to determine the prevalence of symptoms, the related risk factors, the course of symptoms, and, most importantly, serve as a first step in identifying appropriate treatments or prevention measures. Whether there is just one syndrome or several, as suggested by Pearn (2000), clinical research with military personnel on combat, peacekeeping, and peace enforcement operations needs to be conducted. By doing so, the basis for understanding whether there is also a unique set of stressors and symptoms associated with peace enforcement can be explored. It may well be that in turning to the more effective military strategy of green helmet operations, there will continue to be an accompanying reduction in the cluster of symptoms associated with traditional peacekeeping. Empowering professionally trained military personnel, placing them in danger with options in terms of both physical and psychological self-defense, and supporting their efforts at achieving their mission in a complex environment are most likely step not only in the direction of mission accomplishment but also in the direction of overall readiness for future operations.

REFERENCES

Andersen, H. E. (1998). *Danske FN-soldater 2 år etter* [Danish UN soldiers 2 years after]. Copenhagen: Psykologisk Afdeling, Forsvarets Center for Lederskap.

Antonovsky, A. (1987). *Unraveling the mystery of health. How people manage stress and stay well.* San Francisco: Jossey-Bass.

Bache, M., & Hommelgaard, B. (1994). *Danske FN-soldater. Oplevelser og stress-reaktioner [Danish UN soldiers: Experiences and stress reactions].* Copenhagen: Center for Leadership.

Boutros-Ghali, B. (1992). *An agenda for peace. Preventive diplomacy, peacemaking and peacekeeping.* New York: United Nations.

Boutros-Ghali, B. (1995, January 3). Supplement to an agenda for peace. *Position paper of the secretary-general on the occasion of the fiftieth anniversary of the United Nations A/50/60.* New York: United Nations.

Carlström, A., Lundin, T., & Otto, U. (1990). Mental adjustment of Swedish U.N. soldiers in South Lebanon in 1988. *Stress Medicine, 6,* 305–310.

Doutheau, C., Lebigot, F., Moraud, L., Crocq, L., Fabre, L. M., & Favre, J. D. (1994). Stress factors and psychopathological reactions of U.N. missions in the French Army. *International Review of the Army, Navy and Air Force Medical Services, 67,* 36–38.

Egge, B., Mortensen, M. S., & Weisæth, L. (1996). Armed conflicts—soldiers for peace: Ordeals and stress. In Y. Danieli, N. S. Rodley, & L. Weisæth (Eds.), *International Responses to Traumatic Stress* (pp. 257–282). New York: Baywood.

Galtung, J., & Hveem, H. (1976). Participants in peacekeeping forces. In J. Galtung (Ed.), *Peace, war and defense: Essays in peace research* (Vol. 2). Copenhagen: Christian Ejlers.

Giller, E. L., & Weisæth, L. (1996). *Post-traumatic stress disorder.* London: Bailliere, Tindall.

Hägglund, G. (1991, October). Remarks made to *The World Veterans Federations 20th Meeting,* Paris.

Johansson, E. (2001). *The unknown soldier—A portrait of the Swedish peacekeeper at the threshold of the 21st century.* Karlstad: Karlstad University Studies.

Kettner, B. (1972). Combat strain and subsequent mental health. A follow-up study of Swedish soldiers serving in the U.N.-forces 1961–62. *Acta Psychiatry Scandinavian Supplement, 230,* 1–112.

Knudsen, Ø. (1999). *Mission: The former Yugoslavia. A study of Norwegian military nurses' service experiences in the Balkans 1993–98.* Oslo: U.N. PUB Academica.

Litz, B. T., Orsillo, S. M., Friedman, M., Ehlich, P., & Batres, A. (1997). Posttraumatic stress disorder associated with peacekeeping duty in Somalia for U.S. military personnel. *American Journal of Psychiatry, 154*(2), 178–184.

Lundin, T., & Otto, U. (1989). Stress reactions among Swedish health care personnel in UNIFIL, South Lebanon, 1982–84. *Stress Medicine, 5,* 237–246.

Lundin, T., & Otto, U. (1992). Swedish U.N. soldiers in Cyprus UNFICYP: Their psychological and social situation. *Psychotherapy and Psychosomatics, 57,* 187–193.

Marshall, S. L. A. (1947). *Men against fire: The problem of battle command in future war.* Gloucester, MA: Peter Smith.

Mehlum, L. (1995). Positive and negative consequences of serving in a U.N. peacekeeping mission. A follow-up study. *International Review of the Army, Navy and Air Force Medical Services, 68*(10–12), 289–295.

Mehlum, L., & Weisæth, L. (2002, February). Predictors of posttraumatic stress reactions in Norwegian U.N. peacekeepers one year after service. *Journal of Traumatic Stress, 15*(1), 17–26.

Moskos, C. C. (1976). *Peace soldiers. The sociology of a United Nations military force.* Chicago: University of Chicago Press.

Pearn, J. (2000, June). Traumatic stress disorders: A classification with implications for prevention and management. *Military Medicine, 165,* 434–440.

Rikhye, I. J., Harbottle, M., & Egge, B. (1974). *The thin blue line.* New Haven and London: Yale University Press.

Segal, D. R., Furukawa, T. P., & Lindh, J. C. (1990). Light infantry as peacekeepers in the Sinai. *Armed Forces & Society, 16,* 385–403.

Shepard, B. (2000). *A war of nerves: soldiers and psychiatrists.* London: Jonathan Cape.

Weisæth, L. (1979). *Psykiatri og stress hos FN-soldater i Syd-Libanon [Psychiatry and stress among U.N. soldiers in South Lebanon]* (p. 133). Oslo: HQ Defense, Medical Staff, Department of Psychiatry.

Weisæth, L. (2002). Military psychiatry. In U. Schnyder and R. bok Orners (Eds.), *Acute stress reactions and early intervention.* Oxford: Oxford University Press.

Weisæth, L., Aarhaug, P., Mehlum, L., & Larsen, S. (1993). *The UNIFIL study. Positive and negative consequences of service in UNIFIL contingents I-XXVI. Report Part I. Results and recommendations.* Oslo: Norwegian Defence Command Headquarter, The Joint Medical Service.

Weisæth, L., & Sund, A. (1982): Psychiatric problems in UNIFIL and the U.N. soldier's stress syndrome. *International Review of the Army, Navy and Air Force Medical Services, 55,* 109–116.

Wessely, S. (2001). Psychological injury: Fact and fiction. In A. Braidwoos (Ed.), *Psychological injury. Understanding and supporting.* Proceedings of the Department of Social Security War Pensions Agency Conference. London: The Stationary Office.

13

Psychological Interventions in Peace Support Operations: Current Practices and Future Challenges

Megan M. Thompson and Luigi Pastò

The 1990s inaugurated an era of international conflict resolution with new and challenging characteristics. Peacekeeping no longer means providing a buffer between former combatants, but more often interceding in the midst of civil wars marked by deep-seated cultural and religious divisions (Breed, 1998). Peacekeepers are exposed to widespread physical devastation, large-scale massacres, and are themselves the targets of violence. Rules of engagement did not evolve in step with changes in international conflict, and they often provide insufficient guidance or latitude for operational effectiveness and/or personal safety (Bercuson, 1996; Dallaire, 2000; Litz, Orsillo, Friedman, Ehlich, & Batres, 1997; MacKenzie, 1993). These factors have increased psychological problems among peace support personnel (e.g., Adler, Dolan, & Castro, 2000; Baggeley, Piper, Cumming, & Murphy, 1999; Litz, 1996; Lundin & Otto, 1996; Mac-Donald, Pereira-Laird, Chamberlain, Mirfin, & Long, 1998). For example, in a sample of 3,461 American peacekeepers from operation Restore/Continue Hope in Somalia, more than one third suffered from clinically significant post-deployment psychiatric symptoms (Orsillo, Roemer, Litz, Ehlich, & Friedman, 1998). Statistics such as these highlight the link between operational stresses and psychological consequences of peace support missions. Thus the nature and quality of the psychological services provided to troops sent on these missions is critical.

We begin this chapter by presenting a social cognitive theory of stress and coping as a framework for understanding psychological adaptation to stress at each phase of peace support operations. We then describe current mental health interventions across the deployment cycle. Intervention is broadly defined to include training, stress briefings, short-term interventions in the field, as well as traditional long-term psychotherapeutic aftercare. In general, we advocate greater attention to prevention in mental health service delivery. Command consultation is presented as one approach that may be of particular merit in this regard. Stress inoculation training is then outlined as a proactive training intervention with direct relevance to issues of psychological resiliency. The chapter concludes with a discussion of the challenges that continue to face mental health practitioners in the military.

SOCIAL COGNITIVE THEORY

Social cognitive theories of stress and coping emphasize appraisal processes thought to mediate the relation between experiences and mental health outcomes (Bandura, 1982; Lazarus & Folkman, 1984; Meichenbaum, 1985; Taylor, 1983). Accordingly, particular appraisals (i.e., perceptions of current events and expectations of future events) underlie psychological vulnerability and resiliency and are thus related to coping efforts adopted and to the intensity of stress reactions (Catanzero & Mearns, 1999). Specifically, people who make negative appraisals experience decreased positive affect, use less adaptive coping strategies (e.g., excessive drinking), and exhibit more maladaptive behaviors (e.g., hostility; Kassel, Jackson, & Unrod, 2000; Lazarus & Folkman, 1984). Conversely, positive appraisals that help people derive meaning from experiences, gain a sense of mastery, and maintain self-esteem, and that integrate experiences into an overarching narrative of one's life are related to more rapid and complete recovery from negative events (Holman & Cohen Silver, 1998; Taylor, 1983). Moreover, appraisals that are discrepant from actual experiences lead to distress (Pancer, Hunsberger, Pratt, & Alisat, 2000). Appraisals, therefore, must be flexible enough to be revised in the light of disconfirming evidence (see Taylor, 1983). Furthermore, people who appraise their coping resources as inadequate have poorer adaptation outcomes (Bandura, 1977, 1982).

THE PHENOMENOLOGY OF PEACE SUPPORT OPERATIONS

Predeployment

A deployment's impact begins well before military personnel reach a foreign theater of operations (Bartone, Adler, & Viatkus, 1998; Britt & Adler, 1999; MacDonald et al., 1998). Departure dates usually follow months of intensive predeployment training, which coincides with heightened anxiety and psychological distress (MacDonald et al., 1998). Key predeployment appraisals include getting to know colleagues and leaders, as well as the family's ability to cope with the demands of the upcoming deployment (Bartone et al., 1998). Soldiers can feel ambivalent about the upcoming peace support operation if warrior training clashes with the more neutral peacekeeping role and/or when personal and political views of a mission are at odds with one another (Litz, 1996; Litz, King, & King, 1997; Lundin & Otto, 1996). Anxieties can increase as departure dates approach, especially if there is a great deal of uncertainty about the mission.

Deployment

Other chapters in this volume aptly cover the range and intensity of deployment stressors. It is also important to note that the deployment experience "seldom matches expectations, and the discrepancy often requires a reappraisal of the meaningfulness of their preparation and actual involvement" (Garland, 1993, p. 337). Indeed, appraisals may be especially important in the context of a six-month tour, because people have ample opportunity to monitor, assess, and reassess the stressor and their coping efforts to deal with it (Thompson & Gignac, 2001).

The number, frequency, and intensity of traumatic events experienced during a deployment affect the nature of appraisals made and assessments of one's coping resources. These appraisals in turn affect psychological outcomes. For instance, troops who appraised their Gulf War duty with greater threat showed higher distress levels (Solomon, Margalit, Waysman, & Bleich, 1991). Chronic stressors, such as ambiguous rules of engagement, role ambiguity and conflict, restricted activity, crowded or primitive living conditions, extremes of weather, periods of inactivity, as well as interactions with colleagues, civilians, and combatants, may also affect the appraisals troops make of the situation and of themselves (Segal & Segal, 1993). Family concern remains high and is a frequent impetus to seek mental health assistance during a deployment (Pincus & Benedek, 1998). Finally, modern peace support operations are characterized by frequent and rapid changes in intensity (Hall, Cipriano, & Bicknell, 1997) that may increase perceptions of a lack of control, an appraisal particularly linked to psychological distress.

Postdeployment

Troops are often home within 24 to 48 hours of leaving the mission area. The rapid pace of redeployment is itself a stressor (Bercuson, 1996) because it offers little chance to disengage from deployment and adjust to in-garrison and family roles. Conflicted emotions about the tour, generalized hostility, feelings of psychological isolation from others, and feelings of helplessness and powerlessness are not uncommon among returned peace support personnel, at least in the short term (Bartone, 1999; Thompson & Gignac, 2001). These feelings can lead to maladaptive coping such as substance dependence and abuse, antisocial and risky behaviors, and accidents (Adler et al., 2000; Aldwin, Levenson, & Spiro, 1994; MacDonald et al., 1998; Orsillo et al., 1998). Postdeployment adaptation can be further complicated if veterans are dealing with the emotional aftermath of traumatic events (Baggeley et al., 1999; Litz, Orsillo, et al., 1997; Litz, King, et al., 1997).

Research shows that successful postdeployment recovery is largely associated with the nature of appraisals made concerning the deployment. For instance, Aldwin et al. (1994) found a decreased relation between combat stress and PTSD among personnel who were able to recount positive effects of their military service. General positive personal outcomes include recognizing one's ability to cope with adversity, increased self-discipline, resilience, reassessing or deepening key life values, the development of a clearer direction and sense of purpose in life, and a deeper appreciation of peace. Deployment-specific positive outcomes included a belief in the value of the deployment, feelings of contributing to humanitarian causes, and valuing cross-cultural contact (Aldwin et al., 1994; Garland, 1993; Hall & Jansen, 1995; Tedeschi & Calhoun, 1996; Ursano, Wheatley, Sledge, Rahe, & Carlson, 1986).

MENTAL HEALTH INTERVENTIONS ACROSS THE DEPLOYMENT CYCLE

Although the UN and NATO provide general guidelines for peace support operations, the specifics of selection, training, and care are left to individual participating nations. These activities can be constrained by countries' peacekeeping experiences and their political and monetary support of the military (Kidwell & Langholtz, 1998). Although some long-standing contributions of military mental health professionals such as screening, training, and CISD may be justly classified as proactive; the previous section makes clear that the majority of psychological interventions are reactive in nature. That is, military mental health services have largely been called on after stress symptoms are manifested, or at least after negative events have occurred. Services typically involve assessment, treatment, and disposition, are provided in a clinic or hospital setting primarily after referral, and occur in the context of a patient-helper relationship.

Predeployment Interventions: Screening, Briefings, and Training

Screening

Many, although not all, countries (see Ballone, Valentino, Occhiolini, Di Mascio, Cannone, & Schioppa, 2000) have screening procedures to assess soldiers' psychological well-being. Often conducted in the context of the Departure Assistance Group (DAG), psychological screening may be limited to one question determining the soldier's contact with mental health services in the preceding five years (Scanlon, 1995). Other questions may address family concerns, sometimes with the spouse present. Although, in theory, screening refers to the identification and selection of the best-qualified individuals, in practice, the emphasis is often on determining any major impediments precluding a soldier's deployment (Scanlon, 1995). Many military personnel consider the screening process to be perfunctory, especially if there is limited time between the mission notice and deployment date and in times of declining recruitment and retention.

The United States provides a psychological screening program (see Wright, Huffman, Adler, & Castro, in press). Although screening occurs across the deployment cycle, the program has focused on deployment and redeployment. The program involves an initial psychological screening administered to groups of troops. Here questionnaires assess demographics, PTSD, depression, substance use, deployment events, and more recently hostility, quality of marriage, clinical and personal history, as well as peacekeeping and other trauma experience. Questions assessing physical health and sick days are also included. Answers that exceed criteria on at least one of these scales flag individual soldiers for clinical interviews to determine further treatment. Although used in the predeployment phase of two rotations to Kosovo, this program is not designed to screen out at-risk soldiers from deploying on peacekeeping missions but rather to identify those individuals who would benefit from further evaluation or follow-up.

Psychological readiness may also involve the unit commander's assessment of a unit or a particular soldier's readiness. In general, there are no standardized criteria to assist commanders in this screening. The U.S. screening program could certainly be used to assist commanders. The psychological division of the Danish Forces tries to assist commanders in a standardized manner via the development of an observation form to be completed by squad leaders or platoon commanders, a questionnaire completed by the individual soldier, and accompanying written guidelines for commanders (Bache, 1993).

Briefings

Predeployment briefings are lectures that disseminate information concerning peace support deployments in general (e.g., history of peacekeeping, mine awareness) and specific missions (e.g., mission-specific geography, culture, rules of engagement). These briefings serve important psychological functions because the information imparted can establish or realign expectations; this in turn may reduce uncertainty and anxiety.

Briefings specifically addressing psychological issues typically range from one to four hours. These lectures provide definitions of stress and stressors and outline specific types of deployment stressors, including critical incident stress, chronic stressors, and daily hassles. Stress symptoms are reviewed, and general recommendations for stress reduction, including critical incident stress debriefing (CISD) as well as lifestyle management (eating, sleeping, exercise, talking, meditation) are also introduced (e.g., Deahl, Srinivasan, Jones, Thomas, Neblett, & Jolly, 2000).

Training

Specific training in weapon handling, reconnaissance, practical mine awareness training, and so on, is a focus of most predeployment training. One consequence of this training can be decreased physiological and psychological reactivity of these tasks. However, the psychological coping benefits of this training are at best implicit. Specific techniques to minimize stress reactions are almost never taught. Indeed, we found little evidence of specific predeployment skills training with respect to psychological well-being.

Deployment Interventions

Personnel who administer in-theater mental health support vary somewhat across nations but usually consists of medical officers, medical assistants, mental health specialists (e.g., mental health nurses, social workers), and priests or chaplains. Psychiatrists may deploy but more commonly serve in supervisory and consultation capacities, making scheduled visits during tours or in cases of emergency. The integration of these teams also varies, but some countries deploy multidimensional mental health care teams as support to contingents. The Dutch army now deploys a social-medical team consisting of medical officer, clinical psychologist, social worker, medical assistants, and nurses. The United States has deployed similar combat stress control teams (CSC; e.g., Hall et al., 1997; Pincus & Benedek, 1998; Ritchie, Ruck, & Anderson, 1994).

Mental health professionals offer a variety of in-theater interventions including educational briefings on aspects of well-being as needs arise. One-on-one interventions emphasize brief clinical sessions that focus on basic coping techniques such as planning, problem solving, and prioritizing. Where appropriate, medications to treat anxiety, depression, and insomnia are prescribed (Hibler, 1984). Mental health resources are often at a premium in many countries; thus medical staff provide the first line of intervention, referring to mental health professionals who tour camps on a regular basis.

In-theater clinical interventions follow a therapeutic model typically referred to as PIES (proximity, immediacy, expectancy, simplicity; Bache, 1993; Gerardi, 1996; Koshes, 1996). Principles of care include the provision of mental health care as soon as possible and as close to the soldier's home unit as feasible. Lessons learned from the First and Second World Wars showed that soldiers whose treatment was delayed until they were evacuated for rear guard mental health treatment rarely returned to active duty (English, 2000). As a result, members of the mental health team convey an explicit expectancy of return to duty to the soldier. To reinforce this, these soldiers continue to wear uniforms and undertake as many duties as possible. Treatment focuses on immediate problems and avoids in-depth therapy.

First-echelon care may consist of a short-term hiatus from stressful situations focusing on physiological needs such as rest and food. Early intervention is facilitated by increased recognition of stress symptoms by peers and leaders, as well as corpsmen and field medics (Balacki, 1992; Hibler, 1984). Second order care may require the soldier's transfer to a CSC unit co-located with the nearest field hospital. These units set up as close to the home unit as possible and service small groups of soldiers who are suffering from psychological stress. Individual counseling and group discussions allow the ventilation of feelings and train coping skills. Only individuals deemed at risk to themselves or others, or whose psychological problems are severe, are evacuated for further treatment. One report demonstrated the success of a CSC unit in that 85% of soldiers making use of these services quickly returned to duty (Pincus & Benedek, 1998). However, the extent to which these notions have been consistently applied in peace support operations remains unclear.

One of the mainstays of operational mental health interventions is critical incident stress debriefing (CISD), used to avert psychological damage among groups of military personnel after their involvement in traumatic events (see Budd, 1997; Jiggets & Hall, 1995). CISD, a fundamental component of the more comprehensive intervention of critical incident stress management, occurs immediately or soon after a traumatic event and consists of a single session intervention by a mental health professional and co-facilitator (Mitchell, 1983). A forum for an open, confidential discussion is first established. Participants then describe where they were when the traumatic event occurred, and their thoughts, feelings, and physical reactions to the event are serially elicited. Stress management principles are briefed. The session is then summarized and ended. Although some researchers have concluded that the impact of CISD is at best minimal (e.g., Rose, Wessely, & Bisson, 2001), a meta-analysis (Everly & Boyle, 1999) reported a large effect size supporting the effectiveness of CISD in crisis intervention. Others have suggested that the benefits of CISD may be evident with more than one debriefing session (Shalev, 2000) and when outcomes other than PTSD are assessed (Deahl, Srinivasan, Jones, Neblett, & Jolly, 2001). Overall, the consensus concerning the effectiveness of CISD appears to be guardedly positive. However, more carefully controlled research is needed (see Litz, Gray, Bryant, & Adler, in press, for an excellent review of CISD).

As a mission ends, mental health services are often limited to triage, consultation, and emergencies. Mental health evacuations may actually increase at this time because fewer psychological support resources remain and a more relaxed attitude about returning soldiers home may exist (Garland, 1993). Beyond this, the bulk of end-of-mission interventions are often directed toward out-clearance briefings. These lectures, often coupled with medical preventative health briefings, discuss issues such as reintegration into nondeployed roles and family reunions. Stress symptoms are outlined, as are the thoughts and feelings that are a natural part of arriving home. Ideally, end-of-mission interventions should instill adaptive expectations and appraisals concerning homecoming so that troops can properly interpret and address any ambivalence experienced upon returning home.

Postdeployment Interventions: Out-Clearance Briefings, Out-Clearance Screenings, Psychological Debriefings, and Therapy

If out-clearance briefings are not provided before troops leave a theater of operations, they are often provided soon after return home. In addition to lectures, some out-clearance procedures also offer opportunities for more structured debriefings. These differ from the standard lecture format in that veterans gather to discuss deployment events to begin the reintegration of these events into overall life experience. For example, the Netherlands conducts intensive group debriefings for two days immediately after redeployment and prior to reunion with loved ones and leave. Seen as a preventative measure to circumvent or minimize later psychological damage, these structured confidential group discussions with other peacekeeping veterans are meant to validate deployment experiences and destigmatize the feelings and symptoms associated with the tour (Koshes, 1996). The degree to which this approach is popular with Dutch troops, in particular the enforced delay in reuniting with family, remains to be seen. The effectiveness of this approach in preventing subsequent psychological problems relative to traditional debriefing methods also remains to be established empirically.

Out-Clearance Screenings

Many countries' postdeployment out-clearance procedures include an appointment with a social worker. Intended as a rudimentary psychological screening to uncover major psychological problems and provide appropriate referrals, troops often view this technique as perfunctory as predeployment screenings in terms of identifying individuals who are suffering psychological distress. More often the military medical system will be the first point of contact by peacekeeping veterans who are seeking assistance to understand and treat the sometimes confusing physical and emotional symptoms that can occur after redeployment.

As noted earlier, some divisions in the United States have used one of the most comprehensive redeployment screening programs. This large-scale initiative screens for major trauma events, risk factors, and adjustment problems and provides individual follow-up clinical interviews as necessary. Canada has used a similar two-phase psychological screening program during redeployment from a recent humanitarian mission to Eritrea (T. Cook, personal communication, September 18, 2001).

Postdeployment Therapy

Most militaries provide post-theater treatment, often restricted to diagnosed PTSD, although services are being expanded to address other potentially stress-related conditions such as medically unexplained physical symptoms (MUPS) and Gulf War syndrome (Neisenbaum, Barrett, Reyes, & Reeves, 2000). Typical of these efforts are the Canadian Forces Operational Trauma and Stress Support Centers. Here, multidisciplinary teams including psychiatrists, clinical psychologists, social workers, chaplains, and/or community mental health nurses assess and treat a range of problems arising from deployments such as substance abuse, depression, anxiety, and psychiatric disorders including PTSD.

In general, individual-level psychotherapy assists returning peacekeepers in dealing with the aftermath of trauma and with the tasks of reintegration into postmission roles; family therapy is available, as is group therapy on a more limited basis. With respect to PTSD specifically, research shows the most effective therapies targeting PTSD are cognitive-behavioral in nature, specifically exposure and anxiety management therapies (Culpepper, 2000). Medications may be prescribed to target specific symptoms of combat stress reactions (Koshes, 1996). However, antidepressants prescribed to military personnel with PTSD (Culpepper, 2000) often have limited effectiveness (Solomon, Gerrity, & Muff, 1992).

Mental Health Interventions: A Focus on Prevention

Command Consultation

Command consultation reflects the belief that individual-level problems can become unit-level issues that affect operational readiness and effectiveness (Garland, 1993; Hall et al., 1997), and it is characterized by two key features. First, there must be an active and open advisory relationship between mental health specialists and unit command (Conner & Thoresen, 1972). Second, mental health personnel are placed in the operational theater (Garland, 1993; Shivers, Hulsebus, & Havrilla, 1983) to ensure that mental health resources are responsive to current operational needs and that practitioners have credible in-theater experience (English, 2000). Moving mental health resources closer to "the headquarters, the troops, and the real problems" (Conner & Thoresen, 1972, p. 152) is consistent with long-standing principles of effective psychiatric intervention in the context of war (e.g., PIES; Shivers et al., 1983).

In theory, command consultation generally includes assessment, intervention recommendations, and evaluation of interventions (Lenz & Roberts, 1991). Command consultation can be based on objective assessment measures presumed to reflect current or imminent unit mental health maladjustment, including number of mental health or pastoral service referrals, disease rates, unexcused absences (i.e., AWOLs), court-martial, and/or accident rates. Other measures might more directly reflect social-psychological dimensions related to operational readiness and effectiveness such as deployment appraisals and expectations, assessment of coping ability, unit cohesion, unit trust in the leadership, and unit commitment. Aspects of the particular operation may also be assessed, such as intensity, duration, and pace of operations (Hibler, 1984). Notable departures from typical or normative levels on any of these unit-level measures of operational readiness and effectiveness would be discussed with the command structure (Hibler, 1984). Discussions with key unit leaders might uncover underlying reasons for the observed departures, and possible remedies are devised (Bey & Smith, 1971). Interventions may be implemented at the group level (e.g., stress management and prevention training) or at an organizational level (e.g., policy changes with regard to leave). These interventions are aimed at restoring mental health to predeployment levels or better, as well as at reducing the likelihood of similar problems arising in the future. The success of the interventions would be assessed through continued tracking of unit-level mental health.

Although command consultation has been used occasionally in both traditional combat operations (e.g., Vietnam, Operation Desert Storm) and in operations other than war (e.g., Somalia, Haiti), it has not been consistently applied. Operational readiness and effectiveness survey data have been collected in some countries (e.g., Castro, Bienvenu, Huffman, & Adler, 2000; Murphy & Farley, 2000), but typically results have not been fed back to commanders or used to develop immediate interventions. Even within countries that employ it to some effect, the consultation process is not formally organized within the military, nor are clinical psychologists provided "clear active support for their consultative efforts" (Lenz & Roberts, 1991, p. 686). Moreover, when a command consultation process is implemented, the effects of the interventions and of the process itself on unit mental health are not often evaluated in a satisfactory fashion (Lenz & Roberts, 1991).

Some evidence indicates that, when available, commanders do seek consultation with regard to unit-level mental health. During a year-long peace support operation to the former Yugoslavia, two mental health teams made 1,459 command consultations in addition to providing more traditional psychiatric services (e.g., outpatient and combat stress center services; Pincus & Benedek, 1998). In another study, unit-level surveys of mental health measures among U.S. peacekeepers in Haiti were usually followed by additional requests for stress management classes (Hall et al., 1997).

The few examples of command consultation we found occurred exclusively during deployments. However, we envision command consultation as a valuable vehicle for the delivery of integrated mental health services in support of operational readiness and effectiveness (Hall et al., 1997) throughout the entire deployment cycle. During the predeployment phase of peace support operations, consultation could focus primarily on the assessment of operational readiness through objective measures and on training for psychological resiliency. Departures from norms on relevant dimensions would signal the need for interventions tailored to the issues uncovered. Indeed, command consultation before operations may be the most significant contribution of mental health expertise to the prevention of psychological problems, providing an opportunity to influence rates of battle fatigue and return to duty (Garland, 1993).

During deployment, consultation can focus on monitoring and maintaining operational effectiveness levels. Ideally, command consultation would be well integrated within a battery of more traditional operational mental health services and would include administering large surveys to monitor unit-level variables presumably related to operational effectiveness. The focus would be on prevention; identifying, and dealing with minor problems before they become major concerns. With the advent of laptop computers, in-theater computer services, and Internet connectivity, survey data could be rapidly collected, analyzed, and fed back to commanders in the field.

Postdeployment command consultation would emphasize recovery and return to optimal operational readiness. Although the idealized view is that the postdeployment phase is completely positive, as already indicated, feelings of isolation and helplessness, interpersonal problems with coworkers, and declines in perceptions of leadership all define the postdeployment phase (MacDonald et al., 1998). All these indicators are logically linked to unit-level outcomes such as morale, cohesion, and may even be linked to attrition rates, underscoring the importance of postdeployment follow-up. The psychological screening program of the U.S. Army most closely approximates this approach across the deployment cycle, although it is not clear how integrated the links are among research, medical, and command structures and how this information is used in developing unit-level mental health interventions.

The success of command consultation is predicated on maintaining the confidentiality of individual soldier-level information. The traditional separation between command and medical structures has attempted to assure soldiers that their personal problems are not the automatic purview of commanders and will not inevitably affect their careers. Therefore, it must be understood by all involved parties, including troops, medical personnel, mental health professionals, and members of the command structure, that only information aggregated at the unit level and relevant to operational readiness and effectiveness is open for discussion during command consultation. The identities of individual soldiers must be protected, unless the soldier is a risk to himself or herself or to others. This understanding of command consultation preserves the sanctity of the client/health care provider relationship and also ensures that data provided on surveys is an accurate reflection of important psychological dimensions of a unit.

The Role of Appraisals in Preventative Military Mental Health

One theme that emerges throughout our discussions thus far is that appraisals and expectations are instrumental in affecting psychological adaptation before, during, and after deployment. In particular, predeployment expectations may create a crucial mental and emotional set that enhances coping through the deployment cycle. This being the case, predeployment briefings and training must be geared toward reducing uncertainty and establishing largely positive deployment appraisals and expectations that are tempered by realistic evaluations of the challenges and hardships of peace support operations. Personnel who are unable to realign their predeployment expectations in light of operational realities, or whose appraisals of their coping resources are not aligned with the challenges of a deployment, may experience more adjustment problems. Skills training should augment educational briefings, providing personnel with specific coping techniques to foster self-efficacy before, during, and after operations. Stress inoculation training may be a valuable vehicle for the acquisition and rehearsal of a variety of coping skills, including positive appraisals.

Stress Inoculation Training

Stress inoculation training (SIT; Meichenbaum, 1985) is a clinical intervention that focuses on expectation/appraisal processes. According to SIT, stress is the result of negative appraisals and assessments of inadequate coping resources. The initial phase of training involves conceptualizing the event in a realistic fashion; participants are provided with accurate information about a stressful event. The second phase involves the acquisition and rehearsal of coping skills such as practicing relaxation techniques and self-statements designed to regulate emotions and maintain task focus. In the final training phase, the new coping skills are put to the test during a graduated exposure to stressors (Armfield, 1994). The stressors presented during the exposure are strong enough to arouse psychological defenses without overwhelming them and provide the context in which to practice adaptive stress-relevant coping behaviors.

In one of the few published accounts, Novaco, Cook, and Sarason (1983) applied SIT in the context of marine recruits' adaptation to basic training. The SIT intervention included a film that modeled self-statements emphasizing the reappraisal of stressors and the use of coping self-statements to control negative emotions and to maintain task focus. Results showed that recruits who viewed the SIT coping skills training film expected to succeed on a larger number of training tasks relative to those who viewed films only showing the realities of basic training and to recruits in nonfilm control conditions (Novaco et al., 1983). This study supports the notion that the provision of stressor-specific coping skills modeling reduced the overall apprehension of recruits during a very stressful portion of training. Although the link between expectations and training outcomes remains to be established in this context, the larger stress and coping literature has demonstrated that individuals who have positive expectations (facilitated here by specific modeling skills) fare better psychologically (Thompson & Gignac, 2001) and perform at higher levels (e.g., Bouffard-Bouchard, 1990).

Novaco et al.'s (1983) results provide hope that the cognitive, affective, and behavioral markers of psychological resiliency may be identified and specific coping skills to promote psychological resiliency may be modeled and incorporated into standardized training programs. We believe that the preventative benefits of this training will be greatest if provided as early as possible in a soldier's military career (Novaco et al., 1983). Recruit training is a stressful time, characterized by extreme uncertainty and anxiety (Novaco et al., 1983). Thus it presents an ideal opportunity to begin to train and model preventative coping techniques. For example, training in the techniques of progressive muscular relaxation and coping self-statements could be presented in the context of a complete physical and mental fitness program provided to recruits from the beginning of their careers. Ideally, these techniques should be as ingrained and automatic to soldiers as other basic military skills.

FUTURE CHALLENGES

We have suggested that the nature of the appraisals about the peace support mission and about coping resources are critical to long-term psychological adjustment. Carefully tailored briefings, command consultation throughout the deployment cycle, and stress inoculation begun during recruit training were outlined as viable preventative mental health interventions. Each of these programs is aimed at teaching, monitoring, or modifying the nature of troops' appraisals and the links between these appraisals and well-being. However, several challenges remain to be addressed by military mental health professionals.

One feature of modern peace support operations is their volatility. For instance, Rwanda, expected to be a low-intensity tour, escalated into one of the worst massacres of civilians (Dallaire, 2000). Somalia also deteriorated rapidly into a dangerous and very psychologically demanding tour. The operational tempo in the Balkans has increased and decreased over the course of the UN and NATO missions in that area. To meet these changing operational requirements, mental health teams should incorporate flexible staffing policies. An initial cadre of mental health professionals who assist with in-theater adjustment issues could be reduced when the deployment reaches a steady state, but be ready to deploy again in response to increases in operational tempo (see Hall et al., 1997).

Debate continues concerning the effectiveness of psychological debriefing (i.e., CISD). Thus empirical studies should systematically determine the components of CISD that may or may not assist psychological recovery. Alternatively, CISD interventions may need to be modified to include a greater number of sessions and specific coping skills training (see Foa, Hearst-Ikeda, & Perry, 1995). Clearly, further research also needs to be conducted to identify whether there are certain types of individuals for whom CISD is indicated, and conversely, whether there are some individuals who may actually be harmed by CISD.

The specifics of psychological education and briefings need continued refinement. Far too often these stress briefings are taught in general terms and at a junior university level. Presentation must be tailored to specific deployment stressors and events, using terms to which troops can relate. If the briefing points are not made relevant to the peacekeeping context, many troops will fail to see the personal relevance of the information and forget the messages.

Predeployment preparation should also incorporate briefings from experienced peacekeepers willing to discuss the realities of a deployment to that theater. This is an approach implemented to good effect in some training centers (e.g., Peace Support Training Center, Kingston, Canada). Film clips or still pictures of living quarters, general geography of the area, and so on, could augment these discussions. The information provided by these multiple resources will help form accurate expectancies and reduce the uncertainty of the upcoming deployment, particularly for those going on their first mission. Similar discussions led by peacekeeping veterans should be incorporated into postdeployment briefings. In particular, these briefings should specifically highlight the positive outcomes tailored as much as possible to the specifics of the mission. Soldiers should leave the deployment knowing that despite the frustrations and adversities associated with the tour, they have accomplished important goals in terms of the mission and/or in terms of their own personal growth.

Demographic factors may be important for military mental health professionals to consider because they target subpopulations that are at increased risk for stress-related outcomes. Combat units, combat engineers, and medical personnel are more likely to witness traumatic events, and they tend to deploy more often (Castro & Adler, 1999). These factors make particular groups at greater risk for "sequential traumatization" (Baggeley et al., 1999) and burnout, and thus stress-related outcomes (Jones, 1985; McFarlane, 1986; Solomon, Oppenheimer, Elizur, & Waysman, 1990; Ursano & McCarroll, 1990). Augmentees, or military personnel temporarily attached to a unit in order to fill some specific mission goal, are another subpopulation that may be at risk for negative psychological outcomes because this group has traditionally received less organizational and social support throughout the deployment cycle (Thompson & Gignac, in press). Thus particular attention should be paid to monitoring stress-related symptoms and, where necessary, providing additional training and other interventions to these groups.

Perhaps the biggest challenges for military mental health professionals lie at a cultural level. Similar to any culture, militaries are ultimately sustained by an amalgam of fundamental shared values, customs, and traditions. Perhaps the defining feature of militaries is the principle of unlimited liability—a willingness to accept casualties. The culture that has arisen from this feature inculcates physical rigor, loyalty, obedience, discipline, and courage, characteristics assumed to be related to the ability to control or at least mask anxiety in the face of danger. Maintaining these characteristics has also been thought to require vigilance against any perceived softening within the ranks, a condition equated to the eroding of military readiness and effectiveness (Ulmer, Collins, & Jacobs, 2000). Thus soldiers are often reluctant to admit they are less than

100%, as in many occupations it has meant being removed from duties (Budd, 1997) and a loss of face, isolation from comrades, and guilt arising from letting down or even endangering the unit. For all these reasons, signs of psychological distress in self or in others have been considered to reflect inherent character weaknesses, especially in military units that place such a high value on fitness, toughness, and courage (Noy, 1991).

Nonetheless, the reality is that combat stress reactions may be a significant cause of the loss of personnel, often accounting for between 25% and 50% of total casualties in high-intensity battles (Noy, 1991). Despite statistics such as these, military command structures have continued to resist interventions that address more complex psychological models of battle casualties (Lenz & Roberts, 1991). Mental health service providers must also do a better job of presenting mental fitness as an integral part of operational readiness in the way that physical fitness is in order to be seen as a relevant concern to both leaders and troops. Moreover, mental health teams must provide more information and education, to both troops and leaders, with regard to the services and the tangible benefits that an integrated mental health team can provide.

The emphasis in this chapter has been on mental health programs and professionals. However, commanders play an integral role in any system designed to deal with operational stress because they have final responsibility for the system and the personnel under their command (see English, 2000). Commanders need to lead by example, educating themselves with respect to mental fitness. The ultimate goal of all prevention and intervention programs promoting adaptive cognitive appraisals, across a deployment, and indeed throughout a military career, is to significantly enhance commanders' capability to maintain the operational effectiveness of their troops.

NOTE

The authors wish to thank Tonya Stokes-Hendriks for her assistance in the editing of this chapter.

REFERENCES

Adler, A. B., Dolan, C. A., & Castro, C. A. (2000). U.S. soldier peacekeeping experiences and well-being after returning from deployment to Kosovo. *Proceedings of the 36th International Applied Military Psychology Symposium* (pp. 30–34). Split, Croatia: Ministry of Defense of the Republic of Croatia.

Aldwin, C. M., Levenson, M. R., & Spiro, A. (1994). Vulnerability and resilience to combat exposure: Can stress have lifelong effects? *Psychology and Aging, 9,* 34–44.

Armfield, F. (1994). Preventing post-traumatic stress disorder resulting from military operations. *Military Medicine, 159,* 739–746.

Bache, M. (1993). Stress management for military personnel in UN-missions: Psychological support activities in the Danish Armed Forces. FCL report (PCLPUB 133).

Baggeley, M. R., Piper, M. E., Cumming, P., & Murphy, G. (1999). Trauma related symptoms in British soldiers 36 months following a tour in the former Yugoslavia. *Journal of the Royal Army Medical Corps, 145,* 13–14.

Balacki, M. F. (1992). Battle fatigue intervention: A vital role for nursing. *Military Medicine, 157,* 192–195.

Ballone, E., Valentino, M., Occhiolini, L., Di Mascio, C., Cannone, D., & Schioppa, F. S. (2000). Factors influencing psychological stress levels of Italian peacekeepers in Bosnia. *Military Medicine, 165,* 911–915.

Bandura, A. (1977). Self-efficacy: Toward a unifying theory of behavioral change. *Psychological Review, 84,* 191–215.

Bandura, A. (1982). Self-efficacy mechanism in human agency. *American Psychologist, 37,* 122–147.

Bartone, P. T. (1999). Hardiness protects against war-related stress in Army Reserve forces. *Consulting Psychology Journal: Practice & Research, 51,* 72–82.

Bartone, P. T., Adler, A. B., & Viatkus, M. A. (1998). Dimensions of psychological stress in peacekeeping operations. *Military Medicine, 163,* 587–593.

Bercuson, D. (1996). *Significant incident: Canada's army, the airborne, and the murder in Somalia.* Toronto:: McClelland and Stewart.

Bey, D. R., & Smith, W. E. (1971). Organizational consultation in a combat unit. *American Journal of Psychiatry, 128,* 401–406.

Bouffard-Bouchard, T. (1990). Influence of self-efficacy on performance in a cognitive task. *Journal of Social Psychology, 130,* 353–363.

Breed, H. (1998). Treating the new world disorder. In H. J. Langholtz (Ed.), *The psychology of peacekeeping* (pp. 239–254). Westport, CT: Praeger/Greenwood.

Britt, T. W., & Adler, A. B. (1999). Stress and health during medical humanitarian assistance missions. *Military Medicine, 164,* 275–279.

Budd, F. (1997). Helping the helpers after the bombing in Dhahran: Critical incident stress services for an air rescue squadron. *Military Medicine, 162,* 515–520.

Castro, C. A., & Adler, A. B. (1999, Autumn). OPTEMPO: Effects on soldier and unit readiness. *Parameters,* pp. 86–95.

Castro, C. A., Bienvenu, R. V., Huffman, A. H., & Adler, A. B. (2000). Soldier dimensions of operational readiness in U.S. Army forces deployed to Kosovo. *International Review of Armed Forces Medical Services, 73,* 191–200.

Catanzero, S. J., & Mearns, J. (1999). Mood-related expectancy, emotional experience, and coping behavior. In I. Kirsch (Ed.), *How expectancies shape experience* (pp. 67–91). Washington, DC: American Psychological Association.

Conner, D. R., & Thoresen, A. R. (1972). Observations of a mental health command consultation program. *Military Medicine, 137,* 152–155.

Culpepper, L. (2000). Recognizing and treating post-traumatic stress disorder. *Hippocrates, 14*(6), 44–52.

Dallaire, R. A. (2000). Command experiences in Rwanda. In C. McCann and R. A. Pigeau (Eds.), *The human in command: Exploring the modern military experience* (pp. 29–50). New York: Academic/Plenum.

Deahl, M., Srinivasan, M., Jones, N., Thomas, J., Neblett, C., & Jolly, A. (2000). Preventing psychological trauma in soldiers: The role of operational stress training and psychological debriefing. *British Journal of Medical Psychology, 73,* 77–85.

Deahl, M. P., Srinivasan, M., Jones, N., Neblett, C., & Jolly, A. (2001). Evaluating psychological debriefing: Are we measuring the right outcomes? *Journal of Traumatic Stress, 14,* 527–529.

English, A. D. (2000). Leadership and operational stress in the Canadian Forces. *Canadian Military Journal, 1*, 33–38.

Everly, G. S., & Boyle, S. H. (1999). Critical incident stress debriefing (CISD): A meta-analysis. *International Journal of Emergency Mental Health, 1*, 165–168.

Foa, E. B., Hearst-Ikeda, D., & Perry, K. J. (1995). Evaluation of a brief cognitive-behavioral program for the prevention of chronic PTSD in recent assault victims. *Journal of Consulting and Clinical Psychology, 63*, 948–955.

Garland, F. N. (1993). Combat stress control in the post-war theater: Mental health consultation during the redeployment phase of Operation Desert Storm. *Military Medicine, 158*, 334–338.

Gerardi, S. M. (1996). The management of battle-fatigued soldiers: An occupational therapy model. *Military Medicine, 161*, 483–488.

Hall, D. P., & Jansen, J. A. (1995). Stress and arousal in deployment of a combat support hospital. *Military Medicine, 160*, 581–583.

Hall, D. P., Cipriano, E. D., & Bicknell, G. (1997). Preventive mental health interventions in peacekeeping missions to Somalia and Haiti. *Military Medicine, 162*, 41–43.

Hibler, R. J. (1984). Battlefield stress: Management techniques. *Military Medicine, 149*, 5–8.

Holman, E. A., & Cohen Silver, R. (1998). Getting "stuck" in the past: Temporal orientation and coping with trauma. *Journal of Personality and Social Psychology, 74*, 1146–1163.

Jiggets, S. M., & Hall, D. P., Jr. (1995). Helping the helper: 528th Combat Stress Center in Somalia. *Military Medicine, 160*, 275–277.

Jones, D. R. (1985). Secondary disaster victims: The emotional effects of recovering and identifying human remains. *American Journal of Psychiatry, 142*, 303–307.

Kassel, J. D., Jackson, S. I., & Unrod, M. (2000). Generalized expectancies for negative mood regulation and problem drinking among college students. *Journal of Studies on Alcohol, 61*, 332–340.

Kidwell, B., & Langholtz, H. (1998). Personnel selection, preparation and training for U.N. peacekeeping missions. In H. J. Langholtz (Ed.), *The psychology of peacekeeping* (pp. 89–100). Westport, CT: Prager.

Koshes, R. J. (1996). The care of those returned: Psychiatric illnesses of war. In R. J. Ursano and A. E. Norwood (Eds.), *Emotional aftermath of the Persian Gulf War: Veterans, families, communities and nations* (pp. 393–414). Washington, DC: American Psychiatric Press.

Lazarus, R. S., & Folkman, S. (1984). *Stress, appraisal, and coping.* New York: Springer.

Lenz, E. J., & Roberts, B. J. (1991). Consultation in a military setting. In R. Gal and D. Mangelsdorff (Eds.), *Handbook of military psychology* (pp. 671–687). Chichester, UK: Wiley.

Litz, B. T. (1996). The psychological demands of peacekeeping for military personnel. *National Center for PTSD Clinical Quarterly, 6*, 1–8.

Litz, B. T., Gray, M. J., Bryant, R., & Adler, A. B. (in press). Early intervention for trauma: Current status and future directions. *Clinical Psychology: Science and Practice.*

Litz, B. T., King, L. A., & King, D. W. (1997). Warriors as peacekeepers: Features of the Somalia experience and PTSD. *Journal of Consulting and Clinical Psychology, 65*, 1001–1010.

Litz, B. T., Orsillo, S. M., Friedman, M., Ehlich, P., & Batres, A. (1997). Posttraumatic stress disorder associated with peacekeeping duty in Somalia for U.S. military personnel. *American Journal of Psychiatry, 154,* 178–184.

Lundin, T., & Otto, U. (1996). Swedish soldiers in peacekeeping operations: Stress reactions following missions in Congo, Lebanon, Cyprus, and Bosnia. *National Center for PTSD Clinical Quarterly, 6,* 9–11.

MacDonald, C., Pereira-Laird, J., Chamberlain, K., Mirfin, K., & Long, N. (1998). Mental health, physical health & stressors reported by New Zealand Defence Force peacekeepers: A longitudinal study. *Military Medicine, 163*(7), 477–481.

MacKenzie, L. (1993). *Peacekeeper: The road to Sarajevo.* Vancouver: Douglas & McIntyre.

McFarlane, A. C. (1986). Posttraumatic morbidity of a disaster: A study of cases presenting for psychiatric treatment. *Journal of Nervous and Mental Disease, 174,* 4–13.

Meichenbaum, D. (1985). *Stress inoculation training.* New York: Pergamon Press.

Mitchell, J. T. (1983). When disaster strikes . . . The critical incident stress debriefing process. *Journal of Emergency Medical Services, 8,* 36–39.

Murphy, P. J., & Farley, K. M. J. (2000). Morale, cohesion and confidence in leadership: Unit climate dimensions for Canadian soldiers on operations. In C. McCann and R. A. Pigeau (Eds.), *The human in command: Exploring the modern military experience* (pp. 311–332). New York: Kluwer/Plenum.

Neisenbaum, R., Barrett, D. H., Reyes, M., & Reeves, W. C. (2000). Deployment stressors and a chronic multi-symptom illness among Gulf War veterans. *Journal of Nervous and Mental Disease, 188,* 259–266.

Noy, S. (1991). Combat stress reactions. In R. Gal and A. D. Mangelsdorff (Eds.), *The handbook of military psychology* (pp. 507–530). New York: Wiley.

Novaco, R. W., Cook, T. M., & Sarason, I. G. (1983). Military recruit training: An arena for stress-coping skills. In D. Meichenbaum and M. E. Jaremko (Eds.), *Stress reduction and prevention* (pp. 377–418). New York: Plenum.

Orsillo, S. M., Roemer, L., Litz, B. T., Ehlich, P., & Friedman, M. J. (1998). Psychiatric symptomatology associated with contemporary peacekeeping: An examination of post-mission functioning among peacekeepers in Somalia. *Journal of Traumatic Stress, 11,* 611–625.

Pancer, S. M., Hunsberger, B., Pratt, M. W., & Alisat, S. (2000). Cognitive complexity of expectations and adjustment to university in the first year. *Journal of Adolescent Research, 15,* 38–57.

Pincus, S. H., & Benedek, D. M. (1998). Operational stress control in the former Yugoslavia: A joint endeavor. *Military Medicine, 163,* 358–362.

Ritchie, E. C., Ruck, D. C., & Anderson, M. W. (1994). The 528th Combat Control Unit in Somalia in support of Operation Restore Hope. *Military Medicine, 159,* 372–376.

Rose, S., Wessely, S., & Bisson, J. (2001). Brief psychological interventions ('debriefing') for trauma-related symptoms and prevention of post-traumatic stress disorder. *Cochrane Library, 2.* Oxford: Update Software.

Scanlon, R. L. (1995). *Requirements for helping CF peacekeepers deal effectively with deployment stress.* Directorate of Medical Operations, Surgeon General Branch. Ottawa, Canada.

Segal, D. R., & Segal, M. W. (1993). *Peacekeepers and their wives: American participation in the multinational force and observers.* Westport, CT: Greenwood.

Shalev, A. Y. (2000). Stress management and debriefing: Historical concepts and present patterns. In B. Raphael & J. P. Wilson (Eds.), *Psychological debriefing* (pp. 17–31). Cambridge: Cambridge University Press.

Shivers, W. F., Hulsebus, R. C., & Havrilla, J. F. (1983). A command consultation model for community mental health. *Military Medicine, 148,* 159–161.

Solomon, S. D., Gerrity E. T., & Muff, A. M. (1992). Efficacy of treatments for posttraumatic stress disorder: An empirical review. *Journal of the American Medical Association, 268,* 633–638.

Solomon, Z., Margalit, C., Waysman, M., & Bleich, A. (1991). In the shadow of the Gulf War: Psychological distress, social support and coping among Israeli soldiers in a high risk area. *Israel Journal of Medical Science, 27,* 687–695.

Solomon, Z., Oppenheimer, B., Elizur, Y., & Waysman, M. (1990). Exposure to recurrent combat stress: Can successful coping in a second war heal combat-related PTSD from the past? *Journal of Anxiety Disorders, 4,* 141–145.

Taylor, S. E. (1983, November). Adjustment to threatening events: A theory of cognitive adaptation. *American Psychologist,* pp. 1161–1173.

Tedeschi, R. G., & Calhoun, L. G. (1996). The posttraumatic growth inventory: Measuring the positive legacy of trauma. *Journal of Traumatic Stress, 9,* 455–472.

Thompson, M. M., & Gignac, M. A. M. (2001). *A model of psychological adaptation in Peace Support Operations: An overview.* (DCIEM Technical Report No. TR 2001–050). Defence and Civil Institute of Environmental Medicine, Toronto.

Thompson, M. M., & Gignac, M. A. M. (in press). Adaptation to peace support operations: The experience of Canadian Forces augmentees. In P. J. M. D. Essens, A. L. W. Vogelaar, E. Tanercan, and D. J. Winslow (Eds.), *The human in command: Peace support operations.* Amsterdam: Mets & Schilt.

Ulmer, W. F., Collins, J. J., & Jacobs, T. O. (2000). *American military culture in the 21st century: A report of the CSIS International Security program.* Washington, DC: The Center for Strategic and International Studies Press.

Ursano, R. J., & McCarroll, J. E. (1990). The nature of a traumatic stressor: Handling dead bodies. *Journal of Nervous and Mental Diseases, 178,* 396–398.

Ursano, R. J., Wheatley, R., Sledge, W., Rahe, A., & Carlson, E. (1986). Coping and recovery styles in the Vietnam era prisoner of war. *Journal of Nervous and Mental Disease, 175,* 273–275.

Wright, K. M., Huffman, A. H., Adler, A. B., & Castro, C. A. (in press). Psychological screening program overview. *Military Medicine.*

14

Posttraumatic Stress Disorder following Peacekeeping Operations

Brett T. Litz, Matt J. Gray, and Elisa Bolton

The psychological impact of peacekeeping missions varies considerably, given the diverse demands of different missions, the degree of training and preparation, and the unique characteristics of the person and the recovery environment. In this chapter, we delineate the malevolent and potentially traumatic experiences that modern peacekeepers confront and review the literature on the prevalence of posttraumatic stress disorder (PTSD) in peacekeepers. It needs to be emphasized at the outset that the large majority of soldiers cope very well with the immediate demands of peacekeeping and do not develop psychopathology (e.g., Litz, King, King, Orsillo, & Friedman, 1997). As is the case with exposure to any severe stressor, a complex synergy of factors determines risk for PTSD associated with peacekeeping service. Consequently, we provide a depiction of factors that have been shown to increase risk for PTSD. We also provide brief descriptions of assessment measures and effective treatments for PTSD.

In this chapter, we distinguish stressors associated with low impact from stressors characterized as potentially traumatizing events (PTEs), the latter being a necessary but not sufficient cause of PTSD. However, both low-magnitude stressors and PTEs are implicated in the etiology of PTSD (e.g., King, King, Foy, Keane, & Fairbank, 1999). Low-magnitude peacekeeping stressors are experiences that are difficult to cope with, but are generally tolerable (e.g., poor living conditions). However, when the stress of a mission overwhelms an individual's ability to cope, a severe acute stress reaction can develop (e.g., an individual may begin to have trouble sleeping or to feel irritable frequently). Over time, stressful life events can also have a cumulative impact and take an even higher toll (e.g., an individual may develop enduring problems interacting effectively with others). Although low-magnitude stressors are not of sufficient magnitude to cause PTSD directly, they can contribute to a person feeling overwhelmed and unable to cope.

Potentially traumatic life events are more severe forms of stress that are typically considered to be intolerable. According to the *Diagnostic and Statistical Manual of Mental Disorders* (4th ed.) (American Psychiatric Association, 1994; DSM-IV), traumatic events are those in which a person either experiences, witnesses, or is confronted with actual or threatened death or serious injury or is faced with a threat to the physical integrity of self or other and is left with a feeling of fear, helplessness, and/or horror. A defining feature of trauma is the elicitation of intense emotions, however, unresponsiveness to stimulation, a lack of emotional involvement in surroundings, shock, and exhaustion are also characteristics of response to trauma (e.g., Foa, Zinbarg, & Rothbaum, 1992). In essence, trauma involves intense or protracted exposure to some uncontrollable and unpredictable aversive experience, which challenges one's view of the world as orderly and one's view of self as efficacious and invulnerable.

Peacekeeping missions are filled with low-magnitude or malevolent events, only some of which are especially prevalent in this type of context. Stressors common to both peacekeeping missions and traditional war zones include abrupt change in lifestyle, family separation, exhaustion, unfavorable climatic conditions, uncertainty about length of the mission, and demoralization about the efficacy of a mission (e.g., King et al., 1999; Rosebush, 1998). Stressors associated with peacekeeping missions include helplessness about affecting people's suffering and safety concerns, boredom, conflict about roles and duties, taunting and harassment by civilians and uncertainty about rules of engagement, and conditions under which offensive action is appropriate (Bramsen, Dirkwager, & van der Ploeg, 2000; Litz et al., 1997). As an example of changing rules of engagement, in Somalia the initial goal was to assist in the distribution of food to starving civilians, whereas the goal toward the end of the mission was to remove the strongest clan warlords by military means (Litz, King et al., 1997). One of the uniquely stressful aspects of peacekeeping is the proximity required in order to provide humanitarian assistance and protection, and deterrence. Thus the types of defensive military structures that are commonplace in war are often not available in peacekeeping missions, which heighten the sense of vulnerability and anxiety. The emphasis on proximity and restraint rather than protection creates considerable hypervigilance and arousal in peacekeepers and contributes to a general sense of fear. There is also the possibility of additional stress arising from the belief held by many peacekeepers that the stress they experience goes unrecognized by family, friends, and their government (O'Brien, 1994). Yet these experiences of low-level stressors are not inconsequential; research has demonstrated that such low-level stressors contribute cumulatively to the lasting negative psychological impact of military missions, and specifically to the development of PTSD (e.g., King et al., 1999; Wolfe, Erickson, Sharkansky, King, & King, 1999).

During deployment, peacekeepers may also be confronted with traumatic events that are typical of a war-zone, such as unexploded ordnance and land mines, witnessing death and dying, clearing civilian corpses, and being involved in serious driving accidents. They may also be fired on as a result of a misunderstanding, accidentally in crossfire between two armed feuding parties, or during "firing close," which occurs when the opponent wishes to intimidate the peacekeepers in order to keep them away from a certain area. Peacekeepers may also witness atrocities committed against fellow peacekeepers and civilians and the malicious destruction of property. For example, Bramsen et al. (2000) reported that 85% of their sample of peacekeepers in Bosnia had witnessed shootings and 47% had seen dead and/or wounded people. In addition, participants reported a mean number of 4.6 PTEs while on deployment. PTEs that are particularly horrific or frequent are associated with the greatest risk for PTSD and other problems implicated by exposure to traumatizing events (e.g., Kulka et al., 1990).

However, the nature and frequency of potentially traumatic events encountered will vary tremendously with the specific nature of the particular peacekeeping mission. Peacekeeping missions have ranged from very benign observer operations (e.g., Sinai) to highly dangerous peace-enforcement missions (e.g., Bosnia). Not surprisingly, the incidence of exposure to PTEs has varied with the nature of the specific peacekeeping mission (Litz, 1996). Increasingly, UN and NATO peacekeeping missions have required putatively neutral peacekeeping forces to intervene among warring factions in order to establish peace. Such missions necessarily involve greater exposure to traumatic events relative to those that merely require monitoring of firmly established and agreed-upon peace accords. For instance, in a very large sample of U.S. soldiers deployed to Somalia, over half of the sample reported engaging in very dangerous duty 13 or more times during their service (Orsillo, Roemer, Litz, Ehlich, & Friedman, 1998). Moreover, over a third of the sample reported that their unit was frequently fired upon. In a study of Australian peacekeepers deployed to Rwanda, a quarter of the sample frequently had to handle dead bodies, and nearly half believed they were in danger of being killed at least occasionally during the course of their service (Hodson, Ward, & Rapee, in press).

Although exposure to PTEs is invariably perceived as extremely stressful, they typically do not produce severe or chronic PTSD. In most instances, the acute distress that occurs in the immediate aftermath of exposure to PTEs spontaneously remits within a few months after the events. Because exposure to PTEs is a necessary but not sufficient cause of chronic PTSD, attention has been focused on the pretraumatic, peritraumatic, recovery environment, and posttrauma lifespan conditions that create risk for posttraumatic difficulties (Halligan & Yehuda, 2000; King et al., 1999). There is scant comprehensive epidemiological research on the risk factors associated with PTSD from peacekeeping missions. However, it is worth noting research on risk factors revealed from epidemiological studies of PTSD, which deserve special attention in the peacekeeping context. For example, prior exposure to PTEs is a risk factor for chronic PTSD stemming from subsequent PTEs (King et al., 1999; Stretch, Knudson, & Durand, 1998). In particular, a history of exposure to interpersonal violence, in childhood or adulthood, substantially increases the risk for chronic PTSD subsequent to any type of PTEs (Breslau et al., 1998; Green et al., 2000; Nishith, Mechanic, & Resnick, 2000). Dougall, Herberman, Delahanty, Inslicht, and Baum (2000) hypothesized that prior trauma history sensitizes victims to the new stressor, thus potentiating its impact. Thus peacekeepers with a history of PTEs may be particularly at risk for PTSD stemming from mission PTEs. Lack of social support is also implicated in risk for PTSD. Specifically, problems with cohesion and support from fellow peacekeepers and concerns about public support at homecoming have been shown to predict PTSD (Bolton, Litz, Glenn, Orsillo, & Roemer, 2002; Orsillo et al., 1998).

In order for a diagnosis of PTSD to be warranted, persons must report a PTE, and they must report at least one recurrent reexperiencing symptom, at least three avoidance and so-called emotional-numbing symptoms, and a minimum of two hyperarousal symptoms. Moreover, these symptoms must persist for more than a month following exposure to the traumatic event and must be sufficiently distressing so as to impair occupational, social, or other important domains of functioning (APA, 1994). Reexperiencing symptoms entail various guises of "reliving" the trauma in the form of intrusive thoughts or memories of the event, nightmares, flashbacks, or psychophysiological reactivity when reminded of the trauma. Because of the inordinate distress and anxiety resulting from these intrusive reliving symptoms, individuals often go to great lengths to avoid thinking about or recalling the trauma. Accordingly, avoidance and numbing symptoms develop. These symptoms include efforts to avoid thoughts, feelings, and situations that are reminiscent of the trauma. Finally, hyperarousal symptoms are indicators of a stressed or taxed nervous system, under heightened alert or threat: hypervigilance, exaggerated startle, concentration difficulties, irritability or excessive anger, and sleep disturbance.

Because PTSD symptoms are quite common in the immediate aftermath of trauma, these symptoms need to be present for at least a month following the traumatic event to warrant a PTSD diagnosis. Although very unpleasant, PTSD symptoms are so ubiquitous and prevalent immediately after trauma that they are not deemed abnormal. It can be argued that the one-month cutoff is arbitrary; however, the prolonged experience of debilitating symptoms is considered indicative of psychopathology. Although most trauma survivors exhibit positive readjustment and ultimately return to baseline levels of functioning, the immediate aftermath of trauma is generally characterized by some combination of emotional or psychological disturbance, social or occupational impairment, or significant physical pain secondary to injuries incurred during the trauma. The specific problems incurred and the rate of recovery is influenced by the nature of the traumatic experience, biological and psychological predisposition and temperament, and the quality of the recovery environment. For a sizable percentage of trauma survivors, a pattern characteristic of PTSD (e.g., fear and avoidance responses, affective instability, interpersonal withdrawal, and autonomic hyperarousal) persists and becomes chronic (e.g., Koss & Burkhart, 1989).

PREVALENCE OF PTSD FOLLOWING PEACEKEEPING OPERATIONS

Research bearing on the psychological and psychiatric impact of peacekeeping is in its infancy and firm answers remain elusive. No study to date has met rigorous sampling and measurement standards, which limits the generalizability of the findings. In addition, there is tremendous variability in assessment methods, which can partly account for varying rates. Also, it is impossible and for the most part inappropriate to consider the prevalence of PTSD stemming from "peacekeeping," generically defined because of the wide variety of missions. Nevertheless, there are some noteworthy findings (we confine our review here to peer-reviewed studies). Generally, traditional peacekeeping missions, where there is a firm, established peace, are associated with the lowest rates of PTEs and PTSD, and at the other end of the spectrum, dangerous peace enforcement missions are associated with the highest PTEs exposures and PTSD prevalence (Litz, 1996).

An investigation of Norwegian peacekeepers who served in the UN Interim Force in Lebanon documented that 15% of those who completed their service developed PTSD, as did 25% of those who had their service interrupted due to disciplinary, social, or medical problems (Weisæth, Mehlum, & Mortensen, 1996). In contrast, only 3% of Dutch peacekeepers in the former Yugoslavia developed PTSD, although more than one fifth of the sample reported at least some significant symptoms of PTSD (Bramsen et al., 2000). The conclusions we can draw on the emotional impact of such services are limited by the fact that these studies utilized differing cutoff scores on different self-report measures of PTSD. In addition, little information is provided on the selection of cutoff scores, limiting comparisons between the studies and conclusions about their relative accuracy.

Using empirically derived cutoff scores on two psychometrically sound PTSD self-report inventories, a large-scale investigation of 3,461 servicemen and women estimated that approximately 8% of American soldiers in Somalia met criteria for PTSD five months after their return to the United States (Litz, King, et al., 1997). The prevalence rates were not significantly different for male (7.9%) and female (8.8%) peacekeepers. The size of the sample, coupled with the care in selecting measures and deriving cutoff scores in this study, likely provides a very accurate estimate of the prevalence of PTSD among peacekeepers serving on this mission. It bears repeating, though, that peacekeepers' risk of developing PTSD secondary to peacekeeping operations depends largely on the nature of the mission. Moreover, the accuracy of PTSD prevalence estimates following peacekeeping missions will be facilitated to the extent that subsequent studies utilize structured clinical interviews to verify diagnostic status.

Prevalence rates of PTSD following peacekeeping operations may also vary as a function of time elapsed since the mission. During a two-year longitudinal study of New Zealand peacekeepers, it was determined that psychological distress was quite high at predeployment and again at follow-up (which occurred approximately six to seven months after returning from the mission), but was significantly lower during the mission itself (MacDonald, Chamberlain, Long, Pereira-Laird, & Mirfin, 1998). Although this pattern of symptoms may seem to be paradoxical, this observation has been made by others as well (e.g., Rosebush, 1998). The heightened distress prior to deployment is likely attributable to anticipatory anxiety about the mission coupled with concerns about traveling to a distant, foreign land and being separated from friends and loved ones for a lengthy period of time. The reductions in reported distress during the mission are consistent with deficits noted earlier that occur in the face of chronic uncontrollable or unpredictable stress (i.e., unresponsiveness to stimulation, emotional detachment, shock, and exhaustion; Foa et al., 1992). Moreover, soldiers may self-protectively refuse to report or even to personally acknowledge their emotional difficulties during the mission so they can continue to function (Rosebush, 1998). In fact, it has been noted that the presentation rates of psychiatric difficulties during war is quite low, but that many soldiers develop further difficulties after their service period is complete (O'Brien, 1994). Consequently, estimates of the incidence of PTSD immediately or very soon after missions may underestimate the full extent of distress incurred by peacekeepers as a result of their service.

The rates of PTSD following peacekeeping operations are likely influenced by efforts to cope with distress following the mission. In one investigation of 106 British peacekeepers who served in the former Yugoslavia, there were remarkably low rates of PTSD despite the fact that soldiers were exposed to numerous and severe PTEs (Deahl, Srinivasan, Jones, Thomas, Neblett, & Jolly, 2000). Notably, the incidence of PTSD was approximately 10 times less than that reported in other military and peacekeeping studies. Nevertheless, these researchers observed significant increases in alcohol consumption among the peacekeepers, which led them to consider the possibility that reported psychopathology was spuriously low due to a "masking effect," resulting from the abuse of alcohol in an attempt to avoid mission-related distress.

In sum, estimates of PTSD following peacekeeping operations have generally ranged from 3% to 15%, and the largest study to date (Litz, King et al., 1997) using empirically derived cutoff scores and well-validated measures estimated the prevalence of the disorder following a peacekeeping operation to be approximately 8%. Most studies have also demonstrated that many more peacekeepers will suffer from significant, if subthreshold, levels of PTSD symptoms. Thus posttraumatic stress appears to be a very significant and fairly common consequence of modern peacekeeping missions.

RISK AND RESILIENCY FACTORS FOLLOWING PEACEKEEPING OPERATIONS

There are a few studies that have examined risk and resiliency factors in the postdeployment environment for peacekeepers. For instance, in one study of peacekeepers, we found adjustment to peacekeeping to be significantly related to having discussed the experiences, especially with supportive significant others (Bolton, Glenn, Orsillo, Roemer, & Litz, 2002). Specifically, peacekeepers who reported disclosures of their experiences to spouses, family members, and friends endorsed fewer symptoms of PTSD. In addition, we found that adaptation to peacekeeping was positively related to homecoming reception such that those peacekeepers who reported a more positive reception at homecoming reported fewer symptoms of psychological distress postdeployment (Bolton, Litz, et al., 2002). Others have also observed that social support is associated with less distress following peacekeeping operations (Hodson et al., 2001).

In a review of factors that have been found to be associated with poorer psychiatric outcomes of war, O'Brien (1994) cites numerous maladaptive features that typify modern-day peacekeeping operations. He asserts that conflicts that are prolonged, are characterized by changing goals or objectives, involve an ill-defined enemy (e.g., civilian combatants), and that are ultimately unsuccessful are especially likely to result in significant pathology. He notes that witnessing or participating in atrocities in war has been found to be predictive of subsequent psychological distress. Peacekeepers sometimes witness the occurrence of atrocities and frequently encounter the aftermath of atrocities in the form of mass graves. O'Brien conjectures that those peacekeepers who adjust positively after conflict tend to be the beneficiaries of some combination of the following factors: early intervention, peer support and acceptance, and a lack of previous psychiatric difficulties.

Recent studies that have empirically examined these risk and resiliency factors in peacekeepers specifically have tended to corroborate these conclusions. In particular, characteristics of the service environment and perceptions of the meaning of one's service and the impact of the peacekeeping mission have been consistently associated with mental health outcomes. A series of studies of U.S. peacekeepers have illuminated factors in addition to traditional war-zone traumatic events that are predictive of PTSD. For instance, peacekeepers with lower symptoms of PTSD were more likely to feel positive about military cohesion and morale during their deployment (Litz, 1996). Moreover, the strongest statistical predictor of PTSD following the peacekeeping mission was the interaction between the extent of exposure to stressful war-zone events and frustrations with aspects of the mission (e.g., restrictive rules of engagement). This finding underscores the notion that unique features of particular peacekeeping missions can influence the impact of potentially traumatic events encountered (Litz, Orsillo, Friedman, Ehlich, & Batres, 1997).

A related study also documented the fact that low-intensity stressors that characterize the peacekeeping environment can also predict the development of subsequent PTSD. Specifically, negative aspects of the peacekeeping mission were defined as "events, circumstances, or contexts that might have created a sense of personal discomfort, aggravation, or distress or that might have led to a sense of being disheartened but did not pose an eminent threat to life for military personnel" (Litz, King et al., 1997). These circumstances included dealing with the harsh climate, looting of food supplies, and lack of privacy. Such experiences, although not of sufficient magnitude to cause PTSD by themselves, contributed to the prediction of PTSD symptom severity following the mission.

Finally, another study of peacekeepers examined the impact of sexual harassment on the severity of PTSD symptoms (Fontana, Litz, & Rosenheck, 2000). Fifty-two percent of women and 12% of men reported experiencing at least some sexual harassment or abuse during the peacekeeping operation. The severity of PTSD symptoms was impacted by exposure to combat directly and indirectly through fear and sexual harassment. Although sexual harassment is obviously not unique to peacekeeping missions, this type of stressor is often overlooked in studies examining the range of stressors associated with military operations, despite the fact that it is clearly and unfortunately a common experience.

In addition to characteristics of the peacekeeping environment, researchers have begun to examine intrapersonal variables that are associated with a heightened risk of psychopathology. Bramsen and colleagues (2000) conducted a prospective study of personality traits that were predictive of subsequent posttraumatic stress disorder. As these authors correctly noted, although previous investigations have documented associations between personality variables and PTSD, the measures are typically completed after deployment. Accordingly, the relevant personality traits cannot be said to predict PTSD, but simply to correlate with PTSD. It is entirely possible in such instances that PTSD or other pathology secondary to trauma influences scores on personality measures. In the Bramsen et al. investigation, however, Dutch peacekeepers completed a short form of the Dutch MMPI prior to deployment to the former Yugoslavia. The number of PTEs experienced during deployment was the strongest predictor of subsequent PTSD, but two predeployment personality traits were also significant predictors of postdeployment PTSD. Specifically, individuals who scored higher on scales that purportedly assess negativism (a negative, hostile, or generally dissatisfied outlook on life) and "psychopathologic personality" (having paranoid ideas or psychotic experiences) were more likely to develop posttraumatic stress disorder following the peacekeeping mission. Note, however, that individuals with extreme scores on these baseline measures were not deployed. The authors acknowledge that "most MMPI scores were within the normal range" (p. 1118). Consequently, it is doubtful whether those deployed can truly be characterized as having paranoid ideas or psychotic experiences, and the term *psychopathologic personality* is probably not an apt descriptor for those who were actually deployed.

Assessment of PTSD

It is beyond the scope of this chapter to provide a comprehensive review of PTSD and PTEs exposure measures, and other comprehensive reviews are available (Litz, Miller, Ruef, & McTeague, 2002; Weathers & Keane, 1999). Therefore, we discuss select interviews or inventories that are characterized by exceptional psychometric properties and are most relevant for researchers and clinicians working with peacekeepers.

The most common class of potentially traumatic events that a peacekeeper is likely to encounter is war-zone-related trauma. Most trauma checklists have a single item pertaining to combat exposure. Combat exposure rarely involves a discrete traumatic event, and peacekeepers typically have varying levels of exposure. If a researcher or clinician is not interested in obtaining an exhaustive trauma history, but instead wishes to determine the frequency of combat exposure in a peacekeeper population, the Combat Exposure Scale (CES; Keane, Fairbank, Caddell, Zimering, Taylor, & Mora, 1989) can be used, and it can be modified to fit a particular peacekeeping context (e.g., Litz, King et al., 1997). The CES inquires about multiple traumatic events that fall under the rubric of combat exposure, such as being under enemy fire, witnessing combat-related injuries, and being surrounded by the enemy. The CES has demonstrated excellent test-retest reliability, internal consistency, and is associated with greater PTSD severity (Keane, Fairbank, Caddell, Zimering, Taylor, et al., 1989).

It would be a mistake to assume the only traumatic experiences encountered by peacekeepers are stressors traditionally identified with combat missions, however. Peacekeepers may encounter other kinds of PTEs, such as motor vehicle accidents, sexual assaults, and unexpected life-threatening injuries during the course of their service. If broad trauma exposure (i.e., not just war-zone traumas) are of interest, investigators may elect to use a more general trauma screen such as the Traumatic Life Events Questionnaire (TLEQ) developed by Kubany and colleagues (2000). Drawing from existing trauma checklists and utilizing ratings from published experts in the area of PTSD, Kubany and colleagues developed a brief trauma-screening inventory that inquires about a respondent's experience with 21 potentially traumatic events. If an event is endorsed by the respondent, he or she is asked to specify the frequency of its occurrence and is also asked to indicate whether the event evoked intense fear, helplessness, or horror. The TLEQ performed very well in a series of studies assessing its psychometric properties in diverse settings and populations (Kubany et al., 2000).

Once it has been determined that an individual has encountered an event consistent with DSM-IV criterion A for PTSD, it is necessary to ascertain whether the symptom criteria (reexperiencing, avoidance and numbing, and hyperarousal) are also met. For formal diagnostic purposes, structured clinical interviews are generally considered the "gold standard" (Norris & Riad, 1997). Perhaps the greatest advance in the assessment of PTSD is represented by the

Clinician-Administered PTSD Scale (CAPS-1; Blake et al., 1990). The CAPS-1 items provide point-to-point correspondence with the 17 symptoms that comprise DSM-IV criteria for the disorder. Unlike other interviews for PTSD, frequency and intensity of symptoms are not conflated because both dimensions are rated separately for each symptom on a 5-point Likert-type scale. The CAPS-1 provides standard prompt questions, suggests follow-up queries, and behaviorally specific anchors to facilitate clinician ratings. Conveniently, it allows for the evaluation of dichotomous diagnostic status (i.e., caseness) as well as continuous scaling of PTSD severity. Other structured interviews that have very good diagnostic properties yield only dichotomous data and, accordingly, are not sensitive measures of symptom change or subthreshold difficulties. Given the care that went into its construction, it is not surprising the CAPS-1 has been found to have excellent test-retest reliability, internal consistency, sensitivity, and specificity (Blake et al., 1995).

Although structured clinical interviews may provide the most accurate diagnostic information, there are many purposes for which intensive interviews are impractical. Paper-and-pencil measures of PTSD symptomatology are a much more efficient use of resources for large-scale screenings in clinical and research settings, and some demonstrate excellent convergence with diagnostic interviews. Once a subset of individuals with pronounced symptoms has been identified, a structured interview can then be administered if optimal accuracy is desired. Brief self-report measures also allow clinicians and researchers to track symptom change over the course of treatment in an expedient manner. If a researcher wishes to monitor PTSD symptom status longitudinally in a sample of peacekeepers, such measures will allow changes to be tracked relatively efficiently.

Although PTSD measures have not been developed for use specifically with peacekeepers, measures developed for use with traditional combat populations will certainly suffice. Perhaps the best paper-and-pencil measure of combat-related PTSD is the Mississippi Scale for Combat-Related Posttraumatic Stress Disorder (Keane, Caddell, & Taylor, 1988). The Mississippi Scale is a 35-item measure that assesses DSM symptoms as well as associated clinical features of the disorder, such as substance abuse, depressive symptoms, and suicidality. Its ease of administration and excellent psychometric properties has helped establish the Mississippi Scale as the most widely used PTSD measure among veteran populations, and it is now available in multiple languages (Keane, Newman, & Orsillo, 1997).

Another recently developed self-report measure of PTSD that appears to be quite sound and broadly applicable is the PTSD Checklist (PCL; Weathers, Litz, Herman, Huska, & Keane, 1993). The PCL consists of 17 items that correspond to DSM diagnostic criteria for PTSD. Respondents rate the extent to which they have been affected by each symptom during the last month on a scale ranging from 1 (not at all) to 5 (extremely). In an initial evaluation of its properties with Vietnam veterans, it was found to have excellent test-retest reliability and very good convergence with a structured clinical interview (Weathers et al., 1993).

Psychological Treatments for PTSD

Numerous psychological treatments are available for PTSD. Some of these treatments focus on eliminating the conditioned fear response thought to underlie PTSD through exposure to thoughts, feelings, and memories associated with the traumatic event. Other treatments attempt to correct the maladaptive beliefs that may develop in response to traumatic events and to develop additional anxiety management skills. The efficacy of treatments for PTSD in peacekeepers has yet to be empirically assessed; however, treatment of such individuals is likely to be informed by established interventions with combat veterans and survivors of other traumatic events.

The efficacy of exposure therapy for PTSD has been established through several well-controlled studies with veterans (Boudewynns & Hyer, 1990; Cooper & Clum, 1989; Glynn et al., 1999; Keane, Fairbank, Caddell, & Zimering, 1989) and with survivors of various other types of traumatic events (Marks, Lovell, Noshirvani, Livanou, & Thrasher, 1998; Tarrier et al., 1999). For example, Keane and colleagues (1989) found that in comparison to veterans in a wait-list control group, veterans treated with exposure therapy showed significant improvement in symptoms of reexperiencing, depression, and anxiety. Cooper and Clum (1989) found that the veterans who received the combination of standard and exposure therapy reported a decline in their distress associated with their combat experience as compared to those veterans who received standard therapy alone. Boudewynns and Hyer (1990) found that 75% of the individuals who had decreased physiological responding at posttest and who demonstrated improvements on measures of anxiety and depression had received exposure therapy. In addition, Glynn and colleagues (1999) found that individuals in two treatment conditions that received exposure therapy reported a decrease in distress relative to those in the wait-list control group. In general, these studies indicate that exposure therapy is effective in reducing the distress of individuals suffering from PTSD. These studies also indicate that exposure therapy is particularly strong in reducing the reexperiencing symptoms of nightmares and intrusive recollections as well as hyperarousal. However, this treatment appears to be less effective at reducing avoidance and social withdrawal. There is also some research to indicate that exposure therapy is less effective for patients in which guilt or anger is the primary emotion (Foa, Riggs, Massie, & Yarczower, 1995; Pitman et al., 1991).

There is also evidence that cognitive therapy, which focuses on altering maladaptive thinking patterns, is helpful in reducing distress associated with traumatic events. This treatment is based on theories proposing that some maladaptive beliefs create feelings of distress, such as anxiety, depression, anger, guilt, and shame. These cognitive patterns or beliefs, and the emotions they evoke, are thought be the cause of some dysfunctional behavior (e.g., avoidance of safe situations) and distress (e.g., chronic feelings of anxiety and anger). In cognitive therapy, individuals are taught to identify these dysfunctional thought patterns, to challenge them, and to replace them with functional beliefs. Cognitive therapy with survivors of traumatic experiences focuses particular attention on beliefs about safety, trust, and self-worth.

Data from two well-controlled studies indicate that cognitive therapy is effective in reducing symptoms of PTSD. Resick and Schnicke (1992) found that their cognitive intervention, which includes a component of cognitive therapy, was effective at ameliorating symptoms of PTSD, depression, and social adjustment. Marks et al. (1998) found cognitive therapy, exposure therapy, and the combined treatment to be more effective than relaxation therapy, but otherwise equal to each other. Although this evidence suggests that cognitive therapy is an effective treatment component for PTSD, many clinicians and researchers believe that including an exposure component with cognitive therapy is crucial. Dismantling studies to date (e.g., Marks et al., 1998) have not documented incremental treatment gains of cognitive therapy when combined with exposure therapy alone.

Finally, anxiety management is another approach that has been used to treat individuals with PTSD. This eclectic method often incorporates numerous components, such as psycho-education, muscle relaxation, breathing retraining, role playing, and assertiveness training. In general, these treatments have been shown to be less effective than comparison treatments (Rothbaum, Meadows, Resick, & Foy, 2000), which suggests they should not be considered as necessary and sufficient approaches to treating individuals with PTSD.

CONCLUSIONS

Posttraumatic stress disorder occurs in a small but significant percentage of peacekeepers following their missions. A larger proportion will develop at least some significant symptoms of PTSD or other psychological distress (e.g., Orsillo et al., 1998). Although peacekeeping operations have historically been viewed as relatively benign compared to traditional combat missions, they are increasingly characterized by features associated with greater psychological distress. Specifically, these operations often involve changing goals, ambiguous rules of engagement, civilian combatants, and exposure to the aftermath of violence or ongoing atrocities. Research efforts have begun to delineate factors associated with risk and resilience such that negative psychological consequences may be reduced and identification of those individuals most adversely affected can be facilitated. Although assessment measures and treatments have not been designed specifically for use with peacekeepers, empirically validated instruments and interventions have been developed for use with veterans of more traditional combat missions, and they will likely prove effective. In order to elucidate the psychological impact of peacekeeping operations and minimize poor psychiatric outcomes, those working with peacekeepers should utilize established and empirically validated assessment instruments and clinical interventions (see Litz, Gray, Bryant, & Adler, in press).

REFERENCES

American Psychiatric Association. (1994). *Diagnostic and statistical manual of mental disorders* (4th ed.). Washington, DC: Author.

Blake, D. D., Weather, F. W., Nagy, L. M., Kaloupek, D. G., Gusman, F. D., Charney, D. S., & Keane, T. M. (1995). The development of a clinician-administered PTSD scale. *Journal of Traumatic Stress, 8,* 75–90.

Blake, D. D., Weather, F. W., Nagy, L. M., Kaloupek, D. G., Klauminzer, G., Charney, D. S., & Keane, T. M. (1990). A clinician rating scale for assessing current and lifetime PTSD: The CAPS-1. *Behavior Therapist, 13,* 187–188.

Bolton, E. E., Glenn, D. M., Orsillo, S., Roemer, L., & Litz, B. T. (2002). The relationship between self-disclosure and symptoms of posttraumatic stress disorder in peacekeepers deployed to Somalia. *Military Psychology.*

Bolton, E. E., Litz, B. T., Glenn, D. M., Orsillo, S., & Roemer, L. (2002). The impact of homecoming reception on the adaptation of peacekeepers following deployment. *Military Psychology, 14,* 241–251.

Boudewyns, P. A., & Hyer, L. (1990). Physiological response to combat memories and preliminary treatment outcome in Vietnam veteran PTSD patients treated with direct therapeutic exposure. *Behavior Therapy, 21,* 63–87.

Bramsen, I., Dirkzwager, A. J. E., & van der Ploeg, H. M. (2000). Predeployment personality traits and exposure to trauma as predictors of posttraumatic stress symptoms: A prospective study of former peacekeepers. *American Journal of Psychiatry, 157*(7), 1115–1119.

Breslau, N., Kessler, R., Chilcoat, H., Schultz, L., Davis, G., & Andreski, P. (1998). Trauma and posttraumatic stress disorder in the community: The 1996 Detroit area survey of trauma. *Archives of General Psychiatry, 55,* 626–632.

Cooper, N. A., & Clum, G. A. (1989). Imaginal flooding as a supplementary treatment for PTSD in combat veterans: A controlled study. *Behavior Therapy, 20,* 381–391.

Deahl, M., Srinivasan, M., Jones, N., Thomas, J., Neblett, C., & Jolly, A. (2000). Preventing psychological trauma in soldiers: The role of operational stress training and psychological debriefing. *British Journal of Medical Psychology, 73,* 77–85.

Dougall, A., Herberman, H., Delahanty, D., Inslicht, S., & Baum, A. (2000). Similarity of prior trauma exposure as a determinant of chronic stress responding to an airline disaster. *Journal of Consulting and Clinical Psychology, 68,* 290–295.

Foa, E. B., Riggs, D. S., Massie, E. D., & Yarczower, M. (1995). The impact of fear activation and anger on the efficacy of exposure treatment for posttraumatic stress disorder. *Behavior Therapy, 26,* 487–499.

Foa, E. B., Zinbarg, R., & Rothbaum, B. O. (1992). Uncontrollability and unpredictability in post-traumatic stress disorder: An animal model. *Psychological Bulletin, 112,* 218–238.

Fontana, A., Litz, B., & Rosenheck, R. (2000). Impact of combat and sexual harassment on the severity of posttraumatic stress disorder among men and women peacekeepers in Somalia. *Journal of Nervous and Mental Disease, 188,* 163–169.

Glynn, S. M., Eth, S., Randolph, E. T., Foy, D. W., Urbaitis, M., Boxer, L., Paz, G. G., Leong, G. B., Firman, G., Salk, J. D., Katzman, J. W., & Crothers, J. (1999). A test of behavioral family therapy to augment exposure for combat-related post-traumatic stress disorder. *Journal of Consulting and Clinical Psychology, 67,* 243–251.

Green, B., Goodman, L., Krupnick, J., Corcoran, C., Petty, R., Stockton, P., & Stern, N. (2000). Outcomes of single versus multiple trauma exposure in a screening sample. *Journal of Traumatic Stress, 13,* 271–286.

Halligan, S. L., & Yehuda, R. (2000). Risk factor for PTSD. *PTSD Research Quarterly, 11,* 1–2.

Hodson, S. E., Ward, D., & Rapee, R. (in press). Post deployment predictors of traumatic stress—Rwanda: A case study. In G. E. Kearney, M. Creamer, & R. P. Marshall (Eds.), *Military Stress and Performance—The Australian Defense Force Experience.* Melbourne: Melbourne University Press.

Keane, T. M., Caddell, J. M., & Taylor, K. L. (1988). Mississippi scale for combat-related posttraumatic stress disorder: Three studies in reliability and validity. *Journal of Consulting and Clinical Psychology, 56,* 85–90.

Keane, T. M., Fairbank, J. A., Caddell, J. M., & Zimering, R. T. (1989). Implosive (flooding) therapy reduces symptoms of PTSD in Vietnam combat veterans. *Behavior Therapy, 20,* 245–260.

Keane, T. M., Fairbank, J. A., Caddell, J. M., Zimering, R. T., Taylor, K. L., & Mora, C. A. (1989). Clinical evaluation of a measure to assess combat exposure. *Psychological Assessment, 1,* 53–55.

Keane, T. M., Newman, E., & Orsillo, S. M. (1997). Assessment of military-related posttraumatic stress disorder. In J. P. Wilson & T. M. Keane (Eds.), *Assessing psychological trauma and PTSD* (pp. 267–290). New York: Guilford Press.

King, D. W., King, L. A., Foy D. W., Keane, T. M., & Fairbank, J. A. (1999). Posttraumatic stress disorder in a national sample of female and male Vietnam veterans: Risk factors, war-zone stressors, and resilience-recovery variables. *Journal of Abnormal Psychology, 108,* 164–170.

Koss, M. P., & Burkhart, B. R. (1989). A conceptual analysis of rape victimization: Long-term effects and implications for treatment. *Psychology of Women Quarterly, 13,* 27–40.

Kubany, E. S., Haynes, S. N., Leisen, M. B., Owens, J. A., Kaplan, A. S., Watson, S. B., & Burns, K. (2000). Development and preliminary validation of a brief broad-spectrum measure of trauma exposure: The Traumatic Life Events Questionnaire. *Psychological Assessment, 12,* 210–224.

Kulka, R. A., Schlenger, W. E., Fairbank, J. A., Hough, R. L., Jordan, B. K., & Marmar, C. R. (1990). *Trauma and the Vietnam War generation: Report of findings from the National Vietnam Veterans Readjustment Study.* New York: Brunner/ Mazel.

Litz, B. T. (1996). The psychological demands of peacekeeping for military personnel. *National Center for PTSD Clinical Quarterly, 6,* 1–8.

Litz, B. T., Gray, M. J., Bryant, R., and Adler, A. B. (in press). Early intervention for trauma: Current status and future directions. *Clinical Psychology: Science and Practice.*

Litz, B. T., King, L. A., King, D. W., Orsillo, S. M., & Friedman, M. J. (1997). Warriors as peacekeepers: Features of the Somalia experience and PTSD. *Journal of Consulting and Clinical Psychology, 65*(6), 1001–1010.

Litz, B. T., Miller, M. W., Ruef, A. M., & McTeague, L. M. (2002). Assessment of adults exposed to trauma. In M. M. Antony & D. H. Barlow (Eds.), *Handbook of assessment, treatment planning, and outcome evaluation: Empirically supported strategies for psychological disorders.* New York: Guilford Press.

Litz, B. T., Orsillo, S. M., Friedman, M., Ehlich, P., & Batres, A. (1997). Post-traumatic stress disorder associated with peacekeeping duty in Somalia for U.S. military personnel. *American Journal of Psychiatry, 154,* 178–184.

MacDonald, C., Chamberlain, K., Long, N., Pereira-Laird, J., & Mirfin, K. (1998). Mental health, physical health, and stressors reported by New Zealand defense force peacekeepers: A longitudinal study. *Military Medicine, 163,* 477–481.

Marks, I., Lovell, K., Noshirvani, H., Livanou, M., & Thrasher, S. (1998). Treatment of posttraumatic stress disorder by exposure and/or cognitive restructuring: A controlled study. *Archives of General Psychiatry, 55,* 317–325.

Nishith, P., Mechanic, M., & Resick, P. (2000). Prior interpersonal trauma: The contribution to current PTSD symptoms in female rape victims. *Journal of Abnormal Psychology, 109,* 20–25.

Norris, F. H., & Riad, J. K. (1997). Standardized self-report measures of civilian trauma and posttraumatic stress disorder. In J. P. Wilson & T. M. Keane (Eds.), *Assessing psychological trauma and PTSD* (pp. 7–42). New York: Guilford Press.

O'Brien, L. S. (1994). What will be the psychiatric consequences of the war in Bosnia? A bad war from the psychiatric point of view, leading to hidden pathology. *British Journal of Psychiatry, 164,* 443–447.

Orsillo, S. M., Roemer, L., Litz, B. T., Ehlich, P., & Friedman, M. J. (1998). Psychiatric symptomatology associated with contemporary peacekeeping: An examination of post-mission functioning among peacekeepers in Somalia. *Journal of Traumatic Stress, 11,* 611–625.

Pitman, R. K., Altman, B., Greenwald, E., Longpre, R. E., Macklin, M. L., Poire, R. F., & Stekette, G. S. (1991). Psychiatric complications during flooding therapy for posttraumatic stress disorder. *Journal of Clinical Psychiatry, 52,* 17–20.

Resick, P. A., & Schnicke, M. K. (1992). Cognitive processing therapy for sexual assault victims. *Journal of Consulting and Clinical Psychology, 60,* 748–756.

Rosebush, P. (1998). Psychological intervention with military personnel in Rwanda. *Military Medicine, 163,* 559–563.

Rothbaum, B. O., Meadows, E. A., Resick, P., & Foy, D. W. (2000). Cognitive-behavioral therapy. In E. B. Foa, T. M. Keane, & M. Friedman (Eds.), *Effective treatments for PTSD* (pp. 60–83). New York: Guilford Press.

Stretch, R. H., Knudson, K., & Durand, D. (1998). Effects of premilitary and military trauma on the development of post-traumatic stress disorder symptoms in female and male active duty soldiers. *Military Medicine, 163,* 466–470.

Tarrier, N., Pilgrim, H., Sommerfield, C., Faragher, B., Reynolds, M., Graham, E., & Barrowclough, C. (1999). A randomized trial of cognitive therapy and imaginal exposure in the treatment of chronic posttraumatic stress disorder. *Journal of Consulting and Clinical Psychology, 67,* 13–18.

Weathers, F. W., & Keane, T. M. (1999). Psychological assessment of traumatized adults. In P. Saigh & J. Bremner (Eds.), *Posttraumatic stress disorder: A comprehensive approach to research and treatment* (pp. 219–247). Needham Heights, MA: Allyn & Bacon.

Weathers, F. W., Litz, B. T., Herman, D. S., Huska, J. A., & Keane, T. M. (1993, October). *The PTSD Checklist: Reliability, validity, & diagnostic utility.* Paper presented at the Annual Meeting of the International Society for Traumatic Stress Studies, San Antonio, TX.

Weisæth, L., Mehlum, L., & Mortensen, M. (1996). Peacekeeper stress: New and different? *National Center for PTSD Clinical Quarterly, 6,* 12–15.

Wolfe, J., Erickson, D. J., Sharkansky, E. J., King, D. W., & King, L. A. (1999). Course and predictors of posttraumatic stress disorder among Gulf War veterans: A prospective analysis. *Journal of Consulting and Clinical Psychology, 67,* 520–528.

Cross-Cultural Psychology in Peacekeeping

Cooperation and Coordination across Cultures in the Peacekeeping Forces: Individual and Organizational Integrating Mechanisms

Efrat Elron, Nir Halevy, Eyal Ben Ari, and Boas Shamir

Peacekeeping forces, in each and every location and mission, are always multicultural organizations consisting of forces from different nations, speaking multiple languages and representing different cultures. As such, these frameworks represent some of the most extreme cases of culturally diverse organizations, and (as a consequence) some of the most interesting challenges for cross-cultural management both at the level of the organizations and at the level of the individuals serving in them.

The many ways in which cultural diversity influences the effectiveness of organizations has become a prominent issue for both researchers and those directly involved in peacekeeping missions (e.g., Elron, 1997; Knouse & Dansby, 1999; Meschi, 1997; Solomon, 1996). This diversity, combined with the increasing importance of the peacekeeping forces, highlight the need to understand how the forces operate as coherent, coordinated, and integrated structures. In other words, from both practical and theoretical viewpoints, the question of interest is how the multinational peacekeeping forces operate in unity despite the potential for misunderstanding, conflict, and operational difficulties resulting from their multicultural nature. This chapter investigates the integrating behaviors and mechanisms that lead to the overcoming of the cultural barriers via a study done on peacekeepers in several peacekeeping sites and schools.

Based on literature in military psychology, international management, and social psychology, we begin with a discussion of the consequences of cultural diversity in organizations and groups. Next, we describe the extent of cultural diversity in the peacekeeping forces, followed by a description of our study of international peacekeepers, the findings from the study, and their implications.

CULTURAL DIVERSITY IN ORGANIZATIONS

With the onset of that complex trend termed *globalization*, many organizations have increasingly found themselves dealing with a culturally diverse workforce. In recent decades, much scholarly effort in organization science has been devoted to examining the negative and positive consequences of such diversity. Cultures are the deeply ingrained patterns of values, perceptions, assumptions, and norms shared by members of the same group (Schein, 1985). National culture, as an often taken-for-granted product of primary socialization, is thought to be particularly potent, and its effects on individuals are perceived to be particularly resistant to change. Most studies on intercultural interactions conclude that such interactions tend to be especially complex. The differences in the value priorities, goal preferences, and interpretive schema held by members of different cultures have the potential to increase misunderstandings, friction, and even conflicts. Moreover, the language factor can intensify these differences. Stening (1979), in his review of literature on cross-cultural interactions, reports a variety of problems, such as disparities in attributions about causes and intentions of behaviors, communication gaps, stereotyping, ethnocentrism, and prejudice.

In organizations there may be an added complexity as the differences in cultural values can be manifested in different attitudes toward organizational practices, such as motivational techniques and leadership styles (Erez, 1993; Erez & Earley, 1987; Hui, 1990). Moreover, the cultural differences that members bring to the organization imply they are likely to have different assumptions about what a good team is or what constitutes an efficient organization. These differences have implications for the cohesiveness and integration within organizations and organizational groups. Coordination and control can be difficult to achieve in culturally diverse organizations where individual differences of participants are enhanced by differences in their national cultures (Ghoshal & Westney, 1993). Research on international joint ventures (IJVs), the type of organization that has structural similarities to the peacekeeping forces, found that the national culture of partners is a major determinant of IJV success (Fiol & Lyles, 1985; Lyles & Salk, 1996; Parkhe, 1993; Salk, 1996). Differences in partner nationality and culture often lead to conflicts and misunderstandings that can limit the sharing of information and learning, which are crucial to the effectiveness of these organizations.

Conversely, empirical support has also been found for the advantages of cultural diversity (Cox, Lobel, & McLeod, 1991; Elron, 1997; Watson, Kumar, & Michaelsen, 1993). Although most of these studies were done at the level of the work-group, they nevertheless provide evidence for an elevated level of cognitively related aspects of outcomes. The higher levels of creativity, decision making, and overall performance are attributed to the larger pool of cognitive resources and increased attention directed at the decision-making process. The passage of time and the specific context, combined with individual, group, and organizational norms and specific mechanisms that enhance cultural integration, allow culturally heterogeneous organizations to resolve group process issues and capitalize on their culture-related skills to substantially improve their performance, to the extent of exceeding the performance of culturally homogeneous organizations (Earley & Mosakowsky, 2000; Elron, 1997, 2000; Elron, Shamir, & Ben Ari, 2000; Meschi, 1997; Salk & Brannen, 2000; Watson et al., 1993).

The multinational peacekeeping forces are different in several ways from most civilian organizations just described. They are temporary alliances that mostly operate under relatively short time frames, and they are often created with a sense of urgency to deal with ad-hoc problems. Even in more permanent forces there is a frequent rotation of commanders, officers, and soldiers. They are, however, organizations that like civilian organizations have specific missions and goals, and like civilian organizations they perform better when intercultural relationships between the different forces and the individuals within them take the form of cooperation and coordination.

In the past few years, observers of multinational peacekeeping forces have increasingly begun to address issues related to the relationships between the different forces. For example, Palin (1995; also Alberts & Hayes, 1995) talks of the variegated composition of such forces in terms of military capabilities, basic doctrines, ethos, and ability to communicate. In a seminar on cooperation, command, and control in UN peacekeeping operations held in 1997, one of the key problem areas identified was differences in language and culture (International Association of Peacekeeping Training Centers, 1998). Other observers have noted that different linguistic abilities may create problems in the transmission of orders (Downes, 1993; Palin, 1995). Other findings point to a more comprehensive difficulty with trust between peacekeepers and foreign nationals (e.g., Segal & Tiggle, 1997). Given that trust is widely considered a necessary condition for collaboration between individuals and groups (Kramer & Tyler, 1996), its low level as reflected in the survey brings into light the potential cross-cultural difficulties implicit in bringing together international forces.

A deeper understanding of these issues in the specific context of the multinational peacekeeping forces is especially important because of the relatively high intensity of the cross cultural contacts and because the cooperation of the different forces is inherently critical to the peacekeeping missions. This chapter focuses on behaviors and orientations at the level of the individual soldiers and officers that enhance cross-cultural integration within the peacekeeping forces. Moreover, we investigate the ways these individual efforts are related to and embedded in organizational-level integrating norms and mechanisms.

THE STUDY

We conducted our research in several sites: UNTSO (the UN observers' force headquartered in Jerusalem and the oldest mission of the UN), UNIFIL (the

UN force located in Southern Lebanon), UNDOF (the UN force located in the Golan Heights on the Israeli-Syrian border), the Pearson Peacekeeping Center in Canada (responsible for courses on different aspects of peacekeeping given to both civilians and military personnel from around the globe), the Canadian forces, peacekeeping school in Kingston, The United Nations School in the Irish army, the Italian army headquarters in Rome, and the liaison unit of the Israeli army responsible for coordination activities with the peacekeeping forces based in and around Israel. The selection of the sites was based on our wish to achieve a variety of locations, type of missions, size of forces, and circumstances. The interviews took place between 1999 and 2001.

Our understanding of the internal working of the multinational peacekeeping forces in terms of their dealings with cultural diversity relied mainly on 62 semistructured interviews with army officers and UN officials at the different sites. Most interviewees belonged or served in truly culturally diverse environments within the missions. For example, they worked in mission headquarters, served as officers in particular positions of leadership that require such contact, or served on observer missions. These assignments distinguish study participants from most soldiers and junior officers who serve in large national units that are usually stationed in geographically separate areas and operate in a relatively culturally homogeneous environment.

Quotes from the interviews conducted appear in this work, with the officers' nationality and the mission the officer participated in (which was the most recent mission for those who were interviewed in their homelands) in parentheses. To have a better understanding of the missions, we also used written and Internet materials published by the different peacekeeping sites, the homeland forces, or by related agencies (e.g., civilian peacekeeping centers).

IS THERE REALLY AN OPERATIONAL UNITY IN THE PEACEKEEPING FORCES?

In the interviews we asked whether the meeting of people from different cultures led to misunderstandings, disagreements, and conflicts. When responses were positive, we inquired further into the content and nature of the conflicts in order to identify whether they were task, relationship, or process-related conflicts, and what was the level of emotionality experienced (Jehn, Northcraft, & Neale, 1999). Task conflict occurs when group members disagree about the task content (e.g., goals, key decision areas and the appropriate choice for action). Relationship or emotional conflict occurs when group members have interpersonal clashes characterized by tension, annoyance, anger, frustration, and other negative feelings. Process conflict happens when the disagreements are about how to do the task, mainly the assignment or division of responsibilities, roles, and resources.

The analyses of the interviews reveal that in almost all interviews, conflicts that resulted from cultural differences were described as task related. Moreover, most interviewees insisted that conflicts rarely occurred, and what they mostly experienced were culturally related and language-related misunderstandings and disagreements. However, there was a slight increase in the frequency of the conflicts, the levels of emotionality, and the importance attached to the conflict in the more dangerous missions, although even the more severe conflicts were contained and kept at a relatively low level. An example of such conflict was the refusal of some of the troops in Kosovo to cooperate with a unit whose soldiers were known to treat the locals harshly. All the interviewees who were in close outsider positions (e.g., Israeli liaison officers) expressed agreement with the notion that there was (relative) peace within the peacekeeping forces. They did indicate, however, that they feel beneath the surface or behind closed doors there may be more tension than what appears to be: "I didn't see and didn't hear about any tensions between the UNIFIL battalions. . . . There were however some discreet talks about how sometimes it's difficult for a Westerner to receive orders from a force commander who is not."

Although conflicts are kept at a low level, one problem that was reported as a cause for some frictions and uneasy feelings by some of the study's participants was the gap in the levels of professionalism that existed between some of the armies (despite the efforts at some level of standardization taken by the UN). Although this problem is not a cultural one per se, it does have cultural manifestations because it was mostly specific armies from developing countries that were perceived as less professional by officers from the developed countries. This problem was discussed mainly by those officers who participated in the more active and dangerous missions (e.g., Kosovo), where the consequences of being less professional were more severe. It seems that the informal ways to avoid severe conflicts regarding this issue were either to assign the less professional armies less important roles (such as guarding a camp) or separate geographical areas for their activities.

It should also be mentioned that some of the interviewees stated that they did have a preference for working with cultures that are more similar to theirs, while having a harder time adjusting to more distant cultures in terms of values (see also Soeters and Bos-Bakx, this volume). As stated by one of our interviewees, "The Chinese are a lot more of an authoritarian organization than we are, and essentially they obey the senior present, regardless of the situation. Of course, most of the Europeans are not like that and there is a difference" (Austrian officer, UNTSO).

In the next sections we present the different behaviors and mechanisms used by the individual peacekeepers and the organizational frameworks they belong to that help the prevention of conflicts, thus enabling the separate forces to be part of an integrated structure.

Individual Behaviors and Attitudes Enhancing Cooperation and Coordination

Although most multinational organizations usually have members from two or three cultures in different locations or subsidiaries (i.e., expatriates from headquarters, third country expatriates, and locals), the multinational peacekeeping forces' sites are truly multicultural and require individuals to interact with and adjust to many cultures at once rather than to a certain culture. Our basic assumption is that in order for these interactions to enhance the unity of the forces, they need to be based on individual intercultural competence. According to Spitzberg and Cupach (1984), the criteria for intercultural competence are appropriateness (meets cultural expectations and is proper for the context) and effectiveness (the degree to which communicators achieve shared meanings and desirable outcomes). Therefore, intercultural competence is the ability to relate effectively and appropriately in various cultural contexts.

In practice, intercultural competence is based on both behaviors and attitudes (Rubens, 1989). According to a model of intercultural competence defined by Ting-Toomey (1999), culturally sensitive knowledge includes cognitive information about important aspects of the culture such as values, language, verbal and nonverbal communication styles, ingroup and outgroup boundaries, relationship development, and conflict management. The skill set consists of skills that mostly have behavioral manifestations (e.g., observation, listening, verbal empathy, nonverbal sensitivity, constructive conflict skills, and flexible adaptive skills). The motivated mindset refers to attitudinal or motivational factors such as mindfulness when regarding one's ethnocentric tendencies and the social identities of all parties.

Ting-Toomey's model serves as the basis for categorizing our findings. We begin with the description of the behaviors that are related to intercultural effectiveness—because interviews were our main tool for investigation, our strongest evidence relates to actual behaviors, as these can be described in a precise manner by interviewees in relation to both self and others (taking into account that descriptions of self may sometimes be influenced by self-enhancement motivations). The behaviors described in the interviews are based on the model's first two components: the search for knowledge and the set of skills manifested through these behaviors. We then continue with an analysis of the attitudinal and motivational factors required for intercultural effectiveness. Because attitudes are more implied and are harder to pinpoint in interviews, we base our writings on a combination of evidence and past literature.

Interculturally Effective Behaviors

Interviewees were asked what actions they took to bridge and overcome cultural differences and what they did to prevent culturally based conflicts. Most of the behaviors described as effective in the cross-cultural interactions consisted of alternating between behaviors ranging from the more active to the more passive. More specifically, the behaviors described consisted of (1) "integrating differences," (2) "bridging differences," and (3) "tolerating differences." The first behavior, integrating differences, consisted of bringing the different cultural perspectives and preferences together, resolving differences among them, and generating integrative solutions. The second behavior, bridging differences, included communicating across the differences, making an effort at understanding them, and building shared bases. The third behavior, tolerating differences, consisted of passive actions (or inactions) that allow the other the space to act freely according to his or her own cultural values, beliefs, and norms.

Integrating Differences

Finding Integrative Solutions and Compromises

Integrative solutions, elicited by a high concern for both one's own and the other's results, are in many situations the most constructive mode of managing disagreements and conflicts. They reduce the conflict issues and usually improve the relationship with the other party (e.g., Barker, Tjosvold, & Andrews, 1988). Integrative solutions tend to be especially effective if a commander combines them with a degree of direct instruction (Van de Vliert, Euwema, & Huismans, 1994). Certainly directly instructing others is typical of most relationships in the armed forces, especially between commanders and soldiers. Examples of finding integrative solutions in order to take into consideration all different cultures were given in several interviews: "We have negotiating functions, mediating function, and I think that then it is good when you have a problem to solve, that you look at it from different angles, and you find a common way that you want to proceed. I think that that is one of the strong points of multinational forces" (Swiss officer, UNTSO). A closely related style of handling conflict is compromise, where there is concern for all parties involved, but the solution involves a middle ground where each party gains but also loses some of its interests.

Coordination of Communication

Because certain features of communication are different across cultures (Gibson, 1997), the most evident being fluency in English and the different meaning attached to words, intercultural communication is likely to be a particularly complex and demanding process. Two complementary routes to coordinated communication were reported. The first route included individual initiatives in communication coordination. The second route involved individuals establishing unofficial group norms on how to communicate in the multilinguistic context (over and above the explicit guidance from the UN norm that English is the official language in most missions).

The cultural differences in communication are most evident during the first two phases of the communication process (the phases in which messages are constructed and transmitted), and they can be reconciled during the later phases of the communication process, namely the receiving, decoding, and feedback phases (Gibson, 1997). The individual initiatives reported by interviewees who spoke English more fluently include active listening, focusing on the core of the message as it was intended rather than the actual words or phrases used by that person, framing (which involves taking the other person's frame of reference), and following up (accurately repeating the communicator's message). An example of some of this initiative is provided by the commander of one of the forces: "It is very important that when someone gives the message that they make sure that the person is receiving it, that they actually listen, that they have the ability to listen. Then secondly, that they understand what you are saying. You have to do that almost by testing them, asking them 'do you understand?'"

As for group norms, interviewees reported that communication was pervasively treated as a conjunctive task, in which the individual with the poorest performance determines the group product (Brehm, Kassin, & Fein, 1999, p. 270). Accordingly, repetitions, slow pace, and multiple verifications were prevalent in task meetings to ensure understanding of the information transferred by all participants. In some cases protocols of discussions were read and reread by group members who found the conversations difficult to follow. Many channels of communication, both formal and informal, are established and used simultaneously. Another norm that developed was that of consideration: "Even in social settings, when there are two of us who speak the same language that others don't understand, we will always be very careful to adhere to English, although there is no official rule on it" (Polish civilian officer, UNTSO).

Another way to at least partly overcome the communication barriers is the use of the common military background: "Even where there is a language barrier, you can, because of the military signs, symbols and because of the understanding of the military setup you can have a negotiation without even uttering a word of understanding" (Irish officer, UNIFIL).

Bridging Differences

The two main themes of the behaviors that meant to actively reach out to peacekeepers from other cultures evolved around cultural knowledge seeking and the investigation of cultural differences on the one hand, and the finding and creation of common bases on the other hand. Changing one's behavior to adjust to the other's culture is another way that helps create a bridge over cultural fault lines.

Seeking Knowledge and Mapping the Differences

A major challenge for those encountering new cultures is to understand the culture-based assumptions and values of the other and to find ways to get reliable information and expertise. They need to learn the local habits and communicate with people about their lives and values (Janssens, 1995). Most recent models in the social psychological literature view cross-cultural exposure as a learning experience (Furnham & Bochner, 1986). These models state that the major task facing a newcomer is not to adjust to a new culture but to learn its salient characteristics. Kim (1991) took a systems view to the intercultural communication process and emphasized the need for adaptability.

Many of the skills required for intercultural competence also relate to learning—learning about one's own culture and that of the stranger, learning new communication styles and scripts, learning to suspend judgment and perceive new ways of looking at situations, and learning new patterns of behavior. We found two primary learning behaviors in our interviews: engaging in cultural comparisons and addressing cultural differences.

Engaging in Socially Based Cultural Stories and Comparisons

With many cultures represented in the same location, personal conversations about the different cultures were prevalent and many times involved friendly comparisons to individuals' own culture. These conversations were mainly used as a way to understand the culture-based assumptions and values of the other, to learn about habits and norms, and communicate with people about the uniqueness and similarities of their lives. An Indian officer serving in UNIFIL described a typical interaction with an officer from Poland in the following manner "It starts with light talk, what is the culture like in India, what is the army like in India, what are the people there like. And the Polish guy will be telling me what Poland is all about."

Addressing Task-Specific Cultural Differences

In the context of multicultural work-groups, discussions about differences in cultural values, expectations, or norms are most useful when specific aspects of the group task are analyzed (Janssens & Brett, 1997). In our interviews we found evidence that in some cases there were concrete discussions of the underlying dimensions of culture, forming the background of the discussion while the issues are the foreground, rather than vice versa. This helped the discussion of differences become less threatening and was found to be a very efficient way to come to a shared understanding of how to go about these specific issues. It also helps identify which differences made a difference in terms of barriers and leverages. An example of behaviors belonging to this category is given by an officer in UNTSO: "You have to consult, probably more than you would consult in a national environment because you have to understand their reason that they don't want to do it in a certain way."

Emphasizing and Creating Shared Bases

Many of the bridging behaviors peacekeepers engage in fall into the category of creating common bases that exist side by side with the cultural differences. The content of these common bases ranged from mission specific to the more general aspects of military life and social relationships. The similarity-attraction paradigm (Byrne, 1971) provides a basis for understanding why people prefer to interact with those who are similar to themselves. People assume that similar others are easier to work and communicate with, and they also believe that similar others are more trustworthy (Brewer, 1981). The creation of common bases between peacekeepers from different cultures helps in highlighting the areas where there are similarities between the different participants in attitudes, values, norms, goals, experience, and background despite the different cultural backgrounds.

Emphasizing Superordinate Goals

It is a long established finding in social psychology that the institution of superordinate goals, that is, objectives held in common by all groups, is one of the most effective techniques for resolving intergroup conflict and increasing intergroup cooperation (Sherif, Harvey, White, Hood, & Sherif, 1961). This can be translated to an emphasis on the goal at large, in our case the importance and essence of the peacekeeping mission. More specifically, this can be done by stressing common goals, interdependence, and collaboration over individual goals, self-sufficiency, and competition (Ilgen, LePine, & Hollenbeck, 1997). The existence of the superordinate goals in the participants' internal frame of reference is described: "Everybody has a mindset to help to solve this big problem here and we are risking our lives for it, and no one is grateful. So we must as a group, at least, be together and help each other" (Dutch Officer, UNIFIL).

Creating Shared Norms

An important phase multicultural teams should go through to reach maximal effectiveness is recentering (Di Stefano & Maznevski, 2000). Recentering involves providing a common ground in terms of norms on which to build a shared basis for interacting with each other. By recentering, a common view of situations and a common set of norms are developed. When a team is homogeneous, it is fairly safe to assume after a few brief exchanges that everyone is on the same footing. But the more diverse the team is, the more important it is to keep revisiting these issues: "Let's say, if we had a conflict for whatever reason, I would say: 'Let's grab a coffee and sit down.' . . . It was a group norm. People viewed that as a natural way of solving a problem or conflict" (Canadian Officer, UNPROFOR).

Emphasizing and Creating Mission-Specific Shared Experiences

Even when it was not part of the official requirements of the mission to work together side by side, some of the officers reported that they intentionally created opportunities that allowed them to work together with other armies. The goal of these mission-specific shared experiences was both to learn from other armies and to enhance the relationships between the armies: "We had a very good relationship with the Finnish battalion . . . we had joint exercises. We would go out with them. We would share our expertise in terms of mine clearing, bomb disposals. We would use their shooting ranges, and we worked in connection with one another" (Irish officer, UNIFIL).

The Shared Fate of Being "Foreigners in a Foreign Land"

The shared fate of being far away from "home," especially under conditions of threat, can lead to ingroup/outgroup perceptions described extensively in the group dynamics literature (e.g., Rothberger, 1997; Tajfel & Turner, 1986). When discussing their shared fates, participants in multinational peacekeeping forces perceived themselves as the "ingroup" in the context of the people whose peace they have to keep, and their internal cohesion increased as a result. An officer from UNIFIL described in detail the effects of the shared fate and purpose:

We are all in a foreign land and are there for a common purpose. . . . There is a certain commonality, without respect to where you are from—whether you are Irish, Ghanaian, or Finnish—about the way you operate and live your life style. But also another important thing is that you integrate with locals, the Lebanese, and that you understand their culture. And that's important cause at the end of the day you're living in their country. (Irish officer, UNIFIL)

Emphasizing the Common Military Background

The common military background of peacekeepers has a considerable impact on both interpersonal interactions and on the way participants constructed their experience. It was clear from interviewees' descriptions that their shared military profession served as a powerful starting point from which interactions evolved, and peacekeepers reported making deliberate and conscious use of this commonality in order to facilitate interpersonal interactions. What follows are quotes describing officers' feelings about their shared background: "We have a culture that is similar. Military culture is similar. There is a sense of comradeship there. . . . When we talk, we talk not as Canadian and Spanish, we talk as two different officers" (Canadian officer, ONUSAL).

Beyond the strong bonds felt between officers, which in itself served as an integration mechanism, the common military background had additional repercussions on the integration of the forces, such as the conviction that disagreements can be solved: "It doesn't matter whether people come from Africa, India, Thailand, or Russia. If I sit around the table with other soldiers, I will find a solution for any problem. This is my conviction, because we have the same mental process" (Italian officer, UNPROFOR).

The Basic Commonality: Eating and Drinking

In most contexts eating, drinking, and partying are central to the creation of sentiments of cooperation and affiliation. As anthropologists have taught us, eating and drinking signal commonality, afford relaxed circumstances for interaction, and are part of the minute exchanges through which trust is created (Goody, 1982). In our interviews, numerous instances were mentioned in which eating and drinking with members of other national forces was a means to enhance familiarity and create social bonds that also eased the mutual functioning and coordination on the job. Other more unique options are also described: "For example an Indian and Finn became friends by going to the sauna, and now the Indian wants to go every day to the sauna" (Indian officer, UNIFIL). When such social encounters happen between groups or individuals of equal status, they have also been found to contribute to the weakening of prejudices, an important factor in the creation of effective coordination (Amir, 1969).

Self-Monitoring: Changing Behavior to Adjust to Another Culture

A process frequently reported by interviewees is self-monitoring, which is the tendency to regulate one's own behavior to meet the demands of social situations (Snyder, 1987). Our study suggests that a culturally diverse environment raises the frequency of self-monitoring. Individuals' awareness of cultural differences leads in some instances to the adjustment of their behaviors to the other's culture. For example, individuals take what they know about each other's differences and apply it to adapt their own behavior and thinking. They change their conversation style and adapt their interaction behaviors according to the culture of the people with whom they are working: "It's not they who have to change, it is you who have to change. And you have to be different for every single person" (Irish officer, UNIFIL).

A more specific example is described by an Australian officer serving in UNTSO, who related to the concept of "saving face," acknowledging it is more relevant to some cultures than others: "Some countries do not always understand the concept of face, the fact that many of the cultures where you tell them that they are wrong about something; you have to give them a way out."

It is important to note that self-monitoring can be a facilitator of cross-cultural adaptation (Montagliani & Giacalone, 1998). Those who engage in it elicit more positive responses from their counterparts and take part in more cross-cultural contacts, thereby acquiring more culture-specific information that further allows them to behave in accordance with the demands of the culturally diverse environment.

Tolerating and Accepting Differences—Giving Cultural Space

Although integrating and bridging behaviors are indeed critical for the creation of cooperation, internal toleration and acceptance of cultural differences is no less important. Although giving cultural space to others is relatively passive, these attitude-based components of intercultural effectiveness are necessary to create a positive and dignified atmosphere and allow peacekeepers the sense of freedom to engage in their culture-specific practices. The tolerance and respect associated with the behaviors in this category also enable interactions between individuals to proceed more smoothly. These more internal manifestation of cross-cultural competence belong to two categories:

Suspending Judgment

Suspending judgment about the cause of communication problems resulting from differences is the single best predictor of effective communication in diverse teams (Maznevski & Di Stefano, 2000). Despite the advantage that comes from a nonjudgmental attitude, our nearly universal tendency is to react instinctively to differences as bad. "They" are different from "us," "we" are right and good, therefore "they" are wrong and bad and to be blamed when problems occur. Even when people are conscious about cultural or other differences, the evaluative instinct kicks in quickly. Stereotyping in turn does not foster respect because it treats individuals as tokens or representatives of a larger group and depersonalizes interactions and relationships. The fixed and unchangeable identity of a culture does not allow any attention to the construction of an individual's identity in the cultural context (Ely, 1995; Nkomo & Cox, 1996; Turner, 1987). The more active aspect of suspending judgment includes flexible attributions, which is the willingness to update perceptions and beliefs about the other's behavior (Mendenhall & Oddou, 1985).

What the peacekeepers reported as effective was to avoid succumbing to immediate stereotyping, and to try understanding the situation both from a personality and a cultural perspective, rather than simply a cultural one. This attribution style does not necessarily suggest denial, suppression, or assimilation of cultural diversity. Cultural differences are neither concealed nor blurred. Rather, peacekeepers' attributions are interpreted as stemming from their acknowledgment that an individual's identity or personality includes both unique individual characteristics and a cultural component as well. "It's very hard to generalize. I have found in the same country some guys who were superb officers and some guys that were awful. Now, some countries have the reputation of not working, let's say Greeks, I had two guys from Greece in Bosnia and both of them were excellent. But as a nationality, they didn't have a good reputation. . . . So, it's also personality driven, rather then just nationality driven" (Irish officer, Bosnia).

Avoiding Treading on the Other's Cultural "Comfort Zone"

Our natural tendencies toward ethnocentric thinking as a result of our wish to maintain a positive social identity (Janssens & Brett, 2000) can result in convictions that our way is the best way. Moreover, such thinking can lead to exerting pressure on the other to conform and adhere to our own ways and solutions, many times at the expense of treading on cultural "comfort zones." A solution that was practiced by some of the peacekeepers was sufficing with the standards that the task at hand required, and letting different cultural norms prevail when these standards were met rather than insisting there was only one way to go about achieving the mission's goals. This solution allowed all participants the freedom they needed for their specific ways to achieve the best performance, and it prevented situations that made people feel uncomfortable by either not complying with their own cultural norms or even acting against them. What follows are two examples of this behavior, one a more general statement and one more specific:

I accept the fact that I cannot always get my point of view and then I have to back off because that is one of the things I learned in Bosnia. In Bosnia very often you had to move a couple of steps backward to move forward again. (Danish officer, UNTSO)

You have to allow them to go to their mosque, for services on Friday. So, what we did is dropped him outside a mosque, and the other two would continue to patrol and pick him up later. (Irish officer, UNIFIL)

In the next section, based on direct evidence from the interviews, existing theories, and our interpretation of what stands behind the behaviors displayed by the peacekeepers, we describe the skills, dispositions, and attitudes that best support the peacekeeping forces' unity.

Interculturally Effective Dispositions and Attitudes

Being effective and successfully managing relationships in the multicultural environment of a peacekeeping force requires more complexity and sophistication than when working domestically. The encompassing term that describes the skills, dispositions, and attitudes required for such an environment is cosmopolitanism. Taylor and Osland (in press), summarizing the literature on this concept, elaborate on what this orientation requires, reflecting and enhancing the findings of our study and the behaviors just described. Cosmopolitanism is first of all a mindset that indicates an orientation toward the outside world, a willingness to engage with those who come from different cultures. It entails an openness toward divergent cultural experiences. At the same time, however, cosmopolitanism can be a matter of competence, a personal ability to make one's way into other cultures, through listening, looking, intuiting, and reflecting. It also involves the ability to view a situation from several vantage points or perspectives and to acknowledge and accept the differences between people from different cultural backgrounds, subsequently identifying and assessing the impact of these differences on past, current, and future potential dynamics.

These aspects of intercultural sensitivity are related to increased competence in intercultural relations (Bennett & Bennett, in press). It seems that in the context of so many cultures residing side by side during the peacekeeping mission, it is easier for those that are in the midst of this arena to reach a higher level of cosmopolitanism—they experience their own culture in the context of other cultures rather than experiencing their own culture as central to reality, making it harder for them to remain "entrenched" in their own culture. In Bennett and Bennet's (in press) terms, such an environment encourages ethnorelativism rather than ethnocentrism. In terms of the understanding of another culture, people who are ethnorelative are able to search for and identify new patterns in others' behaviors, rather than simply define others' behavior in terms of their own patterns. It also means an ability to examine their own assumptions, place a boundary around them, and operate at least tentatively under other assumptions. Flexibility and being able to adapt to different styles with different people is also crucial, because culture has a strong influence on preferences for relationship styles and leadership styles (Yeung & Ready, 1995).

What was most evident in many interviews, and strongly related to the concepts described here, is the high motivation to engage in cross-cultural contact (although other motivations, like financial benefits, can play an important role too). Moreover, the experience of interacting with people from different cultures is considered positive and desirable, as described by a Swiss officer serving in UNTSO: "It is an absolutely fascinating experience, this multinational surrounding. It is very different from what I'm used to. . . . We have time to socialize, [to be involved in] cultural exchange, learning about other countries and problems they have. To learn how people feel about different things. . . . That is why I like it so much, not only from the work point of view but also from the social point of view."

In the next section we explicate the ways the individual behaviors and dispositions that serve to integrate the forces are related to and embedded in some of the integrating mechanisms used by the forces at the organizational level.

INDIVIDUAL BEHAVIORS EMBEDDED IN ORGANIZATIONAL INTEGRATING MECHANISMS

Although the multinational peacekeeping forces operate in many arenas around the globe, there are actively managed mechanisms used in all sites that help offset the potential problematic effects of the cultural diversity (Elron, Shamir, & Ben-Ari, 1999). These mechanisms are strongly related to the ways the individual peacekeepers interact with their cultural counterparts, and in this section we elaborate on two such examples.

One important organizational mechanism is the voluntary nature of the participation in the missions. In most armies, the officers volunteer for the missions, and observers' missions consist of volunteers only. Indeed, most of the interviewees reported that their participation in a multicultural peacekeeping mission was on a voluntary basis (although for some it was a necessary but not formal requirement to advance to higher ranks). An important implication is that there is an initial self-selection—it is mostly those officers who have the motivation to engage in cross-cultural interactions that will be more willing to volunteer. Another important motivation was to be part of missions in which they generally believed and in which they felt they were useful. Obviously there are other motivations that may be more salient for some of the officers, such as monetary incentives, but for most of our interviewees these motivations existed in parallel to their positive views of the peacekeeping missions rather than being the sole motivating factor that attracted people to the missions. Examples of these motivations are expressed next:

I actually volunteered for that position, I had to put my name on a volunteer list. That's what I joined the military to do, is to go overseas and get mixed up with other cultures . . . and just kind of experience different parts of the world. (Canadian officer, MFO)

It is because they have an interest in something bigger than their national context, and the U.N. is one of the few organizations which gives the scope to go into those operations which are multi-national. (New-Zealander officer, UNTSO)

Another consequence of the voluntary nature of joining a peacekeeping mission is increased commitment to getting along with others and to being more integrated into the mission. According to Brehm's (1966) reactance theory, people want the freedom to think, feel, and act as they (and not others) choose. When freedom is exercised, and the threat of being forced to engage in unwanted endeavors is relatively minor, there is a lesser need for engaging in behaviors that prove the autonomy of the self and greater willingness to cooperate with organizational goals, or in this case, the cooperation between the forces.

Another prevalent and salient organizational mechanism that has become part of the social fabric in the missions is the deliberate cohesion-building activities that come in the form of a range of educational, cultural, and sport events designed to introduce national cultures to each other. These activities help create a common esprit de corps and a unique identity for the specific mission. Furthermore, the allocation of time and space for such activities enhances the potential for spontaneous interpersonal interactions that allow better and deeper acquaintanceship between members of different cultures. There are numerous examples of such activities. The Australian contingent of the MFO, for example, invited force members for a day of games and sport on Australia Day (the day Australia was colonized by the British), and the New Zealanders offered a Maori-style feast on Waitangi Day (the day the British signed a treaty with the Maori people).

The importance of these activities in terms of individual behaviors is their direct and indirect encouragement of social initiatives and activities. They signal that the meeting of cultures in social settings is desirable. An Austrian commander in UNDOF has initiated such an activity with his own group of colleagues and soldiers: "One of the things we have, especially during summer time, every Friday evening, is more or less a small party here in the office, where we are all together. That is the chance to sit together with all your guys and to speak to each other, and that's the moment when people come closer."

Interestingly, these same activities are also a way to enhance cultural sensitivity via the emphasis of cultural differences. The celebration of national days, in which culture-specific food is served, culture-specific music is played, and culture-specific activities take place, serves to differentiate one country from the others and highlight its uniqueness. In terms of our model, then, these social activities allow for both the creation of shared bases and the seeking of cultural knowledge.

CONCLUSIONS AND IMPLICATIONS

As people tend to perceive themselves in ways that set them apart from others in their immediate environment, cultural awareness with its positive and negative implications is likely to be found wherever cultural diversity exists. The sites of multinational peacekeeping forces are an illustration of an organization that in many ways realizes the potential advantages that cultural diversity holds and minimizes its potential damages. The framework proposed in this chapter attempts to increase understanding of the ways individual actions of peacekeepers, and the ways these actions are embedded within the organizational mechanisms and norms, help ease coordination and reduce potential conflicts among the different units within the forces. Applications of such an understanding can result in greater success in the carrying out of peacekeeping missions. Moreover, it has important implications to the operation of all organizations that face the challenge of cultural diversity.

Our data support Salk and Brannen's (2000) contention that cultural differences themselves do not cause problems; rather, it is how the individual peacekeepers' behaviors and orientations channel these differences, combined with the organizational integrating mechanisms and the individuals' acceptance of them. It is important to realize, however, that a crucial contribution to the relative ease of the unity among the forces is the fact that in order for peacekeeping missions to succeed, the multinational forces must be seen as impartial and neutral. In other words, the multinational structure is an inherent part of the legitimacy given to the mission, and hence there is a deep recognition of its critical importance for those who take part in the missions.

The practical implications of the enhanced understanding of the processes that help explain the unity within the forces are mainly in the areas of the selection, training, and socialization of the individual peacekeeper. Currently, the selection of officers to peacekeeping missions is based mostly on professional experience, task expertise, and the officers' willingness to volunteer. Given the critical importance of integration among the diverse national units contributing to the mission, and the convergence on these missions of cultural diversity, foreign environment, novel experiences, individual dispositions and personality, selection criteria related to intercultural effectiveness would seem highly relevant. In the words of an American officer serving in UNTSO: "I think it takes a special kind of individual to do it. Not everybody can do it. We've seen this in the U.N. where people can't adjust to various places . . . some people find it hard to adjust to the culture and the language and end up going back."

Taking our various findings regarding behaviors and attitudes together with the empirical evidence for the relationship between personality and expatriate success (e.g., Caliguiri, 2000), the findings could serve as an initial base for the selection of officers going out on these missions. Behaviors could be assessed through several channels. One example is assessment centers that use simulations of intercultural situations similar to the ones faced in the missions. Another option is giving weight to performance appraisals from the officer's direct commanders in previous peacekeeping missions. These appraisals should rely on evaluation criteria that include the relevant behaviors described in this chapter. Moreover, these appraisals could be further used as a feedback mechanism both on the mission and between missions.

Attitudes are harder to assess, and perhaps one way to go about approximating them is through the use of personality questionnaires. Based on the evidence described previously on both behaviors and attitudes, it seems that one of the most important and encompassing aspects of personality in the multicultural context is cognitive complexity, which involves the ability to handle ambiguity and multiple viewpoints (Osland, Bird, Delano, & Jacob, 2000). In other words, black-and-white thinkers can be detrimental when it comes to dealing with the intricacies of interacting effectively with other cultures. Other important traits that were found to predict the success of expatriate managers are openness to experience, extroversion, emotional stability, and agreeableness (Caliguiri, 2000). These traits encompass both the individual's *ability* to establish interpersonal relationships and the individual's *motivation* and willingness to engage in cross-cultural interactions.

Cross-cultural training increases intercultural adjustment and proficiency, reduces the time necessary to reach such proficiency, and enhances the work performance of those who go through it (Black & Mendenhall, 1990). However, only a portion of the armies uses such training, and in most cases only a few hours are dedicated to cross-cultural issues. Moreover, it usually provides specific information about the country the mission takes place in, rather than deeper approaches related to the meaning of culture and intercultural effectiveness that have been shown to enhance the training's effectiveness (Earley, 1987). We recommend, therefore, that specific and explicit training for multicultural effectiveness within the peacekeeping forces should constitute a more significant part of the overall predeparture preparation peacekeepers go through. It is important to note, though, that intercultural training can only partly remedy cross-cultural insensitivity, and it does not fully compensate for personalities or deeply ingrained attitudes that hinder intercultural encounters, and therefore cannot be used instead of selection but only to complement it.

There are many organizational mechanisms used by the peacekeeping forces to increase integration and unity and socialize peacekeepers into the multi-cultural nature of the missions. An added approach that seems to operate only at the level of the individual peacekeepers and seemed to be very effective is addressing differences in cultural values, expectations, or norms via explicit discussion in the context of specific tasks. Discussing cultural differences as they relate to specific issues confronting the group should help surface cultural differences in a way that actually helps the group break down stereotypes and develop a clearer understanding of each member's unique perspective. These discussions must, at their core, recognize that individual perspectives go well beyond cultural values and include personal and professional values as well (Janssens & Brett, 2000). These kinds of discussions will also sustain those behaviors and attitudes that are effective.

In sum, it is the combination of existing individual behaviors and organizational mechanisms, as well as possibly incorporating our recommended changes, which allows for peacekeepers to derive the maximal benefits from the cultural diversity in the peacekeeping forces. Undoubtedly these benefits will further contribute to the enhancement of the forces' organizational effectiveness.

NOTE

The research at the basis of this chapter was supported by grants from the Steinmetz Center for Peace Research and from the Recanati Foundation of the School of Business Administration at the Hebrew University.

REFERENCES

Alberts, D. S., & Hayes, E. (1995). *Command arrangements for peace operations.* Washington, DC: National Defense University Press.

Amir, Y. (1969). Contact hypothesis in ethnic relations. *Psychological Bulletin, 71,* 319–342.

Barker, J., Tjosvold, D., & Andrews, I. R. (1988). Conflict approaches of effective and ineffective project managers: A field study in matrix organizations. *Journal of Management Studies, 25,* 167–178.

Bennett, J., & Bennett, M. (in press). *Developing intercultural sensitivity: An integrative approach to global and domestic diversity .*

Black, J. S., & Mendenhall, M. (1990). Cross-cultural training effectiveness: A review and a theoretical framework for future research. *Academy of Management Review, 15,* 113–136.

Brehm, J. W. (1966). *A theory of psychological reactance.* New York: Academic Press.

Brehm, S. S., Kassin, S. M., & Fein, S. (1999). *Social psychology* (4th ed.). Boston: Houghton Mifflin.

Brewer, H. B. (1981). Ethnocentrism and its role in interpersonal trust. In M. Brewer and B. Collins (Eds.), *Scientific inquiry and the social science.* San Francisco: Jossey-Bass.

Byrne, D. E. (1971). *The attraction paradigm.* New York: Academic Press.

Caliguiri, P. M. (2000). The big five personality characteristics as predictors of expatriate's desire to terminate the assignment and supervisor-rated performance. *Personnel Psychology, 53,* 67–88.

Cox, T. H., Lobel, S. H., & McLeod, P. L. (1991). Effects of ethnic group cultural differences on cooperative and competitive behavior on a group task. *Academy of Management Journal, 34,* 827–847.

Di Stefano, J. J., & Maznevski, M. L. (2000). Creating value with diverse teams in global management. *Organizational Dynamics, 29,* 45–63.

Downes. C. (1993). Challenges for smaller nations in the new era of U.N. multinational operations. In Hugh Smith (Ed.), *Peacekeeping: Challenges for the future.* Canberra: Australian Defense Studies Center.

Earley, P. C. (1987). Intercultural training for managers: A comparison of documentary and interpersonal methods. *Academy of Management Journal, 30,* 685–698.

Earley, P. C., & Mosakowsky, E. (2000). Creating hybrid team cultures: An empirical test of transnational team functioning. *Academy of Management Journal, 43,* 26–49.

Elron, E. (1997). Top management teams within multinational corporations: Effects of cultural heterogeneity. *Leadership Quarterly, 8,* 393–412.

Elron, E. (2000). *Cultural diversity and political processes in multinational top management teams.* Presented at the Academy of Management Meeting, Toronto.

Elron, E., Shamir B., & Ben-Ari, E. (1999). Why don't they fight each other? Cultural diversity and operational unity in multinational peacekeeping forces. *Armed Forces & Society, 26,* 73–98.

Elron, E., Shamir B., & Ben-Ari, E. (2000). *Cross-cultural differences in the multinational peacekeeping forces: Faultlines or seamlines?* Presented at the Academy of Management Meeting, Toronto.

Ely, R. J. (1995). The role of dominant identity and experience in organizational work on diversity. In S. E. Jackson & M. N. Ruderman (Eds.), *Diversity in work teams: Research paradigms for a changing workplace* (pp. 161–186). Washington, DC: American Psychological Association Press.

Erez, M. (1994). Toward a model of cross-cultural industrial and organizational psychology. In H. C. Triandis, M. D. Dunnettem, & L. M. Hough (Eds.), *Handbook of Industrial and Organizational Psychology, vol. 4* (pp. 559–607). Palo Alto, CA: Consulting Psychologists Press.

Erez, M., & Early, P. C. (1987). Comparative analysis of goal-setting strategies across cultures. *Journal of Applied Psychology, 72,* 658–665.

Fiol, C. M. & Lyles, M. A. (1985). Organizational learning. *Academy of Management Review, 10,* 803–813.

Furnham, A., & Bochner, S. (1986). *Culture shock: Psychological reactions to unfamiliar environments.* London: Methuen.

Ghoshal, S., & Westney, D. E. (1993). Introduction and overview. In S. Ghoshal and D. Eleanor Westney (Eds.), *Organization theory and the multinational corporation.* New York: St. Martin's Press.

Gibson, C. B. (1997). Do you hear what I hear? A framework for reconciling intercultural communication difficulties arising from cognitive styles and cultural values. In P. C. Earley & M. Erez (Eds.), *New perspectives on international industrial/organizational psychology* (pp. 335–362). San-Francisco: The New Lexington Press.

Goody, J. (1982). *Cooking, cuisine and class: A study in comparative sociology.* Cambridge: Cambridge University Press.

Hui, C. H. (1990). Work attitudes, leadership styles, and managerial behaviors in different cultures. In R. W. Brislin (Ed.), *Applied cross-cultural psychology.* Newbury Park, CA: Sage.

Ilgen, D. R., LePine, J. A., & Hollenbeck J. R. (1997). Effective decision making in multinational teams. In P. C. Earley & M. Erez (Eds.), *New perspectives on international industrial/organizational psychology* (pp. 377–409). San Francisco: The New Lexington Press.

Janssens, M. (1995). Intercultural interaction: A burden on international managers? *Journal of Organizational Behavior, 16,* 155–167.

Janssens, M., & Brett, J. M. (1997). Meaningful participation in transnational teams. *European Journal of Work and Organizational Psychology, 6,* 153–168.

Janssens, M., & Brett, J. M. (2000). *Competences and practices to stimulate meaningful participation in transnational teams.* Presented at the Academy of Management Meeting, Toronto.

Jehn, K. A., Northcraft, G. B., & Neale, M. A. (1999). Why differences make a difference: A field study of diversity, conflict, and performance in workgroups. *Administrative Science Quarterly, 44,* 741–763.

Kim, Y. (1991). Intercultural communication competence: A systems-theoretic view. In S. Ting-Toomey and F. Korzenny (Eds.), *Cross-cultural interpersonal communication* (pp. 213–229). Newbury Park, CA: Sage.

Knouse, S. B., & Dansby M. R. (1999). Percentage of workgroup diversity and workgroup effectiveness. *Journal of Psychology, 133,* 486–494.

Kramer, R. M., & Tyler, T. R. (Eds.). (1996). *Trust in organizations.* Thousand Oaks, CA: Sage.

Lyles, M. A., & Salk, J. E. (1996). Knowledge acquisition from foreign parents in international joint ventures. *Journal of International Business Studies, 27,* 877–904.

Maznevski, M. L., & Di Stefano, J. J. (2000). Global leaders are team players: Developing global leaders through membership on global teams. *Human Resource Management, 39,* 195–208.

Mendenhall, M., & Oddou, G. R. (1985). The dimensions of expatriate acculturation. *Academy of Management Review, 10,* 39–47.

Meschi, P. X. (1997). Longevity and cultural differences of international joint ventures: Toward time-based cultural management. *Human Relations, 50,* 211–228.

Montagliani, A., & Giacalone, R. A. (1998). Impression management and cross-cultural adaptation. *Journal of Social Psychology, 138,* 598–608.

Nkomo, S. M. & Cox, T., Jr. (1996). Diverse identities in organizations. In S. R. Clegg & C. Hardy (Eds.), *Handbook of organization studies* (pp. 338–356). Thousand Oaks, CA: Sage.

Osland, J. S., Bird, A., Delano J., & Jacob, M. (2000). Beyond sophisticated stereotyping: Cultural sense-making in context. *Academy of Management Executive, 14,* 65–79.

Palin, R. H. (1995). *Multinational military forces: Problems and prospects.* International Institute for Strategic Studies. Adelphi Paper Number 294.

Parkhe, A. (1993). Partner nationality and the structure-performance relationship in strategic alliances. *Organization Science, 4,* 301–324.

Rothberger, H. (1997). External intergroup threat as an antecedent to perceptions on in-group and out-group homogeneity. *Journal of Applied Psychology, 73,* 1206–1212.

Rubens, B. D. (1989). The study of cross-cultural competence: Traditions and contemporary issues. *International Journal of Intercultural Relations, 13,* 229–240.

Salk, J. E. (1996). Partners and other strangers: Cultural boundaries and cross-cultural encounters in international joint venture teams. *International Studies of Management and Organization, 26,* 48–72.

Salk, J. E., & Brannen, M. Y. (2000). National culture, networks and individual influence in a multinational management team. *Academy of Management Journal, 43,* 191–202.

Schein, E. H. (1985). *Organizational culture and leadership* (pp. 1–22). San Francisco: Jossey-Bass.

Segal, D. R., & Tiggle, R. B. (1997). Attitudes of citizen-soldiers to military missions in the post–Cold War world. *Armed Forces and Society, 23,* 373–390.

Sherif, M., Harvey, L. J., White, B. J., Hood, W. R., & Sherif, C. W. (1961). *The Robbers Cave experiment: Intergroup conflict and cooperation.* Middletown, CT: Wesleyan University Press.

Snyder, M. (1987). *Public appearances private realities: The psychology of self-monitoring.* New York: Freeman.

Solomon, C. M. (1996). Danger below! Spot failing global assignments. *Personnel Journal, 75,* 78–85.

Spitzberg, B., & Cupach, W. (1984). *Interpersonal communication competence.* Beverly Hills, CA: Sage.

Stening, B. W. (1979). Problems in cross-cultural contact: A literature review. *International Journal of Intercultural Relations, 3,* 269–313.

Tajfel, H. (1982). Social psychology of integroup relations. *Annual Review of Psychology, 33,* 1–39.

Taylor, S., & Osland, J. S. (in press). The impact of intercultural communication on global organizational learning. In M. Easterby-Smith and M. A. Lyles (Eds.), *Handbook of organizational learning and knowledge.*

Ting-Toomey, S. (1999). *Communicating across cultures.* New York: Guilford.

Turner, J. C. (1987). *Rediscovering the social group: A self-categorization theory.* Oxford, UK: Basil Blackwell.

Van de Vliert, E., Euwema, M. C., & Huismans, S. E. (1994). Managing conflict with a subordinate or a superior: Effectiveness of conglomerated behaviors. *Journal of Applied Psychology, 80,* 271–281.

Watson, W. E., Kumar, K., & Michaelsen, L. K. (1993). Cultural diversity's impact on interaction process and performance. *Academy of Management Journal, 36,* 590–600.

Yeung, A., & Ready, D. (1995). Developing leadership capabilities of global corporations: A comparative study in eight nations. *Human Resource Management, 34,* 529–547.

16

Cross-Cultural Issues in Peacekeeping Operations

Joseph Soeters and Miepke Bos-Bakx

In a globalizing world, organizations must work together. When these organizations are also faced with reductions in staff levels and resources instead of growth, there is an even greater imperative for cooperation. This is the situation in which most Western armed forces currently find themselves. Not only does cooperation in the defense sector happen jointly among the military services (e.g., the land and air forces), but to an increasing extent cooperation also happens among the military units of several countries. Sometimes this cooperation assumes far-reaching structural forms, such as the Euro-corps or the European Rapid Reaction Forces, which are planned to be operational in 2003. Usually, however, international military units meet as part of a specific mission, on training exercises, and increasingly also on actual missions.

Recent history shows that military operations, whether under the flag of NATO or the UN, are no longer conducted by one single country. Military forces are dependent on one another to achieve their mission goals usually because there is a lack of adequate resources, personnel, and logistics to conduct independent action, and sometimes, as in the case of the United States, because building an international coalition strengthens the perceived legitimacy of an operation.

The result of this increased cooperation is that military operations have become thoroughly internationalized and will continue to be so in the near future (e.g., Moskos, 2001). However, the level of intercultural interaction on international missions may vary. Each contributing country may have its own geographical sector, which limits the extent of intercultural communication to staff units and headquarters, as is the case on the macro-administrative level in Bosnia or Kosovo. True integration at the level of troops may also occur, as in the case of a Bulgarian platoon of engineers being integrated within a Dutch battalion that was deployed to Bosnia.

Regardless of the level at which international cooperation occurs, the know-how regarding international management drawn from the business sector is both useful and applicable to the armed forces. One of those knowledge do-mains concerns the influence of national cultures on the structure and func-tioning of multinational companies and international alliances. In various studies it has been demonstrated that this influence is considerable (e.g., Hof-stede, 2001; Triandis, 1995). In this chapter we apply this type of knowledge to the military, specifically to the conduct of military personnel in international peacekeeping operations. First, we describe key findings regarding the role of cultural differences in values that may impact military operations. Second, we analyze two case reports on peacekeeping operations from NATO operations in Bosnia and a UN mission in Cyprus in which cultural factors have affected the mission. Third, we pursue the implications of culture for the structure of peacekeeping missions, the leadership and command style, and the performance of multinational teams. Finally, we suggest avenues for further research. Through this analysis of the role of cultural values in international military operations, our goal is to contribute to the enhancement of the cultural inter-operability of such missions (e.g., Winslow & Everts, 2001).

One limitation of this chapter should specifically be mentioned. This chapter focuses on cross-cultural issues that occur as a consequence of multinational cooperation in military missions. Obviously, cross-cultural issues also come to the fore when Western armed forces are being confronted with local people from other cultures, such as during Operation Restore Hope in Somalia. The present chapter, however, does not deal with this type of cross-cultural com-munication; other publications do (e.g., Winslow, Kammhuber, & Soeters, 2003).

NATIONAL CULTURES AND THE MILITARY

The importance of analyzing national cultural differences in order to un-derstand the dynamics of international cooperation has its roots in work per-formed about 30 years ago. In the 1970s, the Dutch social psychologist Geert Hofstede (2001) studied work-related values of the employees of more than 50 national subsidiaries of the U.S.-based multinational company IBM. On the basis of data from more than 100,000 respondents he was able to detect four cultural dimensions, covarying independent of one another. The dimensions have been shown to be quite similar to standard anthropological insights on the nature of society. These cultural dimensions are as follows. *Power distance* refers to the perceived and preferred social (in)equality within organizations and societies, and in general this dimension refers to the relation people have to authority. *Uncertainty avoidance* is the extent to which people in a society feel uncomfortable in strange, unknown situations. This dimension refers to primary dilemmas or conflicts and ways of dealing with them (e.g., through rules and regulations). *Individualism as opposed to collectivism* is the degree to which individuals are supposed to look after themselves or, on the contrary, remain oriented toward integration into groups (see also Triandis, 1995). *Masculinity* predominantly refers to achievement motivation and the division of gender roles in society. The opposite of this dimension (femininity) refers to concern with others. Data pertaining to these cultural dimensions are numerous (Sondergaard, 1994). Hofstede's concepts—although not without criticism (e.g., Tayeb, 1994)—have been helpful in the analysis of national differences in legal systems, the degree of democratization, the distribution of roles between the sexes, the outburst of violence and conflict (Hofstede, 2001), and even the safety of national air forces (Soeters & Boer, 2000). In addition, Hofstede's model has been relevant in studying the national differences in defense and security matters. For example, defense spending as a percentage of GNP has been shown to correlate positively with Hofstede's masculinity index (Hofstede, 2001).

Although Hofstede's data are 30 years old, they have not lost their validity. For example, in a recent study, van Oudenhoven (2001) has shown that students, when asked to describe an organization, use "spontaneous" dimensions that highly correlate with Hofstede's indexes. Moreover, the students' descriptions of companies in their country show national differences that correspond to a large extent to what would be predicted on the basis of Hofstede's national culture scores. Apparently, Hofstede's dimensions have a validity going far beyond one or two decades, despite the widespread cultural developments that have occurred in the past three decades.

Hofstede's theory has also been applied to specific subgroups within cultures, including the military sector. In a study among cadet officers of 13, and later 18, military academies in mostly Western countries, remarkable results were found (Soeters, 1997; Soeters & Recht, 1998). First of all, it became clear that the military in the various countries shows substantial international cultural differences. The four Hofstede dimensions were grouped in two categories that are highly relevant to military theory. The first category involves issues related to bureaucracy, and the second category involves the occupational orientation toward military life. Hofstede's power distance and uncertainty avoidance were combined to create indexes of the bureaucracy concept, which varies from a classical or coercive bureaucracy to a more modern, or postbureaucratic style (Jaffee, 2001). Hofstede's dimensions of individualism and masculinity were combined to reflect the institutional orientation toward the military as opposed to a more neutral or occupational attitude toward working within the armed forces.

With regard to these two major categories, interesting differences were found. For instance, the cadet officers in Italy were, comparatively speaking, both bureaucratic (with large power distances and a strong rule orientation) and institutionally oriented. The latter is to say that they are not inclined to high salaries and leisure time, because they are fully dedicated to the institution of the military, as if it were a vocation. In contrast, the cadet officers of the academies in Denmark were less bureaucratic and more occupationally oriented (i.e., they were striving for high wages and ordinary working times, as if working in the military was just another job). In addition, these Danish cadets were also strongly inclined toward pursuing a career in the civilian labor market.

When all of the various academies were ranked from traditional (bureaucratic and institutional) to modern (postbureaucratic, with more emphasis on working in the military as just another job), the United States (West Point) and the Netherlands occupied middle positions, indicating a hybrid cultural profile. The U.S. cadet officers were rather occupation oriented, but at the same time their tendency to avoid uncertainty through rules and regulations was surprisingly "traditional." The UK scores in general were equally hybrid (like those in the United States and the Netherlands), but interestingly enough the power distance in Sandhurst was by far the highest among all 18 academies, including those of Brazil and Argentina. In fact, the British power distance score could hardly be plotted in a normal graph. We have chosen to mention these specific results because the UK, the Netherlands, Denmark, and the United States are each highlighted in the accounts of intercultural encounters on peacekeeping missions presented in the next section of this chapter.

All in all, the cultural diversity among the academies of the 18 countries is considerable. This cultural heterogeneity within the military was found not only among the young cadet officers in the academy study, but also in a quasi-experimental study at the NATO Defense College in Rome (Soeters & Recht, 2001). Nearly 200 Defense College students, between the ages of 35 and 45 and with ranks ranging from major to colonel, filled out a questionnaire at the beginning and the end of their 26-week course at this institute. The same cultural profiles for countries like Italy, the UK, the United States, and Norway were found as in the academy study. More interestingly, however, was that these cultural profiles did not change during the course, although the students were exposed to a multinational environment. Hence an Italian officer remained very much an Italian officer, despite intensive interaction with people from other national backgrounds over the course of six months. Apparently, cultural differences are fairly constant.

Despite evidence that values characterizing nationality are stable, the academy study also showed that there is something like a supranational military culture. In comparison with business organizations, military culture in all countries turned out to be relatively bureaucratic, hierarchic, and institutional (Soeters, 1997). This means that even before entering a specific multinational force, officers may have undergone vicarious anticipatory and actual socialization to work in such frameworks. The consequence of this is that military personnel of different origin can often function with each other without too many problems. Moskos (1976), for instance, found that the most serious tensions during the United Nations Peacekeeping Force in Cyprus (UNFICYP) operation took place between military personnel and the UN civilian staff, not between military personnel of the various contingents. Something similar seems to have occurred in Bosnia and Kosovo (Moskos, 2001). Apparently, there is a certain military professionalism that, at least to a certain extent, can surmount national borders and cultural differences (see also Elron, Shamir, & Ben-Ari, 1999, and Elron, Halevey, Ben Ari, & Shamir, this volume).

Nevertheless, cultural heterogeneity is present in the military, as we have shown, and will still impact international military operations in many ways. Furthermore, certain conditions combine to make the development of a so-called international frame of reference among military personnel fairly difficult. For example, military units must maintain a national line of responsibility, the time frames of the operation tend to be rather tight, the sense of urgency generally is high, and personnel are constantly rotated. Given this balance between an underlying common military understanding (explored in Elron et al., this volume) and pressures that operate against the development of an international military outlook, examples from real-world joint operations elucidate some of the conflicts that can emerge.

In the following section we describe two intercultural encounters that took place in three peacekeeping missions: (1) Anglo-Dutch cooperation in the UNFICYP mission, and (2) Danish-U.S. collaboration in the Implementation and Stabilization Forces in Bosnia (IFOR and SFOR). Although we limit ourselves to western experiences, we are fully aware that similar, or perhaps even more complicated, cultural encounters may occur in other missions, such as the ECOMOG operation in Liberia (i.e., the Military Observer group of the Economic Community of West African States [ECOWAS]), which was composed of troops from various African countries (Olonisakin, 1999).

COMPLEX CULTURAL ENCOUNTERS IN PEACEKEEPING MISSIONS

Anglo-Dutch Cooperation in Cyprus

The UN mission UNFICYP came into being in 1964 and is related to a "property right"—controversy between the inhabitants of the island of Cyprus. Both "mother countries," Greece and Turkey, play a role in the background of this conflict. From its inception, UNFICYP, which is intended to control the border dividing the isle into Greek-Cypriote and Turkish-Cypriote parts, has been supported by troops from numerous countries. At the moment, UNFICYP is composed of British, Argentine, and Austrian troops, each with their own buffer zone. In 1998, the Dutch government decided to make a company available to replace part of the British regiment during a period of three years. The company was put under the command of the British sector commander. The Dutch personnel were attached as national platoons in the British order of battle or had been allocated to platoons that were completely international in composition.

In the beginning, this cooperation did not develop smoothly (Soeters, Op den Buijs, & Vogelaar, 2001). In a limited survey among the Dutch service members of the first rotation, 85% of the respondents stated they did not like the way the British acted. Some 60% disagreed with the statement that the cooperation with the British was smooth. Only 50% found that Dutch and British soldiers got along very well. Language differences did not seem to be the root of the problem. What, then, was the reason for the apparent discord? An analysis based on a number of in-depth interviews with Dutch soldiers (Soeters, Op den Buijs et al., 2001) as well as an account of the experiences of two Dutch lieutenants (Brink & van Rosendaal, 2000) provide some possible explanations.

Most of all, the Dutch military seemed to have problems with the hierarchical customs within the British Army. Recall from the academy study mentioned earlier that the culture of the British Army is characterized by a very large degree of power distance, and as such this fact mirrors the stratified British society. The Dutch soldiers in Cyprus criticized the rank-based separate mess halls and canteens and the prohibition against platoon commanders drinking a beer with the men and women with whom they had worked all day. The authoritarian way in which orders were issued in the British Army was also strange in the eyes of the Dutch. The Dutch military personnel were disconcerted by the typical threat that accompanied the issuing of orders: "If these orders are not fulfilled, disciplinary actions will be taken!" This approach stands in stark contrast to the jovial tone that Dutch commanders generally use when explaining their plans and orders.

The ease with which punishments are given in the British Army were simply not understood nor accepted by the Dutch soldiers. UK commanders have a fairly large degree of discretionary power to punish individuals as well as units. Their penalties may vary from extra duties (painting after normal working hours, running for an hour) to imposing fines that can go up as high as hundreds of pounds. In the eyes of the Dutch, these types of punishment were and are unacceptable, because working hours (including those for extra duties) are subject to strict working time regulations, and financial penalties during peacekeeping operations can be imposed to a limit of 90 Euros only. Furthermore, punishing a whole group because one or two soldiers drank too much the previous night (not an uncommon occurrence) was not considered fair by the Dutch military personnel (Soeters, Op den Buijs et al., 2001).

Similarly, the Dutch perspective on the importance of working conditions and the government policies designed to protect worker-soldiers was also at odds with the British method. In general, Dutch service members are fairly protected by all kinds of rules and regulations, of which the Labor Conditions Act is a prominent one. This act, among other things, forbids Dutch soldiers to work with asbestos. One can imagine the problems arising when a British commander ordered a Dutch service member to clean up a mess containing asbestos.

The culture-related friction in the Anglo-Dutch cooperation in Cyprus can be explained using theoretical and empirical knowledge of both societies and their armed forces (Hofstede, 2001; Soeters, 1997). Dutch society (and the army as well) is characterized by a horizontal orientation (low power distance, concern for others, see also Triandis, 1995). British society, on the contrary, and even more so the British Army, is steeped in a vertical orientation (large power distance, and relatively low concern about others, see also Triandis, 1995). The friction, which emerged, therefore was not that surprising. Nevertheless, during the Anglo-Dutch cooperation, the friction became so tense that the Dutch military staff in The Hague deemed it necessary to intervene. A special commission investigated the situation and prepared a report with various recommendations (published in a circular from the "Section Lessons Learned" from the Dutch army staff, April 2000).

Some of them are presented here:

- One should start to get to know one's own culture, then the other culture, and finally one should search for solutions to deal with the differences.
- One should take into account that a British person higher in rank does not accept contradiction when issuing orders.
- Show your military professionalism, for this will speed up the integration with the British.
- Operate within your own tasks and responsibilities, and do not deal with matters that concern others, as this helpfulness can quickly be explained as insubordinate (take into account that British service personnel hardly take initiatives beyond their own tasks).
- Make use of your national hierarchical channels, even when your own (national) commander is not present for the moment.
- Always be yourself; be open and honest. And be polite when addressing officers and NCOs.

These recommendations, in addition to the advice not to ridicule other customs, have been presented to commanders and were used during training before Dutch soldiers deployed to Cyprus. Dutch military personnel were made aware of the fact that working with the armed forces of another country is not necessarily the same as working with compatriots.

The importance of these recommendations is that they are not ethnocentric, which means that the Dutch way of viewing things is not considered superior to the British perspective. One can safely assume that the British military personnel in Cyprus must have had their own complaints about some of the most stubborn Dutch military habits, such as the habit of always questioning orders and answering back. Recent interviews during the fall of 2002 showed that according to the British military, remarkable differences and the severance of punishments indeed did hamper the binational military cooperation in Cyprus. It is extremely important for the Dutch, or personnel from any nation, to realize that frustration from culture-based behaviors and attitudes occurs on both sides, and that military personnel from the "foreign" culture experience frustration too. Understanding and respecting each other's customs are fundamental steps to realizing effective international military cooperation. The importance of this type of culture-related awareness cannot be underestimated, because the effectiveness of operations may be seriously threatened when not enough attention is paid to it. However, problems will not always be so severe as in the case of UNFICYP, as the following example shows. This example deals with Danish-U.S. collaboration in Bosnia. In this case there were no overt problems; however, culture-related tensions did occur in everyday working life between the vertical culture of the United States and Denmark's horizontal culture (Triandis, 1995).

Tensions in U.S.-Danish Cooperation in Bosnia

Many countries contribute to the SFOR troops in Bosnia, and this multinational presence is reflected in the existence of multinational divisions (MNDs). One of these MNDs is headed by the United States, the so-called Task Force Eagle division in Tuzla, Bosnia. Battalions belonging to this division consist of troops from various countries, including Denmark. At least 30% of the Danish officers, deployed to Bosnia, had regular contacts with American officers belonging to this staff. Although the encounters between the officers of both nations have not produced serious problems, there have been a number of tensions related to cultural differences as noted by the Danish themselves (Soerensen, 1999).

First of all, it is striking that Danish officers use civilian criteria to describe the nature of their job. They refer to result-orientation ("the importance of the accomplishment of a task"), social behavior ("soldiers are first and above all human beings") and a decentralized military structure ("it must be easy for a soldier to get in touch with his superiors"). This Danish military culture, as confirmed by the previously mentioned academy study (Soeters, 1997; Soeters & Recht, 1998), is quite different from that of the U.S. Army. Phrases like "obey orders," "work by the book," and "comply with military law," which are favorite expressions among the Americans, are not seen as the most important qualities to the Danish military. The relative importance of such formal bureaucracy implied by these phrases may be due, in part, to the distance between soldier and superior, which is much more pronounced in the U.S. Army than in the Danish (Soerensen, 1999). This is not a military peculiarity: in civilian supervisor-subordinate relations, the United States is also tighter than Scandinavia (Triandis, 1995).

Generally, the same observations about the U.S. military have been made in the 50 years from the Second World War until the recent operations in the Balkans. Wilson (1989) reports that mission-oriented command still is fairly unknown to the U.S. military, whereas the inclination to "just follow the orders" is more familiar (Soerensen, 1999). Even U.S. generals deployed to Bosnia and Kosovo are not seen as having the authority to change policies and measures according to their own views (Caniglia, 2001). European managers working for U.S. multinational corporations have made similar observations. European managers often complain about the formal reporting systems and volume of written policies and procedures that come down from U.S. headquarters (Schneider & Barsoux, 1997).

These tendencies are consistent with what Hofstede identified as risk and uncertainty avoidance as evidenced by the results of the academy study referred to earlier in this chapter. Others have also observed that Americans display a "check point mania" and a zero-defects as well as a zero-tolerance mentality (Caniglia, 2001; Moskos, 2001). This risk-avoiding tendency comes to the fore in various ways. For instance, if a U.S. soldier wants to get a pizza in downtown Kosovo, he or she will need armed vehicles with cruise-served weapons and at least four soldiers to accompany him or her, whereas a Danish officer will only use an ordinary jeep with two soldiers. This means that the Americans are clearly more directed toward force protection than the Danish, or the British for that matter (Caniglia, 2001; Soerensen, 1999). Bearing in mind the various terrorist attacks on U.S. troops over the past decades, this is not surprising, nor is it unwise. There are, however, more subtle expressions of uncertainty avoidance in the U.S. military.

One expression of this uncertainty avoidance involved the tendency for American officers to be specialists, not leaving their own branch nor even having much regular contact with their counterparts in other branches in the early stages of their careers. Obviously, this is related to the size of the U.S. Army in general and of the branches within this army specifically. The larger an organization, the higher its degree of specialization (e.g., Jaffee, 2001). For the Danish this situation is completely different, because—probably due to the considerably smaller size of their army—they tend to become generalists rather early in their careers (Soerensen, 1999). Hence they develop a tendency to intervene in issues, which strictly speaking do not belong to their own area of responsibility. Such intervention is something the Americans do not like, or at least it is less likely to be understood. This difference in basic orientation is comparable with the point of friction in the Anglo-Dutch military cooperation in Cyprus, which led the Dutch military staff to recommend Dutch personnel only operating within one's own tasks and responsibilities.

A similar mechanism relates to the "up-or-out" career system in the U.S. Army. This system of career progression implies that an American officer's performance in his or her actual assignment is the basis for his or her evaluation. Hence one bad evaluation can ruin an officer's career. Therefore, the American officer or NCO is more vulnerable to criticism that a Danish officer whose overall performance is taken into consideration (Soerensen, 1999). This system may induce greater risk avoidance among the Americans than among the Danish military personnel.

There are important similarities between the Anglo-Dutch experience in Cyprus and the U.S.-Danish experience in Bosnia in terms of the issues that emerge from international peacekeeping cooperative efforts. In both of the case studies, the strict character, the authoritarian manner, and the centralized way of issuing orders was inconsistent with the characteristics of the other military involved in the cooperative effort (i.e., the Danish and the Dutch militaries). In general, Dutch officers go through real culture shock when being confronted with the level of *micro-management* they experience while working in an international context (Duine, 1998). Obviously, this cultural tension relates to the debate about what is the best command style during military operations in general and during peace support operations specifically. The British and U.S. style of commanding certainly seems to be at odds with the more symbiotic and enabling style of issuing orders with which the Dutch and the Danish military are more familiar. This contrast may come as no surprise, because the United States and the UK both have large militaries and share a tradition of combat, as well as general cultural similarities stemming from historical affiliations going back for centuries. Denmark and the Netherlands both have relatively small armed forces, and they share a tendency to favor peace support operations instead of real combat (Soerensen, 1999; Soeters, Op den Buijs et al., 2001), as well as sharing other general cultural similarities (Hofstede, 2001).

All in all, the impact of cross-cultural values on peacekeeping is a complicated subject. More cultural issues may be relevant than can be accounted for using the Hofstede dimensions than were applied in the academy study. Therefore, one should not judge the results prematurely. The question is how this complex subject matter of peacekeeping in an international context can best be dealt with.

The Management of Cross-Cultural Values in Peacekeeping

Because in another chapter of this book ample attention is paid to the macro-dynamics of structuring multinational peace support operations (see Elron, Halevi, & Shamir, Chapter 15 of this volume), we focus on the micro-dynamics here. More specifically, after addressing the structural aspects of multinational military cooperation, we deal with leadership in an international context.

In general, it seems wise to separate national contingents, bestowing on them each their own sector. In the case of the Anglo-Dutch cooperation and after the fairly problematic experiences with the fully mixed Anglo-Dutch structure during the first two rotations, it was decided the Dutch company would be given its own subsector (Soeters, Op den Buijs et al., 2001). In an interview, one Dutch officer went so far as to suggest that mixing troops below the level of the company (some 100 men and women) should definitively be discouraged. Actually, separating troops is precisely what is being done most of the time during peace support operations (e.g., Elron et al., 1999). However, this is not always suitable because of the resources required to staff and support separate units. In addition, at the level of staff units and HQs, this separation is virtually impossible. Hence intercultural encounters simply cannot be completely excluded by means of this type of structuring.

Another issue of a more structural nature refers to cultural differences in legal aspects of military operations. The account of the Anglo-Dutch cooperation demonstrated that many of the disagreements and misunderstandings were related to legal differences, including differences with regard to the rules of engagement. One should pay attention to this, not necessarily in an effort to harmonize legal systems (because that would be a very complicated matter to solve), but at least to be aware of the fact that these differences do exist and should be dealt with. Commanders should display a strictly impartial attitude when it comes to punishments. Obviously, commanders should always be impartial, but in particular they should be impartial when cross-cultural interactions are involved. Also with regard to moral and ethical dilemmas, the commander should refrain as much as possible from prejudiced reasoning and preconceived ideas. As legal rules and moral reasoning reflect the views of a society, there are most certainly nation-related differences among cultural, legal, and ethical ways of reasoning.

To be aware of legal and ethical differences, however, is not the only matter that needs the attention of commanders on multinational operations (Soeters, 1998; Soeters, Op den Buijs et al., 2001). Ultimately, it is important for commanders to follow through on their decisions in order to ensure that the decisions are effectively communicated down the chain of command, understood, and implemented. Many decisions in organizations simply are not carried out because of failing implementation skills: the decisions have been made—often after ample deliberation—but then nothing happens due to a lack of communication and instruction. Commanders, and for that matter managers in the business sector, often forget to translate their decisions to the level of the rank-and-file members of the organization.

While "being there," commanders should do their utmost to infuse the organizational members with central values regarding the direction of the mission as well as the preferred behavior, decision, and communication styles. In addition, commanders in multinational operations should stress—perceptibly and emotionally—some central issues (Soeters, 1998). First, commanders will have to emphasize the *joint* character of the mission. The joint character of the mission should be seen as the superordinate goal for all people involved. In this respect, it seems important to set realistic but challenging goals. If the goals to be achieved are not challenging, cultural friction due to the boredom factor may easily arise (as for instance during UNFICYP, Soeters, Op den Buijs et al., 2001). If the goals are overly ambitious, however, culture-related friction and tension may also surface as a consequence of generally higher stress levels. Hence the mission's goals should be set at the appropriate level, but most importantly, these ambitions or goals should be collectively shared by all people involved.

Furthermore, it is important to emphasize the equal status of all units involved in the multinational operation. This could help overcome prejudicial ideas about the "others" (e.g., Allport, 1958). Such types of prejudice and low levels of acceptance of foreigners have been demonstrated to exist for instance among American citizen-soldiers (Glaser, 1946; Segal & Tiggle, 1997). Other nationalities have similar biases. In a recent Dutch study, a substantial number of Dutch soldiers reported having negative stereotypes about their foreign counterparts on a peacekeeping mission (Kop, Euwema, & de Ridder, 2001). If the status of some contributing countries, for instance developing countries, is relatively low, and if ingroup "virtues" come to be seen as outgroup "vices," it is the commander's responsibility to boost the status of the members of the low-status group. Besides, the commander should make his or her decisions in such a way that every representative of a country can maintain his or her dignity, without loss of face. Although awareness of cultural differences is important, the commander should not exaggerate these differences. Downplaying cultural differences may prevent the development of stereotypes within the unit (Holden, 2002). Finally, various means of cross-cultural training as well as the organization of social events (e.g., exercises, sport tournaments, parties) to enhance mutual acquaintance and cohesion seem to be equally important in order to create some overall esprit de corps. Obviously, these events are likely to be only "fun," but even then cohesion may develop.

A last issue concerns the performance of multinational teams. As mentioned previously, teams in all NATO-HQs and staff units of peace support operations are multinational. Based on information from the business sector, sometimes the performance of these teams is outstanding, but frequently the opposite may be true (Hambrick, Canney, Davison, Snell, & Snow, 1998). This suboptimal performance depends on several variables, including the nature of the task (creative problem solving or implementation), the cultural composition of the group, the maturity of the group, and the existence of curvilinear relationships between group composition and performance. In the case of international military teams, it appears these variables also play a role in predicting effectiveness, but how and to what extent these variables influence group effectiveness needs to be addressed by further research with the military. Although evidence indicates these international teams are generally quite successful (see Elron et al., this volume), the importance of these teams functioning at the optimal level is critical. Thus this issue warrants not only further investigation into the dynamics of teams operating in international staff and headquarters units but early identification of possible performance problems as well.

Avenues for Further Research

It is not particularly spectacular to prophesy that cross-cultural issues will become increasingly important to Western armed forces. The foundation of the

European Rapid Reaction Forces probably is only the beginning of a larger process leading in due time to the formation of an all-European armed forces. Undoubtedly, this increasing multiculturality of the armed forces will provide interesting challenges to the military world, not only in Europe.

It seems important to study these developments thoroughly using longitudinal research designs. One such longitudinal study involved the formation of the 1st German/Dutch Army Corps (from 1995 to 2001). Results from this six-year study showed that various dynamics of intercultural interactions developed over time, including culture shock following an initial period of euphoria (Moelker, Soeters, & Klein, 2003). After the promising first two years of the founding of the binational corps, the two national parties involved developed fairly low opinions of each other, a situation that even seemed to endanger the operability of the corps. Fortunately, this dramatic development was temporary. As a result of excellent collaboration during the Kosovo crisis, as well as ambitious work in the binational headquarters, the two contributing countries started to appreciate each other more (Moelker et al., 2003). Apparently, and in keeping with the well-known contact hypothesis in social psychology (e.g., Allport, 1958), time and experience played a dominant role in learning how to value the other group. In addition, working on a challenging common endeavor affected the intergroup relationships. The precise influence of these integrating mechanisms should be clarified in future studies with militaries undergoing similar restructuring. Providing commanders information on these findings over the course of the formation of the units will enhance commander effectiveness in developing an integrated force.

In addition to considering macro-level interactions among integrated operational forces, these longitudinal studies should also focus on everyday interactions among the service members. To this end, the so-called triangle model of responsibility in peacekeeping (focusing on prescriptions and goals, the occurrence of specific events, and identity images individual soldiers have) may prove to be a valuable frame of reference (Britt, 1998). To enrich this model with cross-cultural values will benefit both scholars and military practitioners.

More work also needs to be done on understanding cross-cultural values themselves. The Hofstede dimensions used in the academy study have been helpful in analyzing the culture-related tensions between so-called horizontally (the Dutch and the Danish) and vertically oriented armies (American and UK). In particular, the dimensions of power distance, uncertainty avoidance, and masculinity/ femininity have proven to be useful concepts. But in understanding the dynamics of peacekeeping, more cultural values may be at stake such as the attitude toward the use of violence. This value is likely to result in considerable nation-based differences (e.g., Soeters, 2001). Another issue of relevance is the attitude toward casualties among the troops. Some nations, such as the United States, generally adhere to a zero-casualty philosophy on peace support operations, whereas other nations such as the British seem to be more willing to accept the idea that soldiers could get killed (Caniglia, 2001).

Some nations also have a recent history of combat, like the UK, whereas others favor the relational aspects of peacekeeping and feel uncomfortable with the use of violence. Future research may succeed in developing systematic knowledge about these value differences and their relationship to operational effectiveness.

In addition, it seems wise to pay more attention to cross-cultural training in general and to the training of multinational teams in specific. In order to create a real sense of togetherness in multinational operations, it would be advisable to experiment with training settings in which military missions are simulated and in which conflicting parties and, hence, uncertainty and danger, are the main elements of the scenario (Soeters & Recht, 2001). For reasons explained extensively by Meyerson, Weick, and Kramer (1996), mutual trust and cohesion are more likely to occur (1) when the level of activities is high, (2) when personnel are drawn from a small labor pool, and (3) when interdependencies are large. These variables could be taken into account when designing training modules for working in an international military context. In combination with elements of conflict management training and with an emphasis on coordinative group tasks, this type of simulated cross-cultural training may enhance the affinities felt by the trainees for one another's culture and their ability to cope with cultural differences within internationally composed military units or organizations.

Designing these modules and studying their effects should provide a considerable contribution to the further integration of Western armed forces. Future victims of conflicts who will have to be protected by these integrated armed forces will be grateful for it.

REFERENCES

Allport, G. W. (1958). *The nature of prejudice*. New York: Doubleday.

Brink, D., & van Rosendaal, F. (2000). *Bi-national cooperation during UNFICYP-II and UNFICYP-III*. Unpublished student thesis, Royal Netherlands' Military Academy, Breda.

Britt, T. W. (1998). Psychological ambiguities in peacekeeping. In H. J. Langholtz (Ed.), *The psychology of peacekeeping* (pp. 111–128). Westport, CT: Praeger.

Caniglia, R. R. (2001, July-August). U.S. and British approaches to force protection. *Military Review*, pp. 73–81.

Duine, J. (1998). Werken en leven in HQ SFOR [Working and living in HQ SFOR]. *Militaire Spectator, 167,* 451–455.

Elron, E., Shamir, B., & Ben-Ari, E. (1999). Why don't they fight each other? Cultural diversity and operational unity in multinational forces. *Armed Forces & Society, 26,* 73–97.

Glaser, D. (1946). The sentiments of American soldiers abroad toward Europeans. *American Journal of Sociology, 51,* 433–438.

Hambrick, D. C., Canney Davison, S., Snell, S. A., & Snow, C. C. (1998). When groups consist of multiple nationalities: Towards a new understanding of the implications. *Organization Studies, 19,* 181–205.

Hofstede, G. H. (2001). *Culture's consequences. International differences in work-related values* (2nd ed.). Beverly Hills, CA: Sage.

Holden, N. (2002). *Cross-cultural management. A knowledge management perspective.* London: Prentice-Hall.

Jaffee, D. (2001). *Organization theory. Tension and change.* Boston: McGraw-Hill.

Kop, N., Euwema, M., & de Ridder, R. (2001). Attituden en vaardigheden van Nederlandse militairen bij vredesoperaties' [*Attitude and skills of Dutch military during peacekeeping missions*]. Den Haag: Instituut Clingendael (Netherlands Institute of International Relations).

Meyerson, D., Weick, K., & Kramer, R. M. (1996). Swift trust and temporary groups. In R. M. Kramer and T. R. Tyler (Eds.), *Trust in organizations. Frontiers of theory and research* (pp. 166–195). London: Sage.

Moelker, R., Soeters, J., & Klein, P. (2003). Sympathy, stereotypes and the contact hypothesis. In F. Columbus (Ed.), *Progress in Sociology Research.* New York: Novascience.

Moskos, C. C. (1976). *Peace soldiers. The sociology of a United Nations military force.* Chicago: University of Chicago Press.

Moskos, C. C. (2001). *Multinational military cooperation: Enhancing American military effectiveness.* Unpublished memo, Northwestern University, Evanston, IL.

Olonisakin, F. (1999). *Reinventing peacekeeping in Africa. Conceptual and legal issues in ECOMOG operations.* The Hague, London, Boston: Kluwer Law International.

Oudenhoven, J. P. (2001). Do organizations reflect national cultures? A 10-nation study. *International Journal of Intercultural Relations, 25,* 89–107.

Section lessons learned. (2000, 10 April). *Working together with British soldiers.* Circular publication from the Dutch Army Staff.

Segal, D. R., & Tiggle, R. B. (1997). Attitudes of citizen-soldiers to military missions in the post–Cold War world. *Armed Forces & Society, 23,* 373–390.

Schneider, S. C., & Barsoux, J. L. (1997). *Managing across cultures.* Harlow: Prentice-Hall Europe.

Soerensen, H. (1999). *Warriors in peacekeeping operations: Points of tension in complex cultural encounters. Danish top officers' experiences from IFOR/SFOR, Bosnia.* Unpublished memo, Copenhagen.

Soeters, J. (1997). Values in military academies. A thirteen country study. *Armed Forces & Society, 24,* 7–32.

Soeters, J. (1998). The commander's responsibility in multinational operations. *Netherlands Annual Review of Military Studies, 2,* 181–191.

Soeters, J. (2001). The Dutch military and the use of violence. *Netherlands Journal of Social Sciences, 37,* 24–37.

Soeters, J., & Boer, P. C. (2000). Culture and flight safety in military aviation. *International Journal of Aviation Psychology, 10,* 111–133.

Soeters, J., Op den Buijs, I., & Vogelaar, A. (2001). The importance of cultural information in multinational operations: a fragmented case study on UNFICYP. *Netherlands Annual Review of Military Studies, 4,* 55–65.

Soeters, J., & Recht, R. (1998). Culture and discipline in military academies: An international comparison. *Journal of Political and Military Sociology, 26,* 169–189.

Soeters, J., & Recht, R. (2001). Convergence or divergence in the multinational classroom? Experiences from the military. *International Journal of Intercultural Relations, 25,* 1–18.

Sondergaard, M. (1994). Research note: Hofstede's consequences: a study of reviews, citations and replications. *Organization Studies, 15,* 447–456.

Tayeb, M. (1994). Organizations and national culture: Methodology considered. *Organization Studies, 15,* 429–446.

Triandis, H. C. (1995). *Individualism and collectivism.* Oxford: Westview Press.

Wilson, J. Q. (1989). *Bureaucracy. What government agencies do and why they do it.* New York: Basic Books.

Winslow, D. J., & Everts, P. L. E. M. (2001). Inter-cultural challenges for NATO. In G. Schmidt (Ed.), *NATO—The first fifty years.* London: Macmillan.

Winslow, D. J., Kammhuber, S., & Soeters, J. (2003). Diversity management and training in non-American forces. In D. Landis (Ed.), *Handbook of intercultural communication.* London: Sage.

17

African Peacekeeping and the Impact on African Military Personnel

'Funmi Olonisakin

The participation of African military personnel in peacekeeping occurs in several forms. In one form, African military personnel serve as part of multinational UN peace operations, within and outside Africa. A number of African countries have contributed troops to such peacekeeping missions since the 1960s. Africans served in large numbers as part of the UN Operation in the Congo (ONUC); as part of the UN Interim Force in Lebanon (UNIFIL), which was also commanded by a Ghanaian general; and in recent times they have served in Somalia and Bosnia, among several other operations. In such operations, they experienced many of the problems commonly faced by peacekeeping personnel in general, including, for example, the monotony of conventional peacekeeping and the frustration of not being able to engage in combat operations, the very basis of their training as soldiers.

In another form, African military personnel have served in peace operations planned and executed by African governments and regional organizations, which are referred to in this chapter as *African peacekeeping*. Such operations planned and executed by African institutions were rare in the Cold War period, and in the real sense of the term, the only case of African peacekeeping occurred in Chad in 1981. However, in the last decade, as the end of the Cold War presented new challenges for Africa, including, for example, more intense intrastate conflict and increased opportunities for conflict resolution in the region, Africans have attempted peacekeeping outside of the UN umbrella in varying degrees. For example, the Organization of African Unity, OAU (now the African Union), with a long history of mediation and conflict prevention, has, in the post–Cold War period, attempted to strengthen its capacity in these areas with the support of small-scale peace operations.

The largest of those small-scale missions has been the OAU Observer Mission in Burundi (OMIB), which consisted of 67 people. A smaller peace force was sent to Rwanda as part of the OAU effort to mediate in the conflict in that country between 1990 and 1992. The OAU Military Observer Group in Rwanda consisted of 55 military personnel (Muyangwa & Vogt, 2000). Such small-scale missions perform roles now commonly recognized as traditional or conventional peacekeeping. However, by far the largest and most challenging African peace operations took place in Liberia from 1990 to 1997 and in Sierra Leone from 1997 to 2000 under the auspices of the Economic Community of West African States (ECOWAS). The ECOWAS cease-fire Monitoring Group (ECOMOG), as ECOWAS peacekeeping forces have become known, consisted largely of military personnel from West Africa except for a period between 1993 and 1994, when two additional battalions from Tanzania and Uganda served as part of the ECOMOG force in Liberia. ECOMOG would later be deployed in Guinea-Bissau to deal with a relatively less intense crisis than those witnessed in Liberia and Sierra Leone.

The operations in Liberia and Sierra Leone have become the best known face of African peacekeeping (see Alao, Mackinlay, & Olonisakin, 2000; Olaiya, 1991; Olurin, 1992, 1993; Vogt, 1992). They represent the most decisive African response to the serious security threat created by the brutal intrastate conflicts that have consumed the region since the end of the Cold War. The conflicts in those countries demonstrated that effective response must move beyond traditional peacekeeping, without waiting indefinitely for the consent of warring parties. And furthermore, those peace forces would use force not only in self-defense but also in the defense of the civilian population by attempting to halt the killing of the innocent. Yet this stance has not been without controversy and not without operational difficulties, and they were bound to be more difficult than those encountered in classical peace operations.

The peacekeeping that takes place in Africa under the auspices of African personnel and regional and subregional organizations varies from UN or other regional peacekeeping only in degree, rather than in substance. The experience of the last decade has shown that African conflict situations, depending on their level and intensity, could require responses at various points on the spectrum of peacemaking. But the conditions that necessitate the type of robust responses witnessed in Liberia and Sierra Leone are by no means limited to Africa. The conflicts in places such as former Yugoslavia and East Timor, for example, have also witnessed brutal acts in which civilians were the focus of the violence.

The African peace operations referred to here have some key features. They occur in brutal internal conflicts, where innocent civilians are often the main targets. All parties to the conflict do not usually grant consent for peacekeeping. Thus peacekeepers have been compelled to use force either in self-defense or to halt atrocities against innocent people. Indeed, it has been difficult to justify all of such acts as peacekeeping. In Liberia, for example, the ECOMOG forces switched intermittently between peacekeeping and enforcement. Thus peacekeeping personnel in such operations are not necessarily short of combat experience, although they still operate under a different set of principles from traditional warfare. The debate about whether this type of operation belongs in the classical peacekeeping category is still ongoing.

African peacekeeping in the form witnessed in Liberia and Sierra Leone is thus vastly different from the peacekeeping initially envisaged by the UN and that has come to be associated with that organization. This chapter argues that despite the frustrations experienced by African military personnel in these operations, given the relatively difficult operational environment and harsh conditions under which they operate, this peacekeeping, organized by Africans for Africans has, on the whole, provided them achievement. However, opinions vary among officers and other ranks as to the extent of impact and sense of achievement. This chapter discusses the various factors that created frustrations for these men and women and the core values that served to give them a sense of achievement despite their frustration. The chapter relies on data gathered from peacekeeping personnel in the field since 1994, first in Liberia, and later in Sierra Leone and during various interviews outside of the mission area with military personnel who served in those operations in various capacities. The rest of this chapter offers an overview of African peacekeeping and the context in which it takes place, outlining the factors that often create particular difficulty and frustration for military personnel. It discusses the various ways in which such personnel are affected by peace operations of this nature.

FACTORS THAT REDUCE MOTIVATION AND SOURCES OF STRESS AND FRUSTRATION

Impact of ECOMOG's Strategy on Peacekeepers

ECOMOG's strategy for dealing with the crisis that emerged in both Liberia and Sierra Leone was an unusual one, which yielded both positive and negative results. This strategy entailed the intermittent switch between peacekeeping and peace enforcement. The positive impact of this strategy was often most visible in the immediate aftermath of the force's change of stance, particularly from peacekeeping to enforcement (Olonisakin, 2000). In Liberia and Sierra Leone, the successful ejection of rebel forces from the capital cities served to halt or reduce atrocities by rebel groups and to create a measure of stability, which allowed humanitarian workers to resume the provision of much needed aid to the victims of the conflicts. The attitudes of civilian populations that had lived under months of terror and suffered indignation at the hands of warring factions that inflicted heavy casualties on them were often characterized by jubilance and euphoria, with praises for the peace force, despite its rough edges. This atmosphere served to boost the morale of the peacekeeping troops, even if temporarily.

However, several other factors relating to the employment of this strategy was a major source of stress and frustration for many of the troops. One had to do with the fact that, in many cases, the same troops that participated in enforcement remained on the ground to implement the peacekeeping phase that followed. Thus there was no period of rehabilitation following a phase of active combat, and they were required to adjust cautiously to a mindset and mood that was conciliatory with the same rebel forces they had faced in combat and to whom they had lost their colleagues. The testimonies of some of the soldiers provide some indication of their concern, stress, and frustration during those operations:

The commanding officer of the Gambian contingent during the ECOMOG operation in Liberia commented, for example, on the problem of switching from enforcement to peacekeeping when the Cotonou agreement was concluded: "The transition from peace enforcement to peacekeeping is not always smooth. We need to look into this. The apprehension was on all sides. You suspect everyone, read in-between the lines, you overreact. We need to look into these areas."

Several ECOMOG officers also commented on the problems of switching between peace enforcement and peacekeeping:

On a peacekeeping mission, a soldier has his mind and whole self built for negotiation and peace brokering and once the warring parties see him that way, this is good. But the automatic switch over to enforcement, which requires force, might have some initial negative effects on the soldier. This can be overcome quite easily and quickly, though, once the troops are threatened. (Sierra Leone major, ECOMOG, 1994)

The combatants you have been fighting against will not trust you. It is difficult to treat well, or be friendly with a person you have seen killing your fellow soldiers or officers. (Tanzanian contingent commander, ECOMOG, 1994)

The problem lies mainly in behavior. Soldiers are tempted to continue with the same behavior that they could get away with during peace enforcement operations. (Ghanaian colonel, ECOMOG, 1994)

From peace enforcement to peacekeeping, enmity is created and the seed of bitterness is sowed in the hearts of the warring factions and the peacekeepers. The psychology of the rebels becomes apprehensive and ruthless. (Nigerian lieutenant, ECOMOG, 1994)

There is the problem of orientation from an aggressive posture to a friendly posture. The situation does not build trust. Where there is no trust, reconciliation is often difficult. (Nigerian major, ECOMOG, 1994)

A human being is not a machine to switch automatically from peace enforcement to peacekeeping. Elements of aggression linger on for some time. Reflex action too continues to make soldiers overreact. Human defensive nature keeps soldiers on the path of war even in a peacekeeping role. (Nigerian colonel, commanding officer, ECOMOG, 1994)

The effects of alternating between peace enforcement and peacekeeping were compounded by the fact that troops were rotated infrequently. Although it was initially agreed the contingents would be rotated every six months, this was not adhered to by all contingents. The Ghanaian contingent rotated most frequently; the Sierra Leoneans, Guineans, and Nigerians rotated least frequently. The average tour of duty for troops in these three countries was about 18 to 24 months, and they remained in the areas of operation in Liberia and Sierra Leone throughout this period. This lowered morale and diminished productivity among these troops. Several contributing states argued it was too expensive to rotate their troops at regular six-month intervals. This was especially true for the Nigerian contingent, which was the largest in ECOMOG, constituting about 70% of the force.

The psychological effects of infrequent rotation on the force were profound, and they were most noticeable in the Nigerian camp, given its size. The problem was more apparent among other ranks than the officers. In theory, officers and other ranks could obtain a pass to travel home to see their families. However, they were expected to meet the costs of this journey from their meager allowance, which was not paid regularly. The cost of transportation to Nigeria prevented the majority of soldiers from going home, whereas officers who so wished often managed to travel home to see their families. Thus a soldier invariably remained in the mission area until he was rotated. This did not enhance morale within the force, and the situation was compounded by the fact that many of the troops remained in the mission area after the enforcement period without any rehabilitation. Commenting on the problems of infrequent rotation, one of the ECOMOG field commanders said, "Having been away from home for too long, they [soldiers] sometimes behave differently at checkpoints. For example they have mood swings. The same soldier, who acts erratically today, may act calmly tomorrow. . . . Rotation is advisable ideally every six months. Lack of this could lead to familiarity, fatigue, boredom, and efficiency diminishes. It is however costly to rotate on the meager resources of different countries" (Nigerian general, 1994).

One other factor that created frustration among ECOMOG officers in particular was that the force was often prevented from pursuing enforcement action to its logical conclusion. Although enforcement phases allowed the troops to utilize their soldiering skills, thus removing much of the monotony that set in during the classical peacekeeping phase, there were serious constraints on the extent to which they could pursue the use of force. For example, following the National Patriotic Front of Liberia (NPFL) attack on ECOMOG and Monrovia in October 1992, the force contained this attack and went on the counteroffensive, wresting the control of several strategic locations such as seaports, which were used for resupply from the control of the rebel force. ECOMOG commanders were convinced they would have ended the NPFL challenge once and for all had the political masters not denied them this opportunity with the order of a cease-fire and the subsequent signing of the Cotonou Accord. This type of frustration is consistent with the usual tension that exists between the military and their political masters, and, not surprisingly, it was a source of frustration for ECOMOG officers.

Logistics and Administration

ECOMOG did not have a centralized logistics distribution. Every troop-contributing state made separate provision for its contingent's logistic requirement. Thus standards were uneven, and there was lack of uniformity in almost all aspects of logistics. There were huge gaps among the logistics capability of the different contingents. ECOMOG officers were concerned not only about the impact of this situation on command and control but also on morale. Another ECOMOG field commander also remarked on this situation: "The lack of centralized logistics has inherent command and control problems for the commander. Besides, it is bad for morale of troops who share the same accommodation or office or checkpoints to have different standards of feeding and welfare amenities" (Olurin, 1992). Yet another ECOMOG commander expressed a similar concern: "[F]inancial constraints have made it impossible for uniformity to be maintained in feeding standards. This tends to reveal inequalities and affects the morale of the troops" (Nigerian general, 1993). Again, given its size in ECOMOG, Nigeria's problem with logistics distribution had an immediate impact on the force.

The issue of operational allowance proved to have the worst effect on morale within ECOMOG and was a major source of stress among the peacekeepers. A small operational allowance of US $5 per day was negotiated at the start of the mission. This came to a monthly average of US $100. It was agreed that each contributing country would be responsible for the payment and upkeep of their own troops. There were, however, noticeable differences both in the amount and the pattern in which some contingents were paid. The Sierra Leonean government paid its troops only US$100 a month on average. This was a source of discontent within that contingent. Sierra Leonean officers and soldiers alike shared this feeling.

The problem in the Nigerian camp was of a different kind. Although operational allowance was paid at the agreed rate of US $5 per day, the allowance was not regular. Troops were sometimes not paid for three months. This had an adverse effect on the morale of troops within the contingent, but its effects on the operation became more apparent during the peacekeeping period that followed.

According to the ECOMOG chief logistics officer (CLO), "Some of the countries are unable to re-supply their people. Nigeria, for example, you need to see some of our soldiers in the bush. Their condition, uniforms and so on, is appalling" (Nigerian colonel, 1994). One ECOMOG field commander commented on the appalling condition of Nigerian troops: "It is however disheartening to note that of all the contingents in Operation Liberty, the Nigerian contingent is the mostly badly turned out. Most of the soldiers had only one pair of boots and uniform. Our troops can easily be seen in tattered camouflage uniforms. Of late they have resorted to purchasing uniforms and boots from Ghanbatt and Leobatt Contingents" (Olurin, 1992).

The concern over the supply problem with uniforms in the Nigerian contingent was shared by officers and other ranks alike. Many soldiers were bitter that they had to resort at times to buying their uniforms with their own money. A Nigerian private, for example, narrated his experience when he was newly deployed to Liberia: "When I arrived here, a Guinean soldier was kind enough to give me one of his uniforms. Although it was a bigger size, it was much better than what I had. Other countries do not have this problem of uniform." A Nigerian lance corporal said, "I had to buy my uniform from the allowance that they gave us. I don't think this is good enough."

There were general problems surrounding the delivery of medical care to the troops. Medical facilities were generally considered substandard. Commenting on this problem, the CLO said, "Apart from consumables, facilities are poor. There are no laboratories to carry out basic tests. Therefore the town hospital is used for this. This has a lot of problems. Blood samples are sometimes exchanged and people receive treatment they are not supposed to."

FACTORS THAT MOTIVATE

ECOMOG's Social Organization: Common Features

In spite of the factors just described, which served to weaken morale and increase the frustration of ECOMOG troops, some factors served to unify the force and provide the troops with a strong sense of achievement. One such factor is a common social origin, which forged coherence within the force. First, all the national contingents that participated in the ECOMOG operations were of sub-Saharan African origin with similar political and economic experiences, and all broadly shared a common African culture. Although variations exist in different African countries, when their culture is subjected to deeper scrutiny, there is much common ground in African tradition. All the ECOMOG troop-contributing countries (unlike Liberia) experienced European-style colonialism and attained independence at about the same period, mostly following the development of nationalist movements. They have passed through similar stages of political development, experiencing military rule or civilian authoritarianism. Guinea, Mali, Nigeria, and Sierra Leone were under military rule at the time, and Ghana was under the civilian rule of the former military leader, Gerry Rawlings. The broad similarities in culture appeared to be a strong unifying feature. The sharp variation in the Liberian culture, especially in the capital, Monrovia, accentuated the cultural similarities among all the contingents.

The similarities in culture among officers and men from contributing nations had some positive effects on ECOMOG. One noticeable area of such influence was that of command within the force. Reflecting on this point, the Gambian contingent commander commented, "[Y]ou cannot complain about discipline from another contingent. A soldier from another contingent gives you respect. The African culture and heritage of giving respect to the elder enhances this."

This natural expression of respect applied even in cases where officers performed similar duties, irrespective of rank. "One thing makes you stand out. That is your rank. My peers are Colonels and Generals. I am considered a son in their midst. There is a bit of pressure to live up to expectation." (The Gambian contingent commander was a captain, one of the most senior ranks in the relatively young Gambian army.)

One noticeable factor within ECOMOG was that, with few exceptions, the force had a common understanding and support for their concept of operations and their strategy, which included the blending of enforcement and peacekeeping. Despite outside criticism during the enforcement phase, they believed their operation differed from conventional warfare, and they were united in their defense of this. In support of their argument that peace enforcement is different from war, the following statements represent some of these officers' reasons for this view:

The tactics, techniques and psychology applied are different in each case. (Nigerian lieutenant colonel)

Enforcement may require an aggressive and frightening approach and if necessary, light offensive on the stubborn faction. A full [*military*] operation entails total offensive to incapacitate the enemy. (Nigerian lieutenant commander, Naval Task Force)

Peace enforcement aims at disarming and demobilizing the combatants, while military operations aimed at defeating an enemy in battle aim at destroying and killing. (Tanzanian colonel)

In peace enforcement, total annihilation and destruction of enemy and its military installations is prohibited. But in defeating an enemy in battle, maximum force and means are employed. (Nigerian lieutenant)

Peace enforcement may be necessary solely when the force is attacked and thus forced to defend itself. The aim is not to defeat the attackers who are not considered as enemies. (Malian colonel)

Peace enforcement is aimed at pressurizing warring factions to honor peace agreement. In military operations aimed at defeating an enemy in battle, consequently, the victor forces set conditions on the losing army to obey without options to refuse, e.g., the Gulf war. (Nigerian navy captain)

Common Ideology

In addition to the developing cohesion just described, there was indeed a strong bond among the national contingents within ECOMOG, which made the sustainment of the mission inevitable, despite the obvious differences within the force. This bond was largely the result of a common ideology, and it offered a psychological boost to the force, particularly at moments when they faced outside criticism. Although it was difficult to identify a military ideology among all the national contingents, common ideological themes were found that helped explain ECOMOG officers' attitudes to their mission. These include a strong sense of Pan-Africanism and regionalism. There was a spirit of African nationalism among all the contingents and participating nations that resulted from shared historical experiences. There was a general perception of the ECOMOG operation as a unique one, which could set precedence for future missions. Accompanying this was a common desire to record such a successful mission on the African continent.

The vast majority of ECOMOG officers and other ranks interviewed in the areas of operation between 1994 and 1999 considered the ECOMOG mission to be considerably different from a UN one. This provided an insight into just how unique they perceived their assignment to be. Some spoke passionately about how and why they considered the mission to be different from a UN one:

You don't have to get all the protagonists to accept your involvement [that is, consent is not necessary]. The overburden of the bureaucracy of the U.N. is avoided, saving time. (Gambian captain)

ECOMOG has more commitment, more integration, and it is more cost effective. (Nigerian major)

Except in Somalia, the U.N. had always preferred peaceful settlement and would want the use of minimum force. . . . Peace enforcement is most desirable for African conflict resolution because this is the only language rebels can understand. (Nigerian lieutenant colonel)

I consider the U.N. missions different from this because they fail to effect the most effective mandate. (Sierra Leone lieutenant)

ECOMOG mission is different in the fact that it does not stand aloof in the resumption of any large-scale war in Liberia. . . . ECOMOG uses force when it is deemed necessary for the general good of all. All these are contrary to U.N. missions. (Sierra Leone lieutenant)

The desire to see a precedent set in Africa, coupled with a strong Pan-African belief, immensely unified the force. African nationalist issues were brought to the fore both at the official and personal levels within ECOMOG, and this factor played no small part in strengthening the resolve of the force to make the mission a success.

At the official level, strong Africanist views were openly expressed: "The reality is that the African solution which the White World community espoused while looking toward the Gulf in 1990 is now confounding them because it is succeeding. They are trying to usurp the gains made by Africans, and President Sawyer and his associates deeply resent this. The Liberians continue to look to ECOWAS for a lasting and acceptable solution" (ECOMOG, 1991).

The personal views of many officers further indicated the strength of their commitment to seeing the success of an all-African mission:

A sub-regional initiative from Africa is as good as any original initiative from developed countries. Despite diversity, ECOMOG troops have successfully operated together. Ideas from within the force are put into practice and success recorded despite adverse cautions on such approach. Despite economic shortcomings, sheer determination by the sub-region has earned it recognition world-wide. Deliberate efforts to frustrate the noble initiatives are glaringly seen. (Nigerian lieutenant colonel)

The ECOMOG operation has taught the whole world that sub-regions all over the world can solve their problems, not necessarily depending on the already over-stretched U.N. (Nigerian lieutenant)

The ECOMOG mission is a very good initiative. It helps bring unity within the sub-region. (Malian colonel)

It is a very laudable idea for countries of the West African sub-region to come together to aid a neighbour in distress. Although there are cultural and language problems, the participating contingents do get on very well and learn from each other. (Ghanaian lieutenant colonel)

African brothers can be a helpmate for others in period of problems and hostilities, and Africans should not rely too much on aid from Western nations. (Nigerian lieutenant)

CONCLUDING REMARKS

African peacekeeping does not differ significantly from other recent peacekeeping operations in terms of the difficult environment in which peacekeepers have to operate. Although both groups face the challenge of logistic support, there are differences in the way in which these challenges are resolved. The real and underlying difference, however, lies in the commitment by Africans, both politicians and the military, to address the crises in their neighborhoods and their readiness to apply the most appropriate strategies even if it has meant incurring serious casualties. This type of response is a recent development in the region, and the states willing and able to commit human and financial resources to it often lack the capacity to manage such difficult operations. Nonetheless, the African experience has offered valuable lessons for other regions.

As a result of such difficult operations, African military personnel have had to endure significant levels of stress and frustration given the conditions under which they have operated. The Liberian and Sierra Leone experience have revealed some of the psychological effects that operations that move beyond traditional peacekeeping can have on military personnel and at the same time revealed the determination to succeed, shown by military personnel bound by a common sense of origin and purpose. This does not mean, however, that there can be no cleavages within such a force. The ECOMOG operations in Liberia and Sierra Leone had cleavages along several lines, but ultimately it appeared that the troops were driven by their individual and group commitment to the people and the mission despite their stress and frustration with the conditions under which they operated.

NOTE

Please note that the views expressed in this paper are entirely the author's and not necessarily the views of the United Nations.

REFERENCES

Alao, A., Mackinlay, J., & Olonisakin, F. (2000). *Peacekeepers, politicians and warlords: The Liberian peace process.* Tokyo: United Nations University Press.

ECOMOG. (1991). *Situation paper on the encampment and disarmament exercise.* ECOMOG Headquarters, Monrovia.

Muyangwa, M., & Vogt, M. A. (2000). *An assessment of the OAU mechanism for conflict prevention, management and resolution, 1993–2000.* New York: International Peace Academy.

Olaiya, A. (1991). ECOMOG mission and mandate. *The Peacemaker, 1*(1), 11.

Olonisakin, F. (2000). *Reinventing peacekeeping in Africa: Conceptual and legal issues in ECOMOG operations.* The Hague, London, and Boston: Kluwer Law International.

Olurin, A. I. (1992). Peacekeeping in Africa: The Liberian experience. *The Peacemaker, 2*(1), 13.

Olurin, A. I. (1993, October). Text of a *Lecture on Military Operations* in Liberia delivered to student officers at the National War College (NWC), Lagos.

Vogt, M. A. (1992). *A bold attempt at regional peacekeeping: ECOMOG and the Liberian crisis.* Lagos: Gabumo Publishing Press.

VII

Future Directions

18

The Psychology of the Peacekeeper: Common Themes and Future Directions

Amy B. Adler and Thomas W. Britt

The study of military personnel deployed on peacekeeping missions to troubled regions presents peacekeeping researchers with both a challenge and an opportunity. By integrating several areas within psychology, peacekeeping researchers are pushed to test the relevance of psychology, to identify the field's limitations, and to optimize the field's ability to address social problems.

As an area of study, peacekeepers provide researchers with a broad venue for applying psychological principles to a real-world issue. Whether viewed at the individual, small group, or organizational level, the issue of peacekeeper motivation, health, and performance sets the stage for psychologists to ask key questions: What is it we already know about psychology that can provide us insight? What is it we still need to know? What new methodological or interdisciplinary techniques do we need to consider in order to address issues unique to peacekeepers?

UNIFYING THEMES

The chapters selected for this volume represent an array of areas within psychology. From social and industrial-organizational psychology to clinical and health psychology, the chapters encompass overlapping but unique specialties within the field. Despite these specialties, several issues emerge consistently across the chapters. First, as almost every chapter in the book highlights, peacekeepers face serious stressors when on deployment (e.g., Adler, Litz, & Bartone; Bliese & Castro; Weisæth). Although some of these stressors are specific to peacekeeping deployments, others occur on different kinds of deployments and still others apply to any work setting. Understanding these stressors is a critical step in defining what Castro (this volume) describes as "the problem" to be studied.

Another aspect of "the problem" that bears examination is the question of outcome measures relevant to the peacekeeper. Several authors in this volume (e.g., Bliese & Castro; Moldjord, Fossum, & Holen; Thomas & Castro; Wisher) address the issue of predicting, maintaining, and measuring performance. Other outcomes of importance include psychological and physical health (e.g., Litz, Gray, & Bolton; Thompson & Pastò). Although the extent to which deployment is associated with elevated levels of distress depends on both the individual and on the nature of the specific peacekeeping operation, there is agreement that exposure to traumatic incidents while on peacekeeping missions can be linked to significant psychological consequences.

The third underlying theme in this volume is the importance of attitudes. Several authors (e.g., Boneiki & Britt; Britt; Galantino) identify the role that attitudes play not only in shaping motivation but also in shaping the impact of the deployment on peacekeepers. Attitudes can indicate both potential problems, as in the case of prejudice, or potential benefits, as in the case of deriving meaning from the deployment. Expanding the discussion of the impact of peacekeeping deployments to include positive effects provides the groundwork for a comprehensive understanding of both the difficulties and opportunities inherent in deploying on a peacekeeping mission.

The fourth theme is the basis for the last section on cross-cultural psychology. In an attempt to place the individual in a person-environment context, these three chapters directly address the cultural environment in which peacekeepers typically perform their mission. These chapters take very different approaches to the same problem. Elron et al. emphasize the positive cross-cultural interactions and adaptations reported by military officers on peacekeeping missions. In contrast, Soeters and Bos-Bakx emphasize the differences in values that drive cross-cultural conflicts on peacekeeping missions. These two chapters are not inconsistent with one another; rather they come at the same question from two different angles. In the final chapter of that section, Olonisakin describes the specific case of African peacekeeping and the role of cultural identity in shaping motivation and attitude. Each of the three chapters identifies the importance of cultural issues in understanding how peacekeepers adjust and operate within the multinational peacekeeping environment.

RECOMMENDATIONS

Taking into account the collective insights of the chapters in this volume, we offer the following ten recommendations for optimizing peacekeeper adjustment and performance during peacekeeping operations. These recommendations are intended for leaders at every level: military commanders beginning at the company level, policymakers, and government, NATO and UN officials involved in planning and executing peacekeeping missions. This list of recommendations is not meant to be exhaustive, but rather highlights the key recommendations that emerge from the chapters in this book.

1. *Be Relevant.* Ensure that peacekeepers see the relevance of peacekeeping operations to their role as service members, knowing that participation in such operations will be rewarded in terms of their career path. Emphasize the need for military personnel to recognize the relevance of the full spectrum of military operations (combat, peacekeeping, humanitarian) to their role in the military, thereby creating a more differentiated conception of what it means to be a service member.

2. *Provide Meaning.* Promote positive attitudes toward peacekeeping operations by placing the operation in a meaningful context, describing the history of the conflict that led to the operation, and letting peacekeepers know how their participation will lead to desirable consequences for the local parties and the peacekeeper's own country. Communicate to peacekeepers how they will know when they have succeeded on the mission.

3. *Train.* Ensure adequate predeployment training for situations peacekeepers are likely to encounter when serving on an operation. This will create a strong sense of efficacy for peacekeepers as they enter the operation. If the guidelines for performance or rules of engagement are likely to change, prepare soldiers for the eventuality, emphasizing flexibility. Retrain professional military personnel in combat tasks during the peacekeeping deployment to maintain their morale and their readiness.

4. *Educate.* Ensure that peacekeepers have accurate knowledge of the groups involved in the peace accord. Broaden peacekeeper knowledge and interactions with local populations beyond conflict-based interactions with individuals antagonistic to the peacekeeping force.

5. *Moderate Stressors.* Although the stressors of deployment will never be eliminated, design interventions that can reduce the impact of stressors through providing clear information, justifiable compensation, opportunity for recreation, and appropriate mechanisms to process psychological reactions.

6. *Support Cultural Competency.* When the operation includes contact with peacekeepers from other nations, capitalize on the common military culture, take into account cultural differences in power distance and authoritarianism, facilitate cultural communication through modeling, adaptability, and respect, and encourage the perception of superordinate goals.

7. *Appeal to Professionalism.* Emphasize that the values and professionalism espoused by the military are consistent across different types of missions. In preparing units for deployment, balance the needs of military personnel motivated by a strong professional combat identity with those motivated by humanitarianism and adventure.

8. *Recognize the Impact of Organizational Decisions.* Acknowledge that decisions made at a political or strategic level can have psychological consequences for peacekeepers on the ground. Consider that the impact of decisions regarding such issues as rules of engagement, timelines for disarmament, and relative deprivation can ultimately affect the adaptation, morale, and performance of peacekeepers.

9. *Intervene Early.* Provide early intervention with military personnel exposed to potentially traumatic events. Supplement clinical support of troops with command consultation.

10. *Encourage Individual Coping Efforts.* Support active coping, adaptive distraction, and social support. Provide alternative social environments that do not necessarily rely on alcohol to bring military personnel together. Contribute to the development of a coherent understanding of the mission and the individual's role in the mission in order to support individual sense of coherence.

These recommendations represent a starting point for addressing the needs of peacekeepers. Each of the issues they represent needs to be considered when military personnel are deployed on peacekeeping missions, although the exact nature of how these issues are addressed may depend on the particular operation or on the particular culture of the nation deploying the peacekeepers. We believe that if these recommendations are adopted and implemented, peacekeeper adaptation and performance will be enhanced. Research will be needed to evaluate empirically interventions designed to improve peacekeeper adjustment and performance.

FUTURE DIRECTIONS

The chapters of the present volume provide a solid research foundation for drawing conclusions about peacekeeper health and performance. However, several topic areas warrant further investigation. These areas include (1) the search for moderators of adjustment and performance during peacekeeping operations, (2) developing reliable and valid measures of performance during peacekeeping operations, (3) identifying mechanisms by which the psychological construct of service members can be broadened to incorporate the role of peacekeeper, and (4) examining similarities and differences in how peacekeepers from different cultures respond and adapt to peacekeeping operations. These areas are each addressed in turn.

Many of the chapters document a relationship between exposure to stressful events during peacekeeping operations and psychological health during or following the operation. However, less research has been devoted to examining factors that may moderate the effects of peacekeeping stress. Bliese and Castro (this volume) present a model emphasizing that moderating variables may be found at the individual, group, and organizational level, and they present evidence for group consensus and job engagement as moderators of the stressor-strain relationship during peacekeeping operations. Numerous other work environment and unit factors that may contribute to either thriving or deteriorating under the demands of peacekeeping need to be evaluated. Examples of such moderators include sense of coherence (a promising individual difference variable described in three of the chapters), a unit's level of cohesion, and the impact of organizational policies such as those that affect peacekeeper safety, rules of engagement, and sense of justice.

Despite the emphasis placed on performance, only the Wisher chapter provides details regarding the actual tasks in which peacekeepers are engaged, and even this chapter does not address how peacekeeper performance can be quantified during an operation. Developing a measure of performance during peacekeeping operations is a difficult task, for the same reason that measuring performance during any type of operation is difficult (see Hodges, 1994). At the level of the operation, a peacekeeping operation succeeds when nothing happens, thereby making performance assessment difficult (Segal, Furukawa, & Lindh, 1990). In the absence of an agreed-upon standard of performance that can be applied to individual peacekeepers, perhaps researchers should develop job criteria that are especially relevant to peacekeepers and then have supervisors rate peacekeepers on the extent to which they are meeting these criteria (see Kilcullen, Mael, Goodwin, & Zazanis, 1999, for an example with Special Forces personnel).

Many of the chapters emphasize the inherent tension between being a peacekeeper and being a combat soldier. Franke (this volume) goes into the most detail regarding how service members might incorporate peacekeeping into their identity as military professionals, but future research is needed to address specifically how the role of peacekeeper can be successfully integrated into a combat warrior's identity without degrading the effectiveness of that original identity. In a related vein, research into the long-term positive and negative impact of multiple peacekeeping deployments on military personnel can identify unit readiness issues of import for future deployments, both combat and peacekeeping.

Those chapters in this book dealing with peacekeepers from different cultures illustrate some of the issues associated with working in a multinational environment in the context of peacekeeping. Follow-up research can identify aspects of the peacekeeper experience that are universal versus culturally specific through a cross-cultural assessment of what peacekeepers find stressful about peacekeeping operations and how stress gets translated into psychological problems. It would also be worthwhile to examine whether certain cultural norms and values buffer or exacerbate the effects of stressors on health and performance.

PEACEKEEPER RESEARCH

The objective of this book has been to understand variables affecting the motivation, performance, and health of peacekeepers through the application of principles from several different areas of psychology. Experts in social, industrial-organization, health, clinical, and cross-cultural psychology contributed to this multidimensional perspective on the psychology of the peacekeeper. By bringing together a multinational team of researchers from different specialties within psychology, the goal has been a comprehensive examination of peacekeepers deployed to troubled regions throughout the world. Furthermore, by integrating academic and military perspectives, the research approach has been both rooted in theoretical principles and real-world applications. Developing the study of peacekeeper behavior and cognition requires nothing less than this multidimensional integration, one that incorporates a wide range of psychological subspecialties to address wide-ranging issues, reflects the multinational nature of peacekeeping operations themselves by integrating an international perspective, and tries to bridge the gap between theory and the real-world experience of being deployed to a remote environment under harsh field conditions with the mission of supporting peace efforts in a troubled region.

Taken together, the chapters in this volume present a basis from which psychology can shed light on the peacekeeper experience. By using psychology to account for peacekeeper adaptation and performance, research-based initiatives can be recommended in order to optimize the adjustment of peacekeepers to the challenge of their mission and, ultimately, to support the success of the peacekeeping mission in sustaining an environment for peace.

NOTE

This chapter was funded in part by the U.S. Army Medical Research and Materiel Command, Fort Detrick, Maryland, and we are grateful for this support. However, the views expressed in this volume are those of the authors and do not reflect the official policy or position of the Department of the Army, Department of Defense, or the U.S. government.

REFERENCES

Hodges, J. S. (1994). Analytical use of data from Army training exercises: A case study of tactical reconnaissance. *Journal of the American Statistical Association, 89,* 444–451.

Kilcullen, R. N., Mael, F. A., Goodwin, G. F., & Zazanis, M. M. (1999). Predicting U.S. Army special forces field performance. *Human Performance in Extreme Environments, 4,* 53–63.

Segal, D. R., Furukawa, T. P., & Lindh, J. C. (1990). Light infantry as peacekeepers in the Sinai. *Armed Forces & Society, 16,* 385–403.

Index

About the Contributors

AMY B. ADLER is a research psychologist with the U.S. Army Medical Research Unit–Europe, Walter Reed Army Institute of Research, in Heidelberg, Germany. She is science coordinator at the unit, has deployed in support of peacekeeping operations, and has a research focus on deployment-related stress and coping.

PAUL T. BARTONE is a U.S. Army research psychologist, currently director of the Leader Development Research Center, U.S. Military Academy, West Point. His research interests focus on individual and contextual influences on health, resiliency, and enhanced performance.

EYAL BEN ARI is an anthropologist with the Department of Sociology and Anthropology at the Hebrew University of Jerusalem. After an initial stint of 4 years with the Israeli army, he served as a reservist for 23 years. He has carried out research on the Israeli army, the Japanese Self-Defense Forces, and multinational peacekeeping missions.

PAUL D. BLIESE is currently the chief of the modeling branch within the Department of Psychiatry and Behavioral Sciences at the Walter Reed Army Institute of Research. While at WRAIR, he has developed and used multilevel analyses to study the Gulf War syndrome, downsizing, the adaptation of soldiers deployed on peacekeeping operations (Haiti), and the impact of new technology implementation.

ELISA E. BOLTON is a postdoctoral fellow at the Boston VA Medical Center and the Boston University School of Medicine. Dr. Bolton's research interests include the psychological adaptation of peacekeepers and risk and resiliency factors associated with PTSD.

KURT A. BONIECKI is an assistant professor of psychology at the University of Central Arkansas in Conway. His research interests focus on the measurement of prejudice as well as the social-cognitive processes influencing the formation, activation, and reduction of negative stereotypes.

MIEPKE P. G. BOS-BAKX is a major in the military psychological and sociological service and lectures on management sciences, with special attention to managing human resources, at the Royal Netherlands Military Academy. Her research interests include human resources and their effects on military personnel.

THOMAS W. BRITT is an assistant professor of psychology at Clemson University in Clemson, South Carolina. He deployed in support of multiple peacekeeping operations as an active duty army research psychologist for five years. His research interests include how engagement in meaningful work can buffer individuals from the adverse effects of a stressful environment, as well as turn stressful experiences into opportunities for growth.

CARL ANDREW CASTRO is a lieutenant colonel in the U.S. Army. He has served on peacekeeping missions to Bosnia, Kosovo, and Saudi Arabia. His research interest includes assessing soldier and family well-being during military operations.

EFRAT ELRON is an assistant professor in organizational behavior in the School of Business Administration at the Hebrew University in Jerusalem. Her research interests include multinational organizations and the ways that cultural diversity influences them and the study of team processes.

LARS KRISTIAN FOSSUM is senior officer in military psychology and military leadership at the Norwegian Air Force Academy, Department of Leadership and International Cooperation. He was educated at the Norwegian Air Force Academy and has a master's degree in psychology from the Norwegian University of Science and Technology in Trondheim, Norway. His research interests are stress, coping, and leadership in military operations.

VOLKER C. FRANKE is assistant professor of political science and international studies at McDaniel College in Westminster, Maryland. He currently also serves as director and managing editor of the Maxwell/SAIS National Security Studies Case Studies Program at Syracuse University. He is the author of a book and numerous journal articles on social identity, peacekeeping, and military socialization.

MARIA GRAZIA GALANTINO is a senior researcher at Archivio Disarmo, Rome, and a Ph.D. student in sociology at University of Rome "La Sapienza."

She has carried out field research on sociological aspects of peacekeeping operations. Her research interests include military sociology and civil-military relations.

MATT J. GRAY is an assistant professor of psychology at the University of Wyoming in Laramie. He trained at the National Center for Posttraumatic Stress Disorder, Behavioral Sciences Division in Boston and has conducted numerous studies examining the symptom course and correlates of PTSD in veteran populations.

NIR HALEVY is a graduate student in the Department of Psychology at the Hebrew University in Jerusalem. Research interests include group processes, intergroup relations, and norms and culture.

ARE HOLEN is a psychiatrist and associate professor at the Department of Psychiatry and Behavioral Medicine, Faculty of Medicine, at the Norwegian University of Science and Technology in Trondheim. His main area of research is posttraumatic stress in relation to disasters and major life events. Other areas of research are bereavement studies and group processes.

BRETT T. LITZ is an associate professor in the Department of Psychiatry at Boston University School of Medicine and the Psychology Department at Boston University, and he is associate director of the Behavioral Science Division of the National Center for PTSD. Dr. Litz's research interests include the psychological adaptation of peacekeepers, the assessment and treatment of PTSD, and emotional and information processing in PTSD.

CHRISTIAN MOLDJORD is a lecturer in military psychology and military leadership at the Norwegian Air Force Academy, Department of Leadership and International Cooperation. He was an officer, educated at the Norwegian Air Force Academy, and has a master's degree in psychology from the Norwegian University of Science and Technology in Trondheim. His research interests include stress, coping, and leadership in military operations.

'FUNMI OLONISAKIN works in the UN Office of the Special Representative of the Secretary-General for Children and Armed Conflict. She obtained a doctorate in war studies from King's College London and has conducted extensive research on African regional security including peacekeeping, civil-military relations, and gender and conflict.

LUIGI PASTÒ is a research psychologist with Defence Research and Development Canada–Toronto. He is a member of the Stress and Coping Group in the Command Effectiveness and Behavior Section. He has traveled to Bosnia gathering information on the deployment-related experiences of Canadian troops. His major interest is psychological interventions for anxiety disorders.

BOAS SHAMIR is a professor in the Department of Sociology and Anthropology at the Hebrew University in Jerusalem. He holds a Ph.D. in social psychology from the London School of Economics and Political Science. His main research interest is leadership in organizations (including military organizations).

JOSEPH SOETERS is professor of social sciences at the Faculty of Military Sciences of the Netherlands' Defense Academy. His research interests focus on international military cooperation, culture in uniformed organizations, cooperation between military and civilian organizations, and organizational change.

JEFFREY L. THOMAS is an active-duty captain and research psychologist with the U.S. Army Medical Research Unit–Europe, Walter Reed Army Institute of Research, in Heidelberg, Germany. He is director of Research Operations and researches occupational stress and health issues, leadership, individual differences, and organizational climate for the U.S. Army.

MEGAN M. THOMPSON is a research psychologist with Defence Research and Development Canada–Toronto. She is group head of the Stress and Coping Group in the Command Effectiveness and Behavior Section. She has traveled to both Bosnia and Greenland gathering information on the deployment-related experiences of Canadian troops. Her research foci include stress, coping and resiliency in military contexts, and the role of individual differences in stress and coping and decision making.

LARS WEISÆTH is a professor in the Division of Disaster Psychiatry, the Department Group of Psychiatry at the University of Oslo. He is also director of the Department of Psychiatry, Medical Staff, of the Headquarters, Defence Command Norway. He has edited books and published numerous articles and book chapters on traumatic stress, deployment, and psychiatry.

ROBERT A. WISHER is a senior research psychologist with the U.S. Army Research Institute for the Behavioral and Social Sciences in Alexandria, Virginia. His research concerns the application of advanced distributed learning technologies to support the acquisition and retention of military skills and knowledge.